Lafayette

OTHER BOOKS BY OLIVIER BERNIER

Pleasure and Privilege

Art and Craft
(Fiction)

The Eighteenth-Century Woman

HERO OF TWO WORLDS

Olivier Bernier

E. P. DUTTON, INC. · NEW YORK

Copyright © 1983 by Olivier Bernier
All rights reserved. Printed in the U.S.A.

No part of this publication may be reproduced or transmitted in any form or by
any means, electronic or mechanical, including photocopy, recording or any
information storage and retrieval system now known or to be invented, without
permission in writing from the publisher, except by a reviewer who wishes to
quote brief passages in connection with a review written for inclusion in a
magazine, newspaper or broadcast.

Published in the United States by
E. P. Dutton, Inc.,
2 Park Avenue, New York, N.Y. 10016

Library of Congress Cataloging in Publication Data
Bernier, Olivier.
Lafayette, hero of two worlds.
Bibliography: p. 344
Includes index.
.1. Lafayette, Marie Joseph Paul Yves Roch Gilbert du Motier,
Marquis de, 1757-1834.
2. France—History—1789-1815.
3. United States—History—Revolution, 1775-1783—Participation, French.
4. Generals—France—Biography. 5. Generals—United States—Biography.
6. Statesmen—France—Biography. 7. France. Armée—Biography. I. Title.
DC146.L2B47 1983   944.04′092′4 [B]   83-14019
ISBN: 0-525-24181-7

Published simultaneously in Canada by
Fitzhenry & Whiteside Limited, Toronto

COBE

10 9 8 7 6 5 4 3 2 1

First Edition

for ROSAMOND

CONTENTS

LIST OF ILLUSTRATIONS

Lafayette in 1782.

The vicomte de Noailles,
and the comte d'Artois.

Three engravings of life under the ancien
régime by Moreau-le-Jeune.

The comtes de Vergennes and de Maurepas.

General George Washington.

American officers: Nathanael Greene
and Benedict Arnold.

French commanders: admirals d'Estaing
and de Grasse and the comte de Rochambeau.

Photographs follow page 202 of text and are reproduced courtesy of the
Prints Division, New York Public Library, Astor, Lenox, and Tilden
Foundation.

AUTHOR'S NOTE

THE SPELLING OF LAFAYETTE

Lafayette seems to have spelled his name both La Fayette and Lafayette; the latter usage is, however, almost constant after 1789. The author has followed local usage, starting with La Fayette, then switching to the compound form after 1789, but always leaving the spelling uncorrected in all documents, memoirs, and letters quoted in the text.

The author has also respected Lafayette's spelling in English, along with his often faulty grammar and Gallicisms, except in rare cases where they obscured meaning. Whenever Lafayette wrote to an English-speaking correspondent, he used English; his letters to French recipients have been translated into English by the author.

PREFACE

There was no need to mention his name, at first, in the United States: to all the Patriots, he was simply "the Marquis," as if there had been no other on the surface of the earth; but soon they couldn't get enough of it. There were Lafayette streets, Lafayette counties, Fayettevilles. He was a hero, the Frenchman who came to fight for the United States, a man who neither feared danger nor sought advancement but selflessly gave of himself that the fledgling country might live, and offered so potent an example that soon all the might of France followed him.

As time passed, those feelings grew even stronger. When Gilbert Lafayette returned to the United States in 1824, he was greeted everywhere by wildly enthusiastic crowds and given a large grant of money and land by an otherwise parsimonious Congress. Then, almost a century later, when the United States went to the aid of France, there was the Lafayette Escadrille and General John Pershing's famous (if probably apocryphal) "Lafayette, we are here."

Today, still, Lafayette's name is taught to schoolchildren across the country as that of a man who loved liberty so truly and so well that he unselfishly dedicated himself to its cause. Of course, few wonder what happened to him after 1781: having helped bring about the victory at Yorktown, he returned home to France and the great epic was over. Except that the young Hero of Two Worlds, as the French called him, after being acclaimed almost as wildly in Paris as he had been on the other side of the Atlantic, lived on for fifty-three more years, during which time he helped dethrone two kings and an emperor. And while in America he is still an unsullied hero, in his own country Lafayette is often considered a fool or a traitor, or both.

Today, as in 1792, the French quickly judge a man by his political stance, and the political extremists often speak loudest. Although Lafayette in his old age claimed he had always been a republican, his opposition to the Jacobins and the abolition of the monarchy in 1792 still rankle among those who exalt Robespierre's achievements; while to those who loathe the Revolution, either because they consider themselves part of the elite, or because, for them, history has stood still since Napoleon, Lafayette, much like Franklin D. Roosevelt in America in the 1930s, is considered a traitor to his class. Indeed, this curious attitude, adopted by Lafayette's own descendants through most of the nineteenth century, survives to this very day.

If one were to read most of the words published in France about Lafayette, one would have to conclude that this selfless genius was a popularity-mad fiend; that this steadiest of liberals was a nincompoop swayed by every political breeze; that this brilliant young leader was stupid, awkward, dull, and incompetent. Surely, then, Lafayette must have been a trial to his family and friends. In fact, nothing could be more wrong: this unfaithful but loving husband, this kind father, this good and true friend was adored by all who knew him well. No one was ever happier or more cherished in his domestic circle, more willing to help the unfortunate, more respected by all those who loved liberty. When the people of France rose, in 1830, against a tyrannical king, they turned instantly to Lafayette: he was a man they could trust, a man incapable of fraud and deceit, a man, finally, utterly devoid of personal ambition. And all over Europe it was to Lafayette that the oppressed looked for help—Italian liberals, Spanish constitutionalists, Polish freedom fighters. All came to the man who stood uniquely for democracy and justice.

Surely, then, the reactionaries who mock him are wrong. But are they entirely so? For Lafayette is also the man who, during the French Revolution, constantly found himself doing things he disliked to retain his popularity; the man who, all through his life, demanded a return to the unworkable Constitution of 1791; the man, finally, who set up a new king, Louis Philippe, and a new régime, only to denounce both, in bitterness and impotence.

In an age when both left and right tend toward an extreme view of the world, it is not surprising to see Lafayette either traduced or ignored: no one likes a true liberal. Still, Lafayette is far more complex—and his positions were often far more ambiguous—than has been supposed. His successes, like his failures, are not without reference to our own situation. Perhaps we still have something to learn from the Hero of Two Worlds.

ACKNOWLEDGMENTS

The author wishes to express his gratitude to the New York Public Library, as always an incomparable help to research; to the Bibliothèque Nationale, Paris; to the Archives Nationales, Paris; to the Archives du ministère des affaires étrangères, Paris; and especially to Mme Chantal de Tourtier-Bonazzi, the curator in chief of the Archives Nationales for sharing her extensive knowledge of Lafayette documentation. He also owes thanks to Elisa Petrini for her painstaking and highly effective work in clarifying the manuscript.

Anyone interested in Lafayette must also acknowledge the immense contribution made by Louis R. Gottschalk in his volumes covering Lafayette's life from his birth to October 1789. His work remains a monument of thoroughness and scholarship.

Lafayette

One

A FORTUNATE ORPHAN

The chateau of Chavaniac, with its round medieval towers crowned with pointed slate roofs and modern central wing pierced by wide windows, was a typical aristocratic dwelling: it retained some parts of the fortress it had once been, but was improved in the new, more comfortable style, which had been in vogue for a century and a half. Without being really grand—it had a few more than twenty rooms—or really glamorous, for its owners were far from rich, it accurately reflected the state of France in 1757: older parts coexisted, often uneasily, with modern thought. And much the way the building towered over the hamlet clustered near its moat, so did the aristocracy dominate the Third Estate, that nine-tenths of the nation that was neither clerical nor noble.

In many ways, though, Chavaniac was unusually primitive. The Auvergne in which it stood was one of the most backward, most isolated provinces in France. It was also sparsely populated, so the castle and its village seemed almost lost in the empty countryside. There were no paved roads going past it, just ruts that became impassable whenever it rained hard.

There were no public monuments, no city gates, no prosperous houses, just a grouping of thatch-roofed huts surrounded by filth. No one cleaned up after the pigs and chickens, and their offal stank as soon as the weather got warm.

In 1757 little had changed since the feudal system had been established some five hundred years earlier. Though the peasants were no longer serfs, it was well understood that they belonged to an order of being altogether different from that of the noble family in its great stone dwelling. They were, for instance, forbidden to mill their own wheat or bake their own bread: instead, they had to use the lord's mill and oven—for a fee. Nor did they own their land. It belonged to the lord, who was entitled to a variety of feudal dues that, together with the tax due the King, came to over half the crop in good years. When the lord was kind and considerate, as at Chavaniac, the peasants were relatively contented, although they went about in rags. You could always tell whom you were dealing with, since anyone from the castle wore fine clothes and had well-dressed hair.

Comfort mattered little. The peasants' huts, of course, were usually overcrowded hovels, but even the castle, modernized though it was, remained freezing all through the long winter. Its great fireplaces did little more than roast you in front while your back froze; and though there was an abundance of servants, they were neither stylish nor efficient. Still, the food was plentiful and good, if plain, and after all the owners, the La Fayettes, were noble.

Birth was everything then, a passport to fortune, fame, and preferment. In the countryside especially, the world was divided between the peasants, whose lot could never change, and the nobles, who might not be rich—the La Fayettes, for instance, were possessed of a relatively modest income— but to whom a career in the army, the church, or the court might bring both wealth and promotion. So it was a good thing for the baby boy born in the old chateau on September 6, 1757, that his parents came from an ancient and noble family.

Still, the La Fayettes, noble though they were, belonged nowhere near the apex of the social pyramid. For one thing, they lived in the wrong place. It might be very well for a thriving merchant to trade in Bordeaux, that center of Atlantic commerce, or for a draper to establish his workshop in Caen, where cloth has been woven for many centuries. A judge might reside in Lyon or in Aix-en-Provence, the site of two of the thirteen parlements, the great tribunals of the ancien régime, but for a nobleman only Versailles would do; and while the army was still mostly officered by the nobility, there wasn't much hope for rapid promotion unless the King knew you.

The system worked very much the way Louis XIV had set it up a century earlier. France was an absolute monarchy and all good things came from the King. If you wanted to become a general, a bishop, a minister, or a First Gentleman of the Bedchamber, you needed the King's favor. This was all right if you were ambitious and liked glamour. Versailles was a dazzling spectacle. There, throughout the great gilded rooms, intrigues and back-biting helped pass the time of those whose sole function was to wait on His Majesty. Of course, there were prerequisites. First, you had to prove that your family had been noble before 1400, an easy enough task for families like the Rohans, the Noailles, the La Rochefoucaulds; then, you must know the customs of *ce pays-ci* ("this separate country"), as its denizens called it. There were special ways to talk, special ways to bow, even a special way to walk (a kind of glide without ever lifting your feet); and anyone from the outside was made extremely unwelcome.

This system resulted in an aristocracy divided into three distinct groups. There were the courtiers, who basked in the golden rays of the King's favor, then came the provincial nobility, often impoverished, who led grim, un-productive lives in their country chateaux, and finally the nobility of the robe, men who had bought a judgeship in one of the parlements and whose functions conferred nobility. While they were often rich, they were despised by the rest of the aristocrats. M. and Mme de La Fayette were both noble, but they belonged to different categories: the marquis to the second, that of the provincial nobility, his wife to the first. Her family, the La Rivières, were courtiers, and so through her connections she was able to provide her husband, a highly competent officer, with a career. By 1759, M. de La Fayette had been appointed a colonel of Grenadiers and was obviously on the way up.

Without his in-laws, the marquis, who had never been a courtier him-self, would likely have remained a captain. This might seem odd at first glance, since the La Fayettes were an illustrious family. Not only did their genealogical charts go back to the year 1000, but they could boast a marshal of France (in the fifteenth century), a lady who was the great love of Louis XIII's life, and the author of the first French novel.

In a world mad for genealogy, however, this pedigree mattered little. The famous La Fayettes had belonged to the elder branch of the family, while the current marquis was descended from a younger brother. Further, unlike some families descended from a younger brother—the Talleyrands, for instance—the two branches had split three centuries earlier, and since then M. de La Fayette's direct ancestors had sunk into obscurity and quasi-poverty. It had only been two generations back that the elder branch had finally died out and the title had come to the younger branch. Even then, because a daughter had inherited the estates, the very chateau had only passed on to the marquis. Except for his wife's relatives, therefore, he had neither cousins nor acquaintances at Versailles: for all the antiquity of his name, he was no better than a newcomer, and was even forced to prove to the royal genealogist that he was indeed noble.

None of this mattered in Chavaniac, however: there, the family was all important and the peasants had no doubts about it. The La Fayettes took pride in their ancient and illustrious lineage, and their attitude became even more pronounced when, on August 1, 1759, without having ever seen his twenty-three-month-old son, the colonel marquis de La Fayette was killed by an English bullet at the Battle of Minden. Now only little Gilbert's life prevented the extinction of the family, and so, to the women living at Chavaniac, he became the most important person in the world.

In a century when children still died in great numbers, Gilbert's survival could not be taken for granted. Exceptional care was taken by his mother and grandmother. The little boy could have no doubts that everything at Chavaniac revolved around him. Not only was he the lord and owner of all he surveyed; not only did everyone treat him with marked respect; he was also the only male in a world of women: his mother, a charming woman in her twenties, his grandmother, the formidable Mme du Motier, and an aunt. Luckily for him, the women in question were loving as well as perceptive and intelligent, so there was no attempt at turning little Gilbert into an overindulged, spoiled child. And within a year, he was faced with his second great loss: Mme de La Fayette left Chavaniac to settle in Paris with her father and grandfather.

It was still the custom, in 1760, for parents and children to lead quite separate lives. Indeed, Gilbert's lot was exceptional in that he was kept with his family instead of being farmed out to a peasant foster mother. So Mme de La Fayette's departure was perfectly normal, especially since she moved to Paris not for her own pleasure but in order to secure little Gilbert's future. The family's income was a mere 25,000 livres* a year ($112,500), not enough to shine at Versailles or even to buy the boy a regiment.† If Gilbert was to succeed later on, the La Rivière connections had to be kept up, and a position prepared for the little marquis.

At least, the boy had one advantage: his income, accumulating through his childhood, would ease his entrance into the great world, and Mme du

---

*One livre is worth approximately $4.50.

†Until 1789, the higher military ranks were both venal and appointive. The King made you a general, but you purchased the regiment you were to command. If he chose, of course, the King could also help you financially.

Motier,* his grandmother, was making very sure that the estate was run productively and efficiently. In fact, partly because of the respect often accorded widowed matriarchs and partly because hers was a strong personality, Mme du Motier was a figure of great authority. She now took over as Gilbert's parent and proceeded to raise him as if he were her own son. As a result, the boy, who hardly knew his actual mother, remained devoted to Mme du Motier for the rest of her long life. He looked to her for love and security, and largely took on her ideas, especially when it came to the importance of the La Fayettes. Then, too, she ran the estate and the daily life of the castle and was regarded by her daughters and servants with awe.

Indeed, this sort of elderly grande dame was not uncommon in prerevolutionary France. "In the provinces far away from the capital," Talleyrand wrote, "a kind of care given to their dignity regulated the relationships of the great families who still lived on their estates with . . . the other inhabitants of the land. The foremost person of a province should have thought himself vile if he wasn't polite and helpful. . . . The peasants only saw their lord in order to receive assistance along with a few encouraging and consoling words. . . . The mores of the nobility . . . resembled its old castles: they had something grand and stable about them."[1]

Mme du Motier, in Chavaniac at least, was just such a personage, and the inhabitants of all the neighboring villages looked up to her. In an age when doctors were few and generally incompetent, she cared for the sick; if catastrophe struck, she helped its victims. The King was impossibly remote. Around Chavaniac, it was Mme du Motier who reigned.

She saw to it that the peasants' rents and dues were paid, but also that they had the seed they needed for planting; she ran the house, hired the servants, settled the menus and the accounts; and to Gilbert she gave not just affection but also standards. She made it plain that he was a *privilégié*, a member of the privileged class, but that duties went along with such privilege. Unlike some nobles who thought the world was made for their pleasure, this often stern grande dame felt responsible for her flock, and she made sure that Gilbert felt the same way. He could expect to lead but must never forget those who followed. Another major aspect of Mme du Motier's personality, however, seems to have made little or no impression on her grandson: her strong religious feeling and frequent devotional exercises. Gilbert was made to attend Mass faithfully, but he seems to have

---

*The full name of the family was now du Motier de La Fayette; the younger branch had called itself plain du Motier, and Gilbert's grandmother, who had married before the extinction of the elder branch, never changed her name.

considered it all an irrelevant bore, and stopped going to church as soon as he was no longer compelled to do so. Also, perhaps because Mme du Motier did such a good job of watching over the family's fortune, Gilbert never managed to develop an interest in it: it was there to be spent, that was all.

That Mme du Motier reigned only on behalf of her grandson, though, everyone knew full well. If she represented the past and present, it was little Gilbert in whom the future was incarnate. From earliest childhood, the little boy to whom all doffed their hats knew that he was a very special person. The women in his family could not transmit the family name or arms; the peasant children around him barely knew who their grandfathers had been; the young marquis alone felt part of an ancient and august tradition, especially so when Mme du Motier launched into her frequent stories about his father and his illustrious ancestors. Further, from the age of seven on, Gilbert's tutor, the kindly abbé Fayon, began instilling in him an appreciation of the history of the La Fayette family.

It was, however, the father whom he had never known that Gilbert especially idolized, and with whom he identified. Colonel de La Fayette had been killed fighting the King's enemies, and one day the young marquis would follow his father to war. Thus, while most other noble children had as their ambition a great position at court, young Gilbert intended to be a soldier.

Of course, soldiers must be brave, bold, daring. So when a terrifying monster, the Beast of the Gévaudan, said to be part-lion, part-wolf, and part-panther (but which eventually turned out to be a large mountain lion), started to terrify the countryside, little Gilbert dreamed of killing it with his own hands. He actually went on long expeditions away from the castle in the hope of encountering it. Luckily for him, the Beast had other business; but Gilbert's ambition was being cast in a permanent mold.

Young La Fayette had another strong reason for wanting to be a soldier: to avenge his father's death. The colonel, he knew, had been shot by an English soldier, and England was still the hereditary enemy. Although the war had ended in 1763, and France had lost nothing more than a few distant colonies in Canada ("a few acres of snow," Voltaire said), it was still considered to have suffered a defeat. Gilbert heard much about the French humiliation, and the next war, which France would win. Like other lessons about his family's greatness, this was a legacy the child promptly made his own.

The little marquis naturally thought he would stay at Chavaniac until it was time to join the army but in 1768 his mother, who was still living in Paris, sent for him. Mme du Motier agreed that the move was necessary, so the eleven-year-old Gilbert, with great dread, made ready to leave his domain. After all, he had not seen his mother for eight years, and now he was to leave his real family, his house, everything he knew, for a city both distant and frightening. It was an enormous shock.

How right he had been to worry quickly became plain to him: soon after the carriage left Chavaniac, he noticed that the people he passed on the road no longer doffed their hats to him. In just a few miles, the little sovereign had become another nobody.

It took well over a week, in 1768, to reach Paris from Chavaniac. For a while the countryside, though more fertile, peopled, and prosperous, looked not unlike the Auvergne. But the child's eyes must have opened wide as he approached the capital. The road ran between parks and lush gardens. The houses and chateaux all looked new and luxurious. At one of the gates of Paris the carriage stopped so that excise controllers could search the travelers' luggage. The city had its own set of customs duties and people went to such lengths to evade them that the tax men had armed themselves with long metal needles that they would thrust into any suspicious-looking package.

Beyond the gate lay the most fascinating city in Europe. People came to Paris from all over the Continent, and from England, too. The city boasted the best artists, the best shops, the most fashionable clothes, furniture, and jewelry, the most advanced thinkers. Its salons set the intellectual tone, its writers' works were read throughout the Western world. Naturally, standards were high, and dullards encouraged to go elsewhere. Foreigners, in the sixties and seventies, were all the fashion, as Horace Walpole discovered to his delight, but provincials were considered subhuman. They dressed badly, talked about last year's books, knew none of the court gossip. Worst of all, they failed miserably when they tried to speak the current jargon, in which everything was wildly exaggerated. If you said you were dying of exhaustion, for instance, you really meant that you were a trifle weary; if you proclaimed that you loved someone to excess, it was not unlikely you were actually rather fond of them; and when a fashionable woman who was busy trying to avoid a provincial cousin told her amiably, "You must come to dinner," she really meant, "I hope I never see you again."

At first, none of this was apparent to Gilbert, although he soon became aware of it. What he did see was a city whose narrow, noisy streets were covered with black, stinking mud; where a dizzying number of carriages, from grand state coaches to fast two-wheeled gigs, were driven at breakneck speed. The city must have seemed to him so immense as to defy comprehension (it was, in fact, the largest in Europe). And even on the drive to his mother's apartment, he must have been dazzled by myriads of servants in sumptuous, gold-embroidered, brightly colored liveries, and by the grand new mansions that were going up everywhere. Although he had no doubt felt lost upon leaving Chavaniac, it must have been as nothing compared to his terror on being driven through Paris. And when he finally reached his mother's residence, the boy knew for sure just how unimportant he really was, for in comparison with the palace he now entered, the castle of his childhood might almost have been a peasant's hut.

The Luxembourg was the most modern of the royal palaces in Paris. It had been built in the 1620s and modeled after the Pitti Palace in Florence; it was smaller than the Louvre but looked more imposing. The main façade was preceded by an elaborate gateway and a grand courtyard; on the other side lay a huge park that was (and still is) open to the public. The center pavilion was crowned with a dome; its stones were carved and ornamented, and all in all it could easily have contained several Chavaniacs. The King, however, did not reside there. Ever since Louis XIV, some hundred years earlier, had moved the monarchy to Versailles, the Parisian palaces had been largely given over to favored courtiers who were assigned rent-free apartments in them. This was where the La Rivières resided.

It must have been an awesome reunion for the young boy. Here was Mme de La Fayette, an imposing figure in her huge hooped skirts and high powdered hair-do topped with feathers and jewels. The terrified Gilbert found himself in his family's salon, a room of enormous magnificence with its white and gold paneling, silk double curtains, lush carpets, and precious inlaid furniture. Besides his mother, Gilbert now met for the first time his grandfather, great-grandfather, and uncle, all polished and sophisticated men. These people spoke very fast about incomprehensible subjects, and behaved with a kind of elaborate politeness. No doubt the boy was struck dumb. And immediately he was forced to adjust. Back in Chavaniac, his hair had only been curled and powdered on a few great occasions; here, every day, his coiffure had to be perfect. Then, too, the wool suits to which he was accustomed were replaced by silk, velvet, and brocade.

Mme de La Fayette promptly revealed herself as kind and maternal, but Gilbert could hardly ignore his transformation from lord of all he surveyed to that of ignorant oaf. He was told he needed both manners and an education. It was the first of many shattering experiences. Indeed, Mme de La Fayette had sent for the child because she realized that, unless he was brought up close to the center of power, his future would be extremely bleak. Now that he was in Paris, he could go to the right schools and meet the right people. The marquis de La Rivière, his grandfather, would use his connections. At the right age, the boy could, with the King's favor, become a lieutenant, and a wife from a good family would also help. This was all sensible planning, but for Gilbert, as he settled in Paris, the future seemed to contain only endless humiliation: the La Fayettes had been so thoroughly forgotten that when, in 1777, a dictionary of the nobility was published, they weren't even included.

At least there was his mother. A young woman still at thirty, she had great charm and intelligence. Although she hardly ever attended the court, she did have her own little salon, and conscientiously set about making her son a proper, civilized Parisian. Of course, she was quite different from the dutiful and austere Mme du Motier, but she very obviously loved her son and made it plain to him that she would do everything in her power to make him a great man. Then, too, the men of the family soon grew fond of Gilbert and paid attention to him and considered him one of their own. Little by little, life grew less uncomfortable, but Gilbert still never felt quite at home in Paris.

Of course, the La Rivières meant him to have a military career, but since advancement depended almost entirely on the King's favor, it was important to make the boy fit to attend the court. So Gilbert was enrolled at the Collège du Plessis, near the Sorbonne, which he attended for the next four years. The curriculum included mathematics, some history and geography and French literature, but it centered on the classics, and Gilbert learned little besides Latin.

Life was hard and unpleasant at the Collège du Plessis. The big rooms were cold and forbidding, the hours long, the masters often harsh. While it was only a small distance from the Luxembourg to the college, the two were worlds apart, and as the boy rode to class—only the poor walked— he must have dreaded the day ahead. Since it was a fashionable school, everybody, it seemed, came from a more illustrious family than his. The humiliated boy pretended to be aloof when really he was ashamed. He made no friends at all. Instead of joining a privileged group, he began to feel the stirrings of revolt. He behaved well but wrote a paper extolling Vercinge-torix, who had led the Gauls against Caesar, at a time when Rome was considered the fount of civilization, and when he was asked to describe the perfect horse, he explained that it was the most independent, most fiery animal and not, as anyone else would have said, the most obedient. Of course when, many years later, La Fayette wrote his memoirs, he claimed that this rebellious fantasy was an early proof of his love of liberty.

Such fantasy was a natural enough response, not only to schoolwork but to the glamorous milieu in which Gilbert was forced to humble himself. Never, perhaps, had French society been more brilliant than in those last years of the ancien régime. Birth and money counted for much, but nothing could replace that combination of wit, grace, and elegance that was the only key to social success. For the silent, gawky adolescent, the soirées in the

gilded salons of the La Rivières' apartments, the balls and court functions
he was made to attend must have been horribly painful. The more he suffered, the more silent he became, and that very silence was an unforgivable
social sin. The participants in this glittering life, these aristocrats with powdered hair, clothes embroidered-in-gold, and dazzling jewels, thought that
manners were all. You were expected to bow gracefully, to dance well, and
to say the right things in the right words at the right time. Youth was no
excuse: one of the darlings of the age was the chevalier de Boufflers, shining
in his mother's salon at fourteen, writing graceful (if singularly empty) verse
at fifteen, and seducing every woman in sight at sixteen. Since, in fact, grace
mattered more than strength, adolescents were thought to be particularly
attractive. But the silent, awkward Gilbert looked at this silken world with
despair and loathing, especially since its splendor left him completely un-
moved. It did not matter to him that one duchess wore a dress embroidered
with real emeralds or that another's head was crowned with diamonds and
the rarest feathers, that the people he saw were dressed in the latest fashion,
that witticisms uttered in his hearing were repeated as far north as St.
Petersburg and as far south as Naples. To Gilbert, this extraordinarily privileged world was simply his private hell. It is no wonder he looked forward
to his summers in Chavaniac in 1769 and 1770. There, at least, he was
somebody.

Then, in 1770, through the vagaries of fate, the world shifted again for
young Gilbert. In late March his mother took ill and, to everyone's surprise,
ten days later she was dead. She was only thirty-two. Although Gilbert had
not really known her long, he was grief-stricken. He was not completely
alone in the world—there were still the La Rivières in Paris, his grandmother
and his aunt in Chavaniac—but a vital support had suddenly been withdrawn. Though he did have guardians, no one was really in charge of his
life anymore.

Then, a few months later, the marquis de La Rivière followed his daughter to the grave. At age twelve Gilbert was left in the charge of a very old
great-grandfather and an uncle by marriage, the comte de Lusignem. Most
important, he had suddenly, at one blow, become one of the richest people
in France. For lack of other male heirs, his grandfather's extensive estate
fell entirely to the adolescent. There was land in Brittany and near the Loire.
There was, as well, a variety of investments. Altogether, Gilbert found
himself in receipt of an annual income of over 120,000 livres or approximately
$540,000. Added to the 25,000 livres a year he had inherited from his father,
the young marquis now enjoyed an income equivalent to well over $600,000.

The once-obscure young man could aspire to anything he wanted, but
first, he had to embark on his military career. Under the ancien régime,

neither age nor ability mattered much if you had the right connections. It was not uncommon for the younger son of a great family to be given a bishopric before he was twenty, and, with the King's favor, children of eight or nine had sometimes been put in (theoretical) command of a regiment. So M. de La Rivière secured Gilbert a commission as a lieutenant in the Black Musketeers, an elite corps of which his great-grandfather had been the commander. The young marquis began to serve on April 9, 1771. Of course, his duties were light: after all, the new lieutenant was only thirteen. Besides, nobles were not expected to take their position in the army seriously except in time of war.

Nonetheless, there were some thrilling moments. The Royal Guard was officered only by aristocrats; as a lieutenant in one of its units, La Fayette was entitled to follow the royal hunt, which is to say that he joined the privileged little group around the King. Better still, Gilbert, as officer of the day, was once actually allowed to approach Louis XV directly and ask him for an order. In a world where the King enjoyed semidivine status, this was a very great moment indeed. As usual, His Majesty looked bored and answered that there were no orders. It made little difference. Lieutenant the marquis de La Fayette had basked in the monarch's reflected glory; if the King became accustomed to him he might listen when asked for a promotion, pension, or court appointment. Although he realized the question was an empty ritual, La Fayette, who had yet to discover republican politics, felt enormously important.

Gilbert's duties as an officer, although they took some of his time, did not prevent him from attending the Collège du Plessis. Those studies continued until 1772. That summer, as the fifteen-year-old set off for Chavaniac, he felt free at last.

Back in Paris, however, M. de La Rivière had decided the time had come to settle his grandson's future, so sensibly, set about looking for a well-connected wife. The sky was the limit, since the combination of proven nobility and a great fortune made La Fayette one of the most eligible bachelors in France. Marriages in the aristocracy (and often in the middle classes as well) were arranged according to the status of the families, for since the family, not the individual, was the basic social unit, its advancement came first. No one expected the future couple to be particularly happy together: the wife was supposed to produce heirs as quickly as possible; after she had done so, she was free to lead her own life. Husbands had mistresses, wives took lovers, and since, within the same large private house, they had separate apartments, they seldom saw anything of each other. Indeed, it was considered bad manners to invite husband and wife to the same parties.

It never occurred to M. de La Rivière that Gilbert ought to be told about his search for a bride, if only because the young man might have followed his heart and made a foolish choice. With proper management, Gilbert might end up a marshal of France and a duke. But for that he would need the backing of a family with solid influence at court. After all, court life was terribly expensive, and an influential duke might well want to marry off a daughter to one of the richest men in France who was also wellborn.

M. de La Rivière knew exactly to whom he must turn. Not only was the duc d'Ayen unfortunate enough to have five daughters, all of whom must be found husbands, he was also a member of Louis XV's intimate circle and belonged to one of the four or five most important families in France.

A very few houses, at the end of the eighteenth century, were so illustrious, so rich, and so constantly in the King's favor that they had actually managed to accumulate not only several titles but also vast estates, large pensions, and huge sums of capital. These families had almost boundless influence at court with which they secured a vast array of plums. They enjoyed the greatest of privileges, those of attending closely on the King's person, and were thus in the best possible position to ask for even more favors.

The greatest of these families were the Montmorencys, the Rohans, the La Rochefoucaulds, and the Noailles, and among them, the Noailles were probably the greediest and most powerful. In 1772, the family was represented, among others, not only by the old maréchal duc de Noailles; his sons the duc d'Ayen and the duc de Mouchy and his grandson the prince de Poix; but also by a variety of other collaterals, including cardinals and marshals of France—all of whom played major roles at court and in the government—people such as the marquis de Noailles, soon to be ambassador to the Court of St. James's, and the comtesse de Noailles, dame d'honneur* to the dauphine,† Marie Antoinette.

Although, as a house, the Noailles were known for their ferocious ambition, both the old maréchal and the duc d'Ayen were polished courtiers with dazzling manners, ready wit, and the willingness to accommodate themselves to the monarch's mistress, whoever she might be. They knew how to keep Louis XV amused when they attended his private suppers and since, for them, the court was the entire world, the King's favor was the only thing that really mattered. Still, they were both decent men who indulged in rather less gossip, backbiting, and intrigue than was the rule at Versailles.

---

*The dame d'honneur was the chief female attendant of a queen or a dauphine and thus held the highest possible place at court for nonroyalty.

†The dauphin was the heir to the throne; the dauphine, his wife.

They were rather fonder of their families than most other great nobles: though they took mistresses, they were kind to their wives, and instead of caring only about the advancement of their house, they actually liked their children, taking notice of them and speaking to them. In sum, it was an unusually welcoming household.

The two dukes shared the office of captain of the Royal Guard, the very highest at court, so that, in procession, they had the right to walk just ahead of the King himself. No one, therefore, could have been in a better position to further the young marquis de La Fayette's career. There were advantages for the Noailles as well. Since the great families liked their fortunes to stay put, a rich (and noble) suitor for one of five daughters was not to be lightly rejected, especially if the suitor was an orphan who could be expected to join the Noailles clan, live in one of the great mansions they kept in Paris and Versailles, and become, so to speak, an honorary Noailles himself.

Still, the duc d'Ayen hesitated briefly when M. de La Rivière approached him. Although he did not have any sons of his own, he intended to have a Noailles grandson. Luckily, there was an available cousin, the vicomte de Noailles. He would be given the eldest daughter, while Adrienne, the second daughter, would become Mme de La Fayette.

A tentative marriage contract was drawn up in October 1772, but it remained unsigned until February 1773. Not only did La Fayette, through his tutor's agency, have to prove that he was as wealthy as he was supposed to be—a time-consuming process given that his estates were scattered all over France—but the duc d'Ayen and the marquis de La Rivière soon became engaged in a ferocious dispute about the amount of Mlle d'Ayen's dowry.

The duke had promised 400,000 livres (about $1,600,000) at the beginning of the negotiations, this being a fifth of his own wife's dowry, but then the lawyers, pouring over the settlement deeds, discovered that his own marriage contract stipulated that the full amount was to go to his eldest daughter. Luckily, the wording was ambiguous, so the duke talked to his wife, who announced she had firmly decided to give 400,000 livres to each of her daughters. The girl's fortune was no longer in question, so the contract could be signed.

At last M. de La Rivière could announce to Gilbert that his future had been settled. Apparently leaving the Luxembourg without regrets, the adolescent moved into the hôtel* de Noailles in Versailles on February 15 and was entered as a student in the riding academy. No other school could have

*A hôtel was a large private house.

served a more useful purpose: the riding academy's star pupil was none other than the comte d'Artois, the dauphin's youngest brother and the most fashionable young man in France. The set that gathered around him was the most select, most elegant, and potentially most influential at court. As a future Noailles son-in-law, and under the protection of his new cousin, the vicomte de Noailles, La Fayette all at once found himself at the very apex of court society. For the erstwhile little provincial, this was a heady rise indeed.

His Royal Highness the comte d'Artois was charming, easygoing, frivolous: he owned more than three hundred pairs of shoes. Pleasure was everything to him. He kept himself busy with racehorses and ballet dancers, was handsome and lithe and completely empty-headed. This was no impediment to being accepted as the leader of the younger set at court and the dauphine's best friend, especially since he was such a pleasant contrast to his two brothers, the dull, awkward dauphin, and the fat, pedantic comte de Provence. Chief among Artois's followers was the vicomte de Noailles.

The vicomte, too, was a handsome man, but he was also intelligent and relatively well read. While Artois played at soldiering, Noailles soon succeeded in becoming a competent, reliable officer. Of course competence may not have been an advantage in the comte d'Artois's circle, but the vicomte was witty enough to make up for it. He was also a good family man and proud of being a Noailles; so when Gilbert turned out to be dull and awkward, Noailles stood by his future brother-in-law, defending him to the others and encouraging him to acquire a little more polish. For Gilbert was as miserable as ever. In a group where grace, dexterity, and good horsemanship counted for everything, he was tongue-tied, shy, and so poor at managing his mount that he soon became a frequent target of Artois's mockery. Still, he was not wholly unpopular: although mostly silent, he was at least polite. Naturally Gilbert soon became devoted to his defender, Noailles. And since the vicomte was not only kind but effortlessly managed everything that Gilbert found so terribly difficult, the younger man (Noailles was three years older) spent the next few years slavishly imitating his mentor.

Curiously, although the marriage contract was signed, and La Fayette was living right in the hôtel de Noailles, the young marquis was hardly ever allowed to see his future bride. The whole world knew of the forthcoming marriage, but Adrienne, the bride-to-be, was kept utterly in the dark. She had been told simply that the young marquis de La Fayette had been taken in as a favor to M. de La Rivière. Gilbert was not allowed to court her, and since he lived in a different wing of the great mansion, he saw the family only on ceremonial occasions. His position was all the more difficult given that the vicomte de Noailles was openly acknowledged as a future son-in-law. Once again, Gilbert was second best.

This time, however, it had little or nothing to do with him: his humiliation was due to his future mother-in-law. For the duchesse d'Ayen had not adopted the mores of her age: in a world devoted to ease and pleasure, she remained austere and passionately religious. While scrupulously fulfilling her obligations as duchess and wife of the captain of the guard, her heart was not in it. She preferred to retire to her own apartments, there to raise her daughters, to think of her soul, and to attend to her very considerable benefactions. She had an unfashionably personal interest in her daughters' future happiness. Consequently, she insisted on sons-in-law whose personality and habits she could approve, refused to allow her daughters to marry while they were still too young to know what they were doing, and actually insisted on obtaining their consent.

All this was trying for the duc d'Ayen, who consoled himself by seeing as little of his wife as possible and by pointing out to his close friends, when provoked, that at least the duchess willingly admitted error when a convincing counterargument could be made. La Fayette was a case in point. At first, the duchess refused even to think of him as a prospective son-in-law. She knew nothing about him and, besides, he and Adrienne were far too young. Luckily, the first objection was easily overcome. When she met Gilbert, she instantly liked him, perhaps because he was so unlike the other young men at Versailles. Her objection to his age remained, however, and it was not until early in 1774 that she told Adrienne why Gilbert had been living with them. Even then, of course, the girl was just fourteen years old.

"We were barely twelve years old," Adrienne wrote, "when M. de La Fayette was offered [to my mother] for one of us; he was only fourteen himself. His extreme youth, the isolation in which he found himself, having lost all his close relatives and being without a guide he could trust, a vast fortune already all his, which my mother considered as yet another danger, all these considerations brought her to refuse him in spite of the good opinion she had formed about him from all that she had learned about his personality. She persisted in her refusal for several months but my father never gave up. . . . And, in fact, once my mother had been reassured by the certainty that her daughter would not leave her for the first few years, once it was promised to her that the marriage would not take place for two years, and that several measures had been taken to complete M. de La Fayette's education, she accepted the man whom, ever since, she has treated as the tenderest and best-loved of sons, the man whose full value she understood from the first moment she saw him."[2]

In the meantime, the duc d'Ayen was active on La Fayette's behalf. In April 1773 the young man was transferred from the Musketeers to the Noailles regiment, where he could feel quite at home since that body, to all intents and purposes, belonged to the Noailles and was commanded by the old maréchal himself. La Fayette's immediate supervisor was his cousin by marriage, the prince de Poix, and his companion, once again, the vicomte de Noailles. Thirteen months later, Ayen pressed further, and, with some reluctance on the part of the War Minister, the young man found himself promoted to captain, a rank left conveniently vacant by Poix when he became colonel. The seventeen-year-old captain had in no way deserved the promotion, and to mitigate the favor, it was stipulated that he would not actually take up his post until his eighteenth birthday. Before that auspicious day, however, the young marquis had become a married man.

The wedding, which took place in 1774 on the same day as that between Pauline d'Ayen and the vicomte de Noailles, was solemnized in the chapel of the hôtel de Noailles in Paris, and it was in one of the wings of the family mansion that Gilbert and Adrienne set up housekeeping. That huge, rambling town palace, with its enormous garden, was both the Paris residence of the Noailles family in all its many branches and a symbol of the family's greatness. Of course, Gilbert found it convenient to have a ready-made home; besides, it was just one more of those moves in which he seemed to have very little choice. His wife was devoted to her mother, and it had been understood that the young couple would remain for a time with the Ayens so that Adrienne could see her mother every day. And, finally, the arrangement was cheap: La Fayette contributed 8,000 livres a year for his share of the expenses, a fraction of what a separate house would have cost him, and a mere trifle compared to his income. There was a drawback, though it was felt, perhaps, by none but Gilbert: as far as the world was concerned, he, too, was now a Noailles.

From the outside this looked like an enviable position. The young marquis now knew he was assured of success in his career. Socially, he belonged to that most envied of groups, the little set around the eighteen-year-old Queen Marie Antoinette, whose husband, Louis XVI, had just that May succeeded to the throne. Further, Gilbert was very rich and he took full advantage of his wealth, setting up a large and pleasant household that "received many people and served very good dinners."[3]

On a personal level, life was not that bad either. Gilbert discovered that his wife was not only pretty, sweet, and intelligent, but madly in love with him, and he soon responded. From their very first night together, Adrienne made it plain that she loved Gilbert sexually. While we do not know exactly how he felt, it seems certain that he reciprocated Adrienne's ardors when he did not provoke them, and found the marriage bed quite as pleasant as she did. Probably the happiest moment of the summer of 1774 came, for him, when he rented a little house where he retired with Adrienne so that they could be inoculated in privacy against smallpox. When the duchess, who found in La Fayette the son she had been missing, joined them, Gilbert was able to display a side of his personality that he usually kept hidden. He was warm, kind, affectionate, caring. He laughed and was amusing to others. Best of all, finding himself the center of a little household for the first time since Chavaniac, he began to feel competent and gifted.

Such rewards were not to be found outside the domestic circle, however. The new social advantages only exacerbated La Fayette's feelings of inferiority. Now more than ever, life was thoroughly unpleasant. First, he dreaded his father-in-law who, like the accomplished courtier he was, valued polish, wit, and grace above all else. Though the duc d'Ayen found all those qualities in his other son-in-law, the vicomte de Noailles, La Fayette suffered by comparison and was often made to listen to his father-in-law's disquisitions on his various insufficiencies. Second, there was life in the army and at court.

In the summer of 1774, Gilbert, along with the inevitable vicomte, went off to Metz, near the eastern borders, to attend maneuvers. Once there he found himself in a hard-drinking set in which, once again, he cut a poor figure. If Metz was bad, Versailles was worse. The Queen was gay, frivolous, and mad for pleasure. Spurred on by the frustration of having an impotent husband, she soon transformed the court: anyone over twenty-five was considered unfashionable and dubbed a *paquet* (a bundle); anyone over thirty a *siécle* (a century). Fashion was all that mattered. Skirts grew wider and wider until they were often twenty feet around; hair-dos reached so far skyward that ladies had to go through doors sideways and kneel in their carriages.

When she wasn't busy planning her wardrobe, the Queen needed constant amusement: dancing, gossiping, gambling for high stakes, men. Marie Antoinette saw to it that she was surrounded only by the most attractive, most amusing gentlemen in France. The group included her brother-in-law, the comte d'Artois, who was conducting simultaneous affairs with an expensive dancer and a number of ladies at court, and told Marie Antoinette all about his adventures. There was the vicomte de Noailles, as charming and amusing as even a queen could demand; the comte de Ségur, whose great scheme it was, for a while, to resurrect the fashions of the late sixteenth century (though Louix XVI for once put his foot down, and the idea came to naught); the prince de Guéménée, a member of the powerful Rohan family, who gave especially splendid parties; the Dillon brothers, whose chief virtue was that they danced so very well. By virtue of his being the vicomte de Noailles's brother-in-law, La Fayette found himself part of this group. He hated every second of it.

At first he imitated the others. They gambled, so did he (and unlike the others, he could afford it). Horseracing became the fashion: he bought horses. Drinking was expected of him: he drank until, one night, he had to be carried back to his carriage, repeating feebly, "Don't forget to tell Noailles how much I've had to drink."[4] In spite of his best efforts, however, La Fayette never felt he really belonged.

"M. de La Fayette carefully sought what he believed to be the most fashionable, both in people and in things," wrote the comte de La Marck, an unfriendly contemporary, "but despite this taste for fashion, he was altogether awkward; he was terribly tall, his hair was red; he danced without grace, rode poorly. . . . At the balls . . . held in Versailles, the Queen took great pleasure in dancing arranged quadrilles. . . . M. de La Fayette was admitted to one of these quadrilles but he was so awkward and gauche [in fact, he stumbled and fell during one of the dances] that the Queen could not help laughing."[5] Soon all the courtiers treated him like a figure of fun.

In fact, though he may have been gawky, La Fayette was not so very tall, nor was his hair so very red, but he was unquestionably made to feel dull, awkward, and inferior. "I was judged unfavorably," he wrote later, "because of my silences and because I neither thought nor heard anything which seemed to me worth saying. The bad effects of my hidden pride and my tendency to observe without participating were in no way mitigated by a gauche manner."[6]

It is hard to judge how much self-justification there is in Gilbert's disclaimer, but it cannot be denied that for a serious young man who wanted to become a competent officer, fashion and dancing were light nourishment indeed. Still, for the first two years of their marriage, both Gilbert and Adrienne behaved as everyone expected. They attended court, participated in all the amusements of Paris and Versailles—balls, dinners, rides in the Bois de Boulogne, concerts, fashionable lectures, even. They spent time and attention, not to mention money, on their clothes and were, apparently, a typical aristocratic couple. The future was secure: Gilbert knew that he would rise in the army through his connections at court, that Adrienne would become a lady-in-waiting to the Queen. With luck and the Noailles influence, he could look forward eventually to being created a duke. Lawyers took care of his estates. He himself would never have to give a thought to money. Very rarely, with his wife, he would visit Chavaniac and display the deepest attention to his grandmother, but it had ceased to be his home.

The La Fayettes' was a classic marriage. The only obvious difference from the norm was that the young couple were very much in love: the arranged marriage was turning into a truly happy union. Alas, this, too, made Gilbert feel unfashionable. His set considered conjugal love simply grotesque. If he wanted to be elegant, he must take a mistress. In itself, this created no problem: having a mistress would not mean he no longer cared for his wife. Adrienne would understand, as all wives did; and he would feel less insecure if he were able to conquer some fashionable beauty. So he started courting the young and gorgeous comtesse d'Hunolstein. He really should have been successful: the fair Aglaé was rapidly gaining a reputation for extreme promiscuousness, no mean feat in a society where women changed lovers almost as often as dresses. La Fayette, however, was considered hopelessly unattractive, and worse, he had a competitor—the duc de Chartres, a member of the royal family.

La Fayette must have cursed his luck. One could compete with another nobleman, no matter how grand, but a royal prince was so much above the run of common mortals that Gilbert really had no hope at all. One evening he had become so frustrated that he awoke his friend Ségur, whose interests were beginning to shift from sixteenth-century fashions to military prowess, from a sound sleep, and challenged him to a duel. Was not Ségur also favored by Mme d'Hunolstein? asked La Fayette. A duel, he said, would at least make him feel better. Since there was no chance of his fighting Chartres, Ségur would have to do. To fight a friend "for the heart of a beauty to which I had not the slightest pretension,"[7] wrote Ségur, was hardly an appealing notion. Ségur refused the challenge and instead stayed up most of the night talking Gilbert out of the idea.

Unfortunately, the duc d'Ayen heard about Gilbert's unsuccessful court-ship. Being a civilized man, he had no objection to Gilbert's taking a mistress, but he loathed ridicule, and the young man had cut a sorry figure. The episode provoked his further scorn, which he hardly bothered to conceal from either the world or his son-in-law.

Still, the Marquis tried to fit in as best he could. He had the consolation of belonging to the Société de l'Épée de Bois, a café that had become a favorite rendezvous for aristocratic young bloods who went there to drink, to make noise, to pick up easy women, and to plan their next pranks. La Fayette was present, for instance, when a group including the comtes de Ségur and d'Artois staged a parody of the way the Parlement of Paris con-ducted its business. Reports of the café sendup were soon circulating through Paris and Versailles, and seemed so shocking that Maurepas, the Prime Minister, asked the King to punish the culprits. As it turned out, the comte de Ségur had already related the episode to his father, who had in turn passed the story on to Louis XVI in such a way as to amuse that rather humorless monarch. As a result, M. de Maurepas was told to leave the young people alone, and the group gained a wholly undeserved reputation for daring and unconventionality.

This café-society prank did not represent mere youthful high spirits. It had a political message as well, which was why it shocked so many. The Parlement was a touchy and powerful, conservative body, all the more defensive of its privileges because all its members were rich judges who had paid as much as 100,000 livres ($450,000) for their offices. Although quite different from the British Parliament in this respect, the Parlement did function as the court of record by registering the King's edicts and could, on occasion, refuse to do so. It courted popularity with the public by refusing to register any new tax edicts, though the edicts in question actually represented the King's attempt to end the tax-exempt status of nobility and clergy and thus lighten the burden of the lower classes. The parlements—there were twelve besides the one at Paris—claimed to be fighting for liberty while they protected their own pocketbooks, and they were not all wrong: for it was the most reactionary elements at court who took the King's side of the disputes. The old-line aristocracy greatly disliked the judges of Parlement, partly because they resented any challenge to the King's authority, upon whom they now depended for everything, and partly because the Parlement men, although legally noble, in fact came from the middle class and thus represented a challenge to the aristocracy's supremacy. In mocking the "jumped-up bourgeois" of the Parlement, Artois, Ségur, and his friends were clearly aligning themselves with the most conservative elements at court. Like the rest of Marie Antoinette's friends, Artois liked things as they were and was determined to resist any change. As a member of this group, La Fayette would have been considered as belonging firmly on the right. In fact, the Marquis was hardly conscious that there was such a thing as politics and was far too busy trying to keep up with the Queen's coterie to care about taxes or the way France was governed.

His efforts to be up-to-date weighed on him, however. Gilbert let a few close friends—Noailles, Ségur—know how unhappy he was. Try as he might, he would never be another vicomte de Noailles, and he knew it. Worse, the duc d'Ayen had so little confidence in La Fayette's military abilities that he decided in 1776 to find Gilbert a position at court where mere proximity would allow him to keep progressing. Gilbert was neither old enough nor grand enough for an appointment in the King's household, but there was always Monsieur,* comte de Provence. The duc d'Ayen went

---

*Monsieur, used without a specific name, was a title reserved for the King's next brother. Artois, who was the third-born, had no specific appellation.

to work and was soon promised that his son-in-law would be made one of Monsieur's lords-in-waiting. Gilbert, when told the news, was appalled, and all the more so because the rest of the family considered it a great coup. He realized with a sinking heart that he was much too afraid of the duc to refuse the arrangement outright. Then after a few days of complete misery, an idea came to him: there was a way out after all.

"When my new relatives found me a place at court, I didn't hesitate to incur [Monsieur's] displeasure in order to preserve my independence,"[8] Gilbert wrote some twenty years later. In fact, distaste for court life rather than a taste for freedom was his motive, but the result, of course, was the same: by offending the comte de Provence, Gilbert would make sure that the promised appointment would fall through. This was easy. Everyone knew that the prince prided himself on his extensive, unfailing memory. A few days after Ayen's announcement of La Fayette's appointment, Gilbert walked up to Monsieur at a masked ball and declared, in contemptuous tones, that only fools who were unable to think for themselves prided themselves on a good memory. Monsieur, of course, was outraged. Still, the Noailles were powerful and good diplomats, and, to Gilbert's despair, they worked out a solution. Monsieur let it be known that he was willing to believe it had all been a mistake, that the Marquis had not realized just whom he was speaking to. The insult, being unintended, would not count. All La Fayette had to do was tell Monsieur he had mistaken him for another and all would be forgiven. Instead, the next day, Gilbert, shaking but determined, walked up to the prince, who was dressed in blue, and said he had known full well whom he was addressing.

"And who was that?" the comte de Provence asked, unbelieving.

"The same person, sir, I see now wearing a blue suit,"[9] La Fayette answered. Monsieur had nothing left to do but give the impertinent young man a frosty look and announce to the duc d'Ayen that the appointment was canceled.

Naturally enough, Gilbert felt triumphant: he had braved every convention and had his way. Unfortunately he had not known how to do it openly, and when the outraged duc d'Ayen gave him a good dressing down, Gilbert was far too scared to explain himself. Instead he sat in respectful silence, which only made his behavior seem more incomprehensible. The prestige of the court, in 1776, was still very great, and turning down a position near the King's brother quite unheard of. The truth was, of course, that La Fayette felt so dreadfully uncomfortable at Versailles that the last thing he wanted was to be stuck there permanently. Later, he was to say that he had always despised royalty: that is pure propaganda. It is nonetheless remarkable that he had the courage and determination to resist both the

duc d'Ayen and general opinion. Of course, he was helped by the con-
sciousness, learned at his grandmother's knee, that the army would be his
road to fame, not some silly court job in which he would always be an object
of ridicule. There was only one way to show the duc d'Ayen and the others
who mocked him just what kind of man he really was—he must lead his
troops to victory. The only problem was that France seemed altogether
unlikely to go to war in the near future.

Two

ANYWHERE BUT HOME

Metz, in the 1770s, was the most elegant of garrison towns. The bulk of the French army was stationed there. In the summer all the elegant young men of Marie Antoinette's set went off to Metz to join their regiments.

Here, as in Paris and Versailles, life consisted mostly of gambling and wenching, while minimal attention was paid to military duty. Still, the young officers did learn some basic lessons: how to give orders, how to maneuver troops so that one half of the regiment didn't march straight into the other, and even a few vague notions of strategy. Little more than courage was expected from them. After all, when it came to the technical side of war, there would always be those dreary officers from the École Militaire, one Napoleon Bonaparte, for instance, noblemen to be sure, but from minor, impoverished families who had neither the means nor the connections to rise to the top.

Just how little actual military merit had to do with promotions was vividly demonstrated in 1775, when both the duc de Noailles and the duc de Mouchy were created marshals of France. As a captain in the Noailles regiment, La Fayette was clearly due for rapid promotion. The curious thing was that he really tried to earn the recognition that came his way; perhaps he wanted to show the Noailles he wasn't as hopeless as they thought; perhaps he really thirsted for glory.

As fate would have it, he had come at the right time—to the right place. The officer commanding the army at Metz was the comte de Broglie. This ambitious and embittered man was anxious to make up for what he considered an unfair lack of rewards. As head of Louis XV's secret diplomacy, he had worked hard year after year, incurred two exiles from court when the ministers, who smelled a rival, had demanded them. Then, at the King's death, instead of being properly praised by his successor, he had found himself completely out of favor because Louis XVI was embarrassed by his grandfather's secrets. On top of all this, Broglie considered himself a genius, and was sure that he alone could govern France properly. Since, however, he also realized that he would never become prime minister, he was now ready to settle for an American throne.

Although the insurgents in the colonies knew that they had not renounced their allegiance to George III only to replace him with another monarch, no one in Europe had yet understood it. It was axiomatic that a monarchy was the only possible form of government because democracies always slid into anarchy. Clearly, therefore, the Americans, once they had won their independence, would need a king. And who better for the new throne, Broglie thought, than himself? The trick, of course, was to lead the American army to victory. That the Americans might have their own competent generals did not occur to him: the new continent, after all, was barely civilized. Only a military mastermind like himself, he thought, could defeat the British army.

This personal ambition, however, was carefully hidden by a cloud of fashionable verbiage. Like most members of Broglie's circle, La Fayette was prattling about liberty in the New World. The word, in fact, had invaded current speech to a surprising degree. We find even the most reactionary courtiers carrying on about liberty as early as 1774, although what they really meant was the liberty of keeping their sinecures and privileges. The word had not yet acquired the explosive meaning it would soon bear as the most important element of the revolutionary trinity, Liberty, Equality, Fraternity. In the seventies, *liberty*, often used in the plural, as in the "liberties of a province," could stand for its exact opposite, *privilege*; but already Rousseau's influence was being felt and the word was beginning to acquire a new and different connotation spurred on by the constitutional notion of the "liberties of the subject" as practiced in England.

Of course, Broglie had no intention of defending liberty against a tyrannical monarch: no such political views marred the pure selfishness of his pro-American stand. La Fayette, however, was too naïve to see Broglie's egocentricity. An eventual American operation was presented as the perfect opportunity for taking revenge on England, something Gilbert had always wanted to do, while incidentally helping a virtuous if uncultured people.

La Fayette also had a personal reason to want to go to America. As an officer of the Noailles regiment he was supervised by his numerous in-laws; in America he would be on his own, or at most under the command of the comte de Broglie, a man who had made it plain he appreciated Gilbert's merits. There would be an opportunity for advancement, and on the battlefield social graces would hardly be necessary. With just a little luck, the young man would return to France a hero. That would show the carping duc d'Ayen, the disdainful Mme d'Hunolstein, and the world in general just what a mistake they had made.

At first, all this remained a fantasy; soon, however, it began to take on more consistency. On August 8, 1775, the comte de Broglie gave a grand dinner for HRH the Duke of Gloucester, King George III's brother, who was on his way to Italy. They invited the prince de Poix, the vicomte de Noailles, and a number of other socially prominent officers. La Fayette had the last place at the bottom of the table. There he heard the duke, who disliked his brother so much that he had adopted a pro-American position, speak at length about the shortcomings of British policy and the merits of the insurgents. This made a deep impression on all the guests: it was the first time they heard the situation explained so clearly, and by so authoritative a source.

Enthusiasm was all very well, but action was more difficult. La Fayette did little more than talk for a year following the dinner; then, on June 11, 1776, as a consequence of reforms being carried through by the new War Minister, the Marquis, along with a number of young and inexperienced courtiers, found himself put on the inactive list. He would be called back in case of war, but for now his military career was at an end; there would be no returning to Metz. At age nineteen, Gilbert was a hopeless failure.

Anyone would have suffered; for the proud heir of the La Fayette tradition, it was a situation that must be remedied at once. Luckily, there was America, for although the Declaration of Independence did not reach Europe until October 1776, it was obvious long before that the insurgents were fighting in earnest. So, after talking it over with Ségur and Noailles, to whom the idea seemed a wonderful lark, La Fayette decided to volunteer as an officer in the American army. Noailles and Ségur enthusiastically followed his lead. Naturally, they had consulted Broglie, "whose heart," La Fayette wrote, "after vain efforts to stop me, followed me with a fatherlike tenderness."[1] We may suppose that the vain efforts were never meant to succeed.

The comte de Broglie, now living in Paris, was giving frequent parties where his elegant young men met with Silas Deane, the American envoy to France, and with Broglie's own aides, Mauroy, du Boismartin, and Johann De Kalb. Deane, of course, was anxious to recruit officers: like the French, he was so convinced of his compatriots' military incapacity that he thought the war would be lost without European officers.

Deane was willing to settle for just about anyone he could recruit, no matter how bad his reputation might be. Broglie, on the other hand, wanted to send over a nucleus of officers he could count on. He would group them around two men in their late forties. One was Johann De Kalb, a German adventurer with a phony title (he called himself a baron) who had ended up as one of Broglie's followers. A self-educated man of considerable intelligence, a devoted husband anxious to give his wife a better life, De Kalb realized that his career in the French army lacked promise, but, as Broglie's adjutant in America, he might do very well indeed. The other, Mauroy, was a real noble, but came from a poor, unimportant family. He, too, had been picked by Broglie as a man with nothing much to lose, and with an obvious need for a protector. Unlike De Kalb, who knew how to make himself pleasant, Mauroy often allowed his resentment to show: his consequent unpopularity made him all the more dependent on Broglie.

Together, De Kalb and Mauroy were to take over command of the American troops, then call for Broglie himself. As for La Fayette and Noailles, both now recruits to the Broglie faction, they were little short of a godsend for the intriguing comte: given their positions and families, they must play an important role in America, and Broglie also knew he could count on them to support his own ambitions. There was, however, an important prerequisite: the young men's families must approve, since more than half their value lay in their connections.

From then on, under the veil of secrecy, the characters of this story proceeded to behave as if they belonged in one of those Marivaux comedies where the young lovers switch places with their servants so as to test each other's virtue. Broglie alternately admitted and denied he knew anything about La Fayette's and Noailles's intentions. Maurepas found out exactly what the young men were planning to do, but first ignored it, then forbade it, then forgot the whole troublesome business long enough for it to start up again. The duc d'Ayen blustered and wavered. Silas Deane first pushed for the young men's departure, then recanted. Had La Fayette not been so deeply committed to his dream, the whole business would have dissolved into the farce it so often seemed. Act One took place in the gilded salons of the hôtel de Noailles—a perfect setting for a society play. Even the characters belonged to the traditional repertory: there was the self-important father-in-law (Ayen), the brilliant young man (Noailles), and his stupid but enthu-siastic friend (La Fayette). The action began when Noailles confessed to his father-in-law that he wanted to go to America. Since the duc was fond of his son-in-law, but disapproved of the Americans as insurgents rebelling against their king, he blew both hot and cold; but when Gilbert told him that he, too, wanted to go over, he made up his mind instantly. If that twit wanted to fight in America, then, clearly, the only right course lay in keeping him in Paris. With much scorn and contumely, the duc forbade Noailles and La Fayette to leave France. About this point Ségur, whose family also dis-approved, simply gave up. La Fayette, however, went straight to Broglie and announced, mendaciously, that he had the duc d'Ayen's blessing. Broglie set about arranging their recruitment and transport through his flunky, De Kalb, while himself pretending to know nothing.

In negotiating with De Kalb, La Fayette and Noailles pushed their bluff still further: the duc d'Ayen, they said, had consented to their joining the Americans only if they both went as general officers. Besides being an utter falsehood, this demand on the part of very young men with no experience of war and precious little military training was almost grotesque. Neverthe-less De Kalb passed along their condition to Deane, who met La Fayette and was hardly reassured—the Marquis was obviously not fit to command. There was a mitigating factor: though La Fayette insisted on being a major general, he would decline any salary, an important consideration since the fledgling United States was stone broke. Furthermore, should the Noailles clan become pro-American, it would almost surely influence Maurepas and the King. Given these considerations, Deane produced, in December 1776, a contract for La Fayette and, at Broglie's request, De Kalb, making them both major generals. De Kalb was experienced; he had fought in Germany and worked his way up from the ranks; as for the Marquis, what mattered was "his high birth, his alliances, his considerable estates in the realm, his personal merit, the great dignities which his family hold at court, his rep-utation, his disinterestedness and, above all, his zeal for the liberty of our provinces."[2] As for the last, Gilbert no doubt pretended to it, although it hardly had the same meaning for him as it did for Deane. What he saw, really, was an opportunity to fight the English and make his reputation; obviously these goals entailed severing of the British connection.

Now a new problem developed. The duc d'Ayen having finally decided to let the vicomte de Noailles, whom he trusted, go over while La Fayette remained in France, had, very properly, asked M. de Maurepas for per-mission. Unfortunately he caught the prime minister in one of his anti-

American moods, and permission was promptly refused. On top of that, news arrived of the crushing American defeat at the Battle of Long Island in August, prompting the French government suddenly to ban all officers from joining the insurgents. To Broglie's deep chagrin, the plan now seemed dead.

Then a new possibility dawned on this ever-ingenious plotter. La Fayette, as everyone knew, was rich. Why not, through De Kalb, talk him into buying his own ship so that he, and a few other pro-Broglie officers, could escape in secret? The main object, after all, was to get De Kalb and Mauroy— who was Broglie's devoted aide—over to America where they could further their patron's ambition. Once again De Kalb approached La Fayette, who loved the idea. Adding *Cur non* ("Why not") to his arms, La Fayette set the wheels in motion once again. Only this time, to avoid arousing suspicion, Gilbert made his arrangements not with Deane himself but with Deane's secretary, William Carmichael; and to preserve secrecy, he saw Carmichael not at the hôtel de Noailles but, most often, during long carriage rides.

Only someone as naïve as La Fayette, however, could have supposed all this would go unnoticed. In no time Maurepas was reading police reports describing the whole transaction. Soon the prince de Montbarey, a high official in the War Ministry, arrived to speak to Gilbert. The young man, shocked at being found out, promptly broke down and confessed his guilt. He promised not to go. Perhaps he was not very convincing. Montbarey appears not to have believed him; nevertheless he had better things to do, and no further measures were taken against La Fayette.

In the meantime another of Broglie's sidekicks, M. du Boismartin, had been sent off to Bordeaux. On February 11, 1777, La Fayette heard through De Kalb that du Boismartin had found a ship named the *Victoire*. This 220-ton vessel had a crew of thirty, was armed with two cannons, and under Captain Le Boursier had already made several trips to America. Now its owner, a rich Bordeaux merchant, was asking 112,000 livres, 40,000 livres in cash and the balance to be paid in June. The price was high, but the Marquis was rich and the deal went through.

Secrecy was now more important than ever, so Gilbert continued without interruption the busy social whirl of the carnival season in Paris. He attended ball after ball, party after party, always as part of the little group around the Queen; it was, in fact, as he came home from a late-night dance that he learned about the *Victoire*. The ship itself would not be ready to sail until mid-March, so Gilbert also proceeded with an earlier plan to accompany the prince de Poix on a visit to England. The young men went off together on February 16.

Meanwhile, although he seemed at times to forget it, La Fayette was still married. Adrienne had given birth to a daughter the year before; now she was pregnant again, but neither she nor the duchesse d'Ayen, faithful champion though she remained, was let in on the secret plan. When Gilbert left for London, Adrienne thought that she could confidently expect his return within a few weeks, well before she was ready to give birth. But La Fayette was typical of his time and class; children meant nothing to him and, in fact, Adrienne was not to see him again for more than two years.

La Fayette's purpose in going to England was not merely to confound the secret police of M. de Maurepas. Curiously, although England was still the hereditary enemy and although France would soon be at war with her again, it had become chic in the late 1770s to go to London. The young bloods of Paris were beginning to copy English habits—horse racing, drunkenness, even the wearing of round hats. It was firmly believed in French society that only English laundresses knew how to wash clothes properly, so that no elegant young man thought his shirt wearable unless it had been sent all the way to London. Unlike the others, La Fayette, out of regard for his father's memory, affected a dislike for the English nation.

Not surprisingly, it was yet another member of the Noailles family who was the French Ambassador, so naturally the two young men went to stay with their cousin the marquis, and were promptly presented to George III. As usual, the gawky, awkward La Fayette did not make much of an impression—a situation soon to be rectified—but he found himself in an altogether delicious position. "At the age of nineteen," he wrote later, "one may be a little too inclined to mock the king one is about to fight, to dance at Lord [George] Germain's house [he was Minister for the American Colonies] next to Lord Rawdon, freshly in from New York, and to meet at the Opera that same Clinton I was to face at the Battle of Monmouth. But while I kept my intentions quiet, I made my feelings very plain . . . and my kinship with the opposition earned me a lunch at Lord Shelburne's."[3] Still, when the King offered to let Poix and La Fayette visit the port installations at Plymouth, the young man declined: it was too close to spying. As for the marquis de Noailles, he reported home that La Fayette was behaving well and attending court regularly.[4]

Appearances notwithstanding, Gilbert was preparing himself for America. He had decided to go directly from London to Bordeaux without seeing his family, so, to explain and justify his behavior, he penned a long letter to the duc d'Ayen that was little more than a string of excuses and omissions.

"You will be surprised, my dear Papa," Gilbert wrote on March 9, "by what I am about to tell you. . . . I have found a unique chance of distinguishing myself and learning my profession: I am now a general officer in the army of the United States of America. My zeal for their cause and my frankness have earned me their confidence. On my side I have done every-thing I could for them and their interests will always matter more to me than my own. In fine, my dear Papa, I am now in London awaiting news from my friends; as soon as it comes, I will leave here and, without stopping in Paris, will embark on a ship which belongs to me. I am overjoyed at having found so fair an occasion to do something and to further my education. I do know that I am making enormous sacrifices and that I will suffer more than anybody at having to leave my family, my friends, you, my dear Papa, because I love you all more tenderly than has ever been done before. But this trip is not so very long, people, every day, take longer ones for pleasure alone, and, besides, I hope to return more worthy of all those who will be good enough to miss me. Farewell, my dear Papa, I hope to see you again soon, keep your tenderness for me, I am longing to deserve it, and already deserve it by the love I feel for you, and the respect felt, until the end of his days, by your tender son, Lafayette."[5] It is impossible to imagine a more fawning appeal for the sarcastic duc d'Ayen's affection.

As it turned out, before he could send it off, Gilbert received the awaited news: the *Victoire* was ready to sail. So it was with the letter in his pocket that, instead of proceeding straight to Bordeaux, secretly he returned to Paris giving as an excuse that he had been taken with the flu. He just could not bear to leave Europe without boasting of his coming exploits to his friends in the capital.

There could naturally be no question of La Fayette's showing his face in Paris, so he went straight to De Kalb's house in Chaillot, just outside the city, and hid there. If the duc d'Ayen had heard about his presence, nothing would have been easier than to obtain a *lettre de cachet*,* and Gilbert might well have found himself spending time in the Bastille; so, triumphantly telling only Ségur and Noailles, Gilbert left for Bordeaux with De Kalb on March 16, dropping off his letter to the duc de'Ayen at the hôtel de Noailles along with a note to Adrienne telling her that the thought of her sorrow was his chief regret, but that having given his promise, he must now keep it. The great escape had begun.

Or so it seemed. In fact, it was almost over with before the Marquis even reached Bordeaux. Naturally enough, the duc d'Ayen had a fit when he read his errant son-in-law's letter: here was rank disobedience wreathed in broken promises. Besides, how would it look in England? The marquis de Noailles was sure to be blamed. The family stood to lose on every count.

---

*A *lettre de cachet* was an order bearing the King's signature and seal; it was often used to imprison people.

Adrienne put it all very neatly: "I was pregnant and loved [La Fayette] tenderly. My father and the rest of the family were all violently angry at the news. . . . [My mother] tried to console me, both by preparing me to hear what had happened, and then by looking for ways to help M. de La Fayette."[6] As for the duc, he went straight to Maurepas and asked for an order restraining Gilbert from sailing, and further commanding him to accompany his father-in-law on a projected tour of Italy.

Maurepas was also enraged: his policy, as distinct from that of Charles de Vergennes, the Foreign Minister, consisted in staying at peace with England; if the war party should win out, Maurepas might lose his place to Vergennes. He was all the more determined to prevent this since, traditionally, dismissal meant exile away from the court, a fate worse than death to someone like Maurepas. And for Vergennes, too, cautiously inching closer to support of the insurgents, this was the very last thing he wanted. The English might protest mildly when fewer than a hundred unknown officers went off to America, but if a member of so important a family as the Noailles followed them, Lord Stormont, the British Ambassador, could be expected to make an enormous fuss; and since Louis XVI was not at all ready to start a war, it might mean the end of the secret help the United States was receiving and possibly the dismissal of Vergennes himself. Finally, there was the King himself, who had no sympathy at all for a rebellious rabble, anti-English though it might be. Predictably, when he heard the news, Louis XVI expressed extreme displeasure, thus aggravating the duc d'Ayen still further since his one great talent in life was pleasing the King. Not only had his dolt of a son-in-law put the family position in jeopardy, he had even put the duc d'Ayen in a difficult situation vis-à-vis the King.

Luckily, for everyone except Gilbert, France was still an absolute monarchy. Maurepas promised Lord Stormont the deluded young fool would be stopped at Bordeaux; Vergennes protested vigorously that he was just as opposed to La Fayette's departure as everybody else; and Louis XVI obligingly signed an order directing the Marquis to Marseilles, there to await the duc d'Ayen and his sister, the comtesse de Tessé, who would be on their way to Italy. Still, despite La Fayette's later claims to the contrary, no one asked the King for a *lettre de cachet*: Gilbert simply wasn't worth imprisoning.

While all this was happening in Paris and Versailles, Gilbert, in Bordeaux, found that the *Victoire* was not yet ready to sail, and although to allay suspicion, he went to stay with the maréchal de Mouchy, his wife's uncle and the governor of the province, he soon found himself forced to tell De Kalb he had come without the duc d'Ayen's consent. De Kalb, who understood what the official reaction was likely to be, demanded that Gilbert write to Paris and find out what was happening there. In the meantime, in the port's register of departures, Gilbert signed out, legitimately but misguidingly, as the chevalier de Chavaniac.

The news from Paris, when it came in a letter from Gilbert's friend, M. de Coigny, was far from good; still, the young man insisted that they set sail. It was a lucky move, for no sooner had the *Victoire* pulled out of Bordeaux harbor than a courier arrived bearing the order obtained from the King. The ship went on to the nearest Spanish port, thus escaping French jurisdiction, while the explosions in Paris continued.

The duc d'Ayen, worried now that his son-in-law's ship would be caught by a British man-of-war and detained indefinitely, sent La Fayette a letter ordering him point-blank to return; this was forwarded by Silas Deane, an indication that even the American envoy no longer backed the young man. As for Louis XVI, always a little slow, he was now so angry that he gave out an order forbidding all French officers to fight in the British colonies and instructing those who had already started on their way, "notably M. le marquis de La Fayette," to return. It looked like a great victory for Lord Stormont; however, the order did not become effective unless and until it was duplicated so that copies existed at both military ministries, War and Navy; and since the Navy Minister, M. de Sartines, was pro-American, he conveniently forgot to forward the order to the War Minister—thus, to all intents and purposes, canceling it. Still, La Fayette was too conspicuous. Duplication or no, he would have to return.

By now the errant young man was beginning to think so, too. Aboard the ship, anchored at Los Pasajes, near San Sebastian, he received a whole packet of letters that included both the duc d'Ayen's and the King's commands. He didn't get much encouragement from his fellow traveler, either. De Kalb, who realized that Broglie's whole plan was likely to be undone, was livid. He told La Fayette that he had indeed better return. At that very moment, in fact, Broglie was loudly protesting he was in no way responsible for Gilbert's flight and disapproved of it quite as heartily as everyone else.

But for all that Broglie and Vergennes protested, the wind was beginning to shift. All the fashionable ladies, who admired La Fayette's boldness, were now supporting his cause: going to America seemed so brave, so romantic, that Gilbert suddenly became famous. It even became axiomatic, in the Paris salons, that if the duc d'Ayen thwarted his brave son-in-law, he would be unlikely to find husbands for his unmarried daughters—and the power of the salons, in 1777, was not to be despised.

Still, Gilbert knew nothing of this. Deeply depressed, he felt, and was told by De Kalb, that he had no choice but to return to Bordeaux; so leaving the *Victoire* at Los Pasajes with De Kalb and some twelve other French officers chosen by Deane and Broglie, he set off by road and entered Bordeaux on April 3. From the ship, on April 1, De Kalb wrote to his wife: "And so he has given up both the voyage and the American war. He is leaving now for Bordeaux. . . . I do not for a moment expect him to return here; and I have advised him to see MM. Raimbaux and Co. who have approvisioned and freighted our ship on his account, to make an arrangement with them and sell it all back if they'll agree to his losing only 20 or 25,000 livres."[7]

As soon as he arrived in Bordeaux, La Fayette went to see M. de Fumel, the commandant of the port, and asked for permission to return to Paris. In what may well have been the luckiest moment of his entire life—had he returned to Paris, Gilbert would certainly never have gone to America—he was told that there could be no question of Paris and that Marseilles must now be his destination. So he sat down and wrote Maurepas a letter worded so humbly and so ambiguously that the prime minister thought it an apology pure and simple while, in fact, Gilbert was merely apologizing for disobeying his order to go to Marseilles. Then, changing his mind in a new fit of depression, he prepared to set off for Marseilles while, in Paris, all were convinced that the escapade was over. Maurepas even wrote the marquis de Noailles to tell him he could now reassure the British government: the marquis de La Fayette, far from sailing to America, was joining the duc d'Ayen on a tour of Italy.

At this point, the story switches to a new genre, something akin to *The Three Musketeers*. Just as our hero, full of self-doubt and despondency, is about to leave for Marseilles, an envoy comes dashing from Paris under a thick disguise. Who should it turn out to be but Mauroy, Broglie's chief aide! Rushing to find La Fayette, he is told that the young man has already left town but, with a last desperate effort, he catches up with him (in a cloud of dust?) and tells him to go on with his noble enterprise. In Paris, he says breathlessly, everyone is rooting for him, and especially Broglie. To be sure, the Noailles family are making a fuss, but that means nothing; even the government is really hoping for the young man's departure (an absolute lie); besides, if he came back now, he would look like a chastised, obedient child. Unlike the cautious De Kalb, Mauroy was perfectly willing to risk La Fayette's future for Broglie's benefit.

Hope dawning in his eyes, our hero listens avidly and, straightening his shoulders, vows to set sail for America after all; but what about the orders? To confuse the inevitable spies, Mauroy and La Fayette ostensibly resume the voyage toward Marseilles. At the first relay, our young nobleman disguises himself as a courier and starts out first riding ahead of Mauroy, but with a slight change of direction—toward San Sebastian. All is well for a while, but when the dashing marquis stops to get a fresh horse at the last inn before the border, he is recognized by the innkeeper's daughter with whom he had chatted on his way to Bordeaux. The suspense mounts! Will the Marquis be betrayed? Will his bold expedition come to a premature end? No! Swayed by the young man's appeals, the innkeeper's daughter keeps the guilty secret to herself, allowing our hero to cross the border undetected and board his ship, still at Los Pasajes, on April 17.

Of course, Mauroy had been lying about the government's wishes, but his goal was to get the ship on its way, and so far, he had succeeded because he had convinced La Fayette. On April 17, De Kalb wrote his wife: "The Marquis has just arrived this instant and will leave with us in a few days. He decided to do so because he has received assurances from Paris that the duc d'Ayen, alone, asked for the King's order; that, on the contrary, everyone else approved of his enterprise."[8] It took another three days for the last preparations to be made, but, at last, on April 20, the Victoire set off toward the west. This time La Fayette was really on his way.

Until this moment, the young man's enterprise had been marked by incompetence, naïveté, and indecision. Instead of the bold defender of liberty described by legend, what we see is a bumbling, not overly clever young man, unhappy at home, whose wish for escape was cleverly manipulated by the comte de Broglie. It was Broglie, after all, who arranged for La Fayette's commission with Silas Deane. It was Broglie who suggested buying a ship and sent one of his aides to make the actual arrangements, and it was Broglie, finally, who managed through Mauroy to send the young man on his way just when he was ready to give up. The reason Broglie went to all this trouble was very simple: of all the enthusiastic young men who wanted to go to America, only La Fayette was rich enough to buy a ship— the ship without which De Kalb could not sail to America and arrange for Broglie's appointment as commander in chief.

Still, once aboard the Victoire, La Fayette demonstrated a new decisiveness. Ships on their way to North America usually made a stop in the French West Indies, where they procured food and water and often sold whatever goods they were carrying. The Victoire was scheduled to make such a stop as well, but since La Fayette was afraid of being detained there on the King's orders, he asked the captain to sail straight to the United States. The captain, who owned a share of the cargo and was afraid of being caught by the British blockade fleet, refused. First La Fayette threatened him, but to no avail; then, by the simple expedient of buying the cargo himself, he convinced the captain to do as he wished. Later in the trip, when a ship in the far distance was thought to be a British man-of-war, La Fayette promptly organized a defense of the Victoire. He was prepared to fight to the last, but as things turned out, the other ship was only a French merchantman and, much to Gilbert's regret, there was no combat.

The crossing, delayed by long periods of dead calm, took a good seven weeks, and for a good portion of it La Fayette, De Kalb, and the other French officers were seasick. Unpleasant as this might be, however, the young marquis, for the first time, was on his own. Even better, as at Chavaniac, he was once again lord of all he surveyed. The ship belonged to him, the captain was following his orders, De Kalb and the others were dependent on him. It was lucky, really, that the vicomte de Noailles had followed orders and stayed in Paris: there was no longer anyone for Gilbert to imitate.

There can be no doubt that La Fayette enjoyed his new position; his memoirs make that quite clear. At the same time, the trip itself was dreary. As he wrote his wife on May 30, Gilbert was no sailor. "I am . . . in the most boring of countries; the sea is awfully sad and we sadden each other mutually. . . . I will keep no diary of my trip: here the days succeed one another and, what's worse, are absolutely alike. Always the sky, always the water, and then, the next day, it's the same all over again."

We have quite forgotten, in this era of jets, what travel could be like in the eighteenth century. The *Victoire*, on which La Fayette spent seven long weeks, was no cruise ship: it was a small, wooden vessel, short of water and food; within two weeks of sailing from Los Pasajes, all fresh meat, vegetables, and fruit were gone, so the crew and passengers were reduced to eating beans, dried vegetables, and salt meat. There were no sanitary conveniences, no place even to walk, for the deck was a small, encumbered area. The cabins were tiny and uncomfortable, and there was absolutely nothing to do except wait for the end of the trip without being able to predict when that might come since all progress depended on favorable winds.

This kind of suspended animation often made for introspection. Gilbert missed his family and friends; he expressed this in the most touching manner when he wrote Adrienne: "It is from very far away that I write you, my dear heart, and the incertitude of the time when I may at last receive your news makes this cruel distance even worse. . . . What fears, what anguish I must add to the already bitter sorrow of having left behind all those I love most! How will you have felt about my second departure? Did it make you love me less? Have you forgiven me? Did you think that in any event I would be away from you as I wandered through Italy? . . . All these thoughts did not stop me from feeling the most painful emotion during those terrible moments when we left the shore. Your sorrow, that of my friends, that of Henriette [their baby daughter], all passed before my soul so as to make it feel it was torn apart. Then, indeed, I failed to find excuses for myself. If you knew how deeply I suffered, the dreary days I passed as I fled from all

I love best in the world! Will this suffering be increased by learning that
you will not forgive me? In truth, my heart, that would make me too pitiful
an object."[9]

All this rings true; and, indeed, why shouldn't it? For the first time,
Gilbert found himself not just without someone to tell him what to do, but
also without anyone for whom he was the center of the universe. At the age
of twenty, he was off on a perilous journey that might well end in captivity
or death. There was no telling when, if ever, he would return to his family.
At the same time, the letter displays a sweetness, a tenderness that is hard
to resist. One can see why the duchess d'Ayen was so fond of her son-in-
law.

It took Gilbert another week to overcome this spasm of sorrow, and
when he did, he remembered just why he was so far away from home. On
June 7, he continued: "Defender of that liberty which I adore, for myself
more than anyone, I bring with me only my frankness and enthusiasm, but
no ambition, no selfish interest; as I work to acquire glory, I am also working
for their happiness. I hope that, out of your love for me, you will become
a good American; it is a feeling appropriate to a virtuous heart. America's
happiness is intimately linked to that of mankind; it will become a safe and
respectable refuge for virtue, honesty, tolerance, equality, and a quiet liberty."[10]

"Quiet liberty," La Fayette wrote: in his eyes fighting the English was
one thing, and a real revolution quite another. The insurgents' fight was no
revolution. The upper class was not dislodged, a new group did not come
to power: the war against England implied no internal radicalization, and
the principles embodied in the Declaration of Independence only confirmed
established practice. Of course, the several states, being part of a monarchy,
had had to deal with royal officials and the British Parliament, but the
monarch was so far away as to be virtually nonexistent, and the governors
he appointed found it almost impossible to govern against the will of the
people. What had happened, in fact, was that after years of virtual independence, the British government was now trying to rule the American
colonies from Westminster. In that sense, the Americans were behaving a
little like the French provinces in claiming their "liberties." From 1774 on,
George III made a convenient scapegoat but, in fact, he had never really
ruled the American colonies.

In America, the prevalent society was so primitive as to be free of feudal
privileges; but there is no reason to think that the Marquis thought this
should become a universal standard. Rather, he was offering his approval of
the fashionable concept of the "good savage," as defined by Rousseau, in a
place so far away from the real world in Europe and so uncivilized that its

customs were bound to remain uncommunicable. What mattered now was to make sure those customs could survive the English onslaught.

That, finally, is the key. It is quite true that since he sought no financial compensation, the Marquis was selfless and disinterested, but our admiration should perhaps be muted by the fact that La Fayette was a very rich man. And like De Kalb and the others, he had embarked for America for selfish reasons. The glory he hoped to acquire would revitalize his military career in France, would earn him the respect of the Noailles clan, and erase the poor opinion of him then current at Versailles. He would also have the satisfaction of avenging his father's death. There was much to be gained, therefore, in helping the United States. Still, when he wrote, "As I work to acquire glory, I am also working for their happiness," he was right; and there, in that little sentence, he was to find the justification of his whole life.

La Fayette, on the high seas, had just met his destiny; but at the hôtel de Noailles, he was still considered an immature, incompetent boy—"insipid of mind and soul," to quote the prince de Ligne—who was so unworldly that he was bound to get himself into trouble and who, furthermore, had deserted his pregnant wife. And from London, on April 8, the outraged marquis de Noailles wrote Vergennes: "My surprise was extreme, M. le comte, when I learned yesterday, in letters sent to me from Paris, that M. de La Fayette was on his way to America. He is luckily so young as to have an excuse for this most unwise behavior; it is the consolation I have in the sorrow caused me by so thoughtless a proceeding."[11] In this case, the ambassador, who had to cope with the anger of the British government, was clearly in a more unpleasant position than the minister, who secretly hoped that France would soon be at war with Great Britain. Still, the Noailles clan and the French court shared the same disgust for La Fayette's improvident ways. On April 28, Maurepas sent a note of reassurance to London: "You will have heard, M. le marquis," he wrote, "how useless our precautions have been regarding M. le marquis de La Fayette; M. le maréchal [de Noailles], whom I had the honor of seeing yesterday, seemed to be as upset as you will surely be. In any event, your house has no reason to reproach itself and the King cannot hold against you the proceedings of a young man whose head others have turned."[12] Still, Maurepas was not the man to stay angry, as long as the flight did not endanger his position; he simply did not care enough. And Vergennes, now satisfied that Lord Stormont's incessant complaints would not cost him his job, or even his policy, wrote to the marquis in London: "I do not know whether the King is aware of this second caprice [first leaving Paris and then disobeying Louis XVI's orders]. I shall take good care not to speak to him about it."[13] Further, in the salons where women were praising the young man's boldness, Ségur, Noailles, and his other friends were also defending him. "It is certainly folly," wrote Mme du Deffand, who, although she did not know the young man, was expressing a consensus, to Walpole, "but it does not dishonor him and, on the contrary, shows courage and a desire for glory."[14] For the first time, the duc d'Ayen was hearing praise of his hitherto hapless son-in-law.

Then, too, Adrienne and her mother defended the absent marquis against the duc's wrath. As it was, the Noailles family were especially kind to Adrienne: she had just lost little Henriette, her firstborn, and, after going through the agony of grief, she now gave birth again: she was entitled to sympathy on both counts, and emphatically did not want to hear her family abusing her husband. And finally, Gilbert's letter arrived. "The first news of M. de La Fayette arrived on August 1," Adrienne wrote, "a month after I had given birth. The consolation it brought me was fully shared [by my mother]."[15] Now, even the duc began to feel sorry for La Fayette. On the assumption his son-in-law was incapable of looking after himself, Ayen actually sent £500 to America so that he would not find himself destitute; he also caused Silas Deane to write General George Washington asking him to avoid La Fayette's "being hazarded much. . . . He is exceedingly beloved and everyone's good wishes attend . . . his expedition. Those who censure it as imprudent of him do nevertheless applaud his spirit."[16] And to Robert Morris, then presiding over the Congress, Deane added: "A generous reception of him will do us infinite service. He is above pecuniary considerations. . . . All he seeks is glory and everyone here says he has taken the most noble method to procure it. You may think that it makes a great noise in Europe and at the same time that, well managed, it will greatly help us. . . . His conduct is highly extolled by the first people in France."[17] In fact, La Fayette, even before his ship came close to the American shore, had already rendered the United States a major service by providing them with publicity. Quite unknowingly, his example was changing the general attitude and atmosphere in Paris and Versailles.

Of course, the little group aboard the *Victoire* knew none of this; but when, on June 13, after fifty-four days at sea, the ship finally entered the bay at Georgetown, South Carolina, exhilaration was the order of the day. The landing was not without its problems, however: between the ship and the landing site lay unnegotiable shallows, beyond which lay apparently virgin forests. There was no sign of habitation anywhere. The dinghies became stuck, and it took hours of wading through the mud and struggling through unruly vegetation before the explorers finally reached a house on the outskirts of Georgetown. It belonged to a certain Major Benjamin Huger, who immediately made the visitors welcome. The extraordinary love affair between La Fayette and America was finally under way.

The very next day, the Marquis, De Kalb, and the other officers made their way to the neighboring Charleston and, after a brief pause, were greeted by the local grandees, Governor John Rutledge, and Generals Robert Howe, William Moultrie, and John Calder. For the next few days, as they prepared to travel north to Philadelphia, where they would receive their actual commissions from Congress, the officers were feted, harangued, and generally treated to the most tumultuous welcome—all, that is, after it had become certain that La Fayette was indeed rich and a genuine marquis. That the reception would have been very different for a poor commoner cannot be doubted; but at that very moment, the *Victoire*, fully laden with cargo, was on its way to Charleston from Georgetown Bay.

Charleston, in 1777, was still a small town; to La Fayette, it must have appeared a quaint, exotic village with its unpaved roads and wooden houses; tiny, poorly supplied shops; and lack of amenities such as theaters, the opera, and public walks. He was ecstatic all the same, and his letters to Adrienne reflected the most thorough optimism.

"My star . . . has just served me in a manner which amazes everyone here," he wrote her triumphantly on June 19. "You may rely on it, my heart, and be sure that it dispels all your fears. I disembarked here after sailing for several days along a coast guarded by countless [in fact, two] enemy vessels. When I arrived here [Charleston] everyone told me that my ship must have been seized by the two English frigates blockading the harbor. . . . Well, by an extraordinary piece of luck, a windburst drove away the frigates for a moment, and my ship came in at high noon without meeting either friend or foe." For the rest of his life La Fayette, like Napoleon, would feel confident in his luck. His star would not let him down. No matter how bleak the present, he must triumph in the end. It followed, of course, that he never need compromise, since his ultimate victory was assured.

"I can only be delighted with the reception I have been given here," Gilbert goes on in the same letter. "The simplicity of manners, the desire to help, the love of fatherland and liberty, a pleasing equality characterize all here. The richest and the poorest man are on the same level." This was indeed a startling fact for a Frenchman accustomed to privilege. There were no peasants doffing their hats here, no one was exempt from paying taxes; all men, in fact, were born equal. And while at home, this might have upset and angered him, somehow, in America, it seemed right simply because it was part of a thrilling new world.

"American women are very pretty, very simple, and of the most charming cleanliness," the happy Gilbert went on. "They rule over all here . . . even more than in England. What enchants me is that all the citizens are brothers. You will find in America no poor people. . . . All citizens have a sufficient income and the same rights as the most powerful landowner.

"Consider how pleasant life is for me in this country, the sympathy which puts me as much at my ease as if I had known everyone here for twenty years, the resemblance of their way of thinking and mine, my love for glory and liberty, and you will see that I am indeed a happy man; but I miss you, my dear heart, I miss my friends; and there can be no happiness for me away from you and them. I ask you whether you still love me, but I ask myself the same question far oftener, and my heart always answers that you do. I hope that it is right."[18]

All in all, this is a touching letter in its blend of superficial observation, enthusiasm, and love. Of course, in those very few days, La Fayette had seen little of the country or its citizens (blacks, of course, were neither citizens nor free); but it is no wonder he saw everything through rose-colored glasses. And he was being treated—he, personally—as the leader of his troupe, a great nobleman, and a brave ally. For the first time, no one could outshine him; the praise and glory were all his. "The Marquis received the honors that one might have given a marshal of France or a protector of liberty," Dubuysson, one of the accompanying officers wrote. After all those snickers at Versailles, it was quite a rise in the world. In his joy, the heir to a great fortune showed he knew how to spend it: before he left South Carolina, he had donated more than 27,000 livres for arms and clothing to the local authorities.

In the midst of all the festivities, La Fayette still found time to buy horses and carriages for the trip north. He was, after all, far too grand to rough it, and must travel in the style of a rich French nobleman. On June 25, the troupe divided itself into several traveling parties; La Fayette, De Kalb, and Mauroy drove off ahead. Soon, they found out that the roads left much to be desired. The climate was impossibly hot and humid, post inns almost nonexistent, the vegetation practically tropical. Within days, the carriages broke down, the horses limped, and often the whole little troupe struggled through forests and swamps on foot. Between the roads, the insects, and the lack of accommodations, it was a bedraggled group indeed the Philadelphians saw trickling in.

Determined to put a good face on the situation, the Marquis wrote that everything was perfect: "I have borne the fatigue of the trip without even feeling it," he informed Adrienne from Petersburg, Virginia, on July 17. "It has been long and dull by land even though everything was even worse when I was aboard my dreary ship. I am now eight days away from Philadelphia and in the beautiful Virginia country. . . .

"I have not yet received a letter from you and my impatience to arrive in Philadelphia so I can find one there is beyond all expression. . . . I can no longer live with this uncertainty. I have indeed undertaken too hard a task for my heart, for it was not made to suffer so much." And on July 23, from Annapolis, he continued: "Farewell, my heart, I know that I love you more dearly than ever, that I needed the sorrows of this separation to feel just how I care for you and that I could give half my blood to kiss you, to tell you myself how much I love you."[19]

No matter how much he missed Adrienne, the exhausted young man who, after thirty days of travel, entered Philadelphia on July 27, had only one desire: to join the American army. The commission given him by Silas Deane was all ready to be handed to Congress; now it was just a question of which army he was to be given. And so it was with the utmost confidence that he presented himself to the authorities, but instead of being greeted like a heroic ally, he found himself treated like an undesirable of whom the United States could not too quickly be delivered. Obviously, something had gone terribly wrong.

Three

AN AMERICAN MARQUIS

Philadelphia was then the capital of the United States, and after Boston, it was the second largest city in the confederation. Its streets were paved, its houses built of red brick, and its statehouse was, relatively, an imposing building, although, to La Fayette, it must all have looked small and provincial. On Sunday, July 27, 1777, it was not a pleasant place to be if you were French. For one thing, the war was going badly. Ticonderoga had fallen, and knowledgeable men expected a quick English victory. Once the British army held both New England and Philadelphia, the rest of the colonies would soon be subdued, and then it would not help to have foreign officers about. Worse still, the English generals could be expected to punish any pro-French Americans with special vigor, and so when La Fayette and his companions, looking thoroughly travel-worn, straggled into the city, it made elementary sense for most prudent men to shun them.

Even the most ardent and careless Patriots, however, had no reason to be happy about the new arrivals. Traditionally, France was the one European nation with which the American states had been at war. George Washington had learned tactics and strategy when he was fighting them. Everyone remembered what a nuisance the hostile Indian tribes, bribed by French gold, had been. For the residents of the colonies, too, they had been a hereditary enemy, and just because a number of French officers had come over to fight with the insurgents did not mean that the old feelings had died out.

Had the French come with supplies, weapons, and money, then, perhaps, they would have been more welcome; but most of the new arrivals were greedy, arrogant, and not particularly well trained. As a result, the Congress, always short of money, felt it was being led into useless expenditures, while most senior American officers flatly refused to obey the odious foreigners. They had a point, too: the men they were dealing with were either discredited adventurers who came to America because they had made Europe too hot to hold them, or, more rarely, competent officers such as the chevalier du Coudray or General Thomas Conway, an Irish-born Frenchman, who felt nothing but contempt for their American colleagues and did not scruple to show it. Further, most American officers, who had had to work hard and long to rise in the army, resented the commissions so liberally dispensed in Paris by Silas Deane.

All this was well known in Congress. Worse still, the comte de Broglie's ambitions were no longer a secret, and while not everyone thought that Washington should remain commander in chief, no one wanted to import a leader from abroad. The situation, in fact, had become so tense that Congress had set up a Committee on Foreign Applications, with the main purpose of sending most foreigners home, and there was a considerable party who wanted Deane recalled.

Back in Versailles, M. de Maurepas might be worrying about the effect of La Fayette's departure, but in Philadelphia, no one knew who he was. They did, however, know that he had come with De Kalb and that De Kalb was Broglie's agent, and so they presumed that La Fayette was part of the plot, as indeed, unknowingly, he was. So on this Sunday, when La Fayette and his friends walked to John Hancock's house—he was the President of Congress—with their contracts, credentials, and a letter of introduction from Silas Deane, they were greeted without enthusiasm and told to report to Robert Morris. Still, they contained their disappointment. After all, the Marquis was carrying a letter asking Morris to act as his private banker in America, and for that reason, at least, he could expect a warm welcome. In fact, he was swiftly dismissed. Morris, it turned out, was too busy to see them. They were told to meet him the next morning at the door of Independence Hall. Even the haughtiest of French ministers would not have asked foreign officers to meet him in the street, so it was a very depressed little group that made its way back to several inns.

The next morning, the situation went from bad to worse. First, although La Fayette and the eleven officers accompanying him were on time, they were kept waiting outside well past the hour of their appointment. When Robert Morris finally emerged, it was in the company of the President of the Committee on Foreign Applications, James Lowell of Massachusetts. Pointing to his colleague, Morris curtly told the visitors: "This gentleman speaks French very well. Therefore you will bring your future business to him,"[1] upon which he reentered Independence Hall, leaving them all standing outside. Before the French officers could say a word, Lowell dealt the death blow. Deane, he told them in excellent French, had exceeded his authority in granting the commissions; they were, in fact, invalid. Besides, he went on, "French officers are a little too eager in wanting to come and serve us without being asked. Last year, it is true, we needed officers, but this year, we have many, and very experienced ones, too."[2] And with these lapidary words he, too, reentered the hall.

La Fayette, still standing there, was stunned. After all his efforts, after crossing the ocean, after the long and arduous trip north from the Carolinas, he had been rejected as if he were nothing more than a crook. By inquiring around the city, he soon found out why he had been greeted with such hostility. His letters of introduction to Congress had been disregarded because De Kalb's connection with Broglie had tainted La Fayette and the others. And that very day, the chevalier du Coudray, whose arrogance excited such hatred among the American generals, struck again. He sent a memorandum to the Congress attacking all French officers in general and La Fayette in particular: it was the best way of eliminating someone who might soon become a dangerous rival. In fact, it simply made the Americans want to be rid of all the French, no matter who they were.

Once again, however, La Fayette's money and position made the difference. As various members of Congress began to read the letters of introduction that the Marquis now arranged to have dropped off at their houses, they realized that he was no adventurer. They might be republicans, but they still felt awe for a real aristocrat. Perhaps the new recruit deserved some attention at least. The very next day, James Lowell, accompanied by William Duer, called on the Marquis to apologize for his earlier rudeness.

This was La Fayette's chance, and he used it well. The two visitors were ready to listen, and he, for once, made a favorable impression. That the Marquis really wanted to fight, really wanted to help the insurgents was obvious, and so was his complete disinterestedness. Here was no arrogant, greedy foreigner, but a young man with a cool, polite demeanor—very different from the other, excitable Frenchmen—who only asked for a chance to be shot at. Still, he was not willing to wait: let Congress confirm his appointment, he said, or pay his travel expenses if he was to go home. After all, he had gone to the trouble and expense of buying a ship just to join the Americans.

Lowell and Duer reported this to Congress, and after a short while Duer returned. He was empowered, he said, to offer the Marquis an appointment as a major general, but dated only from that day, so he would not have seniority over other, American, officers. There could be no question, for the moment, of the young man's actually commanding a division; he would be paid no salary but would be reimbursed for his expenses. Of course, La Fayette accepted. He had no choice, really, since a return to France would have covered him with ridicule and confirmed the duc d'Ayen's low estimation of his capacities, but he stipulated that he would serve entirely at his own expense and as a volunteer, thus proving his disinterestedness and leaving himself an escape hatch. As a volunteer, he was free to leave whenever he pleased.

"So new a style caught people's attention," the Marquis remembered, using the third person to describe himself. "The envoy's dispatches were read and, in a flatteringly worded resolution, M. de La Fayette was made a major general."[3] Indeed, the resolution passed by Congress on July 31 reads like a tribute to the young marquis: "Whereas the Marquis de La Fayette, out of his great zeal to the cause of liberty, in which the United States are engaged, has left his family and connexions, and at his own expense comes over to offer his services to the United States, without pension or particular allowance, and is anxious to risk his life in our cause; *Resolved*, that his services be accepted, and that in consideration of his zeal, his illustrious family, and connexions, he have the rank and commission of a major general in the army of the United States."[4] This was high praise to be sure, but the sting was in the tail: the Marquis was given a commission not just because of his zeal but because of his illustrious family and connections. In Philadelphia as at Versailles, birth came before merit, and La Fayette owed his success in the democratic United States to the aristocratic house of Noailles.

At the moment, though, the young man felt nothing but elation. After the rejection of the first day, his path now seemed clear. The French captain had become an American major general: it was a dazzling promotion. Better still, the new officer was promptly taken to the house where headquarters had been established. There, he met his commander in chief. For La Fayette it was reverence at first sight. "Although Washington was surrounded by a crowd of officers and citizens," La Fayette wrote, "the majesty of his face and his tallness made him known immediately. He was also distinguished by his noble and affable way of greeting people. M. de La Fayette followed him in his reconnaissances; invited by the General to move into his house as a member of his military family, he considered it from that day his own and thus simply did two friends come together, whose affection and mutual confidence were cemented by the most weighty purpose."[5]

La Fayette's reaction that day is hardly surprising. Few Europeans ever met Washington without being impressed by his majestic politeness, and all those who had a chance to know him better joined the large and enthusiastic cohort of the great man's admirers. All the same, the Marquis was lucky, for Washington also took a jaundiced view of foreign officers. "Good policy, in my opinion, forbids the disgusting of a whole corps to gratify the pride of an individual,"[6] he had written to Robert Lee on May 17.

Washington, however, liked having bright young officers about him, especially if they showed admiration and awe. He was a born mentor and needed protégés. When the General asked La Fayette to come and live in his house, of course, Gilbert was thrilled: at Versailles, being given an apartment was a sign of high favor. In America, in fact, it meant little since Washington treated his whole staff very much like family, and, whenever possible, arranged for them to share his quarters.

Even in all the excitement of his new position, La Fayette knew it had only reluctantly been given to him. He did not hesitate to leave his companions behind when, on August 1, he went forth to be given the sash of a major general during a review of the troops and to dine with Washington, or, the next day, when he accompanied his new chief on an inspection of the fortifications outside the city. Speaking in halting English, the young man affirmed his determination to serve, and he was treated by the cool and distant commander in chief with unusual warmth—a warmth due less to Washington's personal feelings than to the material aid the Marquis might offer, but real nonetheless. As for La Fayette, he had at last found the father figure he had been looking for.

When he returned to his inn on that first night, however, Gilbert found his companions in an uproar. Unlike the Marquis, they were being ignored by Congress and army alike. Faced with the probability of having to return home, they complained so bitterly that La Fayette, who felt responsible for them, actually thought of resigning. De Kalb, especially, was outraged. "What is deemed generosity in the marquis de La Fayette," he wrote Congress on August 1, "would be downright madness in me who am not one of the first fortunes. . . . I want only to know whether Congress will agree to me as a major general and with the seniority I have a right to expect. . . . It will look very odd and, I think, very diverting to the French ministry and to all military men to see me under the command of the marquis de La Fayette."[7] After all, more was at stake here than petty envy or personal position, though De Kalb was thoroughly experienced and La Fayette was not; if the comte de Broglie's plan was ever to succeed, then De Kalb, and Mauroy, still waiting in Paris, would have to be in a position to point out Washington's mistakes and suggest a replacement. The two schemers cared little what became of La Fayette. His role was to be that of a Trojan horse, introducing Broglie's men into the American army.

For a few days the young man wavered, for he felt a strong sense of responsibility for his compatriots. But then John Hancock promised that, at some point, Congress would give commissions to his aides-de-camp, and that satisfied the Marquis. A few days later, when General Washington sent him a carriage and an invitation to join him at headquarters for a general review, he went alone, but not without sending the following letter to Congress: "The feelings of my heart, long before it became my duty, engaged me in the love of the American cause," he wrote politely. "I not only considered it as the cause of Honor, Virtue, and universal Happiness but felt myself empressed with the warmest affection for a Nation who exhibited by their resistance so fine an example of Justice and Courage to the Universe.

"I shall neglect nothing on my part to justify the confidence which the Congress of the United States has been pleased to repose in me as my highest ambition has ever been to do everything only for the best of the cause in which I am engaged. I wish to serve near the person of General Washington till such time as he may think proper to entrust me with a division of the army.

"It is now as an american that I'll mention every day to Congress the officers who came over with me, whose interests are for me as my own, and the consideration which they deserve by their merits, their ranks, their state and their reputation in France."*[8]

There was much in this letter to annoy the members of Congress: the importunate pleading for the other French officers; the new major general's singlehanded determination of where he would serve; and finally the assumption that Washington, should he so desire, could simply hand a division over to him, when the appointment to specific commands was one of the most jealously guarded prerogatives of Congress, one that the General would not have dreamed of infringing. Still, when he arrived at the army camp just outside the city, the Marquis soon made himself popular with the other officers. He was not impressed with what he saw. In this village of shacks and tents, "about eleven thousand men, poorly armed and worse dressed,

*This letter, like the rest of La Fayette's communications at this time, was written in English.

offered an odd spectacle: in their disparate and often half-naked state, their
best clothes were hunting shirts, a kind of grey linen coat worn in Carolina. . . . Virtue replaced science and every day increased both experience
and discipline."[9] The American army, in the summer of 1777, was a motley
body of thoroughly untrained men, with little food, clothing, and ammunition; but they were courageous and willing to fight. Instead of expressing
contempt, as the other European officers had done, La Fayette demonstrated
an appealing modesty.

"We must be embarrassed," Washington said as he arrived, "to show
ourselves to an officer who has just left the French army."

"I am here to learn, not to teach," the Marquis answered.[10]

In fact, since La Fayette knew almost nothing, he would have had
trouble pretending he was competent; but because he showed himself so
enthusiastic, so modest, so willing to do everything he could, whatever his
breeding and rank, he was immediately accepted by his new peers; and
because, for the first time since his childhood, he found himself surrounded
by approval, he developed "those engaging manners" Benjamin Franklin
was soon to note. By the end of August, the awkward, gawky young man
was nothing but a memory; only now he had become a pest.

Clamoring for employment would obviously do no good, and so he
blandly informed Washington that Congress meant him to have a command.
The General was far too cautious to explode in front of La Fayette, but he
let himself go, as early as August 19, in a letter to Benjamin Harrison, a
member of Congress: "If I did not misunderstand what you . . . said to me
respecting the appointment of the Marquis de La Fayette, he has misconceived the design of his appointment or Congress did not understand the
extent of his views; for certain it is, that I understood him, that he does not
conceive his commission as merely honorary, but given with a view to command a division of this army. It is true, he has said, that he is young and
inexperienced, but at the same time he has always accompanied it with a
kind of hint that, so soon as I shall think him fit for the command of a
division, he shall be ready to enter upon the duties of it, and in the meantime
has offered his service for a smaller command; to which I may add that he
has actually applied to me, by direction, he says, from Mr. Hancock, for
commissions for his two aides-de-camp [when actually he should have left
this up to Congress].

"What the designs of Congress respecting this gentleman were, and
what line of conduct I am to pursue to comply with their designs and their
expectations, I know not, and beg to be instructed."[11] For the usually cool-
tempered Washington, these were strong words, and for a while La Fayette's
future in the American army looked very uncertain: no matter how strongly

Congress may have felt about its prerogatives, it nevertheless knew better than to interfere in Washington's arrangements. If the General decided La Fayette was nothing but a nuisance, then, obviously, his hopes of a command would vanish.

Soon, however, with the arrival of letters brought to America by Count Casimir Pulaski, La Fayette's position was strengthened. "We are satisfied that the civilities and respect that may be shown to him will be serviceable to our affairs here, as pleasing not only to his powerful relations and the court but to the whole French nation,"[12] Franklin wrote Washington. If the United States wanted French help, in other words, La Fayette could become a means of influencing the Noailles and the court. So when La Fayette returned to headquarters from Philadelphia at the end of August—he had been lobbying in Congress—Washington was far better disposed toward him. When he called him in and explained tactfully that he could not give him a division at the moment but would behave as a father and a friend, La Fayette was elated. No other French officer had been so honored. It seemed to the Marquis that, on his own, he had become the spokesman for all the French in the army and, as a consequence, their leader. Once again, he had been saved by his rank and connections, but he saw only the General's new benevolence.

These were very natural illusions: a young man not yet twenty who attended councils of war and signed their minutes ahead of experienced brigadier generals could be nothing if not exhilarated. When the army passed through Philadelphia, it was La Fayette who rode next to Washington and accompanied the commander in chief on the reconnaissance of August 26, taking part in army maneuvers and living at headquarters. When Mauroy, who had now arrived, and De Kalb, whose applications for commissions had been rejected by Congress, urged La Fayette to go home with them, he refused instantly: he was committed to his new hero.

There is no telling how long Gilbert could have remained with a commission but no command—after all, neither Congress nor the General took kindly to being pestered—if his star had not come to the rescue. So far he had been of very little use to the harried Continentals*; but, luckily for him, he was soon given a chance to show his mettle.

The British, under Admiral Richard Howe and his brother, General

---

*The Continentals were men who had signed a regular, multiyear contract, been properly trained, and could, therefore, be relied on at any time. The militia, on the other hand, was composed of volunteers whose competence as fighting men was at best doubtful and who could and did go home whenever they felt like it; in any event they hardly ever served for more than four or five months.

William Howe, had disembarked a large body of troops in New Jersey with the avowed purpose of taking Philadelphia and thus ending the rebellion. The American army naturally tried to stop them and, on September 11, 1777, met the enemy some twenty-six miles southwest of the city on the banks of the Brandywine. While most of the troops were resisting a frontal attack under General Howe, Washington noticed that a flanking movement led by General Charles Cornwallis was under way and dispatched General John Sullivan, an experienced and competent major general, to deflect it. La Fayette had accompanied Washington throughout the early part of the battle. Now he asked to join Sullivan, who was obviously becoming the focus of the day's main action. Washington agreed and La Fayette set off with the center division.

At four-thirty, Cornwallis attacked with superior force. The center brigade began to waver. True to French habit, the Marquis jumped off his horse and placed himself at the head of his soldiers, urging them to charge and even trying to push them forward by the shoulders when they refused to move. The men, unused to this sort of maneuver, would not obey the frenzied foreigner, but at least they stood their ground with La Fayette's encouragement. Then, in the middle of the action, La Fayette was hit by a bullet just below the calf, but he was so involved in his attempt to repulse the enemy that he noticed nothing until the blood came pouring out of his boot. Remounting, he retreated perforce but then encountered Washington, who was leading the main body of the army, and turned about again to join him. No amount of courage would serve, however: weakened by the loss of blood, he had to dismount once more while Dr. John Cochran, the commander in chief's personal physician, hastily bandaged the wound.

In the meantime, the Americans had given way and La Fayette found himself part of a fleeing mob, but when, some twelve miles to the rear, the army reached a stone bridge over the Chester, the young man halted the retreat and reestablished order among the confused troops. He had just finished doing so when Washington and his staff arrived and took over. At last the brave Frenchman could stop to be properly bandaged.

The wound was not so severe as to endanger La Fayette's life or even his limb, but it was enough to make a hero of the bold young man who, under fire for the first time, had shed his blood for the United States. Washington mentioned the Marquis's bravery in his dispatches to Congress. Everybody was impressed: the French major general had shown a cool courage when faced by a stronger enemy; he had twice rallied his troops; he had continued to serve in spite of the pain caused by his hastily bandaged leg. His behavior was all very different from that of the other French officers, who had shown a marked tendency to avoid actual battles. And the consequences turned out to be everything he could wish for. La Fayette was an American.

He was now perfectly placed to establish himself as that essential man, the link between France and the United States; and he also seemed to acquire greater wisdom and cleverness along with his wound; he managed to make light of it in the most elegant way in a letter to Adrienne.

"I will start by telling you that I am in good health," he wrote, "because I will go on to say that we fought for good and all yesterday and were not the strongest. Our Americans, after having held their ground for quite a long time, were finally routed; and when I tried to stop them, the English gentlemen opposite graced me with a bullet which caused a small leg wound, but it is really nothing, my dear heart, neither bone nor nerve are affected and I am simply forced to stay on my back for a little time, which I resent greatly. I hope, my dear heart, that you won't worry."[13] The letter, he knew, would be read around the Paris salons and, while rallying sympathies to the United States, would make him sound like a modest young hero. He was right, of course: from that moment, the dull-witted young man vanished from memory, to be replaced by a bold and dashing figure.

These heroics were all the more effective in contrast with the plaintive tone of his next letter. "Just think, my dear heart, that I have only had news of you through Count Pulaski one single time. This is really dreadful luck and it makes me cruelly unhappy. Just imagine how horrible it is to be far away from those I love and in so desperate an uncertainty. I just can't bear it and, yet, I know, I don't deserve sympathy. Why was I so wildly determined to come over here? I am being severely punished now. I am too sensitive, my heart, for these sudden breaks."[14] With this letter La Fayette played right into the current fashion for sentimentality: the Marquis was becoming the ideal hero, vintage 1777. Adrienne, moved by her husband's plaints, would work even harder to sway her family's opinion; the suffering young man's wound would become even more praiseworthy. Now that he was unable to move and was alone much of the time, he had little to do but write; it is, however, a revelation of La Fayette's new talents that he was able to convey his feelings in so affecting a manner.

All these complaints, however, were for French consumption. In fact, Gilbert was delighted by his new relationship to Washington. "That respectable man whose talents and virtues I admire more and more as I know him better and better, is willing to be my intimate friend," he went on rapturously, about the General. "His tender interest for me soon won my heart to him. I am established in his house, we live like two united brothers in the midst of a mutual intimacy and confidence. That friendship makes me as happy as I can be while away in this country. When he sent me his personal surgeon, he told him to take care of me as if I were his son, because he loved me like one."[15]

Then, in October, Adrienne received new and detailed instructions. By the first of the month, Philadelphia had been taken by the English and the American cause looked desperate. Always aware that French help, if it could be secured, would make the difference, the Marquis carefully supplied his wife with an official line.

"Now," he wrote, "since you are the wife of an American officer, I have to tell you what to say. People will say, 'They were beaten.' You will answer: 'That's true, but when two armies have *equal numbers* of soldiers and are fighting in a plain, experienced men have an advantage over raw recruits; besides they have had the pleasure of killing more, far more of the enemy than they have lost themselves.' After that, people will add: 'That's all very well, but Philadelphia, the capital of America, the rampart of liberty, has been taken.' You will reply politely: 'You are all absolute idiots. Philadelphia is an uninteresting little town, open on all sides; its port was already blockaded; it was made famous, God knows why, because Congress resided there; that's what this famous city really is; and, by the way, we'll undoubtedly take it back sooner or later.' "[16] It was hardly possible to put a better face on a bleak situation.

Although for the two months following Brandywine La Fayette was barely able to move, he was by no means inactive. Aside from the long letters home, he was in frequent touch with the other French officers, most especially Conway and De Kalb; the latter was finally offered a commission by Congress but took his time accepting it. After all, he wrote to Broglie, even if Broglie joined the American army, it would not further their aims because this appearance of a new superior officer "would be regarded as a crying injustice against Washington and an attempt against the country." He was quite right, of course, and La Fayette, when he pushed De Kalb's claims, remained quite unaware that he was still acting merely as a stalking-horse for Broglie.

The young man's naïveté, in fact, made him look, himself, as if he were joining Washington's enemies. For all his popularity, he still had no understanding of politics or scheming men. Although Washington's strategic retreats in the fall of 1777 would set the stage for later successes, at the time they seemed to prove he was incapable of ever producing a victory. Meanwhile, farther north, General Horatio Gates, a plodding, ambitious officer, was pushing back the British. The commander in chief was unpopular with a substantial section of Congress; various representatives hatched an intrigue to replace him with Gates. This was just the moment La Fayette chose to congratulate Gates on his success and, in his fast-growing role as protector of the French, to praise Conway, who was allied with Gates, and the ambitious De Kalb. On top of these gaffes, he sent another one of his endless letters to Washington reiterating his own claim to a division in the most tactless terms. The General might well have been disgusted, but the Marquis's earlier behavior, his bravery, and his wound served him well. Then too, Washington's affection for the young man, as described in Gilbert's letter to Adrienne, was evidently genuine and no doubt mitigated his response to what would have seemed insolence in another officer.

But La Fayette himself was changing. Marie Antoinette might not have thought much of La Fayette's new wit or elegance, but what seemed lacking in Versailles became dazzling on the other side of the Atlantic, and the Marquis brought with him to headquarters a touch of courtliness to which the General was extremely sensitive.

Even the heretofore critical De Kalb marveled at the transformation of La Fayette. "No one deserves more than [La Fayette] the esteem which he enjoys here. He is a prodigy for his age, full of courage, spirit, judgment, good manners, feelings of generosity and zeal for the cause of liberty on this continent,"[17] he wrote on November 7 to his wife. De Kalb went on to ask that his commission be dated to match La Fayette's, rather than from the earlier date of his agreement with Deane: he did not want to have seniority over the new hero.

So when La Fayette started to pose as the necessary intermediary between France and the United States, no one stopped to reflect that he had left his country against the King's express orders. The Marquis's audacity is sometimes awesome. On October 18, for instance, when he wrote the new President of Congress, Henry Laurens, about a shipment of clothing from France, it was as if he had been appointed Louis XVI's representative in the United States: "I could answer in the name of the nation which furnished them that their destination is for General Washington's army which they can't be taken away from, without robbery."[18] All the while La Fayette dropped names—the King's, Maurepas's, Vergennes's, the maréchal de Ségur's, the maréchal de Noailles's—in such a way as to imply that, back home, he had been very close to the center of power. Of course, in York, Pennsylvania, no one knew how untrue this was. But it did work. By the end of October, everyone, even Conway and De Kalb, recognized that La Fayette was the spokesman for France and the French.

There was, however, one area in which "the Marquis," as he was coming to be known, continued to be stymied: he was still denied a real command and remained a volunteer. Naturally, he tried hard to remedy the situation by pestering anyone who would listen, especially Washington and Laurens to whom, on November 18, he dropped some heavy hints as he described "my known in the whole world love of your cause, my warm patriotism, my sentiments *very warm too* against the English pride."*[19] What La Fayette did not know when he wrote this was that almost three weeks earlier the weightier voice of the commander in chief was already backing his ambitions.

From Whitemarsh, on November 1, Washington wrote: "I feel myself in a delicate situation with respect to the Marquis de La Fayette. He is extremely solicitous of having a command equal to his rank, and professes very different ideas, as to the purposes of his appointment, from those Congress have mentioned to me. . . . I do not know in what light they will view the matter; but it appears to me from a consideration of his illustrious and important connexions, the attachment which he has manifested for our cause and the consequences which his return in disgust might produce, that it will be more advisable to gratify him in his wishes. . . . He is sensible, discreet in his manner, has made great proficiency in our language, and, from the disposition he discovered at the Battle of Brandywine, possesses a large share of bravery and military ardor."[20]

Remaining unaware of Washington's efforts on his behalf, the Marquis grew increasingly bored and dissatisfied; now with the utmost imprudence, he let himself become part of a cabal designed to send Washington back to Mount Vernon. General Conway had just concluded an alliance with General Gates to secure the latter's rise to the post of commander in chief. Gates may well have thought himself more competent than Washington. Conway's motivation was simple. Since Washington disliked him, both because of his haughty manner and his habit of drilling his men constantly and unnecessarily, he obviously stood to gain by a change in command.

Both Gates and Conway realized that La Fayette was devoted to Washington and would eventually stand in the way of their plans, so they decided to get rid of him. First, Conway played on the young man's discontents: the Marquis's services, he said, were obviously not appreciated by the Americans; look, he did not even have his own command yet. He suggested an alternate scheme: Why not invade India? It would be the perfect way to distract the English from the American war, and the leader of the expedition was sure to reap fame and glory. What Conway did not say was that, with La Fayette gone, he would become the senior French general in the United States and could use his influence to secure Gates's promotion.

Anyone familiar with the intrigues of the French Ministry of War would have seen through this scheme, but La Fayette took it up with enthusiasm.

---

*Lafayette's own English.

In a letter on October 24, he suggested the idea to Vergennes, blithely
forgetting that he was persona non grata at Versailles and that in any event
senior ministers were hardly in the habit of listening to twenty-year-old
officers. Although the actual scheme was completely silly—there could be
no question of diverting scarce resources from the actual theater of war while
openly attacking England at the other end of the earth—the tone of the
letter reflected the Marquis's new skill at being presumptuous while sounding humble. His tone, despite the flattery, was that of an equal of the Foreign
Minister: clearly the unimportant young man, in a mere six months, felt he
had become something of a power.

Just as this plot was getting under way, General Gates further strengthened his position by triumphing over General John Burgoyne at Saratoga.
Conway wrote Gates to say that the time had clearly come for a new commander in chief. Unfortunately for Gates and Conway, however, the officers
of the Northern Department did not consider discretion the better part of
valor and promptly forwarded the letter to Washington, who immediately
asked Conway to resign.

At this point Conway, appalled, asked La Fayette for help. The two
Frenchmen were both friends of the marquis de Castries. Conway was
actually his protégé. La Fayette went so far as to put in an appeal to Washington, who then showed him the letter. The Marquis was horrified. La
Fayette broke with Conway and Conway did resign. More important, however, than the break between the two men was the lesson the episode finally
taught Gilbert: that people had ulterior, often dishonorable motives and
could not always be trusted; that intrigue could take on the most innocuous
appearances; that flatterers should not be relied upon. The innocent volunteer was slowly becoming a man of the world.

Luckily for the Marquis, Washington knew and liked him well enough
not to be offended by his early advocacy of Conway. In mid-November,
although his wound was still so far from healed that he was unable to wear
boots, La Fayette rejoined the army. The only action in the fall of 1777 was
in New Jersey. General Nathanael Greene went to relieve Fort Mercer from
Cornwallis's forces; La Fayette asked to serve with him and was placed at
the head of a small body of militia. Once there, as soon as he had gathered
his men, the Marquis went forward to reconnoiter the British positions on
what was to have been a purely routine mission. In no time at all, a fight
was under way.

"I want to acquaint your excellency of a little event of last evening which
tho' not very considerable in itself will certainly please you on account of
the bravery and alacrity a small party of ours showed on that occasion," he
wrote Washington from Haddonfield on November 26. "I came pretty late

into the Gloucester road. . . . My whole body was not yet three hundred. . . . A scout . . . found a strong post of three hundred and fifty hessians with field pieces (what number I did know by the unanimous disposition of theyr prisoners). . . . We pushed the hessians more than half a mile from the place where was theyr main body, and we made them run very fast—british reinforcements came twice to them but very far from recovering theyr ground, they alwais went back. . . . I understand that they have had between twenty five and thirty wounded, at least that number killed amongst whom is an officer some say more, and the prisoners told me that they have lost the commandant of that body. We got yet this day fourteen prisoners. . . . We left one single man killed . . . and only five of ours were wounded. Such is the account of our little entertainment. . . . I wish that *this little success of ours* may please you—tho' a trifling one I find it very interesting on account of the behaviour of our soldiers. . . .

"With the most tender affection and highest respect, I have the honour to be, dear general, Your excellency's most obedient humble servant Lafayette."[21]

It was a small victory indeed, and one of no consequence at all—at best a slight annoyance to the British command; but a time when victories of any kind were so very scarce, it had a pleasant ring to it. As for the Marquis, he loved it all: it had been wonderful sport and confirmed his reputation for bravery and daring. Better still, the very first time he had had men under his actual command, he had made a success of it. And back at headquarters, without wasting a minute, Washington sat down to petition Congress in favour of his protégé with new insistence.

"I should also be happy in [Congress's] determination respecting the marquis de Lafayette," he wrote on that same November 26. "There are now some vacant divisions in the army, to one of which he may be appointed if it should be the pleasure of Congress. I am convinced he possesses a large share of that military ardor, which generally characterizes the nobility of his country. He went to Jersey with General Greene and I find he has not been inactive there. This you will perceive by the following extract from a letter just received from General Greene: 'The marquis, with about four hundred militia and the rifle corps, attacked the enemy's picket last evening, killed about twenty, wounded many more and took about twenty prisoners. The marquis is charmed with the spirited behaviour of the militia and rifle corps . . . [and] is determined to be in the way of danger.' "[22] It was a fine encomium. On December 1, the day Congress received the letter, it passed a resolution stating that "it is highly agreeable to the Congress that the marquis de La Fayette be appointed to the command of a division in the Continental army."[23]

Of course, La Fayette was overjoyed. His ambition was finally fulfilled and, for the first time, his success owed more to his own talents than to his connections. Immediately demonstrating his newfound acumen, he asked Washington for a division of Virginians. It was the best sort of flattery, since the General was notoriously proud of his compatriots. It also should have ensured that the supplies would be forthcoming along with the men. Unfortunately, that turned out not to be the case. Reality, in fact, was once again proving a disappointment. After the brief excitement of Gloucester and his consequent appointment to a division, the Marquis found himself drilling his troops and having a very humdrum time of it. Washington had taken his winter quarters at Valley Forge.

There, La Fayette's 3,086 men lacked everything: training, food, weapons, even clothing, and it quickly became evident that there was very little hope of remedying the situation. The Marquis became very angry indeed when he realized that the meager supplies gathered by the United States were going straight to General Gates and his Northern Department while, at Valley Forge, the army camped in unheated shacks and leaking tents set up in a sea of mud. The men, who lacked both uniforms and fuel, could not keep warm; they were half-starved and La Fayette, although he himself lived in a comfortable house, was acutely sensitive to their hardships.

Desite the impediments, the Marquis did his job conscientiously. He drilled his men regularly, oversaw discipline, and did not hesitate to punish severely officers who failed in their duties, either through carelessness— the failure to post sentries, for instance—or arrogance. He spent his own money on his division, participated in the camp's routine—as one of the few general officers present, he was major general of the day every four or five days—and participated in the war councils. He also wrote Washington at great length on such subjects as where the troops should be quartered for the winter and whether a scheme to attack and retake Philadelphia should be attempted, always signing himself proudly "The Marquis de Lafayette, M.G." On the whole, these letters were sensible and well thought out. In one case, when he argues against the Philadelphia project, the young man becomes positively wise. "Europe has a great idea of our being able to raise when we please an immense army of militia, and it is looked upon as our last but certain resource," he commented on December 3. "If we fall, this phantom will fall also and you know that the american interest has alwais been since the beginning of the war to let the world believe more than we ever expect to be. . . . Therefore we must not let a shining appearance and the pleasing charms of a bold fine enterprise deceive us upon the inconveniences and dangers of the gigantesque and in the same time decisive expedition."[24] Evidently the General felt the same way, and the attack was never made.

"I read, I study, I examine, I listen, I reflect, and from all that I try to arrive at an idea into which I put as much common sense as I can; I will not say much lest I speak nonsense; I will do even less lest I make mistakes,"[25] the Marquis wrote on December 16 to his father-in-law, and it is a fair description of his attitude at Valley Forge. That he was able to say so, of course, shows what a long way he had come since he had left France, although the beginning of the letter is written in the same fawning tone as that earlier message from London; but then, he could also state, accurately, "It is impossible to be better off in a foreign country than I am here. I can only applaud the conduct of Congress toward me, and be more satisfied with it every day. . . . As for the army, I am happy enough to be everyone's friend; no occasion is lost to give me proofs of this."[26] It was true. The Marquis had indeed become respected and liked everywhere, a man of considerable weight and influence; and strengthening his position still further was his unique relationship with Washington.

"Our general is a man truly made for this revolution which could not succeed without him," he wrote the duc d'Ayen. "I am closer to him than any other man in the world and what I see is worthy of his country's admiration. His tender friendship and entire confidence in me about every question, military and political, large and small, with which he is concerned, have enabled me to judge the extent of his business, how much he must conciliate and overcome. I admire the beauty of his character and his soul more every day. . . . His name will be revered throughout the centuries by all who love liberty and humanity."[27] In truth, La Fayette was extraordinarily lucky: all his life he had lacked a father figure; now he had found not just an older man who considered him a surrogate son but one who was a great leader as well.

Still, Washington was busy, and La Fayette did not see him in private quite as often as he claimed when he wrote the duc d'Ayen; there was still plenty of time for missing Adrienne, especially since communications were so uncertain. "You may receive this letter, my dear heart, in five or six years for I am using a complicated route I don't much trust," he wrote her in November. "An officer of the army will take it to Fort Pitt, three hundred miles in the interior of the continent; then it will be embarked on the great Ohio River and cross areas inhabited only by savages; once it arrives in New Orleans, a small ship will transport it to the Spanish Islands; then a ship of that nation will take it, God knows when, as it returns to Europe; but it will still be far away from you and it will first be dirtied by all the filthy hands of the Spanish postmasters before it is allowed to cross the Pyrenees. It will probably be unsealed and resealed five or six times before it reaches you; and then it will be proof to my dear heart that I do not neglect any occasion, even the most unlikely, to give her my news and tell her again how much I love her."[28] Here, too, we see La Fayette maturing: for the first time, he is sure enough of himself to be humorous.

Back in Philadelphia, Washington remained, in most eyes, the indispensable man. But there still was a faction in Congress who felt nothing but contempt for his temporizing tactics, and found a new way to attack him. When, on December 29, Conway's resignation came in, it was accepted; but then he was immediately appointed inspector general of the army, a post that gave him an overview of Washington's every action and disposition. This was an obvious slap at Washington, since the inspector general would be reporting directly to Congress. Unfortunately, La Fayette, at this time, was still thought of as a friend of Conway since they had both pushed the now moribund India scheme. Once again, quite unintentionally, the young man had been caught in someone else's cabal.

This time, however, the scales had fallen from his eyes. He promptly announced that he had neither suggested nor approved Conway's promotion, thus clearly dissociating himself from the anti-Washington plot; and, painfully aware that even in the United States, virtue did not always prevail, he poured his heart out in a long letter to Washington.

"I don't need telling you how I am sorry for all what happens since some time," he wrote on December 30. "It is a necessary dependance of my most tender and respectful friendship for you . . . but another reason to be concerned . . . is my ardent . . . wishes for the happiness and liberty of this country. . . .

"When I was in Europe, I thought that here almost every man was a lover of liberty. . . . You can conceive my astonishment when I saw that toryism was as openly professed as whiggism itself. However I believed at that time that all good Americans were united together, that the confidence of Congress in you was unbounded. Then I entertained the certitude that America would be independant in case she would not lose you. . . . You shall see very plainly that if you were lost for America, there is nobody here who could keep the army and the revolution for six months. There are oppen dissenssions in Congress, parties who hate one another as much as the common enemy, stupid men who without knowing a single word about war undertake to judge you, to make ridiculous comparisons; they are infatuated with Gates without thinking of the different circumstances and believe that attacking is the only thing necessary to conquer. . . . I have been surprised at first to see the establishment of this new Board of War . . . but the promotion of Conway is beyond all expectations. . . . Gal [General] Conway says he is entirely a man to be disposed of by me, he calls himself my soldier, and the reason of such behaviour for me is that he wishes to be well spoken of at the French court and his protector the Mquis de Castries is an intimate acquaintance of mine—but . . . I enquired into his character. I found that he was a dangerous and ambitious man. He has done all in his power by cunning maneuvres to take off my confidence and affection for you. His desire was to engage me to leave this country. . . . I am very sorry whenever I perceive troubles raised amongs the defenders of the same cause, but my concern is much greater when I find officers coming from France . . . to whom any fault of that kind can be imputed. . . .

"[Conway] has engaged me by entertaining my head with ideas of glory and shining projects, and I must confess to my shame that it is a too certain way of deceiving me. . . .

"My desire of deserving your satisfaction is stronger than ever, and everywhere you'l employ me you can be certain of trying every exertion in my power to succeed."[29]

The letter reveals one of La Fayette's most shining qualities, the absolute loyalty he gave to the General and cause. The normally cool Washington answered the very next day (December 31). After speaking of his "friendship and attachment" to the Marquis, and of his "sentiments of the purest affection," he added: "It will ever constitute part of my happiness to know that I stand well in your opinion, because I am satisfied that you can have no views to answer by throwing out false colours, and that you possess a mind too exalted to condescend to dirty arts and low intrigues to acquire a reputation." Then, after denouncing Gates, the General went on: "We must not, in so great a contest, expect to meet with nothing but sun shine. I have no doubt but that everything happens so for the best; that we shall triumph over our misfortunes and shall, in the end, be ultimately happy; when, my dear Marquis, if you will give me your company in Virginia, we will laugh at our past difficulties and the follies of others."[30]

This was an impressive testimonial, and La Fayette took it as such. "Every assurance and proof of your affection fills my heart with joy," he promptly replied, adding, in what may seem at first to be no more than polite self-deprecation, but has the ring of candor, "I never wish'd as heartily to be entrusted by nature with an immensity of talents where I could then be of some use to your glory and happiness as well as to mine own."[31] As long as he followed Washington's guidance, all went well for La Fayette, and his very real qualities came to the fore; it was only when he lost sight of his mentor that he began to go astray. He perceived this accurately but did not always act upon it. When the Marquis was away from the General's leadership, there was no telling where he might wander. Still, his unaffected worship of Washington proves that he recognized greatness and that he was willing to defer to it.

Because he perceived Washington's superiority so clearly, he wrote Henry Laurens a long letter praising the General's talents and denouncing Conway's promotion; but even that straightforward move embroiled him in further complications. Since Conway and Gates realized it was now more urgent than ever to get rid of the interfering young marquis they came up with a new idea: the conquest of Canada, to be led by none other than Gilbert himself.

To the naïve mind, an expedition to conquer Canada seemed to offer a host of advantages. First, it would position an American force at the rear of the British army; second, if successful, it might cause the government in London to make peace with the United States in order to avert the loss of Canada.

The military part of the expedition would be simple, Gates and Conway said. There was an inland British fleet operating on the Great Lakes and adjacent rivers; during the winter, when these waterways were frozen, an American corps armed with straw and torches would burn the ships down where they stood encased in ice; then, the French-Canadians, who were thought still to resent the British conquest of the 1760s, would rise in a body and join the American forces. At that point, the United States would offer to return Canada to France, thus drawing it into the war. Such a war plan would obviously require a French leader for the expedition. Conway selflessly pointed out how uniquely qualified La Fayette was for the role.

When this idea was presented by Gates to La Fayette, with the further enticement that he himself would be allowed to take Montreal all on his own, the Marquis exploded with joy. Compulsively he went around telling everyone how his ancestor the maréchal de La Fayette had killed the Duke of Clarence and many another Englishman besides, back in the fifteenth century. Now he, too, was to strike a death blow at the proud and greedy Britons. Perhaps, fresh from the Conway incident, the Marquis might have wondered why Washington, while not yet attacking the idea openly, refrained from endorsing it in any way; but he was far too excited to think of anything but the glory to be reaped. As always, an adventure seemed irresistible.

Had La Fayette taken a closer look at details, however, he might have had a few questions. First, the enterprise depended on the Americans being able to cross over the frozen waterways; given the slowness and inefficiency of the army's commissariat, there was every prospect that the snows would melt well before the required supplies reached Albany, where the troops would assemble. Second, it was at the least imprudent to use a part of the American army in so remote an area, given the British military superiority in the United States. Finally, there was no guarantee at all that the supposed Canadian uprising would actually occur, and, if it did not, the American expeditionary corps was far too small to have any chance of success. La Fayette suspected none of this, but when, on January 26, 1778, he found out that Conway was to be his second in command, he finally became skeptical. After weeks of blindness, it seemed, Gilbert was finally becoming wise.

"Amongst all the men who could be sent under me Mr. Conway is the most disagreeable to me and the most prejudiciable to the cause," he immediately wrote Laurens, continuing: "How can I support the society of a man has spocken of my friend in the most insolent and abusive terms and does every day all in his power to ruin him."[32] Rather than take on Conway, he was "even" willing to serve *under* the experienced General Alexander McDougall, La Fayette told Gouverneur Morris, who wrote Laurens on that same January 26, "I am deeply surprised at the mature judgment and solid understanding of this *young* man, for such he certainly is."[33] Nor did a letter from Conway arguing that the Canadian expedition would redound to the glory of La Fayette and the United States convince the now thoroughly enlightened marquis. At last, Gilbert knew when he was being flattered, so, inveterate letter writer though he was, he did not even bother to respond to the intriguer.

The very next day, January 27, the Marquis received instructions directly from the Board of War in which he was ordered to leave immediately for Albany: Gates had done his best to remove La Fayette. As it happened, a group of Congressmen was visiting Valley Forge that day. La Fayette went straight to them and told them he did not want an independent command, since it was nothing but a trick to abridge the commander in chief's powers. When queried about the expedition, Washington refused to express an opinion. He would not attack the board's orders in public, but he would not approve of them either.

So La Fayette rode to York, where the Congress had been sitting since the fall of Philadelphia and there he used a potent weapon—the threat that he would resign, return home, and tell everyone that the war was being mismanaged. This was enough to force General Gates and the Board of War to listen to him; and since he was beginning to discover politics, he also lobbied Henry Laurens, who had become his friend; Robert Morris, who was acting as his private banker; and any other member of Congress he could reach. Within a few days, he was successful. The Board of War agreed that the army of Canada was to remain under the ultimate command of General Washington. La Fayette was to be seconded by either De Kalb, who had apparently dropped his pro-Broglie efforts, or McDougall, not Conway; supplies and funds were to be diverted from the Northern Department to the Canadian expedition; and finally, the unrealistic grand design was reduced to a "mere incursion or ravage," which would have a better chance to succeed. Conway's plot had been undercut, and Washington had reason to be grateful.

The Marquis himself felt vindicated. Still convinced, in spite of Washington's silence, that the expedition would be successful, he wrote Adrienne on February 3: "I won't give you long details on the mark of confidence with which America is honoring me. I will simply tell you that Canada is possessed by the English; all that immense country is in the enemy's possession, they have troops, forts, and a fleet there. As for me, I am to go there with the title of General of the Northern Army, at the head of three thousand men, to see if we can do some harm to the English there."[34] This was by no means the only letter La Fayette wrote about his new promotion: he was making sure that all France would know just how important he had become. It was, therefore, essential that he succeed. Unfortunately the plan was bound to fail.

Of course, had Washington spoken up, La Fayette might have spared himself the trip to Albany, but the General had his reasons for remaining silent. "[The expedition] is the child of folly," he wrote a friend on February 8, "and must be productive of capital ills, circumstanced as our affairs are at present; but as it is the first fruit of our new Board of War, I did not incline to say anything against it."[35] The General would not be charged with sour grapes.

By the time this letter was written, La Fayette was already on his way to Albany. The roads in midwinter left much to be desired, and it took fourteen days to cover the six hundred miles from York. Of course, the Marquis stopped often along the way and allowed himself to be charmed by the hospitality, good temper, and egalitarian spirit of his hosts. By then, he had imbibed liberally of the political principles the Americans expounded so eloquently: not that he thought these democratic ideals could possibly apply in France; but in the United States, this second Garden of Eden, they were evidently the very best possible philosophy. The America he was fighting for, he thought, was a country where no man was really poor, where the upper classes used no century-old privileges to oppress the lower class, where crime was virtually unknown, and where comfort replaced luxury. Perhaps this idyllic view owed something to the fact that La Fayette, after all, was a celebrity, and was therefore received with enthusiasm by the most prominent local citizens of the little Hudson Valley towns through which he passed, but he was not altogether wrong. Jefferson's land of small, independent farmers had not yet ceased being a reality, and it made a deep impression on the landowner from the Auvergne.

As soon as the Marquis arrived in Albany, however, this rosy panorama was replaced by a much bleaker prospect. To be sure, here, too, La Fayette was received as the conquering hero. The elderly, experienced General Philip Schuyler invited him to stay at his mansion and gave parties for him; but then, at a strategy meeting, he also told the young man that the proposed expedition was impossible: there were no men, no supplies, no funds, and it was rapidly getting too late to cross the lakes during the frost. General Benedict Arnold and General Conway, who had preceded La Fayette, agreed. Of course, this was a dreadful blow. All Europe now would be expecting La Fayette to conquer Canada. If he never left Albany, he would look like a fool. Hastily he proceeded to inspect the troops and the supplies to see if he could salvage the expedition and discovered that the other generals were right. On February 19, within forty-eight hours of his arrival, he sat down and poured his heart out to Washington.

After reporting that the generals were unanimously against the expedition, he went on with indignation: "I have been shamefully deceived by the Board of War. They have by the strongest expressions promise to me, three thousand (and what is more to be depended upon, they have assured me in writing *two thousand five hundred combattans* [soldiers] *at a low estimate*. Now Sir I do not believe I can find *in all* twelve hundred fit for duty, and most part of these very men are naked even for a summer campaign. I was to find Gal Stark with a large body, and indeed Gal Gates had told me that *Gal Stark will have burnt the [English] fleet before your arrival.* Well, the first lettre I receive in Albany is from Gal Stark who wishes to know *what number of men, from where, for which time, for which rendez vous I desire him to raise.* . . . I have applied to every body, I have begged at every door I could since two days, and I see that I could do something, was the expedition to be begun in five weeks. But you know we have not an hour to lose and indeed it is now rather too late, had we everything in readiness.

"There is a spirit of dissatisfaction prevailing among the soldiers and even the officers which is due to they'r not being paid since an immense time."[36] The outraged Marquis went on to point out that while the army at Albany, such as it was, had already incurred debts amounting to $800,000, only half that amount had been appropriated for the expedition; that the most essential supplies were missing; and that even the straw needed to burn the English fleet was nothing but a fantasy. The military picture was bad enough; the prospect of losing a reputation was even worse, as far as La Fayette was concerned.

"My being appointed to the command of the expedition is known throughout the [American] continent, it will soon be known in Europe. . . . The people will be in great expectations and what schall I answer?" the desperate young man went on. "I am afraid it will reflect upon my reputation and I shall be laughed at. My fears upon that object are so strong that I would chose to [be]come again a volunteer unless Congress offers me means of mending this ogly business by some glorious operation."[37] La Fayette was alluding to an attack on New York City, an idea suggested by Arnold who, at the moment, was too sick to undertake it himself.

At the same time, the Marquis wrote Laurens, complaining about the situation and threatening, once again, resignation and departure; and since, to make it all worse, the hated Conway was now in Albany (De Kalb arrived two weeks later), La Fayette demanded an official report on the situation from him. Conway obliged. The expedition, he wrote, would be "not only hazardous in a high degree, but extremely imprudent."[38] At least, it was plain that the plan had not failed to go forward because of any incapacity or cowardice on the part of its commanding general.

"I fancy (between us) that the actual scheme is to have me out of this part of the continent, and General Conway in chief under the immediate direction of General Gates [thus bypassing Washington]," La Fayette wrote the General on February 23. "How they will bring it up I do not know—but be certain that something of this kind will appear."[39]

Indeed, La Fayette had reason to complain and demand a new, more promising commission. General Gates, whose enthusiastic support of the expedition had convinced him to go to Albany in the first place, had, of course, known all along that both men and supplies were missing. The Marquis had simply been a tool of the anti-Washington cabal. This, added to the December fracas, was a real eye-opener. People were decidely not what they seemed; they lied; they promised what they never intended to deliver. All in all, the world was a more complicated place than the young man had supposed. Once again Gilbert was learning a lesson.

In spite of all these frustrations, however, the Marquis proceeded to show his mettle. A lesser man would have given up and gone back south. Instead, La Fayette proceeded to do everything he could to improve the defenses of Albany. He spent his own money to buy the soldiers clothes, saw to it that some of the debts were paid when he received $200,000 from the Board of War, and did his best to train what few troops he had. De Kalb's arrival was a boost to his morale. Now that he was no longer Broglie's man, this serious, competent officer turned out to be a great help. Strengthening the garrison in Albany was not enough. La Fayette boldly tackled another, often neglected, problem, that of the relationship with the local

Indian tribes: if they could be enlisted against the English, as they had been by the French during the Seven Years' War, they might prove to be an asset. So, early in March, at his request, the elders convened a meeting in Johnstown, New York. It was attended by the Oneidas, the Tuscaroras, and the Onondagas. La Fayette, who was careful to give generous bribes to one and all, was much admired. For the young man who had been raised in civilized France, it was a strange scene. "Five hundred men, women and children," he wrote in his memoirs, "adorned with colors and feathers, with cutout ears, noses loaded with jewels, and almost nude bodies marked with varied figures, were attending the council. The old men, as they smoked, spoke very sensibly about politics. A balance of powers [between the warring English and American troops] would have been their object [so that neither side could oppress them] if only the drunkenness produced by rum, similar to that caused in Europe by ambition, had not often confused them."[40] Liquor notwithstanding, La Fayette's appeals had some effect. The tribes could now be relied on not to attack the Americans. And a number of braves even joined the main army—Washington had asked for them—after La Fayette had paid their wages by sending them a few "French men with black belts and yellow guineas."[41]

At the same time, La Fayette kept himself busy gathering artillery, visiting sites, and giving instructions for building and reinforcing the forts that protected frontier towns from possible enemy incursions. He arranged for exchanges of the sick and wounded with local British commanders. Of course, he was also bombarding Congress with letters, demanding that they officially recognize that the expedition was impossible and asking for a new command that would empower him to attack New York. For a few days, General Gates managed to block this proposal as unlikely to succeed, but La Fayette had many friends in Congress, especially Laurens and Robert Morris, whose debtor he was careful to be. And John Adams was praising La Fayette as a "nobleman who had endeared his name and character to every honest American and every sensible friend of mankind, by his efforts in the rights of both, as unexampled as they are generous."[42] General Gates did not stand a chance: no one wanted La Fayette to resign and go home in disgust. Congress passed a resolution in which it spoke of its "high sense of [La Fayette's] prudence, activity and zeal," adding that it was "fully persuaded that nothing has, or could have been wanting on his part . . . to give the expedition the utmost possible effect." Here was a vindication of a high order, especially when it was followed, on March 13, by another resolution returning La Fayette and De Kalb to the main army, a prerequisite to the planning of an attack on New York, since La Fayette insisted that he must work under Washington's command.

A letter soon came from Washington himself. Written three days before that last resolution of Congress, its purpose was to comfort the young man, and it succeeded. "You seem to apprehend that censure, proportioned to the disappointed expectations of the world, will fall on you in consequence of the failure of the Canadian expedition," the General wrote. "But . . . I am persuaded, that every one will applaud your prudence in renouncing a project, in pursuing which you would vainly have attempted physical impossibilities. . . . The most prone to slander can have nothing to found blame upon. . . . You may be assured that your character stands as fair as ever it did."[43]

Young Gilbert could not have asked for more, and, presumably, the specter of a sardonic duc d'Ayen dissolved into harmless vapor. That the young man had been thinking of his father-in-law is certain: during that busy six weeks in Albany, he managed to have some trees dug up and sent to him in Paris.

Still, before an attack on New York could be seriously considered, one important question remained to be solved: with La Fayette and De Kalb gone from Albany, the commander on this strategic northern front would be none other than the odious Conway. This was clearly not acceptable, so on March 20 the Marquis wrote Laurens a long letter in which he pointed out that if Conway were left in command, it would look as if La Fayette had failed and Conway succeeded—an impression not merely false but especially annoying since, after all, the La Fayettes were a much better family than the Conways, besides being properly French instead of recent Irish immigrants! As it turned out, Gilbert need not have worried: his letter crossed an order from Congress recalling the offending general and sending him to Peekskill, where he would be under General McDougall's command. La Fayette's vindication was complete.

By the time the Marquis left Albany on March 31, he had accomplished much despite the failure of the expedition. First, he had calmly and efficiently reorganized the defense of the whole Albany area; second, he had turned around the anti-Washington intrigues and effectively killed the cabal. Now he was able to return to the main army in Pennsylvania with his head held high. Once there, he found himself third in command.

He immediately made himself useful, upon his return, by assuming a major role in organizing the foreign legions under Count Pulaski, an enthusiastic Polish volunteer, and another French marquis, M. de La Rouërie, who was fighting under the nom de guerre of Colonel Armand; at the same time performing the routing duties—inspection, drill—of a senior major general. But his most important task, in his own eyes, was to stiffen American morale. Clearly, the United States was as far from winning its independence by force of arms as ever, and Lord North, the English prime minister, was beginning to realize that his own troops, no matter how successful, could not hope to prevail. A political compromise seemed the only solution. It was even announced that British commissioners were on their way, and that they were empowered to open negotiations. The question now had become, Were the Americans willing to settle for half a loaf? That, to La Fayette, would have been not only inconvenient but dishonorable as well, so he loudly and eloquently opposed accommodation with the enemy.

Amid all these efforts, La Fayette managed to find time for his two favorite occupations: conversations with the commander in chief, and letters to everyone he knew in France. In December he had told Adrienne, with a little pardonable exaggeration: "Washington finds in me a friend in whose bosom he may unburden his heart and who will always tell him the truth. There isn't a day but he has an important conversation with me or writes me a long letter, and he is good enough to consult me on the most important questions."[44] Now that the Marquis was back in camp, the relationship was resumed and strengthened. We may doubt that the consultations were quite as serious as the young man thought—the General, after all, was accustomed to making up his own mind regardless of advice—but La Fayette was a trustworthy sounding board. Perhaps more important, he was a cheerful and civilized dinner companion. Washington cared greatly about his official family: long, leisurely dinners, with wine and nuts passed around for hours, were his main source of relaxation, the almost only moments when this usually awe-inspiring figure could unbend and rejoin the rest of humanity. Since the General was very fond of his young aide, his presence provided a sense of home for the country squire who stayed away from his beloved estate for so long. In that sense, more, perhaps, than through his political or military advice, La Fayette rendered his adopted father a major service.

More significant was the influence the other way. To La Fayette, Washington communicated his own deep-seated beliefs about free government. For the first time, Gilbert began to understand what liberty really meant, why the people should have rights, why government ought never to proceed without the consent of those it rules. He discovered the need for freedom of the press, freedom of religion, freedom of assembly: in explaining all this, Washington transformed his disciple's life and made his American journey into a life-enduring education.

Although he was now beginning to feel quite comfortable in his "new country," as he called it in a letter to Laurens, La Fayette still missed France, his wife, and his friends. While Adrienne's letters always cheered Gilbert, the news was not always good. In early June, almost a year later, he heard that his eldest daughter had died. "The loss of our poor child is almost always foremost in my mind," he wrote home sadly. "That news came to me right after that of the treaty, and while my heart was heavy with sorrow, I have been forced to receive and take part in the assurances of public felicity."[45]

This sorrow was probably more theoretical than real: Gilbert had scarcely known the baby and taken very little interest in her, and in fact, at that moment, the Marquis was displaying nothing but the most intense jubilation to all his American friends. On June 1, at long last, the news arrived about the Franco-American Treaty of Commerce and Treaty of Alliance concluded at Versailles on February 6: now the United States could be sure of a real ally, with the consequent help in money, men, and supplies amplified by the presence of the French navy. Although everything still remained to be done, it was perhaps not very difficult to forecast, five years before the war actually ended, just what the outcome would be. The celebrations, both at York, where Congress still sat, and at army headquarters, were therefore loud and enthusiastic, giving Washington his first taste of French exuberance. La Fayette, when he heard the news, rushed up to his startled commander in chief and kissed him on both cheeks.

The first consequence of the alliance was a further rise in La Fayette's reputation. Now even more than before, he represented France for the Americans, while in Paris it became an accepted if inaccurate opinion that the Marquis's bold expedition was responsible for the alliance. The truth, of course, was that Vergennes had worked long and hard to convince Maurepas and the King that France had everything to gain by supporting the United States, and he had received the most inspired help from Benjamin Franklin. La Fayette's journey had at best helped to sway public opinion and thus made the new policy a little easier, although it is arguable that by irritating Louis XVI, he had in fact made it harder for Vergennes. Unlike Marie Antoinette who, swayed by fashion as usual, became pro-American, the King took a very bleak view of revolt in any form.* Only the obvious benefits offered by a policy of support to the Americans outweighed his instinctive repulsion for their revolution. Still, in a city convinced that policy was made in the salons, La Fayette's contribution seemed immense.

Paradoxically, the treaty presented the Marquis with a serious problem. All through the lengthy celebrations—a grand dinner with many toasts offered, a special review of the troops, huzzahs for His Most Christian Majesty, and general rejoicings—the Marquis wondered what he should do next. Although France and England were not yet formally at war, it was obvious

---

*He made his real feelings clear by giving the pro-American duchesse de Polignac a then-fashionable medallion of Franklin set at the bottom of a Sèvres porcelain chamberpot.

that they soon would be, and then a Frenchman's place would be in his own country's army.

The invasion of England, which was sure to follow a declaration of war, was obviously something not to be missed—as the Marquis pointed out in many a bloodthirsty letter home. On the other hand, Gilbert faced a very uncertain welcome when he returned: he had, after all, disobeyed the King's orders and must expect some sort of punishment. Then, too, in America, he had become a senior major general, General Washington's adopted son, and a figure whom all respected, while in France he was a captain without a regiment. Luckily, he could find reasons to stay where he was, at least for a few months: the British commissioners were on their way, and who better than the Marquis to warn Congress against their false blandishments? Besides, the spring campaign was about to start: obviously the young man could not abandon his post at such a critical moment. Finally, it quickly became obvious that, for the year 1778 at least, any exchange of hostilities between France and Great Britain would take place either in America or on the water. Apparent selfishness notwithstanding, it made more sense to stay; soon a letter to that effect came from the duc d'Ayen and La Fayette could answer: "Your letter . . . made my decision final and I believe I have done the right thing."

In fact, the Marquis was immediately chosen by Washington for a very important task. Although the British still held Philadelphia, their campaign had hardly been successful. The apparent victories they won by virtue of staying on the field itself were in fact real defeats, in that the Americans always inflicted more casualties than they suffered themselves; this was an especially important consideration because all reinforcements had to come from across the ocean, while American troops found their new men on the spot. Then, too, the insurgents did not seem to understand that once their capital was taken, they were supposed to acknowledge defeat and give up: even the fall of Philadelphia had failed to end the war, and it was hardly possible to occupy militarily every inch of the thirteen colonies. The British, in fact, were confronting what later became a classic colonial war dilemma, one the United States might have done well to remember in Vietnam.

A French fleet could now be expected to sail to America, and British difficulties would then multiply. His Majesty's government, therefore, decided on a two-pronged policy to counter the new alliance. On one hand, it sent commissioners who, with the help of the local Tories, and by offering a few concessions, might end the war by negotiation; on the other, it replaced the unsuccessful General Howe with Sir Henry Clinton, a highly competent officer whom La Fayette had met in London. Howe was so enraged at being relieved of command that when it seemed at the last minute that he could

crush a substantial part of the American army and make La Fayette a prisoner, he jumped at the chance.

Clinton secretly planned to evacuate Philadelphia and concentrate his
army in and around New York, but, on May 18, Howe was still in command.
That was the day Washington sent La Fayette, who commanded some three
thousand men, to reconnoiter the environs of the city to see if he could
intercept the enemy's communications: with the information he brought
back, the General could decide whether or not to make an attempt at storm-
ing the former capital. Washington had made it very plain to the Marquis
that this was strictly an intelligence operation. La Fayette was to take no
risks, avoid any battle with the British army, and never make camp since,
once immobile, he might be surrounded by his much stronger opponent.
La Fayette decided he knew better and, having reached Barren Hill, just
outside Philadelphia, he settled down for a few days. He was not in fact as
reckless as it might appear. His position gave him several roads along which
he could easily retreat if confronted by the enemy. Safe in this knowledge,
he disregarded the General's instructions.

Unfortunately, the militia was not as efficient as the army proper, the
Continentals; it failed to secure La Fayette's escape routes. The British, who
had been watching the incursion, promptly set about blocking them. On
May 20, General Howe, in an ecstasy of joy, invited all and sundry to a
dinner the next day at which the captured marquis would be the guest of
honor.

Shortly after nightfall, while the unsuspecting La Fayette was eating
his supper in a small farmhouse where he had established his quarters, the
British troops surrounded the Americans on two sides. As they moved to
block the last remaining escape route on the third side (the fourth side led
to Philadelphia and the main British strength), they passed the house of a
sleeping surgeon. Awakened by the noise, the man, who, like most local
residents, was a Patriot, looked out and realized what was happening. Soon
he was dashing up the hill in his nightshirt to La Fayette's headquarters,
only to be disbelieved when he reported sighting the enemy. Since he was
quite sure that the area in question was held by a body of militia, the Marquis
assumed that the surgeon had confused their uniforms with those of the
enemy until others confirmed his account: it looked as if the observation
corps was indeed trapped. Seeing all this through his binoculars, Washington
came to exactly that conclusion and prepared to march to La Fayette's rescue.

The third escape route that had been entrusted to the militia was not
yet actually blocked, and if the enemy could be fooled into leaving it open,
the Americans still had a chance. So now it came down to a matter of
cleverness; by remaining absolutely cool, La Fayette gained the advantage.

British troops were always nervous about fighting at night because the enemy usually knew the ground better and often seemed able to appear and disappear at will. So it was no surprise that when their commander, General James Grant, was informed that men were coming through the woods on his flank, he immediately halted his movement well short of his goal, and tried to determine whether or not he was actually being attacked. It was quite a while before he realized he was seeing decoys—what looked like the head of columns to be followed by the rest of the American troops turned out to be very few men. At the same time, the bulk of the corps, under La Fayette, had neatly taken itself out of the trap and, with the main body of the American army now approaching, poor General Grant found himself not only forced to retreat hastily but also suffered a large number of casualties. As for the Marquis, he had outwitted the enemy and behaved with a resourcefulness that evoked praise from Washington in his report to Congress, as well as general admiration—so much so that everybody forgot that he had been careless in the first place. Naturally, the delighted marquis wrote to all his French friends to tell them about his triumph. And his fame grew even brighter.

Once again, however, the Americans' achievement was not so much a victory as the avoidance of certain defeat. With the evacuation of Philadelphia in June by Clinton, at long last, the face of the war changed. For the first time, it was the British who retreated and the Americans who pursued.

To an enthusiastic young man, of course, this seemed like the perfect opportunity. La Fayette promptly suggested that the Americans harass the retreating soldiers and eventually force a battle on them. His proposals were vigorously opposed by Charles Lee, a senior general who had just returned from captivity and thought little of both the Continentals and American independence. Lee favored some sort of compromise with England and was convinced that the Continentals, if put to the test, would be defeated. La Fayette answered with equal vigor that the English were retreating and demoralized; that a surprise attack on their rear was likely to cause panic in the rest of their army; that with a little daring, a major American victory could follow. Lee then pointed to his own greater experience, to his knowledge of the terrain as well as both armies and, to La Fayette and young Colonel Alexander Hamilton's fury, he carried the day. Luckily, General Greene, whom Washington trusted, told the commander in chief he thought inaction a great mistake; and La Fayette, who had quite accurately perceived that in his own reserved way, Washington agreed with him, sent the General a letter on June 24 in which he repeated his arguments and deprecated the conduct of war by council.

This letter, compounding Washington's earlier impatience with Lee's advice, may well have convinced him. The General now decided to put together a corps of four thousand seasoned Continental troops to which he added twelve hundred militia, all to be commanded by La Fayette and used to attack the retreating British. At first Lee agreed to this, but a little reflection quickly convinced him that the young man was likely to have all the glory while he would be made to look like a coward; so, cleverly, he wrote La Fayette, explaining that he would be dishonored if the new corps fought under any command but his own. Taken in by this appeal to his own chivalry, the Marquis agreed to place himself under Lee's command once more if, within the next twenty-four hours, he, La Fayette, was unable to engage the British.

By now, the enemy, who had been moving with such tantalizing slowness, was speeding up its march. Lacking food and ammunition as the commissariat lagged behind, the Marquis was unable to catch up to the British rear, so he waited for General Lee. On June 28, 1778, the battle was joined outside of Monmouth, New Jersey. Although Washington was worried because Henry Clinton had placed the best British troops in the rear, he left the organization of the battle to Lee who, in a first stage, proceeded to lose it through a mixture of confusion, poor coordination, incompetent staff work, lack of communication with his several units, and genuine bad will. Unit after unit, faced by the withering British fire, began to crumple, then flee. In no time, the Americans were retreating everywhere. As for La Fayette, he received what he thought was an order from Lee but actually was not, and moved away from the main body of the army—a serious mistake. For a while, it looked as if the United States was about to endure a major defeat. Then Washington came forward. "The General was never greater in war than during this action," La Fayette wrote in his memoirs. "His presence stopped the retreat, his dispositions brought about a victory. His commanding presence, as he sat on his horse, his calm courage enlivened by the animation produced by the disappointment of the morning, gave him an air very proper to cause great enthusiasm."[46] Putting the Marquis in charge of the second line—which seemed the rear but never really became part of the fight—the General proceeded to trounce the British. That night, still on the battlefield, adopted father and adopted son, sharing the same cloak, slept side by side under a tree.

In itself, the Battle of Monmouth did not change the course of the war. It helped morale, for now the Americans were on the offensive. Unlike the earlier battles in which the Americans were merely winning a war of attrition, it was a classical victory, since the field was left in American hands, and it disposed of General Lee. Within a few days of the action, it had become clear that Lee, who was intensely jealous of Washington and wanted to become commander in chief himself, had actually hoped for a defeat that could be blamed on the General. If anything, he had been disappointed when Washington saved the day. Now, at Washington's request, he was court-martialed and cashiered. Soon afterward, he died, perhaps of jealousy.

The victory at Monmouth reinforced Washington's popularity in Congress because he had, alone, turned defeat into victory, but it led to no new battles. La Fayette's corps went into camp at White Plains, New York, to keep watch on the enemy. The episodic war once again stuttered to a halt. Congress had decisively rejected the overtures made by the British commissioners—it would settle for nothing less than full independence and the evacuation of all British troops—and the Marquis congratulated its president on its stand. "I beg leave to join here my voice to this of all lovers of liberty, all good americans, all true french men, in expressing my admiration and my pleasure at the noble, spirited and ever to be prais'd answer of Congress to the deceitfull and somewhat impertinent address of the British commissioners,"[47] he wrote Laurens on June 23.

Now that he had some free time, La Fayette once again resumed his role as the defender of all Frenchmen in America. For the young man, it was his duty: his eminent position made him, ipso facto, the protector of all his compatriots, even when he himself realized that they were not always deserving. "I know few officers whose merit may be compared to the merit and talent of your country borns," he admitted to Laurens. "But these reflections I will heartily make with Mr. Laurens, but never with the President of Congress as I think it consistent with my duty, with my love for my country, and my sense of the confidence her sons have trusted upon me, to recommend as warmly and forward as speedily as possible the advancement of all French men in our service."[48] Such an attitude was very helpful to countless French adventurers and gave the Marquis a warm glow of sacrifice and self-satisfaction. Despite their fondness for the Marquis, the Americans found this behavior well-nigh unbearable.

"[La Fayette's] countrymen soon find access to his heart and he is but too apt afterwards to interest himself on their behalf, without having a sufficient knowledge of their merit, or a proper regard for their extravagant views," Washington wrote in exasperation to Laurens on July 18. "I am sure you have been severely punished by these importunities as well as myself."[49] And six days later, it was to Gouverneur Morris that he complained, "I do most devoutly wish that we had not a single foreigner among us except the Marquis de La Fayette, who acts upon very different principles from those which govern the rest."[50]

The General's annoyance is understandable. La Fayette's eyes were remarkably clear where principles were concerned. The minute people asked for his protection, however, and especially if they made it plain they considered him a great hero, he went blind.

Luckily, he soon had better work to do. On July 5, a French fleet consisting of twelve ships of the line and four frigates commanded by Admiral comte Charles d'Estaing dropped anchor at Sandy Hook, off the ocean coast of Maryland. Here was the most visible result of the new alliance. La Fayette naturally took over as the liaison between the French and American commanders. This turned out to be the perfect role for him: Washington trusted him, and did not speak French; d'Estaing, who spoke no English, was a very distant relation, and he was soon won over by the young man's charm, willingness, and reputation. For one thing, the major general made it clear that although intensely pro-American, he considered himself French and cared for his own country first and foremost.

When La Fayette first went aboard his ship, the admiral was a very nervous man. He had firm instructions to preserve his fleet at all costs, and knew that the British navy was a formidable opponent. If a significant portion of it caught him in American waters, he was likely to lose his ships, his command, and his reputation. Naturally enough, he was tempted to stay in close reach of the French West Indies. On the other hand, he would appear cowardly and incompetent if he failed to help the Americans. And on top of all this, he did not have a clue as to where or how large the enemy forces actually were. Greatly to his relief, La Fayette provided instant help by hiring spies with his own money; soon the needed intelligence was available and d'Estaing could breathe a sigh of relief.

Now that the French had arrived, some sort of joint operation was obviously called for, preferably one in which the fleet could play an important role. The prime objective seemed obvious: Newport, Rhode Island, a small, prosperous port peopled mostly by Quakers, was surrounded by water and occupied by the British. A combined French-American operation was set up. On the American side, the divisions led by Generals Greene, Sullivan, and La Fayette, after marching through Connecticut, were to start the assault from the land side with the help of French troops from the fleet and the ships' cannon. Agreement on the actual procedure was hard to achieve. The American generals did not really trust the French and insisted on being in charge. The admiral was willing to consider their demand, until La Fayette asked for command of the French troops on the ground. This infuriated Greene and Sullivan on two counts: first, it looked as if La Fayette did not really feel the Continental troops were reliable; second, it would have promoted him over the heads of the other two, more senior, generals. Were the allied troops to be united or separate? they now asked. Admiral d'Estaing, anxious to cooperate when he could, resolved the situation by refusing La

Fayette an immediate command, while leaving him in full charge if he, d'Estaing, should be incapacitated or absent. Having thus soothed all ruffled feathers, he was able to work out a plan with Greene and Sullivan.

At that point, the two generals got together without La Fayette and decided to show just what they thought of the French by ignoring the plan and starting the attack early. Nevertheless, the admiral was prepared to help, but a British fleet appeared off Newport. Leaving the siege d'Estaing sailed out and made ready to fight. As it happened, that was unnecessary: the much smaller British fleet, rather than risk probable defeat, turned and ran, but a violent storm blew up and lasted three days. By the time it was over, the French ships were sorely in need of repair and the siege continued, though without any real hope of success.

D'Estaing wanted to have his fleet repaired in Boston, both because the materials he needed could be found there and because it was safer, but that meant giving up on Newport. The American generals claimed the repairs could be carried out in other Rhode Island ports and were so outraged when the fleet sailed off to Massachusetts that they wrote the admiral an insulting letter. La Fayette, who had been trying to calm everyone, lost his temper and declared he would no longer be associated with officers who offended his national pride. Finally, Greene and Sullivan withdrew the letter.

Once the fracas was over, it became clear that the siege was doomed. General Sullivan was still seething, and in his general order for August 24 he hoped that "Americans will prove by the event able to procure that by their own arms which their allies refuse them assistance in obtaining."[51] Those were fighting words, and once again La Fayette exploded. After all, Sullivan had as good as accused the French of cowardice. Once again, Sullivan caved in: the next day's general orders praised the French. By the end of the month, Greene wrote Washington: "The Marquis' great thirst for glory and national attachment often run him into errors. However, he did everything to prevail on the Admiral to cooperate with us that man could do."[52]

It looked, in fact, as if La Fayette's star was fading. He left Newport and went to Boston to urge a variety of schemes (including that old Indian invasion plan of Conway's) on the admiral—all in vain since d'Estaing knew perfectly well that the young man was in America against the King's orders, and had remained persona non grata in Versailles. Then, to the Marquis's great annoyance, he missed a small battle fought outside Newport, returning just in time to direct, with cool efficiency, the retreat made necessary by the arrival of a British fleet.

Frustrated at missing the action, Gilbert tried to revive his Canadian invasion plan, but met with opposition from all concerned. He had little to do then but continue his role as go-between. Added to all the difficulties he had endured, he now found himself faced with that peculiar phenomenon, a free press, and he found it so annoying that, on September 1, Washington wrote him soothingly: "In a free and republican government, you cannot restrain the voice of the multitude. Every man will speak as he thinks, or, more properly, without thinking, and consequently will judge the effects without attending to the causes. The censures, which have been levelled at officers of the French fleet, would more than probably have fallen in a much higher degree upon a fleet of our own, if we had one in the same situation. . . . Let me beseech you therefore, my good Sir, to afford a healing hand to the wound that unintentionally has been made."[53] It was the voice of wisdom and the Marquis listened to it.

Still, the alliance's failure to achieve much had been very disappointing, so when an opportunity for a bold and well-publicized action appeared, La Fayette rushed to take advantage of it. The English commissioners, headed by Lord Carlisle, issued a statement professing their astonishment "at the calamities in which this unhappy country continues to be involved from the blind deference which their leaders profess toward a power that has ever shewn itself an enemy to all civil and religious liberty." The commissioners had a point, but La Fayette, blindly loyal, considered such language an insult to France; so he wrote Washington telling him he had decided to challenge Carlisle to a duel.

By return post the General begged him to do no such thing. "[I] refuse my approbation to the challenge," he wrote. ". . . The generous spirit of chivalry, exploded by the rest of the world, finds a refuge, my dear friend, in the sensibility of your nation only. But it is in vain to cherish it unless you can find antagonists to support it; and however well adapted to the times in which it existed, in our days, it is to be feared, that your opponent, sheltering himself behind modern opinions, and under his present public character of commissioner, would turn a virtue of such ancient date into ridicule. Besides, supposing His Lordship accepted your terms, experience has proved, that chance is as much concerned in deciding these matters, as bravery; and always more than the justice of the cause."[54] As usual, Washington was right, but this time La Fayette chose to disregard his advice and sent off the challenge. Naturally, Lord Carlisle declined "under his public character as a commissioner"; and in both England and America, everybody thought that the Marquis had made an absolute fool of himself. Not so in France, however, where the challenge was much admired. As for the Marquis himself, to the end of his life he considered his behavior brave and bold, an attitude that only underlines another serious flaw in his understanding of the world: he never quite saw that great issues are not decided by brave words and selfish posturing.

Although this was really a minor incident, and one that Washington soon forgot, it was quite typical of the old-fashioned spirit that still prevailed at Versailles. While the English and the Americans had enough sense to distinguish between personal responsibilities, which might bring about a duel, and public actions, which were shielded by the state, the French did not. Unfortunately, this kind of extreme individualism makes for stormy politics: where principles give way to personalities, compromise becomes unreachable. La Fayette had learned a great deal from Washington about liberty, about war, even about republican government; but the lesson he failed to accept was perhaps the one he needed most of all.

By the end of September, it was becoming evident that the campaign was largely over for 1778, since fighting usually stopped in winter. Also, there was talk of a French invasion of England the following spring. La Fayette began to think seriously of returning home temporarily. Learning of his plans, on September 25 Washington wrote the young man a letter of extraordinary warmth. After thanking him for his many proofs of affection and attachment, he told La Fayette that he felt bound to him by ties of close friendship, and went on: "The ardent zeal which you have displayed during the whole course of the campaign to the eastward, and your endeavours to cherish harmony among the officers of the allied powers . . . deserve, and now receive, my particular and warmest thanks. . . .

"If you have entertained thoughts, my dear Marquis, of paying a visit to your court, to your lady and to your friends this winter, but waver on account of an expedition into Canada, friendship induces me to tell you that the prospect of such an operation is not so favorable at this time, as to cause you to change your views."[55] This was putting it tactfully: the Canadian expedition was finished.

La Fayette did actually decide to go home, but without giving up on Canada. In October, he moved on to Philadelphia, where Congress was now established again, and actually convinced his friends that he should be entrusted with a request to Louis XVI for help in men, weapons, and money so as to mount the invasion. The plan was the result of yet another anti-Washington plot but was hardly likely to lead anywhere: the very last thing Versailles wanted was to see Canada occupied by an American army.

Meanwhile, more proofs of congressional gratitude were showered on the Marquis: a sword encrusted with diamonds to be ordered by Franklin in Paris and many promotions of French officers, as well as permission to go home and return to the United States "at such time as will be most convenient to him," with assurance of his continuing commission as a major general. Henry Laurens, President of Congress, further honored the young man by producing a spectacular testimonial of his services, and addressing it to Louis XVI.

"Great, faithful and beloved Friend and Ally," it began, "The Marquis de La Fayette, having obtained our leave to return to his Native Country, we could not suffer him to depart without testifying our deep sense of his zeal, courage and attachment.

"We have advanced him to the rank of major general in our Armies which, as well by his prudent as spirited conduct, he hath manifestly merited.

"We recommend this Young Nobleman to Your Majesty's notice as one whom we know to be Wise in Council, gallant in the Field, and Patient under the hardships of War. His devotion to his Sovereign hath led him in all things to demean himself as an American, acquiring thereby the confidence of these United States, Your Majesty's good and faithful friends and allies and the affection of their citizens."[56]

However splendid, the commendation was unlikely to do the Marquis much good if Vergennes received, at the same time, a secret plan to invade Canada hatched by La Fayette, and going exactly contrary to French policy. Luckily for La Fayette, his star was once again in the ascendant. First, his trip to Boston, whence he was to sail home, turned into a triumphal procession, and that naturally slowed his progress. Then, as he reached Fishkill, he became quite ill—not so dangerously, perhaps, as he thought—but enough to delay him still further; and, by the time he reached Boston, Washington had found out about the Canadian project and squelched it simply by making his disapproval explicit. This apparent setback drove the Marquis nearly frantic; in fact, though he himself did not realize it, loss of the plan was the best thing that could have happened to him. Now he would be going home in a blaze of glory, without any embarrassing commitments.

He also brought two more letters from Washington with him. The first enclosed a long note to Benjamin Franklin, now United States Minister to France.

"The generous motives," it read, "which first induced La Fayette to cross the Atlantic; the tribute which he paid to gallantry at the Brandywine; his success in Jersey before he recovered from his wounds, in an affair where he commanded militia against British grenadiers; the brilliant retreat by which he eluded a combined maneuvre of the whole British force in the last campaign; his services in the enterprise against Rhode Island; are such proof of his zeal, military ardor and talents as to have endeared him to America, and must greatly recommend him to his prince. Coming with so many titles to claim your esteem, it were needless for any other purpose than to indulge

my own feeling, to add, that I have a very particular friendship for him."[57]
This was a thoughtful letter, since it asked the American minister, in effect,
to defend the Marquis against any remaining anger at his earlier disobedience: more than just public opinion would be on his side when he reached
Versailles.

Meanwhile, in Boston, the authorities were having trouble finding enough
sailors to man the *Alliance*, a thirty-six-gun frigate selected by the United
States government for La Fayette's voyage, but, at last, all was ready. Just
before sailing, on January 11, 1779, the young man sent his great friend one
last, brief letter. "The sails are just going to be hoisted, my dear General,
and I have but the time of taking my last leave from you. . . . Farewell, my
dear General, I hope your French friend will ever be dear to you, I hope
I schall soon see you again, and tell you myself with what emotion I now
leave the coast you inhabit, and with what affection and respect I'l for ever
be, my dear general, your respectfull and sincere friend."[58]

After a well-filled year and a half, the Marquis de La Fayette was at
last going home.

Four

A FRUSTRATING WAR

The young man who stepped off the *Alliance* at Lorient on February 6, 1779, might be famous in America and acclaimed in Paris, but to the French government, which had always been fond of forms, he was no more (for a few days at least) than a disobedient subject; and so Major General the Marquis de La Fayette soon found himself under house arrest. Of course, he endured only a gentle form of incarceration: he was forbidden to leave the hôtel de Noailles for an entire week and allowed to see only members of his family. It is not difficult to think of a worse fate. Gilbert was, in effect, condemned to spend a week in one of the most sumptuous houses in Paris (and one, furthermore, which had a large garden) in the company of an adoring wife, properly respectful in-laws, and a mob of visitors—after all, the Noailles were related to virtually everyone, so the family could be said to include just about the entire court. As a result, the Marquis thoroughly enjoyed himself, even if he was forced to cancel a visit to Franklin, who could not, by the remotest stretch of the imagination, be called a relative.

Such punishment showed how much the world had changed since the marquis de Noailles had written despairingly of La Fayette's departure for America, for while Maurepas felt the King's authority must be vindicated by the appearance, at least, of punishment, there could be no doubt about the young man's status: he was the hero of the hour. That much was obvious the moment he appeared, still covered with dust from his trip, at a ball the prince de Poix, his wife's cousin, was giving in his Versailles mansion on February 11. It became even clearer when, the next morning, Maurepas immediately agreed to see him. By the end of the meeting, La Fayette had become not only the unofficial spokesman for the United States but also someone to be reckoned with at Versailles. As for the eight days' arrest, it was, in the end, no more than a favor to poor Adrienne. She had suffered from her husband's long absence, and on his return he had headed straight for Versailles, the center of power, and not to Paris, where his wife awaited him. She had to take her turn, in fact, after Maurepas and half the court. As soon as the incarceration was over, she lost her Gilbert again, to politics and popularity; but while a lesser woman might have complained, Adrienne, who understood her husband, simply worked hard not to appear clinging.

"When I arrived [back in France]," La Fayette wrote in his memoirs, "I had the honor of being consulted by all the ministers and, much better still, kissed by all the women. The kisses stopped the next day; but I kept the government's ear for a longer time and enjoyed, in Versailles, as much favor as I had fame in Paris."[1] The kisses, in fact, lasted longer than the Marquis is willing to admit: the hitherto recalcitrant Mme d'Hunolstein was fully aware that a hero's love became a great beauty; and upon La Fayette's return, she made it plain to him that the duc de Chartres would henceforth take second place. As for Gilbert, despite all the love letters he had written Adrienne from America, he never thought of being faithful. Soon La Fayette's affair with the beautiful Aglaé became common knowledge.

This, along with the extraordinary and universal acclaim he received, might well have turned the young man's head, but he took it all with great calm and never forgot that he had returned home in order to help the United States. Even his affair with Aglaé, at first, was more for vindication than love. His coolness was all the more impressive since in February 1779, the twenty-one-year-old Gilbert was received everywhere with the wildest displays of enthusiasm. The author of a hit play, *L'Amour Français*, promptly wrote in some extra lines:

> Il renonce aux douceurs d'un récent mariage
> Aux charmes de la Cour, aux plaisirs de Paris
> La Gloire seule échauffe, embrase ses esprits . . .[2]

> He gives up all the bliss of a recent marriage
> The charms of the court, the pleasures of Paris
> Glory alone warms, fires his soul. . .

Not very good verse, perhaps, but effective enough when spoken to the hero sitting in a box, and capped by clamorous applause.

For a while, La Fayette's life became that of the most fashionable man in France. Many parties were given in his honor; he had a large following and was influential at court; the Queen who, after all, set the tone, had quite forgotten about the awkward dancer. Now she treated the Marquis with obvious favor. It was, in fact, through her agency that, on March 3, he was promoted to *mestre de camp*, the equivalent of colonel, and allowed to buy, for 80,000 livres ($360,000) a regiment of the King's Dragoons.

All this acclaim failed to distract the Marquis, however. His task was to help the United States, and this he proceeded to do with vigor and pertinacity. "I told myself that the cost of a fete would have resupplied the army of the United States," he wrote, "and in order to clothe it, I would, as M. de Maurepas once joked, willingly have sold the furniture of the palace of Versailles."[3] In fact, that 80,000 livres La Fayette paid for his new regiment would have bought quite a few bolts of cloth; but he hoped to lead it in the conquest of England and so felt no guilt about spending the money on his own advancement. At the same time, the French government had undertaken to help the United States financially, so there were conferences with Benjamin Franklin and John Adams, schemes to convince Vergennes and Maurepas to do more, to do it faster; and he even made efforts at being the perfect courtier. On February 19, La Fayette wrote the King to apologize for his earlier disobedience and, although the letter was not especially humble, it worked. "If I added to my disobedience behavior which made me still more guilty, it was, Sire, because every Frenchman ought to risk his fortune, his hopes, and even public esteem rather than harm the interests of his country in compromising the government by his conduct."[4] Strong words, since they made a distinction between the King's orders and the welfare of France; but the King had decided on a pro-American policy, and the Marquis was now granted the right to attend his levee, an earnestly sought court distinction.

"I have the honour to acquaint your Excellency that I have received from the Congress their appointment to be their Minister Plenipotentiary at this Court," Franklin wrote Vergennes on February 14. ". . . I have received a number of letters from America all expressing the highest esteem for the Count d'Estaing and the Marquis de La Fayette."[5] From then on, the envoy and his "compatriot" waged a relentless and concerted campaign.

Both knew all too well how weak the Continental army actually was, despite the withdrawal of the British forces from Philadelphia, and how close the United States actually stood to defeat. It would not have done to say so in public, of course, but Vergennes and Maurepas soon found themselves under assault from both sides. Franklin tactfully suggested ways to help the fledgling country while La Fayette bombarded the ministers with a seemingly endless variety of pleas, suggestions, and plans.

There was, of course, the Marquis's perennial favorite, the expedition against Canada, and he tried to revive it as soon as he arrived in Paris; but Vergennes was against it, largely because of the political difficulties it was likely to create between France and the United States, and Jacques Necker, the Minister of Finance, opposed it even more strongly because of the cost involved. Cost was one factor that never ceased to haunt all concerned: Necker, who thought the war was already far too expensive; Louis XVI, who had to listen to Necker; La Fayette and Franklin, who knew how desperately poor the United States actually was; the Congress, whose paper money was depreciating with more than deliberate speed; and General Washington, who had to watch his army melting away for lack of funds. In that respect, France was very much the wrong ally for the United States. Money was the chronic problem of the ancien régime primarily because the rich were not taxed: the entire load of the state's revenue rested on the shoulders of those least able to bear it; nor did it help that M. Necker was a charlatan who pretended to balance the budget while actually financing the war through high-interest loans.

Canada, therefore, was out. At least the French navy and an army corps under the dashing duc de Lauzun had mounted a successful raid on the British establishment in Senegal, which had as its consequence an abundant supply of slaves for the "Southern gentlemen of America," as the Marquis wrote Franklin in a letter of congratulation. Still, something more had to be done, so La Fayette developed a new plan. Like many other influential Frenchmen, the Marquis had been urging an invasion of England, but even he could see that it was a major enterprise requiring lengthy and complex preparations. In the meantime, he suggested raiding a few English ports. John Paul Jones, as it happened, was in Paris: Why should not the two dashing naval heroes get together? France would supply the funds, a few ships, and a few hundred men. La Fayette would provide planning and leadership; and, in the end, a good deal of damage might be done to the hated enemy. For some two months the government gave the plan serious consideration; but then, as it became obvious it would draw on resources that should be husbanded for the great invasion, the idea was abandoned, much to the Marquis's frustration.

Then there was the Irish scheme: La Fayette, who claimed he had contacts in Ireland, thought the island might also rebel against British tyranny. After all, it was a colony, just like Virginia and Massachusetts; better yet, the people were Catholic and groaned under their Protestant masters. "Ireland," he wrote Washington on June 12, "is a good deal tir'd with English tyranny. I *in confidence* tell you that the scheme of my heart would be to make it as free and independent as America. . . . God grant [the Irish] might succeed," and he went on to urge the General to keep all this absolutely to himself since "there are so many people in Congress that one can't unbosom himself safely as he does with his best friend."[6]

Nothing came of the plan to invade Ireland, or of another improbable scheme of La Fayette's. His idea was to rent the Swedish navy. After all, superiority in American waters was essential, and the French fleet was apparently unable to achieve it. When La Fayette presented Maurepas with the idea and the minister pointed out that the King of Sweden might resent having his ships sunk somewhere along the way, the Marquis offered to put up his fortune as a guarantee that the fleet would be returned intact. Maurepas was not convinced.

Even though La Fayette's plans were rejected one after the other, Maurepas kept encouraging him. The aging, cynical courtier knew that appearance mattered more than substance and he appreciated the value of popularity. La Fayette was the toast of Paris, and Paris created public opinion. The war was already far too expensive to continue without popular support; so he listened to La Fayette, encouraged him, treated him well, and paid very little attention to what he said. Since few realized this, it was generally assumed that La Fayette was hand in glove with the Prime Minister. This belief was encouraged still further when, one day, Marie Antoinette asked the young man about the latest secret plan and he answered, respectfully but firmly, that he was not at liberty to discuss it. The Queen was annoyed (briefly) and showed it, and everyone henceforth believed that La Fayette was at the center of power.

In fact, no one really was. The King, as usual, procrastinated. Maurepas, on his side, cared little about actual policy. He was old and tired. Whether or not France had to fight a war, the only thing that really mattered to him was staying in office. Vergennes, of course, was still working diligently but discreetly to align France with the United States, but he was well aware that Louis XVI, if pushed too hard, might well recoil. The War and Navy ministers, on the other hand, were determined to have their invasion of England because it would raise their status in the government and at court; besides, they were able to tell the King that it was a sound project because advance planning had actually begun, in deep secrecy, at Louis XV's orders, around 1765. So, little by little, France drifted toward war.

All this naturally implied friendly relations with the United States, a trend that was, however, slowed by the two military ministers' distrust in the Americans' capacity to fight. Furthermore, the United States was all the way on the other side of the world, while England was conveniently close by. And France clearly had more to gain by a direct invasion of the British Isles. It was therefore decided, almost by default, to go ahead with the invasion plan.

At that point, it became obvious that La Fayette was indeed remote from the center of power. In spite of frantic protests to Vergennes and Maurepas, he was sent to join his regiment all the way off in Saintes, some four hundred miles from Paris. It was a logical move from Maurepas's point of view: the young man was, after all, a mere colonel and had no place at the center of planning. Gilbert, however, considered himself much too experienced and talented to command a mere regiment.

As he frequently pointed out, it was not through a lack of warlike feelings that he wanted to stay in Paris; on the contrary. No one, he felt, hated the English as intensely as he did. On May 19, he wrote Franklin: "But, my dear doctor, tho' I hate the British nation, I however am obliged to confess that those ministers and theyr executors are unhappily of the same nature (whatever corrupted it might be) as the rest of mankind. Don't you feel any shame thinking those people are by their features something like men?"[7] And he felt that neither Maurepas nor Vergennes, on his own, could be trusted to make sufficient efforts. So the moment he arrived in Saintes, he sat down at his desk and began to make up for his absence.

"I should be lacking in candor if I did not admit that my blood boils in my veins,"[8] he wrote Vergennes on June 1, three days after reaching his new post; he meant, of course, that he could do far more as, for instance, the commander of part of the expedition; and, on the tenth, he made his feelings even more explicit to Maurepas. "Remember," he wrote, "that I love the art of war passionately, that I believe I was born particularly to play this game, that I have been spoiled for two years by the habit of being given great commands and much confidence. Remember that I need to justify the favors heaped on me by my fatherland, remember that I adore this fatherland and that the idea of seeing England crushed, humiliated makes me shiver with joy; remember that I am particularly honored by the interest of my compatriots and the hatred of our enemies."[9]

Compared to the fiery marquis, the ministers may have appeared cool and reluctant, but they were, in fact, quite busy: on June 21, Spain joined France in declaring war on England. This was a major step since Spain, by virtue of its extensive Central and South American colonies, was a major maritime power. Now its fleet would reinforce the French navy. As a result, preparations for an invasion of England could be speeded up. A large body of troops was concentrated in Brittany, near the embarkation ports, under the maréchal de Broglie, the brother of the comte, who was still languishing in disfavor; and La Fayette's regiment was moved from Saintes to St. Jean d'Angély, closer to Paris and Brittany. Of course, the Marquis still hoped to be given a major command in the coming operation, but, in the meantime, he set about reorganizing his regiment, which—shades of America—he had found in a shocking state of unreadiness. Soon he extended his pains to a foot regiment left under his command by M. de Voyer, his immediate superior, who had been called to Versailles. Once again, La Fayette made himself popular by his concern for his men's welfare, while at the same time maintaining the strictest discipline. And during every free minute, he wrote letter after letter—to Versailles, but especially to America. He was careful to remain in touch with the various factions in Congress, and never failed to point out that his popularity was one of the United States' best assets. It was only with Washington himself, however, that he dared to be completely open. "What I want, my dear General, what would make me the happiest of men, is to join again American colors," he wrote on June 12 from St. Jean d'Angély, "or to put under your orders a division of four or five thousand countrymen of mine. In case any such cooperation or private expedition is wished for, I think (if peace is not settled this winter) that an *early* demand might be complied with for next campaign.

"Our ministry are rather slow in their operations and have a great propension to peace, provided it is an honorable one, so that I think America must show herself in a great earnest for war till such conditions are obtain'd. . . . For what concerns the royal, ministerial, public good will towards America, I, an American citizen, am fully satisfied with it." And on the very next day, the Marquis received the proof that the ministry was not so slow after all, so he added a postscript to his letter. "I just receive, my dear General, an express from court, with orders to repair immediately to Versailles. There I am to meet M. le comte de Vaux, lieutenant general, who is appointed to the command of the troops intended for an expedition. In that army I will be employ'd in the capacity of Aide Maréchal Général des Logis [Aide Quartermaster General] which is in our service a very important and agreeable place—so that I'll serve in the most pleasing manner, and will be in a situation of knowing everything and rendering services."[10] It was indeed a dazzling position. After meeting with M. de Vaux, La Fayette found out that he was to lead the vanguard in the French invasion of England.

The government had gathered an army numbering thirty thousand men in Normandy and Brittany, with all the needed supplies and ammunition. A joint Franco-Spanish fleet, under the command of the comte d'Orvilliers, was to meet in the Channel. After engaging—and defeating—the British navy, it was to protect the transports as they brought over the men, and La Fayette was given the command of the regiments of grenadiers who were expected to clear the way for the rest of the army. The post became even more exciting when Vergennes promised that a year later, in 1780, France would send an expeditionary force to America. Still, the Marquis felt, promises were too easily forgotten, so, while he was in Paris, he arranged with Franklin to mount a propaganda campaign there contrasting British atrocities and American unity. By late June he was off to Le Havre, where his troops awaited him.

There, once again, the days passed and nothing happened. "I can be calm only on the English shore and we are not there yet,"[11] the Marquis wrote Vergennes on July 1. By mid-month, with no sign of movement, he was growing increasingly discouraged, and so, instead, he tried to convince the government to send an expedition against Halifax, Nova Scotia, and at the same time to dispatch a force to the United States. The Canadian idea fizzled out as usual, but La Fayette displayed an impressive grasp of the military situation in the United States in his argument for the dispatch of troops. The expedition would need, he thought, forty-three hundred men, some artillery, and all the attendant supplies: combined with the Continental army, that should be a force large enough to defeat the British. Besides, he wrote on July 18, "we must have officers who don't mind being bored, who can live on little, will not put on airs and especially not behave in a superior and authoritarian way, who will be able to forego for a year the pleasures, the women, and the culture of Paris; thus we must take along few colonels and people from the court whose manners are not at all American. . . . People will surely say, M. le Comte, that we will be poorly received in that country and disliked by its army. I cannot deny that the Americans are sometimes a little difficult to handle, especially by people with French habits; but if I were to take care of this, I would wager my head that I would avoid all problems and that our troops would be well received."[12]

La Fayette's ambition was clear enough: if he was to be given only a minor role in the French invasion of England, then he would be better off commanding the expedition sent to the United States. Of course, there was no chance of this happening: here, too, there were far too many senior and superior officers who had a better claim, but Gilbert's figures were realistic; and while Vergennes refused to do anything right away, in early September he promised again that in 1780 he would send the sort of military corps defined by La Fayette. Still, he would not allow La Fayette to return to Versailles to discuss the project: even long letters were better than constant interviews.

La Fayette found life at Le Havre increasingly frustrating. There was a bright moment when the sword awarded by Congress was presented to him by Franklin's grandson; but aside from that, very little was happening. The whole French plan was dependent on a safe crossing of the Channel, which was to be accomplished while the British navy was away in the West Indies. The French were so slow, however, that when Orvilliers, the French admiral, tried engaging the British Channel fleet, the English were fore-warned and took refuge in Plymouth Harbor. This effectively prevented any crossing, for the fleet could always sally forth at the wrong moment and attack the French transports. By late September, the weather had worsened, and on October 17, the invasion plan was officially abandoned.

By then, La Fayette had been depressed for quite a while. He missed Washington, especially since, as he wrote on October 7, "my ardent hopes of getting at length a letter from General Washington have been disappointed. . . . Let me beseech you, my dear general, by that mutual, tender and experienced friendship, in which I have put an immense part of my happiness, to be very exact in inquiring for occasions, and never to miss these which may convey to me letters that I will be so much pleas'd to receive."[13] He realized that there were two ways he could return to the United States, so he worked on both at the same time: on the one hand, he kept pressing Maurepas and Vergennes to send off an expeditionary force under his command, and on the other, in that same letter to Washington, he asked the General to recall him. "Nothing could make me so delighted as the happiness of finishing the war under your orders."[14]

Washington, on his side, had been complaining that he never heard from La Fayette; in fact, the letters were simply lost. This difficulty in communicating evoked from the General a rare moment of playfulness in his letter of October 20. "On the 30th of last month I wrote you a letter which, in point of length, would almost extend from hence to Paris. It was to have been brought you by Colo. Fleury; to whom the relationship of some particulars was referred; but the advice of Count d'Estaing's arrival at Georgia, and the hope given us by Congress of seeing him at New York has induced this officer to suspend his voyage to go in pursuit of fresh laurels: of course my letter to you remained on hand and gave me an oppertunity (at leizure hours) to take a copy of it; which is now sent by Monsr. de la Colombe. . . . It only remains for me now to beg the favour of you to present my respectful compliments to *your* (but have I not a right, as you say she made a tender of her love to *me*, to call her *my*) amiable and lovely Marchioness."[15]

La Fayette was finally allowed to leave Le Havre and go home; and on December 24, Adrienne gave birth to a son whom he promptly named George Washington, much to the General's gratification. La Fayette actually felt so elated by the birth that he decided to pay some attention to his wife as well: he spent a week almost alone with her, his first since the summer of 1774. Still, no amount of domestic happiness could distract him from his American mission, especially since the news from the United States was very bad indeed. Not only had the Americans been defeated, yet again, by the British but the army was now poorer than it had been even during the dread winter at Valley Forge. Once more, everything was lacking: money, food, clothes, weapons, ammunition. However, this time the United States had two very effective advocates at Versailles: one was Franklin, of course, whose dependence on the ministers' goodwill forced him to display certain restraint; and the other La Fayette, who shamelessly pestered the ministers for supplies of all kinds. On January 9, 1780, for instance, he spoke to the Minister of War and explained that the United States needed forty thousand guns and the powder to go with them. Apparently the minister listened carefully; eventually, he even acted on the request. On January 18, Franklin asked La Fayette to present a group of French officers who had served in America to the King, and request His Majesty to reward them—recognizing his effectiveness at court. And always, the Marquis courted the ministers. Earlier, writing from the United States, Gilbert had tried to ingratiate himself with Maurepas. Now, his plea for command of the American expedition reads like a love letter. "My heart tells me even more strongly I must submit an opinion to you," he sighed to the elderly cynic, "and I am even more strongly tempted to do so by my tender attachment to you and by the complete confidence you have made me feel for you; I will speak frankly; I will speak not to the minister but to Monsieur le comte de Maurepas and if I were wrong to do so, which I do not think possible, I would count on your feelings for me to reduce the embarrassment I should otherwise feel."[16] Similar blandishments appear throughout La Fayette's voluminous correspondence: time and time again, as he writes some eminent official, he claims to be speaking as friend to a friend, not as subordinate to a superior. The technique often worked: clearly, La Fayette had learned something during his early years at court, and he took full advantage of the kind of fellow feeling that still bound the *privilégiés* together.

Of course, Maurepas was also treated to more solid stuff. The very next day, January 25, for instance, the unfortunate minister received another epistle. "We ought to be ready by the *end of February*; we ought to write to America within a *fortnight*," La Fayette urged, before pleading yet again for his own promotion: "If the French commander should not know how to deal with the sentiments in Congress and the different sentiments in each state, if he should understand neither the prejudices of the people nor the parties formed in the government, nor the way in which to please the army, nor the proper mode of dealing with the civilian authorities—if he should talk to an officer from Boston as he would to one from New York, to a member of the Assembly of Pookeepsie as to one from the self-styled state of Vermont—he would be absolutely sure to give offense, absolutely sure to defeat the purposes of his voyage. But without considering, Monsieur le comte, whether my intimate friendship with the General, or the confidence of the army and the people, in short my *popularity*, to use the English expression, justify my boldness, yet in the event of my commanding the land detachment, I *will answer for it upon my head*, that I shall avoid even a shadow of jealousy and dispute."[17] And a week later, on February 2, the Marquis turned to Vergennes: "If I am in command," he wrote, "you may feel absolutely secure because the Americans know me too well to become unnecessarily worried about me. . . . Otherwise, Monsieur le comte, you would have to start by countering the bad impression made by the arrival of another commanding officer."[18]

Although La Fayette knew more about America than anyone else in France, neither Maurepas nor Vergennes felt they could trust him with a command, so they reached the perfect compromise. La Fayette would return to the United States, but as an American officer, while the comte de Rochambeau, a seasoned soldier who had already spent nineteen years as a major general, would command the French forces, with the understanding that he would keep no secrets from La Fayette and treat him almost as an equal. Just so there could be no rivalry between the two, the King now made Jean-Baptiste de Rochambeau a lieutenant general, the highest rank in the French army short of that of marshal of France, and higher than any in the American army, Washington's excepted.

Once again, La Fayette was on his way to the United States, but this time it was by the King's order and as the representative of France. He was to leave a few weeks earlier than the expeditionary corps and alert the Americans to its eventual arrival, so all necessary preparations would be made to receive it. On March 6 he left a desolate Adrienne behind in Paris; on the tenth he boarded the *Hermione* in Rochefort harbor, and on the fourteenth he set sail for the new continent, but a storm blew up and the ship had to return to shelter. So it was not until March 20 that the journey actually started and this time it went—by the standards of the time—quickly: on April 27, thirty-eight days later, the *Hermione* reached Marblehead, Massachusetts.

The next day, in Boston, the returning marquis was given a tremendous reception. He was greeted by officials of all kinds, including a committee of the state legislature. There were cheers, fireworks, and bonfires. For the second time in his life, the twenty-two-year-old marquis was saluted like a returning hero. He remembered the event fondly in his memoirs: "The arrival of La Fayette in Boston produced great excitement; this was due solely to his own popularity, for no one could guess how much help he had obtained for the United States. Everyone rushed to the shore; he was received with great acclaim and led in triumph to Governor Hancock, from whose house he left for army headquarters. Washington heard about the arrival of his young friend with a deep emotion; when he received the courier who brought him the news tears rolled down his cheeks. . . . Lafayette was received by the army with the greatest joy."[19]

In fact, besides the genuine affection most Americans felt for the Marquis, the people in the know soon had occasion to rejoice: La Fayette had come armed with his King's instructions and commitments. Six thousand infantrymen would soon be on the way, along with abundant supplies of arms, clothing, and ammunition. The expeditionary force, although it was to be led by Rochambeau, through whom all arrangements were to be made, would be considered an auxiliary corps of the American army. Rochambeau would thus be himself under Washington's command—this had been La Fayette's brightest achievement in his conferences with the ministers.

"Here I am, my dear general," he wrote Washington on March 27, "and in the midst of the joy I feel in finding myself one of your loving soldiers. . . . I have affairs of the utmost importance that I should at first communicate to you alone. . . . Tomorrow we go up to town and the day after I'll set off in my usual way to join my belov'd and respected friend and general. Adieu, my dear general, you will easely know the hand of your young soldier."[20]

After making lengthy and complicated arrangements for the reception of the French fleet—the convoy would go to Rhode Island unless the English had returned there, and an intricate systems of flags was arranged to warn the fleet of the current situation—La Fayette was ordered by Vergennes to go to Philadelphia, acquaint Congress with the new developments, and receive new instructions from the chevalier de La Luzerne, the new French minister. And in a separate letter that La Fayette was now to deliver, Vergennes informed La Luzerne that "M. de La Fayette will be leaving any moment for the United States . . . and will develop with [General Washington] a plan according to which our troops and our ships can most usefully be employed for America."[21] There were also some secret but nonbinding instructions that the Marquis brought with him: Florida might be attacked in order to please Spain, its former owner, or else perhaps New York, now held by a small English garrison, since that would bring back the English troops then operating in the Southern states.

La Fayette arrived at the army headquarters in Morristown, New Jersey, on May 10. He was greeted by Washington as a returning son and, in turn, threw himself into the General's arms, then spent the rest of the day and evening discussing the current state of affairs. The next day, Washington notified La Luzerne of the event. "You will participate in the joy I feel in the arrival of the Marquis de La Fayette—no event could have given me greater pleasure on a personal account and motives of public utility conspire to make it agreeable. He will shortly have the honour to wait upon your Excellency."[22]

Unfortunately, La Fayette's arrival was the only good news: the situation at headquarters was as alarming as any since the beginning of the war. "The patience of the soldiery who have endured every degree of conceivable hardship, and borne it with fortitude and perseverance, beyond expectations of the most sanguine, is on the point of being exhausted,"[23] the committee reported on May 25. The position of the army had, in fact, become desperate. There was no money, so the men had not been paid in months. There was no food. Clothing and shoes were almost nonexistent, and most of the men went about barefoot and in rags. Ammunition was in even shorter supply than weapons themselves.

Nor could Congress do much to help. It is important not to confuse the Revolutionary Congress with the institution as we know it today: it was less a representative body than an early version of the United Nations General Assembly. Not only did the states consider themselves virtually independent entities, from the very beginning they had cooperated rarely and reluctantly; they were inclined to resent their confederates for being too bold or too lukewarm. And since the whole point of the early Revolution was to prevent a faraway government from levying taxes, it seemed altogether out of the question to allow a shadowy central authority sitting in a distant city (Philadelphia was a good five days' travel from Boston, for instance) to decide how they were to be taxed. As a result, after an initial burst of enthusiasm, the several states had begun to draw back to themselves the few powers they had delegated to Congress.

The military situation, in May 1780, was exacerbated by the lack of money that derived partly from the fact that in the absence of a national currency, the states printed their own. Since these local banknotes were not backed by gold, they began to depreciate almost as soon as they came off the presses, thus prompting the states to issue ever larger quantities of increasingly worthless paper. Under these conditions, almost any contribution to the common cause began to look like an intolerable strain, and most states became tempted to support their own militia exclusively. Obviously, this was a recipe for disaster—singly, the states were bound to be defeated—but patriotism was still mostly local and people were unwilling to give up their own sparse resources, so the supplies reluctantly promised by the state governments were slow to come when they came at all. Without food and materiel, the army had shrunk to a few thousand men.

Such a state of affairs would have been enough to daunt anyone, but La Fayette was far too enthusiastic to let difficulties depress him: instead, he worked twice as hard to overcome them. Shortly after his reunion with Washington, he set off, in obedience to his instructions, for Philadelphia, where, on May 16, Congress passed a resolution commending the Marquis's "disinterested zeal and persevering attachment." Once there, he instantly started lobbying his old friends. It cannot have hurt, of course, that he brought 10,000 livres in gold with him. Once again, clearly, La Fayette intended to finance his part of the war.

This time, the Marquis was not working at cross-purposes with other scheming compatriots but with an ally, La Luzerne, who was popular and shrewd. Together, the two men achieved a great deal. Of course, the new French force was a great argument: now it was up to the United States to make an effort. Soon Congress was calling on the states for subsidies and instructing its committee at headquarters to cooperate with Washington in securing supplies and militia; better yet, since the militia was made up of volunteers who only served for a short period, often less than six months, the General was instructed to recruit more Continentals, professional soldiers enrolled for the duration of the war. Finally, Congress agreed to provide provisions for the French forces. When La Fayette wasn't busy seducing the Congress, he was directing a steady stream of letters at Vergennes in which he praised the Americans while pointing out how urgently they needed supplies.

When spring came, Washington decided to attack New York, but he still lacked both men and supplies; so La Fayette was pressed into service as liaison with the French command. "It appears to me in the present situation of the enemy at New York, that it ought to be our first object to reduce that post and that it is of the utmost importance not to lose a moment in repairing to that place," he wrote La Fayette on May 16. "I would therefore advise you to write to the Count de Rochambeau and Monsr. de Ternay [who commanded the fleet] in the following spirit, urging them in the strongest terms to proceed both fleet and army with all possible expedition to Sandy Hook . . . unless they have received authentic accounts that the fleet and troops now operating in the Southern states have evacuated them and formed a junction at New York. . . . I cannot forbear recalling your attention to the importance of doing everything possible to engage the Count de Guichen [who commanded the French West Indies fleet] to come upon this coast without delay. . . . With this addition to our present plan we should have reason to flatter ourselves with everything; without it we have a great deal to apprehend."[24] As usual, the General saw the problem clearly: New York could not be taken unless the allies could control its maritime approaches, and that would take the combined fleets of Ternay and Guichen.

On his own initiative La Fayette immediately decided to play a trick upon the English, in an effort to prevent their reinforcing New York: he issued plans for an invasion of Canada. This stratagem seemed all the more necessary because General Benjamin Lincoln, who had been besieged in Charleston by British forces, had capitulated and it was obvious that New York would be Britain's next focus. In fact, on June 24, Clinton did sail into its harbor. And for once his fantasies served him—the British believed that La Fayette's old obsession had surfaced again. They swallowed the Canada story! As for the French fleet, now overdue by several weeks, it was still nowhere to be seen.

In the meantime, the opposing armies marched and countermarched in New Jersey, each carefully avoiding contact with the other. Meanwhile, every day La Fayette wrote impassioned pleas to the several state governments, reminding, begging, cajoling so that supplies might at last be forthcoming. He was surprisingly effective, less, perhaps, because of his powers of persuasion than because the local authorities felt some measure of national pride when prodded by a friendly foreigner; and his efforts may have mattered more than any display of military talents. The entire War of Independence was fought under a burden of great and constant penury against a well-supplied adversary. Washington undoubtedly spent more time in trying to procure gunpowder and shoes than in devising ways to beat the English. In the end, La Fayette's effectiveness at squeezing supplies out of the state governments as well as out of the French ministry did much to help win the war.

On July 4, the Marquis showed his preoccupation with his men's clothing in a lengthy letter to Washington. "You know, my dear general, that I am very anxious of seeing the army well cloathed for this campaign," he began, and went on, and on, and on. "There may be found in the army 4,000 coats and waistcoats which are not absolutely bad, four thousand stoks or cravats and one thousand pretty good hatts.

"We may get from the stores 15,000 overalls, 10,000 pairs of shoes, 3,000 round hatts, and some few shirts.

"There are also six or seven hundred coats of every colour, to which may be added 3 or 400 of the same kind, and some indifferent hats found in the army." After many similar lists, the French marquis finally showed through when he came to his own: ". . . For the Light Division I will beg the leave of wearing a black and red feather which I have imported for the purpose."[25] It is touching to think of the enthusiastic young man carefully laying in a stock of red and black feathers so that, alone in the army, his division might look a little smart.

In fact, the Light Division was a great satisfaction: Major General the Marquis de La Fayette now had under his unique command some 1,850 infantry, 4 cannon, 100 riflemen and 300 cavalry (but only 150 horses) from the Light Horse Corps. The Light Division was indeed one of the best in the army, and by dint of great care, continuous training, and shameless scrounging for supplies, La Fayette managed to mold it into a very respectable fighting force. Still, what good would it be if no fight ever took place? So La Fayette enthusiastically supported Washington's plan to attack New York as soon as the French arrived, and boiled with impatience as they failed to do so.

What had happened, in fact, was that Maurepas, Sartines, the Navy Minister, and Montbarey, the War Minister, who were used to ordinary wars, not expeditions to the far side of the world, had found it very difficult to gather the requisite number of ships and the vast quantities of supplies that were to accompany their men to America. Nor was their task made any easier with their allies across the ocean frantically begging for guns, powder, cloth, and just about everything else that the French government now tried to gather for them. At the end of April, when it became obvious that it was a question of sending only some of the troops or missing the 1780 campaign altogether, five thousand men under Rochambeau and Charles Ternay sailed off. Among the officers were all the "bright young men"—the vicomte de Noailles, the chevalier François René de Chastellux, Alexandre de Lameth, even Count Fersen, Marie Antoinette's great friend, with whom La Fayette had spent his summers in Metz when he was just an awkward nuisance. This time, the crossing to Newport took seventy days: the fleet arrived on July 11 and was, naturally, in poor condition. Many men had become ill over the long voyage, the ships were battered. The whole force, in fact,

looked so unprepossessing that the inhabitants of Newport refused to provide
any sort of welcome until they were told that this was merely a vanguard.

From the moment he reached the American continent, Rochambeau,
most surprisingly considering the backbiting usual among general officers
in the French army, proved a loyal and helpful subordinate to Washington.
He ordered that both the General and the President of Congress be given
all the honors due a marshal of France, adding, however, that he, Rochambeau, would take precedence over all other American officers. And he made
it very clear to his own officers that, after proper discussion, he considered
himself bound to obey Washington. Still, he pointed out, his men were in
no condition to go anywhere before August 15; and Ternay, the cautious
French admiral, who knew that his fleet was smaller than the enemy's, was
extremely reluctant to risk an encounter. It would have been better, of
course, if the two generals had been able to meet, but Rochambeau could
not leave the fleet, and Washington, who was busy trying to enlarge the
army, was needed at headquarters; so, once again, as in 1778, La Fayette
became the essential intermediary, and Washington wrote Rochambeau about
him: "As a general officer, I have the greatest confidence in him; as a friend,
he is perfectly acquainted with my sentiments and opinions; he knows all
the circumstances of our army and the country at large; all the information
he gives and all the propositions he makes I entreat you will regard as coming
from me."[26]

La Fayette, of course, now back at Washington's headquarters, thought
this delay all nonsense since daring was sure to have its rewards; in the July
15 memorandum written by Washington for Rochambeau's instruction and
entrusted to La Fayette, the General even seemed to concur. But Washington also went on to point out that "in any operation and under all circumstances, a decisive Naval superiority is to be considered as a fundamental
principle, and the basis upon which every hope of success must ultimately
depend."[27] The question, therefore, was when and how (if at all) naval
superiority might be attained. Dissatisfied, La Fayette then proceeded to
draft a letter from Washington, which he would deliver to Rochambeau,
pleading for an immediate attack. This initiative infuriated the General, who
promptly delivered himself of a rare but stinging rebuke: "You have totally
misconceived my meaning," he wrote La Fayette (who was just a few tents
away) on July 16, "if you think I have or shall relinquish of enterprizeing
against New York till it appears obviously impracticable from the want of
force or means to operate. . . . What I had in view by discouraging the first
draft of your letter to the French Genl. and Adml. was . . . not to hold up
strong ideas of success which, probably, would not be warranted by the

issue because I never wish to promise more than I have a moral certainty of performing."[28] Unfortunately, this well-deserved reproval failed to make much of an impression on the often-reckless marquis.

In the meantime, La Fayette had been writing Rochambeau on his own, and making a distinctly unfavorable impression. "I received a letter from La Fayette yesterday," the French commander wrote Vergennes on July 17. "It is too voluminous to be copied but is full of bold and contradictory proposals."[29] Clearly, a meeting of the principals was necessary, and Rochambeau wrote Washington to request one, just as the Marquis was setting off from headquarters for Newport.

As was his wont, La Fayette stopped frequently on his journey to ensure that supplies of gunpowder, which the Continental army needed desperately, would be sent on to Morristown. At last, on July 24, he arrived in Newport and promptly met with a whole series of disappointments.

Rochambeau, a veteran general in his mid-fifties, known for his brusqueness, was actually quite amiable toward Gilbert, and Ternay made an exception to his usual taciturnity. In spite of this display of politeness, however, the meetings in the main cabin of the admiral's flagship did not go well. To start with, the two commanders told La Fayette that they had brought only five thousand men—better than the original figure of forty-three hundred but less than the announced six thousand—and left behind most of their supplies with the understanding that they would eventually be sent on. Further they then informed their very junior and overenthusiastic colleague, they expected Clinton to attack Newport: he was bound to come, since his forces were superior to theirs.

Undaunted, La Fayette asked Rochambeau and Ternay to take the initiative instead: attack Clinton first, he pleaded, surprise him. That would make up for the disproportion in men, ships, and supplies. Eying him sternly, Rochambeau answered that he had decided to defend Newport—which he could not risk losing, as it was the only protected harbor available to him. At that very moment, he said, fortifications were being thrown up to protect the town's land approaches. Needless to say, there could be no question of an attack on New York; worse still, Rochambeau actually asked for American reinforcements so that Clinton, if he came, could be attacked from the rear.

In spite of Rochambeau and Ternay's seniority, La Fayette refused to admit he was beaten, so the conferences continued, to no purpose whatever. At this stage Washington decided that if, as the French expected, Clinton moved to Newport, then he himself would attack New York; and since a liaison was needed between the allies, La Fayette was ordered to remain in Newport.

When he heard this, La Fayette naturally pleaded with redoubled fervor for an immediate joint attack on New York, only to be told by Rochambeau that he left the decision up to Ternay. This was entirely in character, since Rochambeau was known for his caution, and since Ternay's command, as admiral, was completely independent. The old general had found the perfect way out: he could not *order* Ternay to attack New York, and he knew that the equally cautious admiral would never risk an engagement with the larger British fleet if he could possibly avoid it.

Poor La Fayette, feeling even younger than his years, now made a fresh proposal. Disregarding Washington's plan for a joint Franco-American attack on New York, he came forth with a complicated stratagem that would allow New York to be taken by an inferior fleet in the very teeth of the British ships. Ternay answered flatly that he would go nowhere until he was able to blockade New York harbor—an obvious impossibility. He did, however, agree to write the Minister of the Navy in Versailles, to ask for four more ships of the line. Rochambeau then chimed in with the announcement that, upon reflection, he could do nothing without his second division—the one still sitting in France.

Throughout these fruitless conversations, La Fayette's usual stream of letters to Washington swelled to a torrent—there were two very long letters on July 26 alone. The Marquis went into endless details about future plans, and about the amount of supplies to be hoped for once the French got around to sending them overseas. Once in a while, his anger against Rochambeau's caution showed through. "Before settling anything, the French Generals want to hear from theyr second division—*don't fear by any means* theyr acting *rashly* and be assur'd you may very far depend on theyr *caution*," he wrote sarcastically on July 29, adding, however, "But our want of arms and ammunitions have made me also very cautious—if the states furnish us with a sufficiency of the first article, and almost a sufficiency of the second which we will make up with the Fleet, than I am most strongly of the opinion that waiting for the second division is altogether wrong and unwarrantable."[30] Time, in fact, was one of the great problems. As La Fayette kept pointing out to the French, the militia were only enrolled for three months: there was no time to waste, therefore, waiting for the hypothetical second division.

At the same time, from Morristown, Washington kept counseling his impetuous young friend: "I perceive . . . you are determined at all events to take New York, and that obstacles increase your zeal," he wrote on July 27. "I am sorry our prospects instead of brightening grow duller. I have already written you on the subject of arms. There is no probability of our getting the number we want from the states, so that without the timely arrival of those we expect [from France], or the assistance of our allies, this alone will prove an insuperable obstacle."[31]

Since the General was now aware that the French fleet had brought neither enough men nor enough supplies, he remained unwilling to engage in any significant action, thus leaving Rochambeau and Ternay to their own devices. Now, as if to make this already complex situation even more impossible, Washington realized that his liaison was advocating new and probably disastrous policies; so he promptly gave La Fayette a warning. "I am persuaded," he wrote, "that however ardent your wishes to undertake the reduction of a certain place, you will not fail to give a candid and full view of the difficulties. We owe it to our allies; we owe it to ourselves."[32] The General was right, of course, and the French understood his position. Unfortunately, they also understood La Fayette's, and the two obviously failed to coincide. At the very moment La Fayette had himself become the problem, however, he was happily congratulating himself on the allies' good relations: "The patience and sobriety of our militia is so much admir'd by the French officers, that two days ago, a French Colonel called all his officers together to desire them to take the good examples which were given to the French soldiers by the American troops . . . on the other hand, the French discipline is such that chiken and pigs walk between the tents without being disturb'd, and that there is in the camp a cornfield from which not one leaf has been touch'd—the torys don't know what to say to it."[33] Neither the General nor the Marquis had forgotten the discord of 1779: this new harmony had much to please them. Unfortunately, it now fell to La Fayette himself to foster discord.

On August 3, Washington, who understood that La Fayette was pushing Rochambeau to adopt his plan, warned him yet again. "I would not wish you to press the French General and Admiral to any thing to which they show disinclination, especially to withdrawing their troops from Rhode Island before the second division arrives to give them a naval superiority."[34] La Fayette would have done well to listen. Instead, he returned to Morristown, there to try to convince Washington, and sent Rochambeau and Ternay a long letter, the last paragraph of which was plainly insulting. "From an intimate knowledge of our situation," he wrote on August 9, "I assure you, Messieurs (as an individual and in my own name), that it is important for us to act during the present campaign, and that all the troops you may expect from France next year, as well as all the plans which you so fondly foster, will not repair the fatal consequences of our inaction now."[35] Implying that the commanders of the French army and fleet were cowards was hardly likely to please, especially when the rest of the letter advocated that same plan of attack on New York which, they knew, Washington had not approved. Rochambeau sent back an indigant letter pointing out that the French were helping the cause by forcing the British to concentrate their strength in New

York prior to attacking Newport, and adding that their very presence had broken the blockade. "At the same time, I wrote General Washington a letter in English," Rochambeau goes on to tell us in his memoirs, "and I asked him to allow all correspondence regarding our business to pass directly between the two of us without any intermediary. . . . I must however say, for Lafayette's justification, that he was substantially expressing General Washington's feelings, and that the General used Lafayette's youth and ardor to express them with more energy."[36] Rochambeau, who wrote this several years after the event, was being too kind: La Fayette, in fact, had very nearly caused a split between the allies, the very catastrophe he was supposedly trying to prevent. By writing in an insulting tone, by advancing his own designs, he had managed to make Washington look indecisive and Rochambeau a timorous fool: it was a good deal worse than the interallied conflicts of 1778. It is no wonder, therefore, that Rochambeau sent La Luzerne a note saying that, henceforth, he would ignore La Fayette and communicate directly with that model of commanders in chief, General Washington.

This time, at least, the young man, who had finally realized the enormity of his blunder, could make sure that the estrangement didn't last. On August 18, he wrote Rochambeau: "If I have offended you, I apologize, for two reasons, the first, because I love you, the second because my intention here is to do everything to please you. Any time I am just a private person, your orders will be my law, and for the least of the French here, I would make every sacrifice rather than fail to contribute to their glory, to their comfort, to their union with the Americans."[37] It was a handsome apology, and Rochambeau accepted it as such. On August 27, he answered: "It is always fine, my dear marquis, to think that the French are invincible; but I will tell you a great secret taught me by forty years' experience: no soldiers can more easily be defeated when they have lost their confidence in their leaders, and they lose it the moment they have been endangered through a particular and personal ambition. . . . You may be convinced of my tender friendship, and that if I pointed out in the mildest way some things that displeased me in your last dispatch, I realized immediately that the warmth of your soul and your heart had somewhat overcome the coolness and balance of your judgment. Keep this latter quality in council and reserve the former for the time of the action. It is always the old father Rochambeau who speaks to his dear son Lafayette, whom he loves, will love and respect until his last breath."[38] Rochambeau was right, and generous into the bargain; but La Fayette took it very lightly.

On October 7, he wrote Adrienne: "A little excessive frankness occasioned a slight difference between myself and [Rochambeau]. Since I saw I couldn't convince him, and that the public good demands that we be good friends, I said to everyone, right and left, that I had been wrong, that I had made a mistake and I apologized in so many words, which had such a wonderful effect that we are now closer than ever."[39] This letter is important, for it shows the depth of self-delusion in La Fayette's personality. He is willing, it seems, for the good of the cause to pretend to be wrong. But he does not in fact believe it, not for a moment. He *knew* he had been right in wanting to land troops on Long Island, right in telling Rochambeau and Ternay that they were dilatory and craven, just as he had been right when he sailed to America in 1777 despite pleas and orders. No matter what others might say at the moment, no matter what he himself might say to achieve his purpose, La Fayette had become convinced that he knew better; nor must he allow his adversaries to shake his conviction since, eventually, they, too, would come around to his views. Besides, Gilbert felt that, unlike most other people, he was selfless and dedicated to a noble cause: there could be no question for him of wanting money, preferment, or promotion; on the contrary, he was helping to finance the war. Thus it became very easy for him to ascribe ignoble motives to other people—they sought personal gain, after all. In 1780, at least, there was one person he so loved and respected that he was willing to listen to him and sometimes even obey him: George Washington. But the General stood alone. And since La Fayette always had a tendency to rush in and think afterward, this rigidity, this excessive self-confidence, combined with frequent blindness to the reality of his position, was very apt to induce the young man into grave error.

The quarrel with Rochambeau did not restrain La Fayette at all. He still looked after his soldiers of the Light Division, drilled them, and looked for nonexistent supplies. "This corps is always kept at full strength and it is distinguished by a red and black feather," he wrote Noailles on September 2. "I should prefer that it be a uniform, or a good pair of shoes, but our skin is visible, and we are sometimes barefoot, not to mention that often the inside is no better garnished than the outside."[40] Still, he managed to find each of his regiments an elegant standard, adorned by a cannon and bearing the device *Ultima ratio*; the *regum** was tactfully left out. John Holker, who, though an American, had been appointed French consul at Philadelphia, gave the Marquis a magnificent white horse, worth 2,400 livres, for which he refused to accept payment, and La Fayette himself provided each of his officers with a sword, cockade, and epaulets. Soon, he was sending to France

---

Ultima ratio regum, "the last argument of kings," is a Latin expression that refers to the use of force.

for uniforms at his own expense—come what might, the Light Division would be the handsomest in the army.

Far more important than fancy uniforms, however, the division must acquire fame and glory. Washington, naturally, got to hear all about it: "You very well know that for many and many reasons both on account of the Country and on that of the French, I think it is very important, Nay, I might say politically necessary that something brilliant be at this time perform'd by our troops," La Fayette wrote on August 14. It is good to know that despite the urgency of his tone, he noted on the envelope: "In case the General was in bed this is not to be given to him before tomorrow morning."[41] In fact, with Washington's concurrence, the army, including the Light Division, was sent off on forage and purposely made to look overextended, but the British commander failed to respond, so once again nothing happened.

Meanwhile there was bad news from elsewhere. General Gates was defeated before Camden, South Carolina, and a British blockade of Brest made it impossible for the second French convoy to sail. The allies, clearly, would not do much in the 1780 campaign since naval superiority continued to elude them, and the British forces in New York refused to come out and give battle. Finally Washington dismissed the militia, whose time of service was nearly up anyway, and agreed, at long last, to meet Rochambeau and Ternay in Hartford.

Taking Generals La Fayette, Hamilton, and Henry Knox with him, Washington set off for Morristown; he stopped to have dinner with General Arnold on the way, arrived in Hartford on September 21, and was met with a thirteen-gun salute and much rejoicing. As soon as the ceremonies were over, he met Rochambeau and Ternay, who had ridden over from Newport, and the three commanders, leaving all the other officers downstairs, closeted themselves with La Fayette as interpreter-secretary in a small room. They immediately agreed on the desperate need for more French help in money, men, and supplies—the very point the Marquis had been making in his letters to the ministers. As for the attack on New York, with one voice they decided to wait until the eventual arrival of comte Luc de Guichen, whose fleet was patrolling in the West Indies.

On the way back to Morristown, La Fayette, who liked Arnold, made a detour to have breakfast with him. As they crossed the Hudson together, he mentioned that he had just learned that a British officer, a certain Major John André, had been captured. André, La Fayette went on, was apparently carrying compromising papers and, at this very moment, was being taken to headquarters where the papers would be read. As the boat reached the shore at West Point, Arnold, who said he had just remembered some urgent

business, told La Fayette go to the fort where Mrs. Arnold was waiting and
to start breakfast without him. As it turned out, he reappeared neither for
breakfast nor for any other meal. He had taken refuge aboard a British vessel:
the compromising papers seized on Major André were, in fact, Arnold's
plans for turning West Point over to the enemy. At first, La Fayette simply
wondered what his friend was doing; but when he sent men out to inquire,
the truth quickly became obvious. Naturally Gilbert was appalled—and
enormously relieved to find himself still free. Without wasting a minute, he
rushed back across the river and gave Washington the dreadful news.

Had he thought out his situation a little more clearly, Arnold might
have warned the British and brought a great catch with him—at worst, La
Fayette alone, at best Washington also. "You will tremble at the danger to
which we were exposed," he wrote La Luzerne on September 26. "You will
admire the sequence of chance and unexpected events that saved us; but
you will be even more surprised when you hear of the participants in this
plot. West Point was betrayed, and betrayed by Arnold; the very same man
who had covered himself with glory by rendering his country the most
important services had lately concluded a dreadful pact with the enemy. . . ."[42]
And to Rochambeau, emphasizing the enormous importance of his chance
remark to Arnold, he added: "We are all stunned by this infamous plot and
admire the miraculous way in which we discovered it. This is the first
example of treason, an extraordinary situation in such a revolution! But this
[unique] example pains us as much as it revolts us."[43]

At least, monstrous as it seemed, Arnold's treachery made for some
excitement, but as soon as it subsided, daily problems started to nag again.
"All this is as monotonous as a European war," La Fayette complained to
the comtesse de Tessé, Adrienne's aunt, on October 4. And complaining
about the continuing lack of supplies, he continued, in an ironic tone: "Without ships we can only wait for an attack and Gen. Clinton seems in no hurry
to start one. As for us, republicans, we preach our sovereign master the
people, so that it may be pleased to renew its efforts. In the meantime, we
are of a frugality, a poverty, a nudity that, I hope, will count in the next
world against our years of Purgatory."[44] Perhaps La Fayette could mock "our
sovereign master the people" more freely to Mme de Tessé because she was
a liberal herself; but, in any event, the words hardly seem those of a real
republican. Of course, the appalling shortage of all necessities was galling;
he came back to it, vividly, in a letter to Franklin written on October 9:
"We are nack'd, shockingly nack'd, and worse off in that respect than we
have ever been. For god's sakes, my dear friend, let us have fifteen or twenty
thousand compleat suits (exclusive of what is expected) and let it be done
in such a way as will ensure theyr timely departure from France. Cloathing

for officers is absolutely necessary. No cloth to be got—no money to purchase."[45]

Despite this poverty, La Fayette was urging Washington to do something, anything. With all sympathy, the General kept refusing. He put it very clearly to Franklin in a letter of October 9. After stating that the Marquis's exertions to "save this country . . . are additional proofs of his zealous attachment to our cause and have endeared him to us still more," the General went on: "He came out flushed with expectations of a decisive campaign and fired with hopes of acquiring fresh laurels, but in both he has been disappointed."[46] And to his adoptive son Washington, once more, preached prudence and wisdom. "It is impossible, my dear Marquis," he wrote on October 30, "to desire more ardently than I do to terminate the campaign by some happy stroke; but we must consult our means rather than our wishes; and not endeavour to better our affairs by attempting things, which for want of success may make them worse. We are to lament that there has been a misapprehension of our circumstances in Europe; but to endeavour to recover our reputation, we should take care that we do not injure it more." And, gloomily, he added, "Arnold's fright seems to have frightened all my intelligencers out of their senses."[47]

Finally, in early November, the General did agree to an attack on New York, but fate was as unkind as ever. British vessels unexpectedly appeared in the Hudson, and the attack was called off. At least, Fort St. George, on Long Island, was taken. After that, it was too late: there could be no campaigning in winter. On November 26, Washington issued an order of the day ending the army's state of activity: "The General presents his thanks to the Marquis de La Fayette and to the officers and men under his command for the excellent order and soldierly disposition which have been conspicuous in the corps. He regrets that opportunities did not offer to avail himself of that zeal and ardor which . . . afforded the strongest assurance of success."[48] It was a handsome compliment, and with it the army went into winter quarters.

All in all, it had not been a pleasant period for the Marquis. Frustration in Saintes, frustration at Le Havre, frustration in America: it began to seem as if the war would drag on indefinitely, as if those hateful Englishmen would never be vanquished. At the same time, Adrienne, to whom Gilbert had written such passionate letters during his first stay in America, now seems to have become less necessary—perhaps because La Fayette was so busy (even if to no avail), perhaps because whatever spare time he had was now taken by endless conversations about the war with his friends, Noailles, Chastellux, Lameth, Lauzun, who were also in America. At any rate, he wrote her far less often, and in much cooler tones. "I will close now my

letter," he told her on October 7, for instance, "but before I seal it I want
to take a moment to tell you about my tenderness for you. General Washington . . . has asked me to convey his tenderest feelings to you; he feels
the same to George. He is very touched by the name we have given him.
We often speak about you and the little family. Adieu, adieu."[49] Poor Adrienne might have been better consoled if the "tenderest feelings" had come
from her husband, not from an American general she had never met.

Although the close of the campaign merely signaled a shift of La Fayette's activities from the military to the political sphere, he could not help
feeling depressed when he looked back at the seemingly endless series of
lost opportunities; worse, there seemed to be nothing but difficulties ahead.
A terrible year was ending, and 1781 hardly looked likely to bring anything
better.

Five

TRIAL AND TRIUMPH

Although the war was a disappointment to La Fayette, he remained as full of schemes as ever. Now that the operations had come to a halt, he was once again surrounded by the same circle of brilliant young men he had known in Paris. It was in their company that he appeared back at headquarters, warning Washington that "these fine officers can, by their status at home, be regarded as the most important people in the French army." All together, the group set off to Philadelphia, there to watch the Congress in action, but not before the General offered a few more words of wisdom about La Fayette's new plan for a Southern expedition. Such a project seemed a good idea since New York was untouchable, and Spain, with its territories in Florida and Georgia, was now an ally. But the joint Franco-American push he envisioned required the support of the slow and disorganized Spanish navy, a very remote possibility. Washington advised La Fayette to go nowhere except Philadelphia without the Spanish navy's support.

The band of French officers that rode away from Morristown could hardly have been smarter, comprising, as it did, the fine flower of Marie

Antoinette's set—and Philadelphia society, which knew a good thing when it saw it, reacted accordingly. From December 1, and for several weeks, the city witnessed a ceaseless round of balls, dinners, and parties of all kinds. Everyone went around in a great whirl of amiability, the French praising the noble simplicity of the Americans, and only occasionally deploring the sad lack of both kept women and prostitutes. They had other surprises, too: in this strange country, balls were preorganized, so that you were told who your partners should be; dinners started early and went on for hour after hour while huge quantities of food and drink were consumed; but they had come to praise, and so they loved it all.

La Fayette also took the time to show his friends the sites of his earlier exploits: there were visits to the Brandywine and to Barren Hill, where he described that glorious retreat Paris had heard so much about. There were conversations, too, with Tom Paine: Chastellux was the author of a highly successful book of political philosophy entitled *De La Félicité Publique* and had much to say to the bold libertarian; and, the American Philosophical Society elected both Chastellux and La Fayette to its membership, a rare and significant honor.

All the while, La Fayette continued plotting his Southern scheme, this time with the help of the ever-cautious chevalier de La Luzerne. "The Cher. de La Luzerne has communicated to me in the *most confidential way* a Spanish plan against St. Augustine [Florida]," the Marquis wrote Washington on December 4, "upon which I am building a letter for the generals of this Nation, and using the best arguments in my power to engage them either to send twelve ships of the line to take us and conduct us to Charleston, or to render theyr operation as useful as possible to General Greene."[1] The plan was never clearly explained, but a bare twenty-four hours later, another letter followed this one. He had written Rochambeau, the Marquis said, to propose a diversion in South Carolina, to be undertaken at the same time as a possible Spanish attack on St. Augustine; all this would happen while part of the Spanish fleet was cruising off Charleston harbor (to help General Greene, who was besieged by the British), and the French West Indies squadron, which had yet to appear anywhere near the continent, was to be convinced to sail past the American coast on its way back to Europe so as to add to the available forces. The plan supposed an extraordinary degree of cooperation among the three allies, and it quickly appeared so very improbable that even the dauntless marquis, who realized how impractical he must have just appeared, felt compelled to add, in another letter written later the same day: "However acquainted I may be with your intentions, I thought upon the whole that I should better wait for your approbation before I present any opinion of yours to the Spanish or French generals in the West

Indias. . . . I confess I don't hope to prevail upon the Spaniards to come here."[2]

Even before Washington began to oppose the scheme, changes at Versailles made it all seem unnecessary, even to La Fayette, who wrote him on December 9: "I have received an intelligence which . . . makes me extremely happy—the Marquis de Castries whom I have sometimes mention'd to you as a man of great worth and my intimate friend has been made Minister of the Navy. . . . We are greatly benefited by the alteration."[3] It was unquestionably good news. Castries was pro-American, and an energetic, efficient minister. At last, France's full naval resources would be thrown into the conflict; and La Fayette had little doubt that he would be able to convince his friend to support his boldest plans. Everyone agreed that the key to victory was naval superiority. Now there was a chance France would really make a significant effort; and if a new fleet crossed the ocean, then Washington would finally be able to attack New York.

All these prospects threw La Fayette into a complete dither since his Southern plans now seemed irrelevant: with added French naval help, the main action might, after all, remain in the North. "I am more than ever puzzled, my dear general," he complained in the same letter, "to know what to do. . . . Every body advises against my going to the south ward . . . there is always the possibility of an expedition where you will want me—I see that the people in whom you confide the most are in a great part for the present far from you—I also candidly confess that private affection for you makes me hate the idea of leaving the man I love the most in the world to seek for uncertainties at a period when he may want me—on the other hand the Southern members want me to go—there is a possibility of being useful and even the love of glory spurs me on—I wait for your answer."[4]

While the possibilities for the coming year were beginning to improve, the situation in America itself was rapidly becoming bleaker. "The Chevalier de La Luzerne's despatches came in time for the post, which is the only means left me for the conveyance of letters, there not being as much money in the hands of the Quartermaster General, I believe I might go further and say in those of the whole army, as would bear the expence of an express to Rhode Island. I could not get one the other day to go as far as Pompton!"[5] Washington wrote on December 14. In truth, after years of deprivation, the army's resources had reached their lowest level yet, and when the Pennsylvania line regiments, whose pay was thirteen months in arrears, were finally given a small sum in worthless paper money, they mutinied and shot several officers.

It seemed possible that the American army would simply disintegrate. On his way from Philadelphia to headquarters, La Fayette stopped in New

Jersey and tried, at considerable risk to himself, to convince the men to end their revolt; but no one really wanted to listen and, in short order, the mutineers told him to leave. As it turned out, the situation failed to be as disastrous as everyone expected. Washington, keeping cool as always, refused to take any troops away from the front line to put down the rebellion and asked Congress President Joseph Reed of Pennsylvania to resolve the conflict; an attempt by Clinton at recruiting the mutineers failed; Washington then firmly refused to put down the rebellion by main force; and finally, General Anthony Wayne, the commanding officer, brought the troops back to obedience by paying them part of their arrears in metallic currency obtained, with great difficulty, in Philadelphia. It had been a very close call, and La Fayette asked La Luzerne to join him in ever more desperate pleas to Maurepas and Vergennes: there was, he said, no money, no food, no clothing, as usual; but there was also no more time.

No sooner was the Pennsylvania mutiny settled than, on January 21, a small section of the New Jersey line took up the rebellion. This time, there could be no attempt at negotiation. Washington decided to stop the movement then and there and gave orders to use force, much to La Fayette's applause: the Marquis, after all, had always been a stickler for discipline.

Just as this latest crisis ended, Congress decided to send Colonel John Laurens, Henry Laurens's son, as an envoy to France in order to obtain loans and supplies. The Marquis entrusted him with a mass of letters, the most important of which was addressed to Castries. Using his well-worn device of writing as a friend rather than a subordinate, La Fayette asked for money before all else. More men, he said, were not needed. Rochambeau was wrong to ask for another corps; he did not understand the great qualities of the American soldiers. Money, La Fayette insisted, would do it all, and he pointed to the recent mutinies to buttress his arguments. As a final note, La Fayette, who feared that continued frustration might make Rochambeau less willing to cooperate, also suggested that the ministers remind him that he was to obey Washington in every particular. It was a desperate letter, written at a time when all the years of patience and effort seemed likely to be wasted—and it worked.

At the same time Gilbert also sent off a letter to Adrienne, but one which, since it was to be circulated in the Paris salons, breathed the most contented optimism. "Many Frenchman have come through headquarters," he noted on February 2, 1781. "They have all been charmed by General Washington and I see with great pleasure that he will be much loved by the auxiliary troops. . . . The vicomte [de Noailles] and Damas have gone on a long voyage over the continent . . . I expect to leave around the 15th for Rhode Island and will accompany General Washington on the visit he will pay to the French army. When you remember what people in France thought of *those poor Insurgents*, when I came here to be hanged with them, and when you think of my tender feelings for General Washington, you will understand how much I will enjoy seeing him received as generalissimo of the combined armies of the two nations.

"I am still admirably treated by the Americans, and there are no marks of affection and trust which I do not receive every day from both the people and the army. . . . I feel for both officers and men a friendship created by a long suite of dangers and sufferings, of good and ill fortune which I have shared with them; our situation has often been as bad as possible; it is wonderful to crown my work with them by giving the European troops a good image of the soldiers who learned along with us."[6]

La Fayette's correspondents all listened to him: the French government agreed to provide more money, Adrienne propagandized dutifully, and America was more popular than ever in Paris. At the same time, it is impossible not to notice that La Fayette now writes his wife in a tone that would be admirably suited for official communications: she had become yet another useful tool, but, clearly, now that her husband was busy and surrounded by his friends, she had also ceased being an object of passionate love. Of course, he may also have been thinking of Mme d'Hunolstein—although there is no remaining letter to her, there is no proof that he never wrote.

In his correspondence at this time, La Fayette always refers to himself as a republican, yet he remained basically a French aristocrat. In 1781 he earnestly hoped that Washington might become dictator; he saw democratic institutions as cumbersome and often annoying. Still, the Marquis was willing to compromise if, after all, his first wish could not be fulfilled. Representative bodies might be a bother, but they apparently were a necessary part of government in America, therefore they must be good. Certainly it had not yet occurred to him that democracy was for export. Whatever he learned in the United States did not include political science. In mid-February, in a letter to an American friend, he argued at length that France was freer than Great Britain—an absolute falsehood—and even went so far as to claim that the French were more tolerant of dissenting religions than the British when, in fact, French Protestants were not even allowed to have birth certificates. More incredibly still, he extolled the French parlements—those assemblies of wealthy, selfish, corrupt reactionaries who bought their offices—as against the British Parliament, a body that, with all its faults, had at least the merit of being elected. The key to this blatant disregard of reality was, of course, La Fayette's burning hatred of England, but it also shows how little, in 1781, he had understood of Washington's respect for the republic.

The British broke the period of inaction, at long last, in February. Clinton sent Arnold to Portsmouth, Virginia, with twelve hundred men in order to establish a base for the reconquest of that state. For the first time since 1776, the British convoy suffered damages when a storm arose that could not be skirted: no ship was sunk, but almost all were severely damaged. Immediately, Washington saw his opportunity: a temporary, limited period of Franco-American naval superiority was in sight, and Portsmouth could be retaken.

It made sense (since the French fleet must be involved in an attack on Portsmouth) to have a French general leading the American troops; so Washington detached twelve hundred men of the Light Infantry from his own army and returned them to La Fayette's command, with orders to start marching south on February 19. The Marquis left the pleasures of Philadephia and joined his corps in Pompton, New Jersey, on February 23. There he found himself in a familiar predicament: his men lacked money, food, and clothes. Further, since the operation had been hastily assembled with the need to surprise the enemy, many of the officers had come without baggage and were thus, as La Fayette put it, "totally unprovided." Nor was it easy to move the men through the muddy countryside. "The detachment had a great trouble to cross the ferry and made afterwards a long march through bad roads—They halted last night within eight miles of the Yellow House, and came up to it this morning—But the rain was so hard and the roads were so bad that I have halted them at this place,"[7] La Fayette wrote on the twenty-third from Pompton. As usual, however, he got the most out of his men. They still felt the esprit de corps that he had managed to create in the fall, and so reacted zealously and without grumbling to his nicely calculated mixture of sympathy and demands.

Arnold, in Portsmouth, was out of the reach of the French fleet because the James River was too shallow to bear large fighting ships. The plan, therefore, was to blockade him from a distance, while La Fayette's corps would approach by land and finish the job. It would take far too long, however, and would be far too great an effort to march the troops the great distance to Virginia, so it was decided to have them shipped from Trenton down the Delaware to Head of Elk, Maryland (today, Elktown), where they would transfer to French ships and be taken the length of the Chesapeake Bay to Portsmouth. The problem was to get them to the head of the bay as fast as possible, since new English warships might show up at any time. This was all of primary importance: control of the Chesapeake implied a hold on most of the state.

Already on March 2, La Fayette, in a letter to Washington, could report impending success. "Your excellency remembers that our shortest calculation on the arrival of the troops at Head of Elk was for the 6th of March," he wrote. "I am happy to inform you that they will be there this day, or tomorrow early, and notwithstanding the depth of the mud, and the extreme badness of the roads, this march which I can call rapid . . . has been performed with such an order and alacrity that . . . two men only have been left behind and yet these two men have been embarked at Trenton with some remains of the baggage."[8] Along with the troops had come twelve pieces of heavy cannon, some medicine and even—miracle of miracles— fifteen hundred pairs of shoes. Of course, none of this would have been possible had not the Marquis, leaving his little army, gone to Philadelphia to beg, plead, and cajole Congress into producing at least some of the necessary supplies, a sport in which he had become the undisputed champion.

Better yet, in Philadelphia he had convinced the states of Virginia and Maryland to help with both men and supplies and, now in Head of Elk, he charmed a group of Baltimore merchants into advancing funds for the purchase of supplies. Then, as usual, everything went wrong. First, the weather became even worse. "Contrary winds, heavy rains, disappointments of vessels and every inconvenience to which we had no remedy have been from the day of my arrival combined against our embarkation from Head of Elk,"[9] La Fayette wrote on March 7. And the British fleet, which had been damaged by the storm some four weeks earlier, had now been repaired and sailed to Portsmouth, so the French squadron dispatched by Ternay prudently returned to Newport. Still, La Fayette had thirty boats standing ready, so he started embarking men and supplies. At that point, news came from Friedrich von Steuben, a German general in the American service who was already besieging Portsmouth, that success was assured if only the sea could be blocked, now a manifest impossibility.

La Fayette was anxious to see battle at last—he always was—but this time his anxiety was shared by the commander in chief. It was no mere British general whom Steuben was besieging but Arnold, the traitor. How fitting, how spectacular it would be if the forces of the United States under La Fayette were now able to capture him, try him, and punish him. Even the French, who cared little about Arnold, felt some excitement: boldly, they sent a large squadron under Charles Destouches, and aboard the ships were eleven hundred soldiers under Vioménil, Rochambeau's second in command. Finally, with this move, hopes ran high.

Then, once again, a problem cropped up. With all the French help, what would be left for the two corps of American troops as a whole, and Major General the Marquis de La Fayette in particular, to do? Destouches would blockade Portsmouth, Vioménil would take the city, while the Continental troops would serve merely as an added security against a British attack by land. The thought of missing the action was devastating, and La Fayette lost no time in communicating it to Washington. "Baron de Vioménil will also want to do every thing alone . . . for the Honour of our Arms [I] think it would be derogatory to it, had not this detachment some share in the enterprize—this consideration induces me to embark immediately,"[10] he wrote on March 8, and promptly sent his men on their way twenty miles to Annapolis. This, he explained, was safe enough, since his boats would have cannon on board and would be staying in waters sufficiently shallow to exclude British warships. Having encamped his troops at Annapolis, the Marquis himself, too impatient to wait, set off with M. de Charlus—chosen because he was the son of Castries, the French Navy Minister—and rode for three days to Yorktown, where Steuben had installed his headquarters. From there, on March 15, he sent Washington his appraisal of the situation. It was positive and, as usual, a little rash: his own troops added to Steuben's five thousand militiamen would be quite enough to take Portsmouth; and as long as a French squadron stopped the British from reinforcing the town, there was not even any need for the French expeditionary corps. The French ships were actually on the way, and although, tactfully, La Fayette refused to take command until his corps had arrived, he could now feel pretty sure that he would have the glory of capturing Arnold.

Then, on March 20, the long-awaited squadron anchored off the capes at the tip of the Chesapeake Bay. Only it was not the fleet La Fayette was expecting: once again, the British navy had proved faster and now it was ready to relieve Arnold. Still, the Marquis remained undaunted: the French fleet, he had heard from his correspondents in Newport, would soon arrive, so taking every possible precaution, he simply waited. In fact, the French squadron he was expecting simply sailed into the path of the enemy. On the sixteenth, the two fleets, each consisting of eight ships of the line, met, fought, and came to a standoff. The French retreated briefly, and, two days later, La Fayette finally heard about the battle.

Nothing loath, the French tried all over again, or so the army thought for a brief moment when they heard a cannonade that lasted more than three hours. No French ships appeared, however; instead, it was a fleet of warships and convoys flying the British flag that sailed up the bay. La Fayette and his officers reluctantly admitted to themselves that what they had heard was nothing more than a thunderstorm. Clearly, there was nothing more to be done, so a very disappointed marquis set off for Annapolis, where his troops awaited him, and Arnold was safe.

At this point, La Fayette found himself with two possible courses of action. He could march his troops from Annapolis through Virginia into the

Carolinas and join General Greene (who, as senior officer, would be in command), or he could return to headquarters. Just which of these possibilities he favored he made clear to Washington on April 8. "The troops I have with me being taken from every northern regiment," he wrote, "have often (though without mentioning it to me) been very uneasy at the idea of joining the Southern Army. They want cloathes, shoes particularly, they expect to receive cloathes and monney from their States. This would be a great disappointment for both officers and men. Both thought at first they were sent out for a few days and provided themselves accordingly. Both came chearfully to this expedition, both have had already their fears on the idea of going to the southward. They will certainly obey but they will be unhappy and some will desert. . . .

"These considerations, my dear general, I beg you to be convinced are not influenced by personal motives. I would most certainly like better to be in a situation to attack New York . . . but I think with you that these motives are not to influence our determination if this is the best way to help General Greene. . . . By the letters I have received from my two friends Marquis de Castries and Comte de Vergennes I am . . . led to hope that having a naval superiority the army under your immediate command will not remain inactive."[11] It was a good try, but Washington knew full well that an attack on New York was, at best, far in the future, while General Greene, with insufficient forces, faced a substantial British effort in the Carolinas. On April 11, he gave La Fayette firm orders to communicate with Greene, whose instructions he was to follow so that the two armies could come together, adding: "You must endeavour to get shoes."[12]

That last was not so easy; and the Marquis, while obeying the orders regarding a conjunction with Greene, felt compelled to point out on April 14: "Your Excellency mentions the propriety of remaining at Head of Elk until shoes can be collected. But the prospects I have from the Board of War are not flattering enough to encourage this measure. On the other hand, General Greene is pressing in his advices and will soon be so in his orders to me."[13] Once again, everything was lacking, not just shoes, but hats, and even shirts. On April 16, having sent his troops ahead to Baltimore, La Fayette joined them there and raised £2,000 on his own bond so he could buy cloth; he even convinced the ladies of the city to fashion the linen into shirts. Once more, in a desperate moment, La Fayette, with absolute generosity, was coming to the aid of the United States.

Perhaps the shirts helped; at any rate, the Marquis, although far from Washington, now became more cheerful: he heard from Greene that he was to fight against General William Phillips, the very same man who had commanded the battery that, at Minden, had killed La Fayette's father. The dream which Gilbert had cherished as a little boy now seemed about to come true: he would avenge his father's death. And a letter written by Washington on April 21 can only have raised the young man's morale since it held up almost intoxicating hopes. "It was with great reluctance I could resolve upon seeing you separated from headquarters," the General explained. "My friendship for you makes me desirous of having you near me. . . . If you proceed forward I shall have one consolation which is that from the present aspect of things it is perhaps most probable the weight of the war this campaign will be in the Southern States, and it will become my duty to go there in person where I shall have the pleasure of seeing you again."[14]

By the next day, however, the prospects were looking markedly grimmer. "I am extremely concerned at the temper of your detachment and the desertions that are taking place,"[15] Washington wrote in answer to La Fayette's letters informing of low morale, and he had good reason to worry. The men, who were being ordered to march to the south, were increasingly unhappy. In fact, the army, being composed of local units, always resented being forced to move far away from home. When this problem was compounded by the lack of money and supplies, the men tended to leave, and La Fayette found his force melting away. There could be no question of using force to stop the desertions: this would merely have made the situation worse. Instead, the Marquis gathered his men and informed them that they were quite free to go back north; only, of course, if they did so, they would miss all the action. Others, he added, would be fighting the decisive battles of the war, and that against an enemy "far superior in numbers, under difficulties of every sort."[16]

As he now discovered, Gilbert had a real talent for addressing an unruly crowd and turning it into a mass of followers. The device was relatively simple: instead of making empty promises, the Marquis appealed to their pride and patriotism. By assuming openly that they were capable of enduring greater hardships than anyone else around, he created such a sense of invincibility that the tired, disgruntled men became, in fact, well-nigh heroic. It was leadership of the first order, and a revelation to everyone. From that day on, the desertions ceased, and the men, much to their general's surprise, even forgot their prejudices against the Virginia militia which eventually joined them.

As usual, speed was of the essence, so La Fayette took his men south on forced marches, with his cannon and most of his own baggage following; the cannon, lagging far behind, was safe, but his baggage, which had been moved faster, was seized by an enemy party. In every little town he passed, he begged for the supplies he needed, impressing the goods when begging didn't work, and apologizing afterward for the behavior forced on him by the necessities of war. By April 21, his Light Infantry had reached Alexandria; on the twenty-fifth, it entered Fredericksburg, then went on to Bowling Green, where La Fayette met an aide of Steuben's and found, to his dismay, that his colleague's command was down to one thousand militia while the enemy, under Arnold and Phillips, numbered twenty-five hundred seasoned troops. La Fayette then moved his men on to Richmond, an obvious target for the British forces since it was the capital of the state. They reached the town on April 29. The very next morning, the enemy appeared across the river in Manchester: by the speed of his movement, La Fayette had saved the city.

It was not until May 5 that Washington heard about the Marquis's maneuvers in Maryland and Virginia, and when he did, he sent another of his impressive, well-deserved testimonials: "I am extremely rejoiced to learn, that the spirit of discontent is so entirely subsided, and that the practice of desertion would probably be totally stopped among the Troops under your command. . . .

"For my own part, my dear Marquis, although I stood in need of no new proofs of your exertions and sacrifices in the cause of America; I will confess to you I shall not be able to express the pleasing sensations I have experienced at your unparalleled and repeated instances of generosity and zeal for the Service, on every occasion."[17]

In fact, La Fayette needed all the encouragement he could get, since, as was standard in this war, the American troops were facing an enemy who was not only superior in numbers, but better armed, better financed, better supplied, and backed, furthermore, by the apparently unbreakable power of the British navy. Against this formidable array, the Marquis found himself, as usual, short of all the necessities, having to plead for every morsel of bread from reluctant state and local authorities and deprived of safe and rapid communications with his commander in chief. He therefore deserved all the more credit as a tactician when General Phillips launched an attack on Richmond from across the river, and La Fayette was able to beat him back and secure, for a while at least, the city's security. Convinced that the strength of the American position made a further attack useless, the enemy now withdrew altogether. Keenly aware, as usual, of the uses of propaganda, La Fayette promptly celebrated his victory by holding a grand review; after which, more prosaically, he tried to fortify Richmond by building a redoubt on the James River and stationing militia at Williamsburg. He then moved his troops toward the Chickahominy River and away from Phillips so as to give himself more room to maneuver and, at that point, received the supplies he had bought earlier in Baltimore.

This appearance of victory, however, was deceptive. In short order, Cornwallis, the British commander and a general of European repute, decided to join Phillips at Petersburg, forcing La Fayette to return to the relative safety of Richmond. The Marquis was confronted by a vastly superior force led, furthermore, by an extremely capable general, and worse yet, the rigors of the terrain made it extremely unlikely that a fleeing army could escape unscathed. To survive, La Fayette had to avoid the stronger enemy, so ease and rapidity of movement were essential, but the combination of marshy land and rivers constituted an almost impassable obstacle. The only hope, therefore, lay in the cooperation of the population with the American forces: they could delay the enemy's progress by destroying bridges while easing La Fayette's passage by repairing them and showing him hidden roads and fords. Obviously, the situation was critical. Wayne's Pennsylvanians were the nearest American corps, and La Fayette sent him an urgent plea for help. "Hasten to our relief, my dear Sir," he begged in a letter marked "Public Service. This letter being of grim importance must be forwarded day and night."[18]

In spite of its inscription, the letter traveled very slowly indeed, and when it finally reached Wayne, the general was in no position to heed its contents: the Pennsylvania line, which had just been paid in worthless paper dollars, had mutinied again. Once more, the shortage of funds was proving fatal to the war effort. La Fayette, left to his own devices, did the best he could. Clearly, the only possible strategy consisted in shadowing Phillips so as to slow him down while always avoiding an actual encounter. This proved unexpectedly easy because Phillips, sensibly, decided to wait for Cornwallis, who was on his way from New York, but once again the desperate shortage of supplies added enormous difficulty to even the simplest of maneuvers. And to the Marquis's ever more desperate requests, Governor Thomas Jefferson could only answer, truthfully, that he had done all he could: the Virginia legislature would not grant any more funds for supplies. Taxes, it seemed, were to be avoided even more strenuously than subjection to England. Apparently, the local aristocracy and middle class, whose resources were not seriously impaired, saw little reason to make real financial sacrifices to the cause of independence.

Since the legislature refused to provide, La Fayette simply resorted to impressing. Wars cannot be fought—or won—without a mobile force; the infantry, by definition, is slow and the Americans had no cavalry. So the Marquis simply requisitioned horses, saddles, and even boots, and set about creating his own Light Cavalry. In the meantime, he begged the Virginia militia, a highly ineffective body of volunteers sluggishly moving around the state, to impede Cornwallis's movements as much as possible without fighting an actual battle. At that point, at last, good news came from General Greene. Although he had been beaten near Charleston by Francis Lord Rawdon, Cornwallis's second in command, the victory had proved so costly to the British force that it was now in retreat to the south—a familiar pattern; and so, Greene wrote, La Fayette was to stay in Virginia. At long last the Marquis had his own independent command. It was now up to him to show what he could do.

Typically, La Fayette set about reorganizing his little army. In collaboration with Steuben, with whom he maintained an elaborately polite relationship, since neither was subordinate to the other, he created decent hospitals for the wounded, an efficient commissary, and an improved quartermaster corps, and his mini-cavalry (less than forty men) began to operate. Of course, the Marquis was only rearranging scarcity, since his entire force consisted of a mere nine hundred Continentals, some twelve hundred to fifteen hundred militia (untrained and always liable to go home), and a mere six pieces of artillery. Clearly, nimbleness would have to replace force.

On May 15, Phillips suddenly died of a fever, probably malaria, caught in the Virginia marshes, and Arnold succeeded him; but when the new commander, continuing a well-established custom, sent La Fayette a letter relating to an exchange of prisoners, the Marquis simply refused to receive it. He would not communicate with the traitor, and Washington, on May 31, fully approved. As for the Marquis, disappointed though he was at losing his chance of beating Phillips, he was at the same time pleased to be fighting Arnold.

The difficulties of the campaign, which rested entirely on La Fayette's shoulders, now began to transform him into a mature, clever commander. Well aware that a defeat would be disastrous, he developed new restraint. "I become timid in the same proportion that I became independent," he wrote Greene on May 18. "Had a superior officer been here, I would have proposed half a dozen schemes."[19]

In late May, Cornwallis at last made his junction with Arnold and took over the command, thus much increasing the pressure on La Fayette. The Marquis now tried, more frantically than ever, to get more troops, but Wayne had still not arrived and the Virginia militia would yield no more. Busy as he was getting his army in shape, the Marquis could not help feeling a burning worry, less about a possible defeat than about his reputation. Would people think him lacking in boldness? Would they make fun of his prudence? The situation was not helped when he received a copy of a song satirizing his affair with Mme d'Hunolstein, which had likely been written by the comte de Provence. Louis XVI's brother had not forgotten or forgiven the young La Fayette's remarks about pedants and their memory.

On May 24, the Marquis wrote Washington twice to explain his new position. "The junction of Lord Cornwallis with the other army at Petersburg," La Fayette explained, "was an event that from local circumstances and from theyr so great superiority it was impossible to prevent. It took place on the 20th and having lost every hope to operate a timely stroke in conjunction with the Pennsylvanians, my ideas were confined to defensive measures. I therefore moved up to Richmond where precautions were taken to remove every valuable property either public or private. . . . It is impossible that 900 Continentals and 400 horses with a body of militia by no means so considerable as they are reported to be and whom it is so difficult to arm, be with any advantage opposed to such a superiority of forces, such a number of cavalry, to which may be added theyr very prejudiciable command of the waters."[20]

". . . I ardently wish my conduct may meet with your approbation," he went on in the second letter. "Had I followed the first impulsion of my temper I would have risked something more. But I have been guarding against my own warmth, and this consideration that a general defeat . . . would involve this State and our affairs into ruin, has rendered me extremely cautious in my movements. . . .

"Public stores and private property being removed from Richmond, this place is a less important object. I don't believe it would be prudent to expose the troops for the sake of a few houses most of which are empty. But I am wavering between two inconveniences. Was I to fight a battle, I'll be cut to pieces, the militia dispersed, and the arms lost. Was I to decline fighting, the country would think herself given up. I am therefore determined to scarmish, but not to engage too far, and particularly to take care against their immense and excellent body of horse whom the militia fears like they would so many wild beasts. . . .

"Was I any ways equal to the enemy, I would be extremely happy in my present command. But I am not strong enough even to get beaten. Government in this state has no energy and laws have no force."[21] Even before receiving these letters, Washington had come to the same conclusions. "*No rational person* will condemn you for *not fighting* with the odds against [you], and while so much is depending on it; but all will censure a rash step if it is not attended with success,"[22] he wrote on June 4.

Luckily for La Fayette, Cornwallis was less interested in crushing him than in destroying his supplies, since he was aware of the critical shortages constantly hampering the American forces; so an elaborate cat-and-mouse game began, with the cat, in this case, more interested in starving the mouse than in gobbling it right away. Once he had destroyed the stores and arsenals of Virginia, Cornwallis reasoned, he would be able to cut the United States in two. The separated halves would then be forced to surrender. Thus, he set off on a quick march of devastation, with the long-range intent of meeting with Clinton in front of Philadelphia and recapturing the capital. Finding himself outflanked by the British, La Fayette moved out of Richmond (whence the government had moved to Charlottesville) and marched northward so as not to be cut off from Wayne; but, afraid that the militia would defect, he still carefully avoided giving battle. At first, he simply followed a route parallel to that of the enemy, cutting bridges and doing all he could to slow it down; then he moved to protect Fredericksburg because it had stores and an armament factory.

Cornwallis, cutting a wide swath through Virginia, moved on to Charlottesville, where he caught only seven slow-footed legislators. The rest of the government had moved to Staunton, causing the Marquis to comment ironically to Greene that the legislators were "less dilatory in their motions than they had been in their resolutions."

When Cornwallis, who felt he had pretty much achieved the destruction he sought, returned to Williamsburg, La Fayette followed. At last, Wayne arrived there on June 10. Now the mouse was almost as powerful as the cat: the American army numbered two thousand Continentals, three thousand militia, and a decent body of cavalry. The game was becoming more even. So when the British moved toward Old Albemarle Courthouse, where most of the Continental and Virginia military supplies had been concentrated, it was with renewed vigor that the Marquis interposed himself. His militia had found him an old, disused, but still passable road, and although he had a longer way to go, he could make better time than the British. So, for the first time, La Fayette actually foiled the enemy's plan—Cornwallis sent a body of horse under the feared Tarleton to ravage Old Albemarle Courthouse, but when he realized his cavalry was facing the entire American force, he prudently withdrew.

Although the British force was still unquestionably the stronger and seemed sure to remain so, the balance now began to shift. For one thing, Jefferson's term expired. As governor, he had been faced by a reticent legislature composed of the very people—large and middling landowners— whom he most respected, and who reinforced his fear of an overly powerful government. The new governor, William Nelson, had been commanding La Fayette's second line and was therefore far more energetic about supporting the army. Secondly, La Fayette asked Steuben to bring his troops from behind Richmond to join the force at Old Albemarle Courthouse. Much to the Marquis's annoyance, it took the German more than a week to do so; Steuben had made himself widely hated, and since his men had been deserting at every opportunity because they did not trust his military skills, his corps became far more effective as part of the main force than it had been as an independent unit. Finally, the Americans gained a psychological advantage when Cornwallis moved back to Richmond and La Fayette shadowed him closely: it looked as if the British were retreating before a superior enemy. This was not the case at all—Cornwallis had, in fact fulfilled his goals. As so often in war, perception was more important than reality. The Marquis still avoided giving battle, but now he looked victorious, and thus won support and applause from the legislature and, eventually, Congress itself.

All through the campaign, both Washington and La Fayette had complained bitterly about the uncertainty of their communications. Every message had to be sent in duplicate or triplicate because the enemy was likely to intercept one of the couriers. In early June, this nuisance unexpectedly turned to advantage. A letter written on May 31 by Washington to La Fayette was seized by Clinton, who reeled in horror at what he read and promptly changed his dispositions. The key passage of this letter explained that, in a meeting with Rochambeau, it had been agreed that "an attempt upon New York with its present Garrison . . . was deemed preferable to a Southern operation as we had not the command of the water. The reasons which induced this determination were, the danger to be apprehended from the approaching heats, the inevitable dissipation and loss of men by so long a March, and the difficulty of transportation; but above all it was thought that we had a tolerable prospect of expelling the enemy. . . . The French troops are to march this way."[23] What Clinton had always feared was at last happening: he was about to be attacked by a combined Franco-American force; so, instead of reinforcing Cornwallis as he had planned to do—and thus ensuring La Fayette's defeat—he now ordered his second in command to take up a defensive position in or about Williamsburg and send back as many of his men as possible to New York.

Of course, La Fayette knew none of this at first, though he did notice that Cornwallis was retreating to Williamsburg. In fact the retreat was not merely a result of Clinton's order. Cornwallis was convinced he had done all he could, and even before the letter from Clinton, he had decided to regroup closer to the shore in order to husband his resources while he waited for reinforcements. Meanwhile, La Fayette received excellent news from France: Louis XVI had finally committed himself fully and publicly to fight on until the thirteen states were fully independent from Great Britain. Since that obviously meant the subsidies to America would be increased, and that more men and more ships would be sent, victory, complete and final, became a possibility once more. Emboldened by all this, the Marquis now tried to provoke a battle with Cornwallis near Williamsburg. This time, it was the

English general who avoided an encounter, and Cornwallis managed to reach Williamsburg without a serious fight. What had merely looked like a retreat just a few days earlier had now, in fact, become one.

With the end of June came the harvest season for wheat and tobacco, so the militia—more than half of La Fayette's army—began to melt away: you could always fight the English, after all, but if you missed the harvest, you lost everything. La Fayette, once again, found himself with a substantially inferior force. Still, with his usual love for a show, he celebrated the Fourth of July with parades, speeches, and a banquet.

Shortly after the celebrations, and much to the Marquis's surprise, the British force left Williamsburg and retreated to Portsmouth; La Fayette's spies reported that transports were continuing to come in. The implications were clear enough: Cornwallis was sending his troops northward and the focus of the campaign must be moving to New York. Thus on July 20, 1781, La Fayette wrote Washington three successive letters in which, after pointing out he had done a good job to date, he went on to surmise that the war in Virginia was, to all intents and purposes, ending. Therefore, he asked, let the General recall him to New York and give him a command in the combined army "*of the North*": thus he might end the campaign "in the most *brilliant* manner."[24] As an afterthought only, he went on to give a detailed account of his actions in Virginia. Obviously, La Fayette was afraid the action was moving on, and he felt entitled to a prominent place in the final attack on New York.

It took the three epistles ten days to reach Washington, and then the General answered fully with two letters of his own. The first was a note of praise. "You ask my opinion of the Virginia campaign? Be assured, my dear Marquis, your Conduct meets with my warmest approbation, as it must that of every body. Should it ever be said that my attachment to you betrayed me into partiality, you have only to appeal to the facts to refute such charges."[25] In the second letter, he answered La Fayette's plea to be recalled to the main army. "I am convinced that your desire to be with this army arises principally from a wish to be actively useful. You will not therefore regret your stay in Virginia until matters are reduced to a greater degree of certainty than they are at present, especially when I tell you that, from the change of circumstances with which the removal of part of the enemy's force from Virginia to New York will be attended, it is more than probable that we shall also change our entire plan of operations. . . . Our views must now be turned toward endeavouring to expel [the enemy] totally from [the Southern] States. The difficulty of doing this does not so much depend upon obtaining a force capable of effecting it, as upon the mode of collecting that force to the proper point, and transporting the provisions, stores necessary for such an operation. You are fully acquainted with the almost impractibility of doing this by land; to say nothing of the amazing loss of Men always occasioned by long marches, and those toward a quarter where the service is disagreeable. I should not hesitate, however, in encountering these difficulties, great as they are, had we not prospects of transporting ourselves in a manner safe, easy and expeditious. Your penetration will point out my meaning which I cannot venture to express in direct terms."[26] One wonders why not, as even Clinton would have realized if he had intercepted this letter that obviously Washington was alluding to a French fleet. If Washington's entire army could actually be moved south, if the French fleet blockaded Portsmouth, then, clearly, the British were in for a major defeat.

While it waited for those alluring prospects to turn into reality, however, La Fayette's little army came close to being beaten itself, through Wayne's imprudence. Near James Island, outside Portsmouth, in early August, the British had set a trap by appearing to have allowed a small body of men to lag behind the main force. Wayne foolishly attacked, only to find himself facing the entire enemy force. He was soundly beaten, losing 139 men killed and wounded, many horses (even harder to replace than the men), and two cannon. Luckily, Cornwallis, who was under orders to get back to New York with all possible speed, did not press his advantage, instead continuing his retreat and allowing La Fayette to occupy Williamsburg. The defeat passed unnoticed, and even better, since Virginia was now free, it looked as if the Marquis had chased the British away. La Fayette was becoming more popular than ever.

As the British retreated, of course, La Fayette advanced, surrounding Portsmouth. The city was so well defended that there was no hope of taking it, especially with a small force, since it takes fewer men to defend a fortress than to storm it. But the Marquis, who knew that Admiral François de Grasse and the French West Indies fleet had just defeated a British force in a naval engagement, now urged the admiral to sail to Virginia; and, on July 30, he wrote Washington a short sentence that shows how thoroughly he understood the situation. "Should a French fleet now come in Hampton Road, the British army [some half of the total forces in America] will, I think be ours."[27]

As for Lord Cornwallis (Mylord, as La Fayette usually called him), his position on land was becoming more difficult day by day as the forces against him grew larger. Instead of returning to New York, which he could still do safely since the British commanded the waters, he found himself ordered to keep a foothold on the Chesapeake to be ready for a future attack on Philadelphia. And although he could see that his position was deteriorating, the habit of victory was so strong and the superiority of the British navy over the French so well established that the possibility of an actual defeat never really occurred to him. Since he had to keep an easy access to deep water and the ships of the line,* he moved again, this time occupying Yorktown and Gloucester closer to the mouth of the bay; he was unimpeded since he had managed to fool La Fayette into preventing a nonexistent march toward Baltimore. By the time the Marquis realized his mistake, it was too late, and the two towns were in enemy hands. La Fayette, who was still unaware of Clinton's orders, mistakenly assumed the English had left Portsmouth because they feared de Grasse's fleet, and settled down to besiege Yorktown. It was the right move. On August 15, Washington wrote La Fayette to keep the enemy bottled up, blocking any possible retreat through North Carolina while keeping de Grasse's arrival a dead secret, since the French ships could then catch the British transports unaware. Slowly, the trap was beginning to close: Cornwallis was already blocked by La Fayette on the land side; soon, the sea would be controlled by the French and there would be no exit from Yorktown.

While Cornwallis was busy reinforcing the defenses of Yorktown—he realized just how precarious his position had become—La Fayette was having trouble managing his disparate forces. "The Pennsylvanians and the Virginians have never agreed but at the present time it is worse than ever," he complained to Washington on August 11. "I receive every day complaints, some from the executive I have been obliged to take notice of. The Governor and council have told me they would insist upon having justice by me from General Waïne's proceedings. General Waïne thinks he and his people have not been well used. In a word, I perceive the seeds of a future dispute between the states."[28] As usual, the scarcity of supplies was to blame— General Wayne had helped himself to the stores gathered by the Virginians for the exclusive use of their own militiamen, as seemed only natural; but the Virginians took the view that whatever the Pennsylvanians wanted they ought to get from home. With great care, La Fayette managed to settle the dispute, but it revealed yet again the fragility of the confederation.

Still, this time, the possibilities for victory looked good. "Lord Cornwallis's abilities are to me more alarming than his superiority of forces," La Fayette wrote General Knox on August 18. "I ever had a high opinion of him. Our papers call him a mad man, but was ever any advantage taken of him when he commanded in person? To speak plain English, I am devilish afraid of him."[29] And on August 21, Washington was sending anxious rec-

---

*A ship of the line was a battleship armed with cannon—it was able to be part of the line of battle.

ommendations. "As it will be of great importance towards the Success of our present Enterprize that the Enemy, on the arrival of the Fleet, should not have it in their power to effect their Retreat I cannot omit to repeat to you my most earnest Wish, that the Land and Naval forces which you will have with you may so combine their Operations, that the British Army may not be able to escape you; the particular mode of doing this I shall not at this Distance attempt to dictate."[30] There was good reason for Washington to worry; after all, the United States army had a long record of last-moment failures. Sensibly, La Fayette decided to make sure all decisions were taken in common by himself and the French commanders.

The Marquis had demonstrated both prudence and spirit in his command, and his respect for Cornwallis was perhaps the best guarantee he had that he would avoid making a mistake. Even the critical Rochambeau could write Vergennes on July 26 from Newport: "M. de La Fayette . . . has behaved perfectly during his entire Virginia campaign." Now everything depended on preventing the British from escaping by land while stopping the British navy from evacuating them by sea. This last, of course, was dependent on the arrival of the French fleet, which would make it so superior to its British enemy as to be safe from attack. But on the land side La Fayette took every precaution although he was, as usual, desperately short of supplies: he now had twenty-five hundred Continentals, one hundred Continental dragoons, and two hundred horsemen, far and away the best force of the entire campaign; as for the militia, its members were still fluctuating.

As soon as Cornwallis had moved out of Portsmouth, the Marquis had had its fortifications razed, thereby denying him that particular asylum should he attempt to retreat. He hired spies, as always, to keep up with the enemy's intentions—one was a servant in Cornwallis's own house—and, encouraged by news of Greene's successes in North Carolina, which meant there could be no relief for Cornwallis from that quarter, he continued to pester Governor Nelson and the Maryland authorities for supplies of all kinds.

All through the month of August, the British, while fortifying Yorktown, remained on the defensive and waited for the arrival of their fleet. While the Marquis watched untiringly over his prey, he found time to write Adrienne yet another propaganda letter in terms clearly meant to consolidate his reputation for modesty. "I would accuse you of undergoing a terrible burst of vanity (since, after all, we hold everything in common, you would be vain if you esteemed my merits too highly) if you had not trembled about the dangers I incurred," he told her on July 26. "I speak now not of gunshot but of the far more dangerous and masterful trick I expected from Lord Cornwallis. It wasn't reasonable to entrust me with such a command; had I been unlucky, the public would have called this partiality blindness. . . .

Without the virtue, the zeal, and the courage of my regular soldiers, I could never have managed. I can never stress my obligation to them enough, especially to those with whom I began this exhausting campaign. I am very pleased with our little army and hope it is pleased with me."[31] In truth, the constant efforts lavished by the Marquis on the Light Infantry had paid off, both by improving its quality as a fighting body, and by cementing its loyalty to its commander. It is easy enough to pursue a fleeing foe; but retreats and feints, followed by rapid forward movements, shadowing the enemy without provoking him, require control of a high order. La Fayette was right to praise his troops, but he deserved much of the credit for their good behavior. At the same time, by exaggerating Cornwallis's skills, La Fayette was puffing up his own merits. Under the guise of modesty, his letter is in fact a long cry of pride.

At the very end of August, finally, the long-awaited reinforcements came. General Louis Duportail, one of Rochambeau's aides, arrived at La Fayette's headquarters with the news that both French fleets, under Admiral Louis de Barras and Admiral de Grasse, were at that moment converging on Yorktown and bringing with them Rochambeau, Washington, and their armies. The whole might of the alliance was being brought to bear upon the unfortunate Cornwallis. But there was one problem: the combined fleets, Duportail announced, could only stay for three weeks, since it was expected that the British would send naval reinforcements, thus regaining their earlier superiority. Although this was not, in fact, the case, the French admirals' fear of the British navy was a powerful help to their enemy. Yorktown would therefore have to be taken within that period, so it was more essential than ever not to let Cornwallis escape.

Just how close to the goal the Americans had now come and how desperately nervous they felt is quite vividly expressed in a letter from Washington to La Fayette: "I am distressed beyond expression to know [that is, I wish I knew] what is become of Count de Grasse and for fear the English fleet, by occupying the Chesapeake, should frustrate all our flattering prospects in that quarter. . . . Should the retreat of Lord Cornwallis by water, be cut off by the arrival of either of the French fleets, I am persuaded you will do all in your power to prevent his escape by land. May that great felicity be reserved for you!"[32] In fact, on September 2, the very day Washington wrote his letter, Admiral Count de Grasse arrived near Cape Henry with twenty-eight ships of the line, six frigates, and twenty-one hundred marines with eight cannons. The marquis de Saint Simon, who commanded the marines, promptly sent La Fayette a message saying he was putting himself under the Marquis's orders, although he was the young man's senior officer.

Now, at last, everything was going well. De Grasse, who was full of enthusiasm, immediately offered to give La Fayette eighteen hundred sailors as well as the marines* so the Marquis could immediately storm the besieged city. The normally impetuous young man refused. It was too risky to launch the operation without further preparation, he said, and besides if he took Yorktown, he would unfairly deprive Rochambeau and Washington of their share in the forthcoming victory.

It must all have been like a dream: after months of hardships, La Fayette found himself at the head of a very sizable army—fifty-five hundred French and Continentals, some six thousand scattered militia—an army, furthermore, in which harmony reigned between the allies. The tall, well-equipped, well-uniformed French troops were greatly admired by their American counterparts, who willingly gave them flour and horses, often themselves doing without both—quite a contrast to the squabbling usually going on within the American army itself. Immediately, the Marquis marched his men closer to Yorktown and reorganized his disposition as he waited for Washington. The Light Infantry formed the right wing, the Pennsylvania and Virginia Continentals held the center, while the French marines were placed on the left wing. On September 6, 1781, an attempt by the British at relieving Cornwallis failed: a small fleet under Admiral Thomas Graves sailed into the bay and was soundly beaten by de Grasse. After that, it was too late: the waters around Yorktown were now firmly in allied control.

Almost simultaneously La Fayette, who had been campaigning in malaria-infested marshes for many months, finally fell prey to the disease. Doing his best to ignore the fever, he dragged himself out of bed to greet Steuben, who arrived back from a sweep in Virginia on September 9, and to try resolving through the usual appeals the severe shortage of food, due to the large size of the army. Then, on the fifteenth, Washington, Rochambeau, and Chastellux, preceding their troops, made a solemn entry into camp before the assembled troops. La Fayette, who had been awaiting them, rushed up to the General and embraced him "with ardor not easily described."[33] That same day, the fleet commanded by Barras arrived from Newport and combined with de Grasse's ships: the French could now align more than forty large vessels and thus vastly outnumbered the British fleet. The reunion was beginning to look like a huge party. Long tables were set up in tents, food was actually found, and the commanders sat down with their officers, exchanging many toasts and much praise. The troops were

---

*Marines were actually army soldiers based on a ship; sailors sailed the ship but also fought in hand-to-hand combat when necessary.

reviewed by Washington, who was repeatedly greeted by musket salutes, while behind him a cohort of French and American officers followed. The French visited the Americans, the Americans reciprocated. After years of travail, the alliance had burst into bloom. And through it all La Fayette shook with fever, but refused to stay in bed.

No matter how ill he may have felt, the Marquis thoroughly relished Washington's order for September 15; the General expressed satisfaction "on joining the army under the command of Major General the Marquis de La Fayette with prospects which (under the smiles of Heaven) he doubts not will drown their toils under the most brilliant success."[34] The always cautious commander in chief was hardly tempting the fates: there really seemed to be no way for Cornwallis to avoid a crushing defeat.

Of course, with the arrival of both Washington and General Lincoln, La Fayette had lost his command and was again the leader of a mere division, but for a week more he stayed in the seat of power while Washington and Rochambeau met aboard the *Ville de Paris*, de Grasse's flagship, to discuss details of the siege, the Marquis himself being too sick to accompany them. "Your approbation of my conduct emboldens me to request that as General Lincoln [the senior general officer under Washington] will of course take command of the American part of your army, the division I will have under him may be composed of the troops which have gone through the dangers and fatigues of the Virginia campaign. This will be the greatest reward of the services I may have rendered, as I confess I have the strongest attachment to those troops,"[35] La Fayette had written Washington on September 8. Of course, Washington agreed; the arrangement became effective on the twenty-second.

When Washington and Rochambeau returned, they had convinced de Grasse to take the risk of meeting the large British squadron he so dreaded, keeping his fleet in place until late October, and leaving Saint Simon and his marines under Washington's command—to the latter's great pleasure. And then, one more time, the French ships threatened to disappear. De Grasse, who had just heard of the British Admiral Digby's arrival in New York with a considerable fleet, decided he must leave rather than face the possible loss of a naval battle. This was appalling news since, without the French ships, Digby could easily sail in and evacuate Cornwallis, who would be able to hold out as long as necessary; Rochambeau and Washington, now both on land, promptly wrote de Grasse and sent La Fayette who, by then, had almost recovered, to convince the reluctant admiral to stay. As it turned out, by the time the Marquis reached the *Ville de Paris*, de Grasse, under pressure from his general officers, had reversed himself. And Admiral Digby, who also feared losing a battle, stayed in New York. Now de Grasse agreed to move his ships out of the York River to Cape Henry, where they could most effectively prevent the relief of Yorktown, as had been suggested at the commanders' conference; but when La Fayette, always greedy for greater victories, suggested attacking Charleston, South Carolina, after Yorktown, the admiral very properly put off making a decision.

It was a triumphant La Fayette who returned to the combined armies on the morning of September 28. Although a day before La Fayette reached him, Admiral de Grasse had written Washington and Rochambeau promising to stay, the young man was convinced it was he who had saved the situation. Reinvigorated, he threw himself into the siege work. He now found himself on the extreme right of the American army, with two brigades of Light Infantry and with Lieutenant Colonel Alexander Hamilton as one of his subordinate officers. The general disposition was quite simple. Rochambeau and the French formed the left wing, the Americans under Lincoln the right, the Continentals were in the front line, the militia to the rear. Over all was Washington as commander in chief.

In Yorktown itself, Cornwallis remained cool and efficient, busily strengthening his defenses. He was confident that Digby would come to relieve him, so he waited: there was obviously no sense in risking a battle he was likely to lose since the allies now far outnumbered his troops. This position would have made sense if the context had not changed drastically: for the first time since 1776, the British navy no longer controlled the waters. Blissfully unaware of this, he watched the labors of his enemies without alarm. After all, they, too, were conducting the siege according to all the proper rules of war. It was a familiar situation, one that Cornwallis felt quite able to handle.

The way to take a besieged city, as everyone had known since Vauban, was to dig a series of trenches so that the fortifications could be approached safely, since a trench was too narrow to make a good target for defending cannon. This principle was so sound that it was still generally applied during World War I. Accordingly, La Fayette and Vioménil set fifteen hundred men to digging, while at the same time warning Washington that ships should be sent to prevent Cornwallis from crossing the York River.

On September 30, Cornwallis gave up his outer fortifications—they could only be defended at great cost—and the allies occupied them. On October 6, the operations began in earnest. The first parallel* was opened

---

*A deep trench that, through a zigzag pattern, allowed the attackers to come closer and closer to the wall, while shielding them from the defenders' cannon because it was parallel to the wall.

and the Light Division manned the trenches the next day. On October 10, a prolonged allied bombardment silenced or destroyed the artillery within the town and eliminated all enemy shipping still remaining in the York River. A second parallel was opened the same day, which could, however, not be completed as the soldiers came under fire from two enemy redoubts. Also that day, La Fayette, always living for the future, assured an emissary from General Greene that he would try to convince de Grasse to attack Charleston next.

Since the two British redoubts were now the main obstacle, Washington gave the Light Division the order to attack and take them. Hamilton was put in charge of the main assault group, the comte des Deux Ponts leading the French, with La Fayette directing the operation from the rear. The attack started as night fell, for the darkness made it harder for the defenders to shoot their targets down. To the Marquis's "unspeakable satisfaction," the Americans fought brilliantly. Not even bothering to shoot, they simply fixed their bayonets onto their guns and charged; almost immediately, the redoubt they were attacking fell into their hands. Rochambeau described it to de Grasse in this way: "The smallest of these two works has been taken by the Americans under M. le marquis de La Fayette, and it contained the battery that was the most dangerous on the York River."[36] The French, who found the going a little more difficult, were equally successful in the end; Vioménil, who commanded them, praised La Fayette and his soldiers in the report he sent off the next day. It was a famous achievement, and Washington, on October 15, thanked both La Fayette and Vioménil "for the excellency of their dispositions and for their own gallant conduct upon the occasion."[37] With the redoubts silenced, work on the second parallel could now be brought to completion.

As the experienced soldier he was, Cornwallis realized how hopeless his position had become. He knew, at last, that the French fleet controlled the bay and that, therefore, Digby would no longer come; unrelieved, Yorktown could hardly be defended against a determined siege. In desperation he decided to try at least one sortie. On the night of the fifteenth to the sixteenth, the British streamed out of their fortress and attacked the allies under cover of darkness. But the besiegers were ready and quickly repulsed them, with only minor damage to a few allied cannon. With dawn on the sixteenth, the steady allied cannonade resumed. By the seventeenth, it was clear to everyone that the siege must end soon. Cornwallis sent out an officer to ask for a suspension of hostilities. La Fayette, who happened to be in the trenches with the Light Division, promptly passed the request on to Washington. By noon on October 19, the capitulation was signed. The British had endured a resounding defeat.

Now, at last, the Americans, for whom the British had felt and demonstrated endless contempt, had won the upper hand. The French, to whom Cornwallis tried to surrender (he thought it less humiliating to give in to a proper European army), very fittingly refused: it was Washington's day. And under the terms arranged by Colonel Laurens and the vicomte de Noailles, the garrison was refused permission to march out of the captured city with the full honors of war; as La Fayette and others pointed out, when General Lincoln had surrendered Charleston, he had been made to sheathe his standards and march out to a tune other than his national anthem. The same conditions were now applied to the English. At 2:00 P.M., with the bands ironically and aptly playing "The World Turned Upside Down," the vanquished army began to march out of Yorktown—without Cornwallis, who had pleaded illness so as to avoid sharing his men's humiliation. To underline the reversal, the Americans arranged for it to be General Lincoln who received the new prisoners. When La Fayette, who stood at the head of his troops, noticed that the British soldiers made it a point to look toward the French units as if they were surrendering to them, he ordered his band to play "Yankee Doodle" as loud as they could. The British, startled by the noise, turned back to the Americans.

It was a great triumph, and well deserved, too; but the happy outcome was due less to La Fayette's skill, or Washington's plans, than to Clinton's mistake. Had he not reacted as he did to that seized letter, Cornwallis, who sent half of his men north, would have had the strength to beat La Fayette before de Grasse arrived. In the end, it was the English commander who set the trap that closed with such a resounding clang upon his subordinate.

"The play is done, Monsieur le comte, and the fifth act has just ended. I was a little uneasy at the beginning, but my heart has really enjoyed the end and it feels equal pleasure in congratulating you on the successful outcome of our campaign. I will not give you the details, Monsieur le comte, but rely on Lauzun to whom I wish as much felicity in crossing the ocean as he felt when he rode over Tarleton's legion,"[38] La Fayette wrote Maurepas in exultation on October 20, and to Adrienne, with far greater restraint, he commented: "The capture of Cornwallis is a most agreeable reward for me."[39] In fact, he was almost mad with joy: the long, long effort, begun at Bordeaux in 1777, had finally borne fruit. Next to Yorktown, all the Marquis's earlier successes paled into insignificance: here was no skirmish, no well-conducted retreat, but a signal victory that resounded across both continents. More than just the guarantee that the United States would be free, it was also the revenge of Minden, proof that Major General the Marquis de La Fayette deserved his rank, the affection of his commander in chief, the respect of his peers, and the adulation of the French. Vergennes, on December 1, could write with truth to the young marquis, "M. de Maurepas [who died just two days afterward] was still living when M. le duc de Lauzun arrived. He enjoyed for a moment the satisfaction given us all by the glorious events he had come to announce. People feel great joy here, and throughout the nation, and you may be sure that your name is venerated everywhere. It is noted with pleasure that, although you did not have the command in chief of this operation, your prudent behavior and your preliminary maneuvers prepared its success. I have followed you step by step, M. le Marquis, throughout your whole Virginia campaign; I would often have trembled for you had I not been reassured by your wisdom. It takes great skill to have resisted, as you did, for so long against Lord Cornwallis, whose warlike talents are so generally praised, and this in spite of the extreme disproportion of your forces. It was you who led him to the fatal end where, instead of making you his prisoner, as he might well have expected, you forced him to surrender instead."[40]

This was strong praise, but, after all, Vergennes had always been pro-American. Five days later, however, the same language came from another, more exalted—and much less pro-American—quarter. "The King being informed, Monsieur, of the military talents which you have repeatedly displayed when you commanded the several army corps which were entrusted to you in America, of the wisdom and prudence which have marked the different decisions you have had to reach relative the interests of the United States, and of the confidence you have earned from General Washington; His Majesty has commanded me to tell you that the praise you deserve on all points has fixed his attention, and that your behavior and your success have given him, Monsieur, the most favorable opinion of you. . . . His Majesty, wishing to give you a particular and flattering assurance of this has decided to give you the rank of a *maréchal de camp* [brigadier general] in his armies,"[41] wrote the Minister of War. A brigadier general at twenty-four: it was more than the French army had seen in many years. Back in Virginia, the fall of Yorktown was marked by celebrations: dinners, toasts, reviews, and speeches. The French praised Washington—the prince de Poix, Adrienne's cousin, for instance, extolled "his genius, his greatness and the nobility of his conduct"—and, while they were at it, his troops and his country. The Americans praised Rochambeau, de Grasse, and the valiant French forces. And everybody agreed on the infinite merits, the courage, the skill, the prudence, the cleverness, the generosity, the foresight of the one man who, in his person, united the two nations: the Marquis de La Fayette.

Even while the festivities were going on, however, La Fayette was trying to convince de Grasse he ought to attack Charleston, or at least

Wilmington, Delaware, but being quite alone in wanting him to do so, he got nowhere. At first, de Grasse reluctantly agreed to try Wilmington if it could be done before November 1, the date on which he intended to sail for the West Indies. Then he looked at his charts and decided he could not do it, after all. And so, suddenly, there was no more fighting, anywhere. The campaign had ended, and La Fayette decided to go home so as to plead, once again, for a bigger fleet and more men with which to undertake the next year's campaign. For now, with winter soon to begin, the fighting season was over.

On his way north he was greeted with cheers, speeches, and praise in town after town. On November 5, he reached Baltimore, where he was met by a complimentary address and appropriate festivities. On the eighth, in Philadelphia, he was asked to preside over the court-martial of Laurence Marr and John Moody, two Tory spies; they were convicted and sentenced to die. There were also lighter tasks. The Marquis conferred with Robert Morris about finance and was brought up-to-date on the dire state of the Treasury; he consulted Robert Livingston about the foreign policy of the United States. He also asked Congress for its permission to take a leave of absence; as in 1779, it was granted in notably friendly terms. The resolution praised La Fayette's "jealous attachment to the cause . . . his judgment, vigilance, gallantry and address . . . his merits and military talents."[42] The letter to Louis XVI, dated November 29 and signed by John Hancock, stated: "Major General the Marquis de La Fayette has in this campaign so greatly added to the reputation he had before acquired that we are desirous of obtaining for him, on our behalf, every notice in addition to that favorable reception which his merits cannot fail to meet with from a generous and enlightened Sovereign, and in that view we have directed our Minister Plenipotentiary to present the Marquis to Your Majesty."[43] Even better, the Secretary of Foreign Affairs was to instruct the United States ministers at Versailles—Benjamin Franklin, John Adams, and John Jay—to "[consult] with and [employ] the assistance of the Marquis de La Fayette in accelerating the supplies which may be afforded by His Most Christian Majesty for the use of the United States."[44] The Marquis, whose £2,000 debt to the merchants of Baltimore was now taken over by Congress, was to ask Louis XVI for a loan or subsidy of 10 million livres; to which Washington, who had joined his protégé in Philadelphia, added a request for greater naval and land assistance so that the 1782 campaign might at last be decisive. This was just what La Fayette had always wanted: he had now become the official go-between for his two countries.

Then there were more honors. The General Assembly of Virginia passed a resolution thanking Washington, Rochambeau, de Grasse, and La Fayette, and ordered that a bust of the young man be made and presented to him. In Boston, where he set sail in early December, and everywhere along the way from Philadelphia, the hero was acclaimed. The government, who had selected the *Alliance* for the Marquis's return to France, had some trouble finding sailors to man it because there could be no question of loitering in order to capture a British merchantman whose cargo they would share, but at last it was done and the little group of French officers prepared to sail. Along with La Fayette, and a witness to his triumph, was the vicomte de Noailles: the tables had indeed turned.

Finally, on December 23, the *Alliance* cast off. "We are going to sail and my last Adieu I must dedicate to my Beloved General—Adieu, my dear General, I know your heart so well that I am sure no distance can alter your attachment to me—With the same candor, I assure you that my love, my respect, my gratitude for you are above expressions, that on the moment of leaving you I more than ever feel the strength of those friendly ties that for ever bind me to you. . . . Your respectfull and tender friend, Lafayette,"[45] the Marquis wrote his adopted father. The war was not yet won, there remained much to be done, but as the ship headed toward Europe, La Fayette had good reason to be proud.

Six

THE HERO OF TWO WORLDS

This time, when the *Alliance* docked at Lorient, on January 17, 1782, there was no question of atoning for disobedience, or being confined anywhere. The Marquis de La Fayette had become the celebrity of the hour. Among those who mattered at Versailles, from monarchs to ministers to the entire Noailles clan, La Fayette could count on the warmest of welcomes; in fact, this "republican" was by way of becoming one of the Queen's favorites.

"Place my affectionate respects at the feet of the Queen," he wrote the prince de Poix on August 24, 1781. "Tell her how proud I am if I have had the necessary opportunities and talents to deserve her kindness by service to the common cause. . . . If to deserve it were necessary merely to love, then, my dear prince, never has sovereign had a more deserving subject."[1] The most experienced courtier could hardly have said it better; and when, on January 18, 1782, the Marquis heard that after twelve years of marriage, Marie Antoinette had at last given birth to a son, he wrote Washington: "The birth of a Dolphin [dauphin] has given a general satisfaction to the

French nation, and from attachment to the Queen I have been made particularly happy by this event."[2]

The very day—January 19—the Marquis reached Paris, in fact, the King, the Queen, and the court, including Adrienne as part of Her Majesty's suite, were celebrating the birth of the dauphin at a great banquet given by the City of Paris. When La Fayette heard the news, he realized that he was not likely to see his wife for a while: etiquette, the unbreachable, paramount etiquette made it impossible for Adrienne to leave the Queen until she dismissed her attendants for the night. At best, he thought, he could bow to the monarchs and get a glimpse of his wife as the procession passed by the hôtel de Noailles; and he was standing before the door when, to his amazement, Marie Antoinette's carriage stopped right in front of him. More amazing still, there was Adrienne, with the Queen, when her rank entitled her to no such privilege: the news of La Fayette's return had reached the royal party at the Hôtel de Ville and, breaking every rule, the Queen had taken Adrienne with her, ordering her on the way to leave the procession and stay with her husband. At a court where etiquette was considered inviolable, there could be no clearer mark of favor. Overcome by the joy of seeing her husband again, Adrienne stepped down from the carriage and fainted right into his arms. It made a pretty picture, but the young woman saw to it that it did not happen again and, from then on, did her best to control her feelings: it would not do to become importunate.

Adrienne was hardly alone in her happiness at her hero's return. All France felt the same. "The reception I have met from the nation at large, from the King and from my friends will, I am sure, be pleasing to you and has surpassed my utmost ambition. The King spoke of you to me in terms of so high a confidence, regard and admiration, and affection, that I cannot forbear mentioning it. I have been the other day invited at the maréchal's de Richelieu, with all the maréchals of France where your health was drunk with great veneration and I was requested to present you with the homages of that body,"[3] one of whom, the maréchal de Noailles, was Adrienne's grandfather, La Fayette wrote to Washington on January 30. Imitation being the sincerest form of admiration, he was able to add that "all the young men of this Court are solliciting a permission to go to America."

This great wave of praise and admiration seemed, for a while, to engulf everyone. There were pamphlets and poems praising the young man. Painters and engravers vied to render his features; everywhere he went, he found himself surrounded by applauding crowds; on February 10, as he sat in his box at the opera, he watched Mlle Dorlay, the leading soprano, crowning a bust of himself that had been set up on the stage. Only Voltaire, in extreme

old age, had been given such a reception. Then, of course, there was Mme
d'Hunolstein, more willing than ever. Everyone knew about the affair, by
now, including Adrienne, who decided that discretion was the better part
of valor. Infidelity, after all, was the rule among the upper classes. She
concealed her jealousy and worked hard at being loving without seeming to
cling.

Even the fair Aglaé and universal applause, however, failed to distract
La Fayette from what he considered his primary duty—advancing the American cause. First, though, he had to straighten out his own slightly awkward
military status. The King had appointed him a maréchal de camp, with
seniority dating from the fall of Yorktown; but the promotion was not to take
effect until the end of the war. It was obviously out of the question for him
to resume the command of a regiment, however, so he sold the King's
Dragoons to the vicomte de Noailles for 60,000 livres, 20,000 less than he
had paid himself. And when he heard that many senior officers were outraged
at his being promoted over their heads, he wrote the War Minister offering
to give it up. He was spared that painful sacrifice, however, because the
marquis de Castries felt that giving in to the protest would injure his authority. Still, amid all the adulation, such sour grapes were the precursor
of an eventual anti-La Fayette faction. For the moment, the grumblers were
fueled by nothing more than envy; but then envy, at court, was one of the
most powerful forces.

Where it mattered, though, La Fayette was wholly popular. Louis XVI
liked him, saw him often, and listened to him with care; the ministers, now
that Maurepas had died, were more pro-American, and Vergennes had the
King's ear. Thus encouraged, the Marquis promptly embarked on a new
series of pleas—more men for Rochambeau's army, more ships, and, above
all, more money. At first, the prospects looked bleak. The war had been
terribly expensive, and, from Versailles, it looked as if the Americans were
not pushing themselves hard enough, La Fayette reported to Washington,
but he persisted—"with greater weight than I could possibly do,"[4] Franklin
informed Robert Morris—and he succeeded, at least in part. He had asked
for a loan of 10 to 12 million livres: early in March, Vergennes told him the
ministers had agreed on 6 million, to be paid quarterly starting that very
month. And on April 18, at Vergennes's request, he furnished the Foreign
Minister with a *Mémoire sur les Affaires d'Amérique*, in which he argued
against retrenchment, and for attacks on Charleston, New York, and Canada.
He had never before been so effective, and he knew it.

"However sensible I am that our cause may be better served by my
presence here than it could possibly be at this period by my presence in

America, I cannot refrain from a painfull sentiment at the sight of many French officers who are going to join their colours in America,"[5] he wrote on April 12. He was perfectly right about his own usefulness being in Paris. Although the government now felt genuine friendship for the United States, it naturally put French interests first. Franklin, clever and eloquent though he was, had only limited access to the ministers, and he remained, after all, a foreigner. Only La Fayette could always reach both King and government, only he could plead shamelessly and endlessly for the American cause: he had, in fact, become an irreplaceable liaison.

An even more exciting role soon offered itself to the young man. Anxious as he was for military glory, La Fayette had always wanted to play a major diplomatic role; and early in 1782, Great Britain let it be known it was ready to start negotiating. An envoy would have to be sent to London: one had been sent to negotiate the peace in 1763. While the Marquis realized he could hardly speak for the United States, when it came to representing France surely there could be no one better qualified.

Once again, however, La Fayette had launched himself unto a sea of illusions. The American ministers, anxious though they were for his help when it came to money and supplies, did not want him to interfere with the peace negotiations; and Vergennes, who liked the Marquis, knew his impulsiveness and love for the United States far too well to send him on so difficult and delicate a mission. In the end it was Rayneval, Vergennes's assistant, who crossed the Channel. Even then, as it turned out, it was months before that happened: in April, de Grasse's fleet was soundly beaten by Admiral George Rodney, thus encouraging the British government to be more difficult; and the preparations for the negotiations soon became a virtual comedy of errors.

It was all a question of the right formula. The powers given the British envoys were carefully worded to include, as possible partners, only France and Spain. Since it had long been official that neither France nor the United States would negotiate separately or until independence had been publicly recognized, both Franklin and Vergennes declared that these powers were inadequate. There was a delay while messengers went back and forth, and a new set of powers finally arrived, but they were addressed to the King of France and "any other Prince or States." The new formula was ambiguous since England had yet to recognize the former colonies as a state; so Franklin, who had the flu, sent La Fayette to Vergennes with a protest, and the British envoy was asked for further clarification. All through this, La Fayette thrust himself forward whenever he could and produced endless advice for all concerned: he wrote John Adams on May 7 to congratulate him on his success

in Holland,* and to report that Louis XVI, "the other day . . . [spoke] of
you in terms of the highest regard," but mainly to ask him if he could come
to Paris with all possible speed. He met with all parties including Sir Thomas
Grenville, the British envoy, to whom he was studiously polite, and he
required the American envoys to state at regular intervals that his presence
in France, instead of the United States, was absolutely necessary—a demand
that Franklin began to find increasingly annoying.

On a social level, the Marquis went on being the toast of Paris and the
court. He was in higher favor than ever with Marie Antoinette; when the
tsarevich and his wife (under the incognito of Count and Countess of
the North) visited France, and a great ball was given at Versailles in their
honor, La Fayette was chosen as one of the Queen's dancing partners, a
major distinction, and one which must have finally eradicated earlier unhappy memories of a young La Fayette stumbling and falling. A few days
earlier, Adrienne, who was accompanying the Russians on a visit to the
Parlement of Paris, was the object of an impromptu, but fervent, speech
lauding her heroic husband. And, of course, Mme d'Hunolstein made sure
the young man did not lack for extramarital bliss. Life was so pleasant, in
fact, and so little like war, that, on June 25, 1782, La Fayette, with a strong
note of underlying guilt, found it necessary to justify himself to Washington.
"How it is possible for me to be here at this period you will hardly be able
to conceive," he wrote, "and I confess I am myself more and more surprised
at the strange delays. Both duty and inclination lead me to America, and
tho' it is not probable you are active in the field, yet the possibility of it is
to me a torment. . . . I would have . . . sailed, when negotiations have kept
me here and the American Ministers have declared they wanted my presence
in this part of the world. I . . . know, in case of a treaty, I may better serve
our cause by the situation I am in. . . . I therefore have thought . . . that
you will approve my submitting to remain a fortnight longer."[6] In fact, the
American ministers did not particularly want La Fayette's help, and Vergennes never even thought of consulting him, although he did keep him
apprised of developments. He stayed on for many more weeks than two.
Once again, rushing about and being officious, the Marquis was repeating
an earlier pattern, that of 1780, and with just as little effect: while he was
now a past master at obtaining help and supplies for the Continental army,
he knew nothing of diplomatic methods; and Vergennes, who had clear war
aims in mind, required no assistance from La Fayette. As for Franklin, he

---

*He had just won recognition there for the United States.

was perfectly willing to go on making Gilbert feel needed, just in case the war flared up again.

The negotiations game continued right through July and August. Luckily, things were quiet in America and Washington tactfully quieted the anxious young man on October 20: "I ceased [to write you] expecting the more agreeable pleasure of embracing you in America. . . . I approve very highly, the motives which induced you to remain at your Court, and I am convinced Congress will do the same.

"The campaign, as you supposed, has been very inactive. . . . I had prepared a beautiful Corps for you to command [but] we have done nothing more than keep a watch upon the enemy."[7] Washington, too, understood La Fayette's potential value in case of renewed fighting. By then, at long last, the British envoy had received a commission to treat with the "Thirteen United States of America." It had taken an Enabling Act to allow the government to use the formula, but Parliament had passed it, and with excruciating slowness, the peace negotiations actually got under way. The great news—independence was now a fact—of course pleased La Fayette. So, in a more private way, did the birth of his daughter Virginie on September 17, 1782. Earlier, he had named his son after Washington; now his daughter was to be a homage to the General's state, prompting, eventually, an approving word from Mount Vernon: "Virginia, I am perswaded, will be pleased with the compliment of the name; and I pray as a member of it she [the child] may live to be a blessing to her parents."[8] Franklin, meanwhile, sent compliments and best wishes on the very day of the birth, adding, mischievously, "While you are proceeding, I hope our states will some of them new-name themselves. Miss Virginia, Miss Carolina and Miss Georgiana will sound pretty enough for the girls; but Massachusetts and Connecticut are too harsh even for the boys, unless they were to be savages."[9] As it turned out, Virginie was to be the La Fayettes' last child, and the world was spared that tongue-twisting possibility.

Franklin was good-humored enough when it came to naming babies, but both he and John Adams took a much more jaundiced view of the new father's political activities. La Fayette's constant interference in the negotiations, his obvious desire to represent both France and the United States, began to look more like vanity than helpfulness. Adams made note of it in his diary. "This unlimited ambition will obstruct his rise," he wrote about the Marquis. "He grasps at all, civil, political and military, and would be the *unum necessarium* in every thing; he has had so much real merit, so much family supports and such favour at Court that he need not recur to artifice."[10] And, indeed, the once-insecure young man was beginning to feel he was meant to run France. Curiously, it was not so much actual power he yearned for, but the appearance of power; more important still, he wanted constant confirmation that he was right and that the policies he advocated were not only patriotic but virtuous.

Luckily, a new expedition to America was in the wind. Since de Grasse's defeat in April had resulted in a less forthcoming English attitude, the French government felt a major allied victory was necessary to bring about peace. Planning began for a huge combined Franco-Spanish operation. The two fleets would join in Cadiz, then sail to the West Indies, where they would proceed to take Jamaica, then go on to attack Charleston, New York, and perhaps even Canada. This time there was to be no scrimping: the forces coming together in Cadiz were to number twenty thousand men—a very large army by the standards of the time—and fifty ships of the line; by the time they met the French already on the other side of the ocean, the allies would number sixty-six ships of the line, possibly the largest gathering of warships ever seen in European history.* As for La Fayette, he was to be given a major role—to be, in fact, quartermaster general and second in command to Admiral d'Estaing, who was to lead the allied forces. It was a rather complicated way of getting back to America: the Marquis had to ask the American commissioners for the authorization to serve, temporarily, in the French army—after all, he was still an American officer—and, rather shamefacedly, he gave Washington the news on October 24. "I . . . think it consistent with my real zeal for our cause, and my obedience to your intentions to take a round about way to serve our military purposes. Under these circumstances, I have accepted to go this winter with Count d'Estaing, but tho' I am to reenter the French line as a Maréchal de camp from the date of Lord Cornwallis's surrender, I will however keep my American uniform, and the outside as well as the inside of an American soldier. I will conduct matters, and take commands as an officer borrowed from the United States, as it were occasionally [that is, for the occasion] and will watch for the happy moment when I may join our beloved colours."[11] The truth was, of course, that the "beloved colours" were at the moment seeing no action, while there was fame to be gained in the d'Estaing expedition.

Before he left Paris in November 1782, La Fayette pressed Vergennes for another loan to the United States, and although it had been well understood by everyone that the Treasury, which had already been bled white, could provide no more subsidies, the Foreign Minister actually agreed to consider lending another 6 million livres, but by then, the Marquis's rela-

---

*The Spanish Armada may have been about as large.

tionship with the American commissioners was already so tense that both parties assumed success was due solely to their own efforts, and each felt bitter at not being credited by the other.

In any case, La Fayette was anxious for Washington's approval. The normally reserved general always treated Gilbert with fatherly tenderness; so even if he actually agreed with Adams and Franklin, he was careful never to let this appear in his correspondence with the young man; besides, behavior that might irritate at close range was more acceptable from afar. From Brest, on December 4, while he waited for favorable winds, La Fayette wrote the General: "I have the honour to send you the copy of a letter to Congress. I hope you will be able to tell them you are satisfied with my conduct. Indeed, my dear general, it is necessary to my happiness you will think so." Then, he went on to lay bare, in two brief sentences, the main reason for his success so far. "When you are absent, I endeavour to do the thing you would have advised had you been present. I love you too much to be one minute easy unless I think you approve my conduct."[12] Of course, this was hardly the first time that the young man set down his affection for his adopted father, but now he revealed more of himself than ever before. Probably because his differences with Franklin and Adams had made him feel insecure, Gilbert was again turning to Washington, the stern but comforting father figure. But while he had learned to please the General, and had pleased the world at large as he did so, he still had not been able to develop his own rules, his own standards. By himself, he never knew whether he had chosen the right course; as a result, La Fayette often seemed oddly robotlike. Talleyrand, that shrewd observer, noted: "His acts don't seem to belong to his nature; it feels as if he's always following advice."[13] The obvious problem with this system was that La Fayette's sense of judgment depended on the General's real or epistolary presence.

It was not only his mentor whom La Fayette missed as he waited in Brest; for the first time, in a letter to the prince de Poix, he complained of his sadness at leaving his friends. The plural was polite; he was really thinking of Mme d'Hunolstein, with whom his affair was reaching a stormy crescendo. Unfortunately, it was also causing a lot of scandalized gossip. Because Aglaé did not live with her husband, because her affair with the duc de Chartres (a prince of the blood royal, after all) had been so notorious, and because, finally, she had had a number of affairs besides those with Chartres and La Fayette, she had managed to shock even the tolerant Parisians. Even though Paris society considered it normal for a young woman to have a number of lovers (preferably consecutively), certain rules had to be observed. Among them was that publicity was only permissible under two conditions: one, if the lover was so august as to discourage attack (this applied to the duc de

Chartres) or, two, if the liaison was old and well-established, a sort of marriage without vows. By flaunting herself publicly with someone as much in the public eye as La Fayette, Mme d'Hunolstein had broken the second rule.

Had Gilbert been really loved her, he might have conducted the affair with the required discretion, but the truth was that he actually cared little for his mistress. What really pleased him was to have his name openly linked with that of one of the prettiest women in Paris, and one, furthermore, who had rejected a prince in his favor. Since, however, that was not the most laudable of attitudes, Gilbert convinced himself that he was the most devoted of lovers, and frequently protested to Aglaé that he was passionately attached to her. And even if they weren't linked by great depth of feeling, there was always sex.

In a time when people discussed sex freely and enthusiastically, La Fayette was known for his almost puritanical reticence. Not that he was chaste: there is every evidence that he went on sleeping with Adrienne until shortly before her death many years later, while, concurrently, having a mistress whenever he was not in the United States. It is, however, interesting to note that there is not a single reference, in contemporary letters and memoirs, to Gilbert's sexual performance. Other well-known young men—Noailles, Lauzun, and many others—were known to be technically satisfying lovers. It seems likely, therefore, that Gilbert thought first of pleasing himself and thus proved something of a disappointment in bed to all but the adoring Adrienne.

Since Aglaé was nothing if not experienced, she must have yearned, at times, for a more competent lover. As a result, when her family, horrified by the scandal she was causing, asked her to break off the affair, she listened. Once before his departure, Gilbert had been told that it was all over; but he begged, she relented, they made love, and the affair was on again.

When a letter from the prince de Poix announced that people were talking more than ever, the Marquis was deeply upset: this is undoubtedly why, after he arrived in Cadiz on December 23, he remained chaste while all his friends were having amours with the local ladies. The final depressing note came when La Fayette realized that going on the expedition meant he could not be named envoy to London. In a last-ditch effort he wrote to Franklin from Brest to ask for his recommendation, yet he must have known that he had lost his chance of getting that particular mission.

Despite the melancholia from all such disappointments, La Fayette immediately set to work. Since as quartermaster general he was in charge of gathering the necessary supplies, there was much for him to do, and he was busy getting a wide variety of items ranging from rope and food and tar to cloth. Of course, he always found time to write and on January 1, 1783, a letter went off to Vergennes in which the Marquis, after acknowledging the importance of his current work, goes about the real business of buttering up the powerful: "My heart follows you in all you undertake, and my friendship for you is joined to my patriotism in wishing your success."[14] After all, it was the Foreign Minister who would oversee the negotiations with England.

By the end of January 1783 the fleet was ready to sail. King Charles III of Spain had approved its successive goals, refusing only to appoint La Fayette governor of Jamaica once it had been wrested from the British. Rebels were the same everywhere, he felt, and someone who fought to free one colony might well do the same in another. "He'd create a republic there!" the horrified monarch exclaimed, thus showing how little he really knew Marie Antoinette's friend. Spain had good reason to worry about republics, though: its American colonies stretched all the way up to the Mississippi, and it dreaded a contagion from the North. Despite the anti-British alliance, the Madrid government had so far refused to recognize the independence of the United States.

Still, the fleet and troops were ordered to action. La Fayette was actually on board his ship when, suddenly, on February 5, the news arrived from Paris that, eleven days earlier, the peace preliminaries had been signed. Of course, the actual treaty was still being negotiated, but unquestionably, the war was over. On February 10, La Fayette congratulated Washington: "Were you but such a man," he wrote, "as Julius Caesar or the King of Prussia [Frederick the Great], I should be almost sorry for you at the end of the great tragedy where you are acting such a part. But with my dear General I rejoice at the blessings of peace where our noble ends have been secured. . . . What a sense of prid and satisfaction I feel when I think of the times that have determined my engaging in the American cause! As for you, my dear General, who truly can say you have done all this, what must your virtuous and good heart feel on the happy instant where the Revolution you have made is now firmly established." Noble words, and, on the whole, sincere, but the Marquis did not forget to reach for a little more acclaim. "Amongs the many favours I have received, I would take it as a most flattering circumstance in my life to be sent to England with the ratification of the American treaty. . . . If any sedentary [that is, permanent] minister is sent, I shall have the pleasure of introducing him. This . . . is entirely confidential."[15] It is not hard to envision the pleasure La Fayette must have felt when he envisioned himself triumphing over the English in their own capital: it would be compensation indeed for not having negotiated the peace. In the United States, however, people took a different view. In his inimitably public-minded style, Washington did his best to promote his protégé; there can be no doubt that he really wished to please Gilbert, but the welfare of the Republic always came first. "How far [La Fayette's mission] is consistent with our National honour, how far motives of policy make for or against sending a foreigner with [the ratification]; or how far such a measure may disappoint the expectations of others, I pretend not to determine, but if there is no impropriety or injustice in it, I should hope that Congress would feel a pleasure in gratifying the wishes of a man who has been such a zealous labourer in the cause of this Country."[16] As Hamilton promptly wrote him in reply, the proposal did seem contrary to the national honor. There was nothing left for Washington to do but send La Fayette the news in such a way as to coat the pill with sugar. On April 16 he argued, "Private gratification should ever, in my opinion, yield to public considerations . . . and I am perswaded that the Marquis, however ambitious and eager he may be in the pursuit of glory, will readily acquiesce to a refusal which is made upon public grounds."[17] The Marquis duly did, of course, but Washington, fond of Gilbert though he was, must have been reminded of those days in the summer of 1777 when an importunate young foreigner kept clamoring for his own division.

Communications between Europe and the United States were so wretched that La Fayette's letter had been the first with the news of the peace. And in Spain itself, where there was further work to be accomplished, he proved, once more, that he could be useful. William Carmichael, the American envoy to the Spanish court, had been unable to obtain recognition because Charles III was unwilling to concede the independence of the United States. In an effort to influence the King through a piece of calculated bluff, La Fayette sent Carmichael a letter by regular post, knowing full well it would be opened and read by government agents. In the letter he told Carmichael not to worry: France would soon make Spain see the light. Since the Spanish Prime Minister wanted French backing for its territorial claims up to the Mississippi, this was an effective threat, and the Marquis followed it up by traveling from Cadiz to Madrid where, after a good deal of effort, he convinced the count of Floridablanca, the chief minister, to receive Carmichael officially. This would have happened sooner or later, but there can be no doubt that La Fayette speeded up the process substantially, and his visit to Charles III gave him occasion to write Mme de Tessé, on February 13, a letter in which he made fun of the Spanish court and its etiquette: "I went and paid court to the King this morning and, in spite of my Insurgent title and uniform, I saw some Grandees looking very small, especially when they were down on their knees: it is enough to make an independent mind sneeze,"[18] he noted sarcastically. No doubt, this amused Mme de Tessé and comforted La Fayette's own image of himself as an "American republican"; but it rings more of the usual French tendency to make fun of foreign customs than of attachment to democratic mores. After all, the Marquis was still perfectly content to bow as deeply, and kiss as many hands, as any other nobleman at Versailles.

Before he left Cadiz, La Fayette, who, until recently, had found the possession of slaves perfectly normal, came up with an idea that had a double advantage: it was enlightened; and it would tie him closer to his adopted father. Why shouldn't he buy an estate together with Washington, he asked the General, on which they could experiment with the freeing of slaves and thus offer an example to the world? It must have seemed a very light-headed proposal to the careful owner of Mount Vernon. Washington, like many of his Northern contemporaries, acknowledged that slavery was wrong; at the same time, since slaves were a form of property, he hardly saw how they could be freed, so he eventually answered that they had better postpone the plan until they met and discussed it. Whether they ever did, no one knows, but nothing came of it. It is interesting, however, in one respect. Now that the war was over, La Fayette realized he needed a new field of activity; being the benefactor of mankind evidently suggested itself as an acceptable role.

Freeing the slaves had to wait; in the meantime, La Fayette, who now returned to Paris, decided to extricate himself from two increasingly difficult situations: he broke with Mme d'Hunolstein and moved out of the hôtel de Noailles.

The liaison with Aglaé had been growing increasingly burdensome. Although he was still attracted to her, La Fayette now began to realize that, in a city full of beautiful and willing women, neither the effort nor the scandal was worth continuing. Since Mme d'Hunolstein, by 1783, found salon after salon closed to her, her mother demanded that she break off the liaison, and actually went to see Gilbert and asked him to give up her daughter. La Fayette promptly agreed to do so; but then he arranged for a farewell meeting, and because Aglaé had become inaccessible, he naturally desired her all the more. In no time at all, the two were in each other's arms (later Aglaé claimed to have been virtually forced by the ardent Gilbert), and their pleasure was evidently such as to give the affair a new, enthusiastic life. They even had fights in which Aglaé dissolved into tears, reproached Gilbert for ruining her reputation and her social standing, and begged him to be gone; we may perhaps guess that the tears were not such as to give Aglaé unbecoming sniffles, and that the scarf covering her heaving bosom somehow got disarranged: the pathetic pleas apparently gave way, every time, to desire, and the scene ended not in separation but renewed embraces.

In a letter written from Chavaniac on March 27, Gilbert pointed out to Aglaé that their "quarrels ended like all lovers' quarrels, but although carried away by passion, I remembered the reproaches of your family and the efforts I had had to make in order to win you again."[19] Gilbert is being polite, but what he really is saying is that Aglaé's reluctance now no longer excited him; that others were more willing, and that he was tired of playing the role of the wicked seducer. There was nothing left to do, therefore, but to break off the affair, and consideration for Adrienne may well have played a role in his determination. While he could see no reason to be a faithful husband, there was a great difference between one or more discreet liaisons and an affair that had become a public and universal subject of gossip in the very salons attended by Adrienne.

Because the Marquis also had found, upon his return from America, that women were even more interested in him than before, Aglaé's tantrums became especially irksome. He may well have had a brief affair with the princesse d'Hénin, a young and fashionable member of Marie Antoinette's circle—probably a brief fling in and out of bed that lasted some two or three weeks. He had, in any event, met the comtesse Adélaide de Simiane, for whom he felt an immediate attraction. So, in that coaxing way of his, La Fayette refrained from telling poor Aglaé that he had found a more appealing mistress. Instead, he let her know that he had decided, most reluctantly, to accede to her own wishes and stop seeing her. And because he often combined kindness and selfishness, he was exceedingly tactful, even if, as a result, his letter sounds a little confused. "For more than a year now you have tried to break our connection," he wrote after many protests of passionate love. "You have wanted this, be satisfied therefore . . . and may your life at least be peaceful since we may not be happy. . . . But at least my heart is my own, dear Aglaé," he added gallantly, "and all you are, all I owe you justifies the tenderness I feel for you; nothing, not even you, can stop me from adoring you."[20] It is easy to see why the French were famous for their politeness. Truthfulness was another matter: before many weeks had passed, Mme d'Hunolstein was well and truly forgotten.

It would be wrong to think, in spite of all this, that La Fayette was neglecting Adrienne, or more, at any rate, than custom allowed. That they continued to be, in the fullest sense, husband and wife is proved by Virginie's birth, and in fact they struck all who saw them as a happy couple. With all his schemes and all his ladies, La Fayette spent a great deal of time at home, and never took up the almost invariable rule according to which husband and wife lived absolutely separate lives. The link with Adrienne was further strengthened by Gilbert's obvious—and uncommon—concern and love for his children. Rousseau's theories notwithstanding, children were not popular

in late eighteenth-century Paris. All the visitors to the La Fayettes commented on the unusual visibility of their offspring and the tenderness and
respect with which their parents treated them. Adding to his pleasure in
being at home, in May 1783, Gilbert finally bought his own house and made
it a center for the Americans who came to Paris and for the young nobles
who had fought in the United States. Since Adrienne was his hostess and
visibly adored him, this, too, brought them closer.

This move to their own house, after all the years at the hôtel de Noailles,
was the direct consequence of Gilbert's coming of age—the requisite age
in those days being twenty-five. At last the young man had full control over
his fortune—not that his guardians appear to have bothered him much before
this. Nor did Gilbert's habits change noticeably. He reappointed Jacques-
Philippe Grattepain-Morizot as his man of affairs and proceeded to spend
as merrily as ever. And he was well able to do so: although his American
exertions had cost him the huge sum of 700,000 livres (roughly $3,150,000)
La Fayette, in 1783, had recently inherited his great-grandfather's estate in
Brittany and so found himself as well off as ever: for the next few years he
could count on an income of 128,000 livres. He remained one of the richest
men in France. Still, like so many members of the landed aristocracy, he
was often relatively short of cash—in this case, partly because Grattepain-
Morizot had been rounding out his properties by the acquisition of still more
land; so when he decided to buy himself a Paris house, he had to sell another
house that he owned but could not live in because it was fully rented. Still,
it never occurred to him that money might be something to think about: it
was merely something you told M. Grattepain-Morizot you needed; you
assumed that if the sum were large there would be a few moans but that
the money would be forthcoming promptly. Comfort, beauty, and elegance
did matter, though. The Marquis spent 200,000 livres ($900,000) buying the
private house at 183 Rue de Bourbon (today, Rue de Lille) and another
100,000 livres ($450,000) refurbishing and redecorating it. We may surmise
that the furniture was handsome since it, alone, cost 50,000 livres ($225,000),
a very large sum, and the French *ébénistes*, then, were the best in the world.
And while, in all other respects, the house was typical of any grand Paris
establishment, its library boasted a very unusual feature: there, occupying
one half a complete frame, hung a copy of the Declaration of Independence.
When visitors asked why the frame was only half complete, La Fayette
would answer that he was leaving room for the future French Declaration
of Rights. However spectacular this may have been, it was, however, little
more than an empty gesture. There was still, at this time, a dichotomy
between La Fayette's declared opinions and his actual behavior: if asked
when the frame would be filled, he probably would have looked absolutely

blank—at some time in the very distant future, he might well have said, the King would no doubt grant his subjects all desirable liberties.

Of course, like other liberal nobles he attended the salons of Mme de Tessé, Adrienne's aunt and a liberal herself, and of Mme Necker, the wife of the erstwhile Minister of Finance, where a financial reform of the state, to be carried out by M. Necker, naturally, was often discussed. Since politics and economics were much in fashion, there were frequent talks in the salons about abstruse subjects such as the system of taxation or the deficits and the merits of constitutional government. However, no one was prepared to do anything about these ideas. La Fayette also frequented another salon, that of the prince de Conti, largely because his friends Poix and Ségur had taken him there. It was a nonpolitical gathering, presided by Mme de Boufflers, Conti's mistress, and one of the most amiable women of the age. Many of its habitués were competent musicians, but they were spurred on by the example of all the greatest composers and performers—Mozart played there— so much time was given to music and to the kind of society theatricals of which the eighteenth century was so fond. Many a duke, if suddenly bereft of his estate, would have made a very satisfactory actor; so the salon of the prince de Conti, while apolitical, was just as enthralling as all the others.

As for the hôtel de La Fayette, the atmosphere there was slightly atyp- ical, but that the La Fayettes had their own salon was a recognized fact. It was less formal than most French houses, and there was neither card playing nor gambling of any kind. It was, of course, a center for all the young noblemen who had fought in America—Noailles, now a strong liberal; Poix, more frivolous than ever; Ségur, who was fast developing military ambitions; Charlus; Chastellux, that earnest, democratic, atheistic intellectual; occa- sionally Lauzun boasting about his women; and also Franklin, Jay, the Adams family, and any other American of note who came to Paris. There were regular Monday night dinners, but callers also came by every day, although they seldom found La Fayette at home because he was so busy. The La Fayettes also saw Adrienne's sisters and the various members of the Noailles family, so it was varied and well attended. It was, of course, pro-American and liberal, so in that sense, it was unlike some of Marie Antoinette's other friends' gatherings; but while reforms might be discussed, nothing ever took place that might upset the court. La Fayette was more in favor than ever at Versailles. One evening in October 1783 the La Fayettes gave a dinner that would remain a subject of conversation both in France and in England for many years afterward. On that day, only a month after the peace treaty had been signed on September 3, 1783, the La Fayettes were hosts to William Pitt, a rising political force in England, and the virtuous William Wilberforce, along with Benjamin Franklin, Mme de Tessé, the vicomte de

Noailles, and a few others. Thus did Pitt, the future champion of conservatism, and La Fayette, the future defender of the French Revolution, meet face to face, but since neither had yet taken up his later position, the conversation remained wholly friendly.

With the exception of a trip to Chavaniac to see his grandmother in the summer of 1783 during which Adrienne, for the first time, accompanied her husband, the Marquis considered himself as still being in the American service. Washington kept writing him reassuring letters. "I am fully persuaded . . . of your zeal in the American Cause . . . and I shall express to Congress . . . my entire approbation of your conduct,"[21] he had written on March 23, following this testimonial with an invitation to stay at Mount Vernon; and when Congress wrote La Fayette and asked him to intervene so that the debts owed by Americans to British merchants might be included in the treaty's final arrangements, the Marquis rushed to Versailles and started pestering Vergennes all over again, without any result, as it turned out, since the British envoys lacked the power to deal with private debts. Then, too, with the coming of peace, commercial questions began to take on major importance. The French government wanted to encourage its new allies to trade with France instead of Great Britain, while patriotic American traders felt France might be just the new market they needed. As usual, La Fayette was the perfect go-between. Soon he was directing his attention toward Charles de Calonne, the new Finance Minister. Since France still followed Jean-Baptiste Colbert's old mercantilist policies, all importers had to pay substantial duties. Gold was the sole real measure of wealth, and the way to be prosperous was to keep exports high, earning foreign gold, while importing nothing, thus retaining your own. This situation was made substantially worse by the fact that every French port had its own set of enormously complicated charges, and every province in France had its own customs and duty system. Thus a piece of merchandise traveling from Brest to Paris had to pay taxes as it left Brittany to enter Normandy, then again as it left Normandy, and one more time as it entered Paris. The result, of course, was that the foreign goods, even if they had been cheap when they left their country of origin, ended up prohibitively expensive by the time they reached the capital. This was the system the American merchants were rightly complaining about, and La Fayette set about to change it. "I am collecting the opinion of every American merchant within my reach," he wrote Washington on November 11, "and my exertions are bent upon representing what may be most advantageous in mercantile regulations, for tho' one cannot hope for a compleat success, yet it pleases one to think that some good measure may be influenced by a proper representation."[22]

The first step, La Fayette soon realized, was to open some ports to

American trade by making them duty-free entry points. In the early fall, he suggested that Bayonne, Marseille, Dunkirk, and Lorient be chosen; at the same time, he requested, and received, a memorandum from Vergennes defining the status of a duty-free port. The second step affected the French West Indies: their ports, the Marquis suggested, should also be open without duty to the American trade. Of course, no decision was taken. Not only was the course of government exceedingly slow, but one of the most powerful groups in France was fiercely opposed to this new policy: the fermiers généraux. These "farmers," so called because the King "farmed out" the collection of certain taxes to them, signed contracts every few years in which they promised to give the Treasury certain sums at stated intervals; they were then allowed to keep the difference between what they actually collected and what they had undertaken to pay. Not surprisingly, the observation "rich as a fermier général" had become a common saying.

Many of the taxes that La Fayette wanted to see abolished went straight into the till of the ferme générale. When, in October 1783, Calonne took on the finances, the prospects for reform looked especially bleak: the new minister was known to be the ferme's best friend. But appearances were deceptive. Calonne was anxious to foster trade with the United States, and so, for political reasons, were Castries and especially Vergennes. Still, the Foreign Minister, as usual, wanted a stalking-horse, and La Fayette could always be manipulated; so Vergennes convinced him to write his *Observations on Trade between France and the United States* in which he argued, in essence, for free trade, still a revolutionary notion. His treatise condemned all internal tariffs, as well as the monopolies (of tobacco, for instance) that had been granted to the fermiers généraux. This little pamphlet, the Marquis thought, would serve a triple purpose: it would convince the public; it would convert the government; and, most important of all, it would get him an official American mission. Not only did he send his *Observations* to Congress and many of his influential American friends, but he let McHenry, his old associate, know that he would appreciate an appointment from the government of the United States. In this last purpose, his failure was total, but he did, in fact, help to change French policy. Armed with his new arguments, which happened to parallel those of the then-popular Physiocrats,* Calonne, Vergennes, and Castries convinced Louis XVI that a new policy was necessary; at the same time, the Marquis was spending a great deal of time at

---

*The Physiocrats were philosophers-economists who argued that the real wealth of nations lay in their agricultural production, not in the possession of gold; and they defended free trade since it opened new markets for wheat and other grains.

court, ingratiating himself with both King and Queen. Early in 1784, Calonne was able to promise that the four duty-free ports would soon be granted— except that Marseilles would retain a tobacco duty; and that the ferme générale, in its purchases of tobacco, would be instructed to give the United States preferential treatment. It was a major victory for the Marquis and, on May 3, 1784, Congress recorded "the high sense [it] entertains of his important services relative to the commerce of France and these United States."[23]

This was very gratifying, but La Fayette was not easily satisfied. Now he wanted more. All through the first half of 1784 he kept pestering Calonne. He asked to have Le Havre declared a duty-free port as well; he wanted the port fees canceled; he insisted it was time to abolish all internal tariffs; he complained that the ferme générale was buying Ukrainian tobacco. As Calonne pointed out, however, there was little he could do: not only were the port fees rather modest but they were also the perquisites of various official bodies who would scream if they were touched. At least the Finance Minister saw to it that the decree concerning the four duty-free ports was published on May 14.

La Fayette threw himself into this work with enthusiasm. With the end of the war, any cause of friction between La Fayette and the American envoys disappeared. Franklin, on December 25, 1783, could write happily to Robert Morris that "the Marquis de La Fayette . . . loves to be employed in our affairs, and is often very useful";[24] and back in America the Marquis's popularity was greater than ever. On October 2, the chevalier de La Luzerne was writing Vergennes that Pennsylvania had just named one of its counties after La Fayette, adding: "It is impossible to be more generally loved throughout the United States than M. le marquis de La Fayette."[25] As for Washington, he remained as much of a friend as ever; only now, lighter subjects crept into his correspondence. On October 30, for instance, he wrote his young friend and asked him to buy a set of silver plate; but soon there was a legacy of the war that threatened to cause trouble.

As soon as the hostilities had ceased, Congress had disbanded the army, much to Washington's and La Fayette's disgust. Its officers, loath to give up their wartime friendship, decided to form a society that would be open to any officer who had served for at least three years in or along with the Continental army. Since, like Cincinnatus (after having taken up the sword to defend their fatherland), they had "returned to the plow," they called their new organization the Society of the Cincinnati. Each member was to contribute the equivalent of a month's army pay, and would be entitled to wear a badge adorned with an eagle. Immediately every officer who was eligible, and a good many who were not, applied for membership. In France,

La Fayette was put in charge of admitting all the officers who had served in the American army, while Rochambeau did the same for those who had belonged to his expeditionary corps.

A host of problems promptly arose. First, there were applicants who had served less than the required three years, such as General Conway, the erstwhile plotter against Washington. After much correspondence between Paris and Mount Vernon, he was finally admitted. Then, it was forbidden to wear foreign orders in France, so La Fayette talked to Vergennes, who talked to the King, and, on December 18, the council gave the necessary approval.

After that, everything went wrong. The first meeting of the Order in France, to La Fayette's jealous rage, was convened by Rochambeau. The badge, some thought, looked ugly. Franklin, in fact, who thought the eagle an immoral bird, would have chosen that useful fowl, the turkey, and often said so. Rejected claimants set up an outcry.

Worse still, a great many Americans, and quite a few French led by that brilliant but amoral publicist the comte Honoré de Mirabeau, pointed out that the society's statutes were retrogressive and antirepublican because they included a heredity clause: the eldest male heirs of the original members were, in their turn, to become members as if by right. This, the critics thundered, was nothing less than the creation of a military aristocracy. Nothing could have been more embarrassing. La Fayette studiously avoided being drawn into the controversy by claiming everything was up to General Washington, that whatever the commander in chief decided was all right with him. In fact, at a general meeting, the heredity clause was dropped and the storm died away, but La Fayette, extremely touchy about matters of honor, no doubt remembered Mirabeau's attack, especially since it had also been directed at him.

Whatever the embarrassment, at least the society occupied his time, which was just as well: La Fayette was sorely in need of new projects now that the war was over. Luckily, the aimless marquis soon found himself another new enthusiasm, which demanded both credulity and lack of thought. In the winter of 1783, a charlatan from Austria named Mesmer became all the rage in Paris. His so-called discovery, animal magnetism, was supposed to be a mixture of cure-all and psychic inspiration: in fact, he seems to have chanced upon an early application of mass hypnotism. His method was as showy as it was simple. In the middle of a large dramatically lit room stood a big vat filled with water and pieces of metal from which rods protruded. In the next room a band played appropriate mood music. Once every rod had been grasped by a client, Mesmer, looking properly magnetic himself, would talk and watch as his patients fainted or went into convulsions, only to wake up refreshed and, they said, healthier. For an idle society with vague mystical longings in which fashion was everything, Mesmer was the perfect fad. Eventually, after some three years, he was declared a fraud by Dr. Joseph Guillotin, who is better known today for the machine he was just then inventing than for his exposure of Mesmer, and back to Austria he went; but in the meantime, La Fayette had become one of his most devoted adepts along with the princesse de Lamballe, Marie Antoinette's friend who was famous equally for the beauty of her fair hair and her utter stupidity. Like other members of the group of special adepts, the Marquis contributed some 2,400 livres to the Order of Harmony, and looked thoroughly foolish.

All through 1783, Washington had been asking his adopted son to come and visit him. On February 1, 1784, he did so again in a letter describing his new way of life. Until then, the tone of his correspondence had been businesslike; now a new elegiac tone crept into it, along with sentences of almost Proustian complication.

"At length, my dear Marquis," the General wrote, "I am become a private citizen on the banks of the Potomac, and under the shadow of my own Vine and my own Fig-tree, free from the bustle of a camp and the busy scenes of public life, I am solacing myself with those tranquil enjoyments of which the soldier who is ever in pursuit of fame, the Statesman whose watchful days and sleepless nights are spent in devising schemes to promote the welfare of his own, perhaps the ruin of other countries, as if this globe was insufficient for us all, and the courtier who is always watching the countenance of his Prince, in hopes of catching a gracious smile, can have very little conception. I am not only retired from all public employment, but am retiring within myself; and shall be able to view the solitary walk, and tread the paths of private life, with heartfelt satisfaction. Envious of none, I am determined to be pleased with all; and this, my dear friend, being the order for my march, I will move gently down the stream of life, until I sleep with my Fathers. . . .

"Come with Madame La Fayette and view me in my domestic walks. I have often told you and repeat it again, that no man could receive you in them with more friendship and affection than I should do."[26] On April 4, Washington wrote separately to Adrienne urging her to accompany her husband to America. In this, at least, he failed. Much as La Fayette may have loved his wife, she would only have been an encumbrance on a journey designed for the greater glory of America's marquis: La Fayette wanted no one to share the attention he craved. And so, on June 28, La Fayette, accompanied only by an aide, sailed to the United States for the third time.

From the evening of August 4 to that of December 21, La Fayette's

journey through eleven of the thirteen states consisted of one long, unin-
terrupted triumph. In New York, Philadelphia, Baltimore, Richmond, Yorktown, Providence, and Newport, to cite only the highlights, the Marquis
was greeted with parades, artillery salutes, speeches, banquets, and delirious
crowds. He addressed several state legislatures; he was awarded the degree
of doctor of laws by Harvard College; he was made a citizen of Maryland,
Virginia, Massachussetts, and given the Freedom of the City of New York;
he was offered countless toasts and endured countless speeches; and everywhere, always, there were crowds, crowds, crowds, cheering loudly and
long. This was a period when the United States seemed to be on the verge
of dissolution, when most Americans thought of themselves as citizens of
their sovereign states, not of the nation, and La Fayette was perhaps the
only real American: because he came from no particular state, he belonged
to all. He was the symbol of victory and the common effort. By cheering
the Marquis people cheered not only for the Hero of Two Worlds but for a
country as yet only dimly perceived. And La Fayette, who understood this,
spoke again and again in favor of a stronger union. "A Federal union . . . will
show to the greatest advantage the blessings of a free government,"[27] he
told the Pennsylvania legislature in early August, and on October 28, in
New Hampshire, he was saying, in a toast: "May we never withhold from
government the essential powers of doing good from jealous apprehension
of doing evil."[28]

That, in fact, was the keynote of his visit. It was becoming obvious that,
for lack of an effective federal government, the United States was fast sliding
toward financial ruin and political anarchy, that too little power was just as
bad as too much. "To avert these evils," Washington had written him as
early as April 1783, "to form a Constitution that will give consistency, stability
and dignity to the Union; and sufficient power to the great Council of the
Nation for general purposes is a duty which is incumbent upon every Man
who wishes well to his Country."[29] This subject was, no doubt, discussed at
length when La Fayette and Washington were joyfully reunited at Mount
Vernon on August 17. The General naturally showed Gilbert around the
estate, taking him for walks along the river and through the fields; and the
two once again shared the lengthy dinners that started at four and went on
until nearly midnight. Throughout this time, Martha Washington, although
actually present, seems to have made virtually no impression on La Fayette—perhaps she was too restrained and silent for his taste. The two men
did not lack for subjects of conversation, however, such as the settling of
the West, the policy to be adopted toward the Indians (harsh), the Spanish
prohibition of free navigation on the Mississippi (it was really a good thing,
Washington thought, as it would encourage the settlers to look north and

east), and, finally, a grand new scheme for linking the Potomac, the James, and, eventually, the Mississippi by a network of canals.

The visit was all too brief. On August 28, Washington was off on a long-projected visit to the West, and La Fayette went east; but for the young man there was one visit at least that promised not to be pure pleasure: the first Indian powwow with the new United States government that was to be held at Fort Schuyler, in upstate New York at the end of September. Because La Fayette was French and had developed such good relations with the Six Nations back in 1778, it was thought his presence would be helpful. The powwow had become necessary because the boundary between the United States and Canada ran through Indian territory, and the British still occupied some forts there, but also because the relations between the tribes and the white settlers needed mending—of late, the settlers had been under frequent attack. As things turned out, the Marquis's role was mostly ceremonial. The United States envoys arrived late, he did not know what their policy was or, therefore, what he was supposed to say, so he confined himself to generalities about cooperation and loyalty to the new nation. When the envoys did come, at their bidding he also urged the Indians to sell their land to the settlers, a policy he knew to be against the tribes' interest. At least, he was able to take an Indian boy back to Paris with him, much to the fascination of all his guests for the next few years. By 1790, the boy, who had received an excellent education, was sent back to the United States.

On his return to New York, La Fayette visited the Shaker community at Nishaguna where he witnessed what he took to be an example of natural magnetism, since the sect, like Mesmer's disciples, was much given to shaking and even convulsions. As a confirmation of Mesmer's methods, the Shakers' habits were very gratifying, especially since, a little earlier, La Fayette had had the pleasure of addressing the American Philosophical Society, of which he was a member, on the virtues of animal magnetism. When told about his friend's new mania, Washington seems to have remained unconvinced; there was little hysteria in the General. Perhaps Louis XVI had been right when he had asked the Marquis, at his farewell audience, "What will General Washington think when he learns you have become Mesmer's chief apothecary?"

Even if Washington thought his young friend sometimes silly, he no doubt kept it to himself, and certainly enjoyed both that first visit and a brief second one, from the twenty-second to the twenty-fourth of November. The two men must have discussed freeing the slaves; La Fayette, as he passed through Richmond, had intervened in favor of one of his spies during the war, who was always referred to as "the Negro James," more from the feeling of loyalty he always had toward his men than from his liberal principles. It took a little while for the Assembly to act, but James was actually and officially freed in 1786. And then the two friends separated again.

That the General was deeply affected by La Fayette's departure is certain. Although Martha Washington had had children by an earlier marriage, the General himself was childless, and while he was fond of his extended family, no one in it could begin to compare with Gilbert. Now, more than ever, the Frenchman was the son he had never had. Further, because he was highborn and rich, La Fayette appealed to a half-hidden side of the General's nature: this believer in democracy always remained an aristocrat at heart. The separation was therefore painful, all the more so, in fact, since Washington, for all his steadfastness, usually expected the worst to happen: partings, for him, were not temporary. This is what he wrote La Fayette from Mount Vernon on December 8. "In the moment of our separation, upon the road as I travelled, and every hour since, I have felt all that love, respect and attachment for you with which length of years, close connexion and your merits have inspired me. I often asked myself, as our carriages separated, whether that was the last sight I should have of you? And though I wished to say no, my fears answered yes. I called to mind the days of my youth and found they had long since fled to return no more; that I was descending the hill I had been 52 years climbing; and that, though I was blest with a good constitution, I was of a short lived family and might soon expect to be entombed in the mansion of my fathers. These thoughts darkened the shades, and gave a gloom to the picture, and consequently to my prospect of seeing you again. But I will not repine; I have had my day."[30] It is impossible to read this letter and not feel moved: evidently the General's talents were not limited to war and government. On the twenty-first, La Fayette answered, with considerably less style, but just as warm a feeling. "No, my beloved General, our late parting was not by any means a last interview. My whole soul revolts at the idea—and could I harbour it an instant, indeed, my dear General, it would make me miserable. I well see you will never go to France—the inexpressible pleasure of embracing you in my own house, of well coming you in a family where your name is adored, I do not much expect to experience—But to you, I shall return, and in the walls of Mount Vernon, we shall yet often speack of old times. . . . Adieu, adieu, my dear General, it is with inexpressible pain that I feel I am going to be severed from you by the Atlantick—every thing that admiration, respect, gratitude, friendship and filial love can inspire, is combined in my affectionate heart to devote me most tenderly to you."[31]

The Marquis had enjoyed his visit, not just because he had seen Washington, but because of the huge outpouring of popular love. "He . . . was received in triumph in all the cities and towns,"[32] La Fayette later wrote of himself, and it was true. Marbois, the French chargé d'affaires, reported to Vergennes on August 15: "The reception given by the magistrates [i.e., the officials] and the people to M. le marquis de La Fayette is surpassing anything that has been done before on this kind of occasion. No more has been done for General Washington himself, all the classes of the citizens are equally ardent in giving him the proof of their affection. Even the Pennsylvania legislature, now sitting, has sent a deputation to congratulate him. This extraordinary distinction has met with general approbation."[33] In fact, La Fayette's trip had produced a shared catharsis. It also enhanced his fame in Europe, where accounts of his reception were soon printed, and taught him, even more thoroughly than before, just how satisfying popularity can be: few rewards in life compare with those unstintingly given by an adoring crowd, and few are more addicting.

Once he returned to France, La Fayette again confronted a certain aimlessness. Of course, he immediately took up his position as chief helper of the United States, but even that was not quite enough. French politics offered no openings: people were beginning to assume that one day La Fayette would become one of the King's ministers, but that was obviously still some years in the future. Instead the Marquis took up a new cause, religious toleration; but since he was a good courtier, he felt he must tread cautiously.

Again, too, he took up his campaign to create duty-free ports in the West Indies. He taught himself as much as he could about trade and government finance so he would be able to argue convincingly and found himself, as a consequence, philosophically in close agreement with Necker. The former minister, that year, had published a little book, *De l'Administration des finances de la France*, advocating, among other things, free trade. It became immensely fashionable because it was aimed at the salons, whose denizens were blind to its technical faults. Although meant to prepare the return of M. Necker to the ministry, it failed. Three years would pass before Necker reached his goal, but, in the meantime, it brought La Fayette even closer to the Necker coterie.

The Marquis's most urgent goal, in 1785, was to dispel the coolness that resulted from the American traders' continued preference for doing business with England: old habits were not merely dying hard, they were not dying at all. To counter this trend, La Fayette worked hard to create opportunities in France for any American who had anything to sell. There was Mr. Boylston, for instance, and his spermaceti; General Greene and his lumber; and always the sore problem of the tobacco monopoly. The Marquis proved highly effective in all areas: Mr. Boylston was awarded a contract to furnish a large quantity of whale oil that would be used in streetlighting;

General Greene sold a great many oak planks to the French navy, whose minister was still the pro-American marquis de Castries. Tobacco, of course, was a tougher problem since it involved the ferme générale, but La Fayette fought on tirelessly.

It is wholly to La Fayette's credit that he used his unique position to help American trade: whale oil and tobacco, after all, are not subjects that usually have much appeal for a young general, and the Marquis still thought of his future career in military terms—but he understood the importance of commerce in linking nations and was anxious to see his cherished United States prosper. Jefferson, who came to Paris as the American minister in March 1785, testified to the help he received. "My duties at Paris were confined to a few objects," he wrote in his autobiography, "the receipts of whale oils, salted fish and salt meats on favourable terms; the admission of our rice on equal terms with that of Piedmont, Egypt and the Levant; the mitigation of the monopolies of our tobacco by the Farmers-General and a free admission of our production into their islands, were the principal commercial objects which required attention, and on these occasions, I was powerfully aided by all the influence and the energies of the Marquis de La Fayette, who proved himself equally zealous for the friendship and welfare of both nations." In 1824 he added: "I only held the nail, he drove it."[34]

On May 29, 1785, the Marquis was granted the much-coveted privilege of the grandes entrées at the King's lever. This meant that he was one of a small group of great aristocrats who surrounded the King the moment he rose in the morning and stayed with him until, fully dressed, he left his bedroom. This unique opportunity to speak directly to the otherwise inaccessible monarch was granted usually only to powerful dukes and certain special favorites. La Fayette had now joined this glamorous group.

To protect his position, therefore, La Fayette was exceptionally—and uncharacteristically—careful when he took up the Protestant cause. Ever since Louis XIV's Revocation of the Edict of Nantes in 1688, Roman Catholicism had been the only legal religion in France. Not only were the Protestants forbidden to hold services, even in the privacy of their homes, but they stood in constant danger of arrest and imprisonment; and since the church was in charge of all birth, marriage, and death registers, the Protestants had no legal existence at all. That, at the end of the eighteenth century, was an obviously grotesque situation, and, secretly, even the pious Louis XVI thought so; but change had become almost impossible at the end of the ancien régime, so the situation was allowed to continue. La Fayette's interest stemmed from his experience in America, where he had learned about religious toleration. Also he was, at best, a lukewarm Catholic. Even Adrienne, although intensely religious and a good Catholic, encouraged her husband in his new ideas. In June 1785 the Marquis traveled to the south of France, where most of the small Protestant population lived, and met the two key ministers, old Paul Rabaut and his son, Rabaut Saint-Etienne. To both he promised he would do everything he could to promote religious toleration.

Of course, La Fayette was not alone in his enterprise. Chrétien de Malesherbes, who had been Garde des Sceaux (Minister of Justice) in the late 1770s; Miromesnil, the current Garde des Sceaux; Louis de Breteuil, the Minister of the King's Household (and thus a very powerful man); Castries; and Vergennes, all were sympathetic but cautious. Still, it was an influential group, and one, furthermore, that could boast of having the King's ear. On the other hand, there was much opposition to any measure of toleration from the conservatives, the church itself and, within La Fayette's family, the elderly, autocratic and obeyed maréchale de Noailles, Adrienne's grandmother. La Fayette kept up his contacts with Rabaut Saint-Etienne, who soon came to Paris to consult with his protectors, and with all the pro-toleration group, but everyone decided to keep quiet at least a while longer for fear of unleashing a powerful Catholic reaction, especially since no one realized that Louis XVI was open to ideas of religious freedom. In fact, the whole topic seemed so explosive that when La Fayette wrote Washington to tell him about his new cause, he felt compelled to do so in cipher.

In the meantime, life had its pleasures. There was the courting of Mme de Simiane, soon to be rewarded with success, and the usual amounts of popular applause. On June 22, for instance, the Marquis, returning from his meetings with the Protestants, was given a hero's welcome by the city of Lyon, and a few days later, in Paris, he was sitting to Jean-Antoine Houdon for the bust commissioned by the Virginia legislature.

None of this was enough to satisfy the impatient marquis, however, and on July 9, leaving Adrienne behind as usual, he set off once again for Prussia; this time he would be pressing on into Austria. Months later, on February 6, 1786, he sat down and gave Washington a vivid account of his journey: "At Cassel," he wrote, "I saw our Hessian friends, old Knip among them [General Wilhelm Knyphausen had commanded the Hessian corps during the war]. I told them they were very fine fellows. They returned thanks and compliments—Ancient foes ever meet with pleasure, which, however, I should think must be greater on the side that fought a successfull cause— At Brunswick I got acquainted with the Duke . . . who is now arrived at the height of military knowledge, and of the confidence of the Prussian army, in which, altho' a sovereign, he acts as General. . . . To Potsdam I went to make my bow to the King [Frederick the Great], and notwithstanding what I had heard of him, could not help being struck by that dress and appearance of an old, broken, dirty Corporal, covered all over with Spanish snuff, with his head almost leaning on one shoulder and fingers quite distorted by the gout. But what surprised me much more is the fire, and sometimes the softness of the most beautiful eyes I ever saw, which give as charming an expression to his physiognomy as he can take a rough and threatening one at the head of his troops—I went to Silesia where he reviewed an army . . . of thirty thousand men. . . . For eight days I [had] dinners of three hours with him, when the conversation was at first confined pretty much to the Duke of York [one of George III's sons], the King and myself, and then to two or three more—which gave to me the opportunity to hear him throughout and to admire the vivacity of his wit, the endearing charms of his address and politeness, so far that I did conceive people could forget what a tyrannic, hard-hearted and selfish man he is—Lord Cornwallis being there, he took care to invite him at table to a seat by me, having the British King's son on the other side, and to make thousands questions on American affairs."[35] What La Fayette forgets to mention here is that, one evening, after he had explained at length and with some animation that the United States would always be free of both monarchy and aristocracy, Frederick II turned to him and said: "Sir, I once knew a young man who, having visited countries where liberty and equality were the rule, then decided to defend these principles in his own country. Do you know what happened to him?"

"No, Sire," the Marquis answered.

"Well, Sir," the King said with a smile, "he was hanged."[36] Evidently Old Fritz had lost none of that sardonic humor that had once delighted Voltaire.

"From Silesia," the Marquis continues, "I hastened on to Vienna where I only stayed a few days, had a very long conference with the Emperor [Joseph II], saw Generals [Gideon] Laudon and [Francis] Lacey, and my uncle the Ambassador [the marquis de Noailles] with Prince [Wenzel] Kaunitz, and after these objects were fulfilled, I posted off through Prague and Dresden to Potsdam, where troops were to make sham fights and every kind of warlike maneuvres—Had I stayed in Prussia, I might have gone often to the old King's who has been most peculiarly kind to me, but the very day I arrived at Potsdam, he fell sick and was near dying—The Maneuvres went on, however—and there I had new opportunities to know the Hereditary Prince of Prussia [Frederick William, Frederick II's nephew] who is a good officer, an honest man, a man of plain good sense but does not come up to the abilities of his two uncles—this second uncle Prince Henry [of Prussia] I have kept for the last because he is by far the best acquaintance I have made. . . . To abilities of the first rate, both as a soldier and as a politician— to a perfect literary knowledge, and all the endowments of the mind—he joins an honest heart, philanthropic feelings, and rational ideas on the Rights of Mankind."[37]

In fact, La Fayette, whose own literary culture was nil, was hardly able to judge Prince Henry's. As for the prince's amiability, it was due in all probability to a desire to annoy his brother, Frederick the Great, whom he had long bitterly resented. Once again, La Fayette was unable to see through appearances and was therefore completely taken in.

In Vienna, the Marquis had given great offense by making it very clear he found Prussia far more interesting. The marquis de Noailles had to explain, mendaciously, that the young man's quick visit—it only lasted a few days—was merely a preliminary to an extended stay the following year, and he put the best possible face on the situation in his report to Vergennes: "I went to court yesterday, M. le comte, to present the marquis de La Fayette to the Emperor. . . . The Emperor spent a long time questioning M. de La Fayette about his American campaigns. The conversation about the recent maneuvers in Silesia was not as extensive. The Emperor never mentioned it at all. M. de La Fayette is only here for a very few days; he must be back at the Potsdam maneuvers by the 20th of this month. It is not given to everyone to combine the most opposed elements [Austria and Prussia were bitter enemies] with as much wisdom as M. de La Fayette. He came from Berlin and will return there when he leaves here without having exactly aroused ill will."[38] Even so seasoned a diplomat as the marquis de Noailles was clearly using a compliment to conceal the Marquis's carelessness in nearly offending the Austrians, but in spite of that, La Fayette actually convinced Kaunitz, the chancellor, that the monarchy needed a treaty of commerce with the United States, and only the lack of interest displayed by the Americans caused the attempt to fail.

Even if La Fayette had not really learned much about the art of war in Prussia, thanks to "the good reception, and the flattering testimonies [La Fayette] had met from those crowns, staffs and other great personages,"[39] the journey added to his already large reputation in France. When in June 1786 Louis XVI went to Cherbourg for the inauguration of a new dike, La Fayette was one of the small party accompanying the monarch, the others being the ducs de Rohan-Chabot, de Liancourt, de Mortemart, de Guiche, and de Polignac; better yet, he was actually asked to travel back in the King's own carriage, clearly the height of favor. Naturally, people began to make assumptions; and when, later that month, he bought the estate, village, and feudal rights of Langeac, in the Auvergne, a purchase that the inhabitants had begged him to make some three years earlier and that cost him 188,000 livres, everyone thought they had put two and two together. La Fayette's plan, they said, was clear: he was working toward his elevation to the eminent status of a duke and peer of the realm. What other goal—aside from being made a marshal of France—could he possibly have?

In fact, they were quite wrong: La Fayette never even thought about becoming a duke. All through 1786, he had other plans. He resumed his efforts to improve the conditions of trade between France and the United States and, in September, received a tangible reward. Because he had convinced Calonne to lower the duties of imported whale oil, the inhabitants of Nantucket Island were once more able to earn a living, so "as a very feeble in truth, but sincere testimony of [their] affection and gratitude"[40] they all gave up one day's worth of milk, and sent their benefactor a 500-pound cheese. The La Fayettes owed this bounty, in fact, to the work of a new commission which had been set up at the Marquis's urging. Along with La Fayette, its twelve members included Calonne, Castries, Vergennes, Dupont de Nemours, and two fermiers généraux, and it proceeded to make major new steps toward a new commercial agreement between France and the United States.

La Fayette's involvement in these problems had a double consequence. First, he began to understand not only trade but government finance; second, he met a new group of people. Until then, the Marquis's friends had been either young noblemen like himself or American officers and politicians. Now he was introduced to what, today, we would call left-wing intellectuals, people like Condorcet and Jacques Brissot, freethinkers who could see much that needed changing in France. Soon, he began to understand that the tax system was grossly unfair; and putting that together with what he had learned about representative assemblies in the United States, he began to think that perhaps people ought not to be taxed without their consent, and also that it was wrong for the government to give huge pensions to already rich members of the upper class. In May he acted on his new beliefs. Ever since his father's death at Minden, he had been in receipt of a 720-livre pension from the Treasury: this he now publicly gave up. And in August, he bought a plantation in Martinique, La Belle Gabrielle, with its slaves so as to start on his great liberation experiment. The slaves were to be given training, then, gradually, freed. Adrienne shared enthusiastically in her husband's goals and, from the start, assumed a large part of the responsibility for the estate.

La Fayette's new friends admired his American successes and welcomed his understanding of constitutional government; they naturally made him even more famous because they were willing and able to write about him. Brissot, a lawyer, writer, and publicist, in his *De La France et Des Etats-Unis*, had this to say: "Let us now address to this young and generous Frenchman the homage of that humanitarian philosophy which has ever admired military exploits only when they further the goal of enhancing liberty, and with liberty the progress of mankind and reason. M. de La Fayette, by his courage, has helped the Americans to take their revenge; may he always with equal success continue these useful endeavors!"[41] Even a man less sensitive to praise than La Fayette would have been flattered. And since his achievements were linked with freedom—political in America, commercial and financial in France—he began, almost unconsciously, to equate being morally right with staying on the left.

Soon the fermiers généraux provided him with another lesson in the unfairness of the system. While most of France was subject to an extremely high tax on salt, a few provinces, for complicated historical reasons, were exempt—the Auvergne was one. In order to stop the smuggling going from the Auvergne into neighboring provinces, the ferme générale asked that it be allowed to control the salt supply there as well. The inhabitants protested, and so did La Fayette and his friends the Neckers. What would seem a minor incident was actually a significant challenge to the policies of the ancien régime, which, always starved for money, was bound with unbreakable chains to the ferme générale, the only body in France that could provide cash quickly when needed. Questioning this new, minor extension of its tax-collecting caused La Fayette to study the entire tax system.

In 1786, however, La Fayette's resistance to the salt monopoly looked to the government like a very familiar attitude: it was simply a lord protecting his people, who, after all, had complained of one imposition or another since the beginning of time; and so the Marquis continued in the King's favor. It was, in fact, probably due to his excellent standing at Versailles that he owed his inclusion in the *Assemblée des Notables.*

This gathering, announced by the King and Calonne in September 1786, was an innovation or, at any rate, a revival of a form of consultation so ancient as to have fallen into desuetude. The necessities it was supposed to address, on the other hand, were thoroughly modern. The Treasury had run out of money, the deficit rose ever higher; taxation, resting as it did on the poor, was already excruciatingly harsh; and while, in theory, the King was all powerful and could therefore modify the system if he pleased, the theory had stopped coinciding with reality. This was due in part to a general reaction against the autocratic government set up by Louis XIV: the aristocracy had been taking advantage of the King's weakness to regain both power and prerogatives, the middle classes felt unjustly ignored, and resented it; as for the peasants, they were reaching the end of their long patience. And besides these hostile interests, the parlements made sure the system became unworkable.

The eleven provincial parlements usually followed the lead given by the Parlement of Paris because all their members shared a common desire to extend their powers while remaining tax exempt. Although their members were actually supposed to be judges, not politicians, anyone with enough money could buy himself a seat. The parlements' main function had remained judicial: they were courts of law, whose judges received official bribes (the *épices*), relied on torture as part of the questioning process, and invariably favored their own kind. Their only claim to a political role came from a technicality. Before any of the King's edicts became law, it had to be entered into the parlements' registers, which, in the absence of any formal code of laws, served as a legal and constitutional record. Naturally, some of the edicts were controversial, and the parlements had the traditional right of presenting "remonstrances," pointing out the faults of the new legislation to the King. According to custom, this was to be done only *after* the edict had been registered. If the King then found the remonstrances to be justified, he could modify his earlier decision, but all through the eighteenth century, the parlements had been reaching for greater powers. By the 1740s, they were remonstrating first and refusing to register unless forced to do so by the King in a solemn ceremony called a *lit de justice.** Soon, they refused to register even when a lit de justice was held. This represented nothing less than a transfer of the legislative power from the King to the Parlement, and Louis XV, who understood this, was finally driven, in 1771, to abolish the rebellious institution. When he died three years later, his successor, Louis XVI, in a moment of typical weakness, reinstated the parlements, carefully specifying, however, that remonstrances must never precede or impede registration.

Within the month that reservation had become a dead letter. Because their members were rich, and ex officio noble (that is, tax exempt), the parlements were actually the most reactionary of institutions, intent on preserving their own feudal privileges. But since it appeared to the misled populace that they alone dared stand up to the all-powerful King and because they refused to register any new tax laws, they acquired immense popularity. The truth of the matter was, of course, that the new taxes would have fallen far more heavily on the rich than on the poor, but it is always easy to sway public opinion by announcing virtuously that the government is spending too much and that taxes must be cut. As a result, the efforts made repeatedly by Louis XVI and his ministers to reform the system came to naught. By

---

*A plenary session of the Parlement, presided over by the King in person, and at which, in theory, obedience was compulsory.

1786, the system had reached a state of paralysis. France was the richest country in Europe, yet its government was on the verge of bankruptcy.

In convening the Assembly of Notables, Calonne and the King attempted to bypass the Parlement: since the notables would be far more representative than the parlements, Calonne hoped that their decisions would be so popular as to force registration, despite Parlement objections. At first, La Fayette's name was not among the 144 members, but he protested vigorously to Calonne and, although the King thought him a little too young, his name was put on the list in place of that of the marquis de Noailles.

The upper classes were, just then, determined to resist the loss of their privileges, while demanding a greater voice in government, and cloaked their fight for continued privilege in words about liberty and despotism borrowed from the *philosophes* of the Enlightenment. It was therefore extremely difficult for Calonne to find anyone to support the moderate reforms he was advocating. A popular story had it that the owner of a parrot who could say "Long live the King" had been told to hide her bird. "Why?" she asked. "Because if you don't, Calonne will make him a notable," came the answer.

La Fayette, it was generally thought, would do as he was told by Calonne: he was, after all, a Noailles, or as good as one; he had been an assiduous courtier; he had no experience other than the military and knew how to take orders. Even La Fayette's best friend concurred in this estimate. Thomas Jefferson, whom Gilbert had first known in the United States during the war, was now one of the American envoys in Paris, and, as such, even more closely linked with the Marquis. And since governments and their constitutions were among his many interests—architecture, wine, and women came next—he watched the new political developments in France with acute interest. Not even Jefferson, however, understood La Fayette: he expected the Marquis to support the government and be asked, eventually, to join it, although he added a by now familiar warning note. "His foible is a canine appetite for popularity and fame," he wrote James Madison on January 30, 1787.

Popularity was something Calonne no longer enjoyed. Except for Louis XVI, who was notoriously weak and changeable, no one much liked Calonne's policies anymore. On the right, the Queen had seen with dismay her favorite minister join the long list of statesmen who felt a measure of reform was absolutely necessary; on the left, the liberals distrusted Calonne as a reactionary who merely pretended to believe in reform so as to raise taxes; and almost everyone resented the spendthrift way in which he had been managing the Treasury. As for the Parlement, it was naturally furious since it was temporarily superseded by the notables. It might have seemed possible, therefore, that La Fayette would join the ranks of the minister's enemies, but, because people at Versailles still thought in terms of royal favors and court positions and had yet to realize that public opinion was a mighty power, it seemed probable, on the whole, that the Marquis would follow Calonne.

He was one of a very small group of nobles to be given a coveted apartment within the Palace of Versailles for the duration of the Assembly, and the fact that he was placed in the second commission (there were seven in all) seemed significant: its president was to be the comte d'Artois, the King's youngest brother and possibly the most reactionary person at court. But La Fayette had known Artois since the faraway days of the riding academy; it seemed reasonable for Calonne to expect that La Fayette would respectfully support Artois's position and Artois, in turn, would uphold the policies of his brother, the King. In 1784 the Marquis had been given the Order of Saint Louis, the highest military decoration in France. Now it seemed likely that if he behaved he would be raised to a dukedom at the close of the Assembly.

Seven

THE PEOPLE'S GENERAL

The year 1787, in which so many other changes took place, opened with the death of Vergennes. It was a great loss—for France, for the King, whose chief minister he had actually become, and for La Fayette. The only immediate effect of the death was a brief postponement of the notables' meeting but, on February 22, the first session was opened by Louis XVI with all the pomp and ceremony inseparable from the King's person during the ancien régime. The etiquette to be followed that day was so complex and so detailed that it filled an entire book. After all, it was not merely a question of who was to sit where or of when to sit and stand. Even the proper costumes were defined in great detail: the nobles, for instance (as distinct from the clergy or the Third Estate),* were required to wear large plumes on their hats and long cloaks that, however, must not be the same dark blue as those belonging to the ceremonies of the Order of the Saint Esprit.

---

*The Third Estate included everyone who was not a member of the First Estate (clergy) or the Second Estate (nobility)—some 98 percent of the population.

After the King opened the Assembly, Calonne now, to all intents and purposes, the head of the ministry, delivered himself of an enormously long speech and eight weighty reports that it took him several days simply to read. The gist of his position was simple: after all the explanations about government finance and foreign trade he was proposing a rationalization of the tax system. Instead of relying on complex and disparate impositions from which the nobility and clergy were practically exempt, with some "noble" land not being taxed even if its owner was a commoner, there would be a universal, equal land tax to be paid by all landowners at the same flat rate, and partly in commodities. While this plan may seem regressive to us because, proportionately, the rich paid no more than the poor, at the time in France, Calonne's proposal was no less than revolutionary. If he had his way, both the nobility and the clergy would pay up like the lowliest peasant. There could be no cheating since land could not be hidden; France was still a preindustrial, agricultural society in which land was the main source of wealth. At long last, the rich would help to finance the state. This was a direct attack on the most powerful groups in France, and they were not likely to give up their privileges of their free will, especially in order to reinforce the King's government. By 1787, it was obvious that change could come only through the Treasury's desperate need for additional income. The conservatives wanted to recoup the power lost by the aristocracy to Louis XIII and Louis XIV; the liberals wanted a representative government. Simplifying the tax system to make it more productive, therefore, was the very last thing most notables wanted.

After Calonne's presentation, the assembly divided itself into seven bureaux, or committees. La Fayette's bureau was charged by Calonne with reporting on the *taille* (the personal income tax paid by members of the Third Estate), the *corvée* (a feudal obligation of peasants to work for at least a week a year building roads), and the circulation of wheat and other grains. In short order, the bureau recommended lowering the taille, abolishing the corvée, and freeing the grain trade from all internal custom duties and prohibitions. Appearances notwithstanding, this was not really a liberal move: it simply resulted from the age-old resistance to any kind of tax and made the Treasury's plight even more desperate, thus weakening the government, while at the same time it earned the bureau some easy popularity. After that, the bureau took up an old idea of Necker's: the establishment of provincial assemblies who would provide the government every year with complaints and suggestions, and allocate the rate of tax payments within the province. This, it must be clear, in no way implied that the assemblies could approve (or even discuss) the nature or amount of the taxes: they were merely to decide which part of the province was to pay what. Immediately, the bureau started discussing how these new assemblies were to be elected; whether, like the old Estates-General,* they were to consist of three separate estates, each having one vote, or whether there was to be one single meeting with each deputy having one vote; and whether the Third Estate was to have the same number of deputies as the other estates, or double the amount. Voting by estates meant that clergy and nobility could combine to stop all progress; doubling the representation of the Third Estate meant that it would equal the two other estates, and thus have real power. La Fayette, who now remembered that he believed in a representative government, argued for a yet more democratic solution—one meeting with simple majority vote—because it more closely resembled the American system. The reactionary comte d'Artois, who presided over the bureau, wanted the estates to have only one vote each. The discussion never had a chance to become acrimonious, though, since on March 12, Calonne called a general meeting of the notables and, firmly ignoring everything the bureaux had done so far, came out with a whole new series of proposals for them to discuss. Even to so unrepresentative an assembly this was an intolerable insult because it confirmed their earlier suspicions: the notables had been assembled as a sort of window dressing. They were to approve blindly whatever projects Calonne chose to send them instead of really expressing the country's opinion. Furious at seeing that their deliberations were ignored, and that they, themselves, were taken for granted, the bureaux immediately met and sent a protest to the King.

So far, La Fayette, if anything, had seemed to line up with the ministry. After all, he owed his very presence in the notables to Calonne's friendship, and he joined with the minister in favoring freer trade; besides, he was an assiduous courtier, and the King liked him. In 1787, it still seemed unthinkable that anyone would jeopardize his future when it all depended on the King's goodwill; and since, at the moment, Louis XVI was backing Calonne, it seemed obvious that La Fayette would follow the monarch's lead. Indeed, in his bureau's deliberations, he had seemed to do so, especially regarding trade and taxes. He still believed that both the King and his minister wanted true reform and had a "patriotic," that is, liberal view, as we can see clearly in a letter he wrote to Washington on January 13: "You easily conceive that there is at bottom a desire to make monney . . . on account of the sums squandered on courtiers and other superfluities— But there was no way

---

*The Estates-General had met at irregular intervals ever since the thirteenth century, at the King's behest, to help solve the crisis of the moment; they were a last vestige of the medieval notion of consensus government, and had been dormant for some 150 years.

more patriotic, more candid, more noble to effect those purpose—The King and M. de Calonne deserve great credit for that—and I hope a tribute of gratitude and good will shall reward this popular measure."[1] So, from the south of France, where he was traveling, Jefferson wrote the Marquis on February 28, recommending the English constitution as the model to be imitated and adding: "If every advance is to be purchased by filling the royal coffers with gold, it will be gold well employed. The King, who means so well, should be encouraged to repeat these Assemblies."[2] In fact, La Fayette, aside from his ties to the ministry and his belief in Louis XVI's good intentions, was laboring under two added burdens. The first was a bout of pulmonary disease, probably tuberculosis, which was to continue afflicting him, on and off, for the next two years; the other, his distaste for what he was beginning to perceive as the reactionary views of the opposition aristocracy. Curiously, although the Revolution was now only two years in the future, the main attack on the regime came not from the left or the oppressed lower classes but from those privileged orders that sought to extend their privileges still further. As a result, the land tax never had a chance: neither the nobility nor the clergy had any intention of bearing the weight of taxation; and so La Fayette, because he didn't share in those attitudes, looked like a government patsy.

Early in March, the Marquis also had another good reason to keep quiet. The comte de Simiane had just committed suicide, presumably over his wife's well-publicized affair with La Fayette. This extreme behavior hardly seemed rational to the dissolute society of the 1780s, so it was generally assumed that the count had somehow gone mad; still, there had been an embarrassing moment.

Luckily for Gilbert, however, Mme de Simiane, who cared nothing for her late husband, was in no mood to discontinue their affair: far from harming her position at court, it made her all the more fashionable and brought her in touch with all the great issues of the day. Since current salon gossip now concerned politics more than sex, La Fayette was the perfect lover; and one cannot help feeling that this mattered more to her than Gilbert's skill—or lack of it—in bed. In all probability, she thought of the Marquis as a future prime minister, and being his mistress would then give her an unassailable position at court; so, promptly forgetting her late husband's lack of manners, she continued to encourage him.

It is no doubt thanks to Adélaide's encouragement that, on March 28, Gilbert felt able to stake out a new political position for himself. Boldly separating himself from the ministry, he read a memorandum on the abolition of the salt tax and, while he was at it, he asked for the liberation of all the galley slaves who owed their term at hard labor to their evasion of the tax.

The salt tax was one of the Treasury's major sources of income, and the galley slaves were considered essential to the manning of France's Mediterranean navy—so opposing these institutions amounted to a declaration of war on the government. At one blow, La Fayette had recovered his political status: no longer a ministerial toady, he was clearly, instead, a force to be reckoned with, for he spoke with the authority of the Hero of Two Worlds. At the same time, Calonne was beginning to realize that the tame gathering he had so carefully composed had become a hotbed of opposition, and he now asked the King to dismiss the notables who were studiously ignoring all his proposals. Louis XVI, on his side, had been watching the proceedings with growing dismay. Calonne had promised him a docile assembly that could be counted on to approve all necessary taxes; instead, he found himself faced with ever stronger attacks on the ministry. Unwilling to face the outcry sure to follow upon a dissolution of the notables, the King, inaugurating a long series of cave-ins, decided to dismiss Calonne in the hopes of thus buying the Assembly's cooperation. What happened can be gathered from a letter La Fayette sent to Washington on May 5: "The moment we entered into the business [of taxation], the less possible it was for the ministry to do without us. To the Assembly the public looked up, and had the Assembly been dismissed [Calonne's] credit was gone. As we were going to separate for the Easter days, I made a motion to enquire into bargains by which, under pretense of exchanges, millions had been lavished upon princes and favourites. The Bishop of Langres seconded my motion. It was thought proper to intimidate us and the King's brother told us in His Majesty's name that such motions ought to be signed. Upon which I signed the inclosed.

"M. de Calonne went up to the King to ask I should be confined to the Bastille. . . . I was getting the proofs of what I had advanced when Calonne was overthrown from his post and so our dispute ended."[3]

The "exchanges" La Fayette speaks about concerned the King's domain. These were a new practice, according to which the King and various great nobles would exchange estates, but recently, the land the King had been receiving had been very much less valuable than what he was giving up. The royal couple's most cherished prerogative was their ability lavishly to recompense people they liked for nonexistent services to the state. After the outcry raised by the huge amount of the courtier pensions listed in Necker's published budget in 1781, it had become politically difficult to keep handing out large sums to undeserving aristocrats; so, instead of pensions, land, in the form of exchanges, went to selected favorites because the Queen insisted on being as generous—some said wasteful—as ever. As the capital value of the King's domain shrank, so did the income derived from it; and that shortfall had to be made up through taxes. It is easy, therefore, to see why La Fayette objected to these exchanges, but he had chosen to attack the most sensitive of issues—one that personally involved the King and Queen.

Marie Antoinette's friends, especially the coterie gathered around her beloved duchesse de Polignac, were outraged; the Queen automatically took up their defense; and the King, as usual, listened to his wife. When, further, the Marquis said that "those many millions abandoned to depredations and cupidity are the product of the people's sweat, tears and perhaps even blood,"[4] the comte d'Artois was genuinely horrified. Not only had La Fayette brought up a taboo subject, but he had done so in a way that simply wasn't polite, since it was a thinly veiled attack on people they all knew. Even the unintelligent Artois eventually came to realize that it was the entire political and financial structure of the monarchy that La Fayette now boldly criticized. The King was just as appalled as Artois and, like many weak people, nursed his resentments.

Luckily for La Fayette, who would otherwise would have been moldering in the Bastille, not only was Calonne dismissed but the King replaced him with Loménie de Brienne, the Archbishop of Toulouse, who had also been part of Artois's bureau and was on very friendly terms with the Marquis. He described the new minister, in fact, as "a man of the most upright honesty and shining abilities,"[5] thereby letting his enthusiasm get the better of his judgment. Brienne, as it happened, was an arch-intriguer who, in short order, demonstrated his complete lack of capacity.

Now that Calonne was gone, the notables continued to sit; soon, at their request, Louis XVI decided upon the establishment of provincial assemblies, "not to vote the taxes, but to divide them,"[6] as La Fayette wrote Washington. It was a step toward liberalism, as was the King's consideration of a motion, adopted by Artois's bureau at La Fayette's suggestion, that the penal laws against the Protestants be abolished. Then, the comte d'Artois asked his bureau to suggest ways to reduce the national deficit, now that Calonne's solutions were dead. At that, La Fayette stood up to ask that the rich be taxed and the poor given help, and went on to add that since, within five years, the current contracts with the ferme générale would expire, the King ought to call a "National Assembly" to vote the new taxes. This was virtually lèse majesté because it implied a limitation on the monarch's absolute powers. After a dreadful silence, the disbelieving comte d'Artois asked: "What, monsieur, you are asking for the convocation of the Estates-General?"

"Yes, monseigneur," La Fayette replied, "and even better than that."

"You actually want me to write down and say to the King, M. de La Fayette is making a motion to call the Estates-General?"

"Yes, monseigneur," La Fayette answered coolly.[7] It was an incredibly bold demand to make. The Estates-General had last met in 1614, and it was generally considered that the autocratic system set up by Richelieu and then Louis XIV precluded their ever being called again. Even this, however, was not enough for the bold marquis. By saying "better than that" he was implying that he wanted a real parliament, not a gathering divided into estates where the clergy and nobility could always outvote the Third Estate. In fact, he was the first man in France to use the term "National Assembly."

This time, La Fayette had really made himself persona non grata at court and among the conservative nobility. Questioning the property exchanges had been bad enough, but now it was the King's actual authority, and not his ministers' failings, that the Marquis had attacked. Well intentioned as he was, Louis XVI had no doubts at all about the preservation of his God-given autocracy. By suggesting it was time to curb it, La Fayette had committed an unforgivable sin. And the Marquis, though well aware of his offense, no longer thought it mattered. "The spirit of liberty," he reported to Washington on August 3, "is prevailing in this country at a great rate. Liberal ideas are cantering about from one end of the Kingdom to another. Our Assembly of Notables was a fine thing. . . . You know the personal quarell I had respecting some gifts made to favorites at the expense of the public. It has given me a great number of powerful and inveterate enemies. I have since that period presented some opinions of mine in very plain terms. I can't say I am on a very favorable footing at Court, if by Court you understand the King, Queen and King's brothers, but am very friendly with the present administration. . . . The King's council is better composed than it has ever been."[8] Indeed, Brienne, in a typically thoughtless move, promptly gave the Marquis a proof of his friendship—and of the fact that he had discounted the young man's attacks—by putting him on the list of the new members for the provincial Assembly of the Auvergne. He did so although at the closing of the recent session of the Assembly of Notables, the Marquis, when it was too late to do anything about his demands, had asked for universal taxation, elected provincial assemblies, economies of at least 40 million livres, the end of all provincial custom duties and, worst of all, the publication of the budget and the list of pensions.

Exciting though they were, however, these new developments were still not enough to fill La Fayette's days, although he did complain to Washington about being overworked. He still found time to prove his continuing pro-American feelings by pursuing the new Finance Minister about the regulations Calonne had prepared, but never issued, regarding trade with America; time to attend the Neckers' salon and talk there with their daughter, Mme de Staël, about the new politics; time to see Mme de Simiane, lovelier

and more fascinating than ever; time, even, to be amiable to the visitors at
the hôtel de La Fayette. Xavier de Schoenberg, a young man of nineteen,
described the atmosphere there. "We went to M. de La Fayette's house.
. . . Today, he embraced me and received me beautifully. . . . I felt as if I
were in America rather than in Paris. He had a quantity of English and
American visitors, for he speaks English as if it were his mother tongue. He
has an American savage dressed in his native costume . . . who only calls
him Father. Everything in the house breathes an air of simplicity. Marmontel
and the Abbé Morellet [leading intellectuals] were dining there. Even his
daughters speak both English and French although they are still very young.
They were playing in English and laughing with all the Americans and would
have made an admirable subject for an English engraving. I admired the
simplicity of so distinguished a young man when so many people, who have
not done anything, are as vain as he is natural."[9]

The "simplicity," of course, was not as spontaneous as it looked. Ever
since the beginning of his American adventures, La Fayette had been con-
sciously building the image of himself most likely to impress the public—
that of the young hero whose modesty is as great as his achievements. And
while anyone who knew him well could see the fevered ambition hidden
beneath the apparent selflessness, to the world at large it looked as if La
Fayette wanted only to help others. This illusion was strengthened by two
highly unusual characteristics: the Marquis, far from needing or wanting
money, was always willing to spend it freely for whatever cause he was
involved in—always a good way of putting himself forward—and while he
longed for honors, recognition, and popularity, he really was not as interested
in power itself as in having the appearance of possessing it. Becoming one
of Louis XVI's ministers held very little temptation for him; he was far more
anxious to ensure the triumph of his new, liberal ideas, especially since then
he could hope to humble the King without having to shoulder any of the
responsibilities of government. And he could indulge his craving for popularity without a bad conscience since, after all, he was working for the
benefit of mankind, and not for what most people would consider selfish
purposes.

Still, there had been a switch, during the Assembly of Notables. Ambition or no, La Fayette had, until then, been a conscientious courtier, a
friend of the Queen's and, if not an actual conservative, a man who was
perfectly willing to work within the system. Why, then, the sudden change?
Partly, no doubt, because his new acquaintances—Condorcet, Brissot, Morellet—had strongly reinforced what the Marquis had begun learning in the
United States, so that he began to have real notions about what a constitutional government actually meant; partly because, by 1787, France had

clearly entered a major crisis from which some changes were likely to emerge, and he could see a role for himself that would bring new popularity and fame, along with that delicious feeling of being right; and finally, most importantly, because he had solved the problem he had been faced with ever since the end of the war, that of being aimless, of lacking a goal. Not only would the Marquis now model himself after Washington but he would actually *become* Washington. Like the General, he would give his country free institutions; like him, he would retire from the cares of state as soon as his goal had been achieved. No longer would La Fayette need to ask himself what Washington would have done in a similar situation; he would actually be the French Washington.

La Fayette's attempt was admirable in many ways. As an aristocrat, he stood to lose a good deal of money from any thoroughgoing reform; he had deliberately given up royal favor, and many of his relatives were angered and horrified by his position. But, where Washington had finally been successful because of his quick and close contact with reality and his willingness to forgo, temporarily at least, popularity and recognition, La Fayette, who needed constant approval, was a bad judge of both men and events. Since his new principles, like Plato's ideas, existed outside of time and space, he had to decide how they were to be applied to the government of France in 1787, a problem that, in the end, he found almost impossible to solve. He knew, for instance, that a republic was the best possible form of political organization, but even in the United States, at this time, it was not working very well. In France, a much more populous country with an ancient monarchy, it was, he realized, a clear impossibility; so he looked, instead, to an English-style constitutional system. But France lacked a parliamentary and constitutional history with its traditional protection for the liberties of the subject, as well as an open aristocracy constantly replenished by the upper-middle class that helped to define the balance between the crown and the English people. Clearly, France would have to develop its own, idiosyncratic institutions; and this was where confusion set in. Still, at the beginning at least, there were some obvious goals: religious toleration, no taxation without representation, and no spending of public funds on grasping favorites would do admirably as first steps.

La Fayette's demands notwithstanding, neither King nor ministers so much as considered, in the summer of 1787, the possibility of calling a National Assembly or even a meeting of the Estates-General, but the provincial assemblies might provide something of a substitute. No one thought, yet, that their members should be elected. Instead, the King nominated the President and half the participants; that half then met and nominated the second half; even when complete, the Assembly's powers were strictly limited. The assemblies would act as a release valve while remaining unable to challenge the royal autocrat.

The first meeting of the provincial Assembly of the Auvergne lasted a week only, from the fourteenth to the twenty-first of August, and was held, in theory, for the sole purpose of selecting its other members. However, partly at La Fayette's instigation and with his warmest encouragement, the Assembly addressed a protest to the King: recalling the province's ancient but almost forgotten right to have its own estates decide on the amount and form of the taxes to be paid: "As we receive with happiness a form of administration which is as desired as it is advantageous, we hope that the rules which have been announced will give our zeal a free course, and our assemblies the proper dignity; we take the liberty of observing that our province was one of the last to exert its rights to hold meetings of its Estates. . . . We think it mandatory to beg Your Majesty that you deign to declare to our province that you do not mean, as we ourselves do not, these new rules to infringe upon the ancient and ineradicable rights of the Auvergne."[10]

"The Law is what I say it is," Louis XV had told the Parlement of Paris in 1766, and, according to constitutional usage, he was right. Now, the Assembly was telling Louis XVI that two centuries of royal supremacy were to be annulled. Paradoxically, the Assembly, while boldly affronting the King, was doing so not in the name of liberty (a newfangled notion) but in that of its ancient privileges. Far from being a revolutionary act, the Assembly's protest seemed to be, in fact, the purest reaction, a return to a time when the central government had not yet become absolute. Still, La Fayette was pleased.

Here, at least, was a beginning. The people—actually, in this case, the nobility—were taking a first step to a French Magna Carta; and even though the Third Estate was still very much the least powerful section of the Assembly, it, too, asserted its right to be heard. "Many abuses may be destroyed, liberal principles be adopted and a great deal of good be done," the Marquis wrote Jefferson from Chavaniac on August 27, adding, with obvious surprise: "There is in the tiers-état more dignity than you perhaps imagine, and although they are not well disposed towards the new Nobles, there is a very good understanding between the ancient Noblesse and the last order."[11] Unwittingly, La Fayette was pointing out the very class division that helped ensure the paralysis of the existing system. The "new nobles" were rich, upper-middle-class men who had gained their status because they belonged to a parlement, and when they bought some ruined noble's estate, as was often the case, they revived every forgotten feudal right, to the peasants' great dismay. They loathed the old nobility because only true aristocrats were allowed at court. While at this stage La Fayette would have been perfectly happy to see the King's powers curbed by a strong, liberal aristocracy, something like the English oligarchy, such a development in France was impossible because the nobility was composed of two different and warring elements.

At the same time, change was obviously on the way. On October 9, La Fayette sent Washington a long analysis of the situation, and even to this less than acute observer, some things were just too plain to ignore.

"The affairs of France," he wrote, "are still in an unsettled situation. A large deficiency is to be filled up with taxes and the Nation are tired to pay what they have not voted." Then, after a description of the King's current dispute with the Parlement de Paris over taxation and the comte d'Artois's general unpopularity, he went on: "The Provincial Assembl[ies] have held their first meeting. Regulations were given to them by the King. Whereby they were intirely submitted to His Majesty's intendants* in each province. We made loud complaints and the regulations are mending. You see that the King is often obliged to step back, and yet the people at large are unsatisfied. So great is the discontent that the Queen dares not come to Paris for fear of being ill received."[12] La Fayette was right in perceiving, this early, that the King could be made to give in, but he completely failed to see what this implied, that royal power had largely become an appearance. It was in fact not the King who needed to be pushed so much as the two privileged orders, since the clergy and the nobility, far more than the bewildered Louis XVI, had blocked all reforms during the Assembly of Notables.

The Marquis had estranged himself from the King and Queen by his behavior at both assemblies, but since he was still on friendly terms with Brienne, he had yet to feel the monarch's displeasure. His popularity was greater than ever, as his triumphal reception when he passed through the little Auvergne town of Aurillac early in September, for instance, abundantly proved. It might have been America all over again: there were banquets, a ball, receptions, and much popular acclaim. La Fayette seemed more interested in the loudness of the applause than the actual state of the province, but local observers noted that, much to the chagrin of the ladies at the ball in Aurillac, he spent the entire evening talking instead of dancing.

Although it now supplied La Fayette with a new, overriding goal, reform was hardly a full-time occupation for a military man. And, indeed, a golden

---

*The intendants were the central government's direct and all-powerful representatives in the provinces. Submission to the intendants meant submission to the King.

opportunity for glory seemed to present itself when the Dutch republic went
to war in 1787. The Princess of Orange was the wife of the stathouder* of
the Netherlands and the sister of the new King of Prussia, Frederick William
II, whom La Fayette had met at Potsdam. She had just been briefly placed
under arrest by the Dutch for plotting to alter the Dutch constitution, making
the nation into a monarchy. Although she was quickly released, the King of
Prussia considered that his honor was at stake, and in short order, he invaded
Holland. The new French Foreign Minister, Montmorin, was well aware
that the bankrupt government in France was in no state to support a war,
and so, to La Fayette's disgust, he decided to remain neutral but only after
hinting that he might well intervene on the side of the Dutch. Since the
Netherlands needed a commander in chief for their army, the Marquis let
it be known he would be happy to oblige; he even started north but was
stopped by news that the Dutch had chosen someone else. It was just as
well, really, since the army of the Netherlands was a joke: in no time at all,
the Prussians were in Amsterdam and the war was over. But La Fayette,
whose belief in his own military talents was highly unrealistic, still regretted
the lost appointment, convinced that under his leadership the Dutch army
could have beaten the Prussians. Because Holland was a republic—actually,
an oligarchy—La Fayette also felt for it the special kind of sympathy he
usually reserved for the United States, and thus was all the more upset to
see it lose the war; in the end, however, Holland remained a republic.

Once again, the Marquis had been willing to leave France for a possibility of personal advancement and greater fame: it mattered very little to
him where he commanded as long as he could distinguish himself further;
given the chance, he would have dropped his French position without a
second thought. He was so restless, in fact, that, at the very moment he
hoped to be called upon by the Dutch, he was busy developing a scheme
for the conquest of North Africa through a landing in Egypt.

The Egyptian project died a natural death, but in France itself, the
system was breaking down a little more every day. At the beginning of the
summer the Parlement of Paris had refused to register the new taxes that
Brienne wanted. The King held a lit de justice in which he came in person
to the Parlement and ordered it to register his edicts. In a break with
precedent, Parlement refused; the King ordered many of its members exiled
to the provinces. Then, in the autumn, a compromise was reached, and one
of the three new taxes was registered. It was at this point that the Protestant

---

*The *stathouder* was a hereditary ruler who served only at the pleasure of the States-
general, the legislature; his was a position of honor rather than power.

agitator, Rabaut Saint-Etienne, returned to Paris and warned La Fayette
that he would wait no longer for reform from above. Now he would circulate
a petition. La Fayette passed on the information to Brienne, who evidently
felt he did not need another kind of turmoil. On November 19, the King
issued an edict returning legal existence to the Protestants, while still forbidding them to hold ceremonies in public. Despite the restrictions, this
was obviously major progress, and La Fayette could, with justice, claim a
good part of the credit for it. Of course, the Parlement, true to its reactionary
beliefs, refused to register the edict because it still considered the Protestants
as heretics ripe for extermination, but eventually the Enlightenment prevailed, and there was such an outcry in Paris that it finally did its duty. By
the end of January 1788 the edict was law.

In the meantime, the Auvergne provincial Assembly, whose August
session had been purely technical except for the address to the King, met
again; and on November 8, La Fayette joined the rest of the deputies. Each
deputy now had one vote and since the Third Estate had twice as many
members as either the clergy or the nobility, there could be little doubt
that it would prevail. La Fayette was elected to the Welfare, Agriculture,
and Commerce Committee, and then the Assembly resumed the anticen-
tralist attitudes it had adopted in its earlier session.

As its first order of business, it promptly confirmed its August resolution,
which had never officially been presented to His Majesty, but now would
be, because the earlier Assembly was not empowered to do anything more
than co-opt the missing half of its membership. Then, on its own initiative,
it decided to elect a Committee of the Twentieth, and put La Fayette on it
as well. The "twentieth" in question was the new tax, one of three that the
King had just convinced the Parlement to register, calling for payment of a
twentieth (5 percent) of everyone's income—a definite step toward tax reform. Without actually refusing to pay the tax, the committee, led by La
Fayette, objected to the tax because it had not been approved by a representative body and framed a resolution decrying its "exorbitant calculation."
The deputies pointed out that while the province had been assessed for
2,038,000 livres, it was too poor to pay more than 1,298,493 livres. This was
in direct defiance of the King: rather than merely distributing the tax, the
Assembly was attempting to determine its amount. Further, while still using
thoroughly respectful language, the deputies called on the "justice of Your
Majesty and the protection of the laws." Now, in France, the King's will
was law: by claiming the "protection of the laws," therefore, as if the law
were somehow distinct from the King, the Assembly was taking a revolutionary stance. To make matters worse, the resolution claimed that the
Assembly was unable to raise the taxes without all the taxpayers' consent.

Bold stuff from Auvergne, but events were speeding up in other parts of the country as well. In Paris, on November 19, Louis XVI went to the Parlement and asked it to register a loan edict; in exchange, he promised that before the end of the five-year period during which the loan would be floated, he would call the Estates-General. Apparently still in his reforming mood, he then sent the Assembly of the Auvergne a message asking it to work on a fairer distribution of the tax burden; the improvement or creation of roads, canals, and grain silos; the adoption of modern methods of growing crops and looking after livestock; and he appealed to rich landlords to set an example for the poor, and conservative, farmers. While these recommendations seemed to represent advanced liberal thinking, however, they were nothing of the kind. The King was willing enough to have a more rational system of production, a more prosperous peasantry, and a tax system that yielded more taxes, but only as long as his power remained unchallenged. As soon as he realized that the Assembly was making political demands, he reacted. Two days later, on December 6, another royal message was read to the Assembly: not only did it set an adjournment date for December 10, but Louis XVI rebuked the disobedient deputies in no uncertain terms. "The Assembly had gone beyond the functions the King had allowed it to discharge under his authority and it must now work with more care and measure on justifying his confidence,"[13] the declaration said. Clearly, the ministry had understood exactly what the Auvergne was doing: it had denied the government the funds the Treasury needed so desperately, thus claiming to itself the very first privilege of any parliament—that of refusing money.

Instead of promptly complying with the King's order, the Assembly, more shockingly still, persisted in its claims. On December 10, it sent the King an answer that, though written in the most respectful style, was an act of open defiance. "[The Assembly's] only consolation in its sorrow is that each of its members . . . has listened only to the voice of his conscience. A better distribution [of the tax] would undoubtedly help the unlawfully taxed contributors [that is, everyone, since there had been no consent to taxation] . . . but [the Assembly] could not feel that the aggravation of the tax made this possible."[14] The Assembly was thus telling the King, first, that the tax was so heavy that it made all fair assessment impossible, and second, that his actions were illegal. It then adjourned without setting a collection schedule. This was no longer mere disrespect but open rebellion.

Curiously, the French aristocracy was almost alone in underestimating the gravity of the situation. The English Revolution, which had ended with the beheading of Charles I, had started with a refusal of funds. On April 28, 1788, a worried Washington wrote La Fayette: "I hope the affairs of France

are gradually sliding into a better state. Good effects may, and I trust will
ensue without any public convulsion."[15] In Paris, Jefferson, who was watching events carefully, now fully expected serious trouble—and soon.

La Fayette, however, perceived none of this. "The disposition of the
people," he wrote Washington on January 1, 1788, "are working themselves
into a great degree of fermentation, but not without a mixture of levity and
love of ease. . . . I am heartily wishing for a constitution and a Bill of Rights
and wish it may be effected with as much tranquillity and mutual satisfaction
as possible."[16] Since the King would never willingly temper his absolute
power, the clergy and nobility would not give up their privileges, and the
people were increasingly dissatisfied, it is a little difficult to see how La
Fayette's wish was to be achieved. The Marquis, however, continued on his
usual rounds. On December 29, the new trade regulations were at last issued.
In the first months of 1788, La Fayette became worried because De Kalb's
son had applied to become a member of the Society of the Cincinnati, thus
raising once again the specter of heredity; in the end an exception was made
and the young man was admitted. Then, since so little seemed to be happening, La Fayette decided to devote himself to his philanthropic interests:
he tried to improve conditions on his estates but dealt only with his bailiff.
Rents were readjusted in certain cases, some of the feudal dues (for the use
of the mills, for instance) were allowed to lapse, and provision was made for
anyone who was likely to starve. He also gave 12,000 livres to a Paris hospital
and, along with Adrienne, joined the French Society of the Friends of the
Negro, which was founded by Brissot and Etienne Clavière in order to bring
about the emancipation of all black slaves. In March 1788 he decided he
might as well go back to the army, and on April 1, he was given an infantry
corps in the Languedoc-Roussillon commanded by the duc d'Ayen. He saw
no reason to stay in Paris, for he felt sure the government would not call
the Estates-General before the summer of 1792, although he hoped the
pressure of public opinion might bring it about as early as mid-1789.

These peaceful prospects were abruptly shattered in April 1788 when
Brienne, in a fit of exceptional and misplaced honesty, decided to publish
the budget. Of course, it showed an enormous deficit. Since the Treasury
had been functioning on the proceeds of loans obtained from both financiers
and the public, and the news of the deficit scared all the lenders away, the
crisis was grave and immediate. Once again the King found himself forced
to take action. The parlements were still refusing to register any new taxes
beyond the Twentieth, so he decided to replace them with a plenary court
that would be forced by law to register all financial edicts without remonstrances. On May 8, 1788, Louis XVI held a lit de justice and compelled
the Parlement of Paris to register its own dissolution. La Fayette was out-

raged—all the more so since, as he wrote to Washington on May 25, "The people in general have no inclination to go to extremities. Liberty or Death isn't the motto on this side of the Atlantic."

At least now the Marquis felt he could break with Brienne and the ministry, which he did, while rejoicing publicly in the fact that many of the people appointed to the new plenary court were refusing to serve. All such stirrings were minor, however. The real beginning of the Revolution came to La Fayette from Brittany, where he owned several large estates; but at the time the news seemed so unimportant that the Marquis gave it just one sentence in the postscript of his May 15 letter: "I have just received an official communication of a resolve signed by more than three hundred gentlemen of the order of Noblesse in Brittany *declaring it infamous* to accept a place in the new Administration—to which I very plainly have given my assent."[17]

It is not, perhaps, the least of the paradoxes that were to mark the French Revolution that it was begun by a group of reactionary aristocrats in the very province that later fought a civil war rather than accept the Republic. Brittany had become French in the late fifteenth century by the marriage of its duchess, Anne, to the King of France. Ever since then it had considered itself an independent duchy that just happened to share its sovereign with its neighbor; and its parlement, always the focus of resistance to the central government, was considered indispensable to the liberties of the province. When, therefore, Louis XVI abolished all parlements, the nobles, who could see taxation coming their way, simply rebelled. Since La Fayette was a Breton landlord, he was asked to join the movement.

Annoyed though it was, until then the court had treated him with great moderation, but this time the Marquis had gone too far. La Fayette compounded the court's displeasure when he also contrived to insult the Queen. The French, almost as xenophobic then as now, held Marie Antoinette's Austrian origins against her, especially because she was well known to have retained all her Austrian sympathies. She was now called *l'Autrichienne* in the streets of Paris, an epithet of the most virulent hatred. Shortly after signing the Breton manifesto, La Fayette went to Versailles, where the Queen told him she had been surprised to hear of his involvement, since she had always thought he was from the Auvergne. "Why, Madame," the Marquis answered, "I am as Breton as you are Austrian." Ostensibly, he was only reminding the Queen that his mother's family came from Brittany; in effect, he was flinging an insult in her face. As for the Breton protest, the King simply refused to receive it so, he said, that he wouldn't have to punish the signatories, but since La Fayette had made himself so conspic-uous, Louis XVI did manifest his displeasure by withdrawing his letters of service as a maréchal de camp. For the second time, the Marquis's military career had come to an end.

This rebuke had no effect on either La Fayette's stand or the disorders in Brittany. As Rennes, the capital of the province, was taken over by the rebellious aristocracy and the parlement continued to sit, Louis XVI resorted to wrist slapping; he had inaugurated the policy he would stick to until the end, that of punishing just enough to irritate, without actually frightening anyone. The King's council gave orders on July 5 that research be started into the history of the Estates-General: since they had not met in 175 years, no one quite knew how they worked anymore. It immediately became obvious that this was a delaying tactic since the research was expected to take months, and possibly years; as a result, the disorders that the promise was supposed to appease simply grew worse, while available funds remained impossibly low. On August 8, the King signed a decree convoking the estates; on September 23, the date of the first meeting was set for May 1, 1789. Meanwhile, the plenary courts were suspended and the parlements reinstated. Almost by accident, Louis XVI had blundered into the most liberal measure possible.

The liberals' victory became more satisfying still when Brienne was fired on August 26, because the Treasury was empty. Necker acceded to the ministry. It was generally, albeit erroneously, agreed that the new minister was a financial genius, so Louis XVI assumed that he would find money, while the liberals, who knew Necker was opposed to the Queen's squandering ways, expected immediate reform. For years now, Mme Necker and her daughter, Mme de Staël, had presided over one of the most successful salons in Paris. They were accustomed to molding public opinion, so they explained that the crisis had been solved: Necker would reduce the deficit, the Estates-General would create a constitutional monarchy, and all would be for the best in the best of all possible worlds.

Only, things were not so easy. One of Brienne's last acts had been to declare a semibankruptcy: the King's debts were halved with a stroke of a pen. This infuriated La Fayette, who, having become reconciled with Brienne on August 8, had been going around guaranteeing there would be no diminution of the debt; once again he broke with Brienne. Of course, even Necker's accession to the ministry failed to provoke miracles. All the lenders who had just been scalded were now doubly shy, and the financial crisis remained as pressing as ever. And now an incredibly thorny question suddenly arose about the way the Estates-General were to be composed—in 1614, each estate had one vote and an equal number of deputies, which meant the votes would be totaled within each estate, then the three of them would cast a single vote apiece in the final balloting. Since there was a conservative majority within the clergy (First Estate) and the nobility (Second Estate), that meant their two votes would always overpower the Third Estate's single vote. But there was another possibility, a new, more democratic way: each deputy would have one vote, and the Third Estate would have as many deputies as the two other orders combined. Thus, the liberal minorities in the clergy and the nobility could combine their votes with those of Third Estate deputies and reach a majority. On September 9, La Fayette visited Necker, who advocated an easy way out: he would ask the Parlement to decide on the shape of the Estates-General. "It is believed M. Necker will manage until then by working miracles thanks to his talent and the public's confidence," La Fayette wrote Mme de Simiane, on whom he depended more than ever for advice, adding, "You are worried about my situation at court. Here it is: M. de Calonne has thrust me out of his circle and the Archbishop of Sens [Brienne] is displeased with me; these two powers have been mutually attacking the other, but both agree as much as you like that I am wrong. My justification can never come out of these circles, nor can my conscience fit into them."[18] In fact, the lines were drawn. Calonne and Brienne now joined the absolutist group, which also included the comte d'Artois and the Queen, while Necker and La Fayette were at the forefront of a liberal group that also numbered two of La Fayette's adversaries: the duc d'Orléans, formerly the duc de Chartres, Mme d'Hunolstein's lover from before the American war, who had succeeded to his father's title; and, most surprisingly, the comte de Provence, he of the supposedly faultless memory.

Even before Necker's new measures began to prove inadequate, however, La Fayette received a cautionary letter. From the remote shores of the United States, Washington saw the situation more clearly than did the Marquis in Paris, and he proceeded to give the best of advice. "I like not much the situation of affairs in France," he wrote. "The bold demands of the Parliaments, and the decisive tone of the King show that but little more irritation would be necessary to blow up the spar of discontent into a flame, that might not easily be quenched. If I were to advise, I would say that great moderation should be used on both sides. Let it not, my dear Marquis, be considered as a derogation, from the good opinion that I entertain of your prudence, when I caution you, as an individual desirous of signalizing yourself in the cause of your country and freedom, against running into extremes and prejudicing your cause." He went on to hope for "a gradual and tacit Revolution, much in favour of the subject by abolishing lettres de cachet and defining more accurately the powers of the government."[19] The oracle had spoken, and La Fayette listened. For a few months, while remaining a steadfast liberal, he sought a course that would result in a representative government, but only in slow and easy steps.

If, however, he now became far less conspicuous, it was not simply because of his newfound prudence, but because an old lung problem was acting up again. As the Marquis lay in bed being periodically bled, the Parlement, now reassembled, at last showed its true colors by taking a firm stand in favor of constituting the Estates-General as they had been in 1614. At last the supposedly "populist" body had shown where its true interests lay, and the result was an immediate loss of popularity. Since Necker genuinely wanted reform as the only way out of the financial crisis, he advised the King to call back the notables, who would advise him on what to do. Not surprisingly, they came to the same conclusions as the Parlement. Except that now, with petitions circulating in favor of doubling of the Third Estate, one of which La Fayette signed, a few young, liberal *conseillers* in the Parlement, the so-called Americans,* pushed through a new resolution that the conservative majority, appalled at its loss of popularity, reluctantly swallowed. In deliberately confused language, the Parlement now expressed its confidence "in the King's wisdom to decide upon the measures necessary to effect the changes that Reason, Liberty, Justice, and public opinion may demand." It was hardly very bold. but it gave the King, who was still controlled by Necker, the opening he needed. On December 27, evading the question of how voting was to proceed within the Estates-General, Louis XVI edicted the doubling of the deputies in the Third Estate.

Almost immediately, it was time for the elections, which took place according to the various local traditions, after which the deputies of each estate were to hold meetings and come up with a list of grievances. In December, La Fayette, who as a noble had the choice of being elected by the nobility or by the Third Estate, decided to stay within his order. More evidence of his moderation could be seen in the letter he wrote Rabaut Saint-Etienne in early January. Louis XVI, he noted, had earned "the gratitude, affection and confidence" of his people, but then he added, "It is in fact this certainty of the King's justice and goodness that confirms me in the idea that the best of monarchs cannot achieve good without the support of the Nation."[20] A constitution, he pointed out, would provide that support. Even so temperate a stand, however, was by no means popular among the nobility of the Auvergne, as the Marquis soon found out. By March 8, he

---

*People's attitudes to America had become the litmus test of their political convictions. To be called an American meant that one was a liberal.

was writing to Mme de Simiane to complain, "There is nothing but division and jealousy here between the orders, the localities and the individuals. I have had the disadvantage of an audience that was partial, full of preventions and prepared against my opinions. Already some noblemen among my friends have warned me that, if I were to compromise, I would surely be elected but not otherwise. I answered I was there to convince, not to flatter. The Third Estate wants to go far, and that is a chance of gaining some fame for myself; but I have preached moderation at the risk of displeasing."

Even though he was actually elected in the balloting later that month, the Marquis was hardly out of trouble, since the electors proceeded to instruct the deputies. "I think I will undo the deliberation by separate orders by posing a few great English and American principles. They have added a sentence which spoils everything. . . . They have put down [in the instructions to the deputies] 'the plurality of the *votes of the Nobility*' but I had already resigned once so that they would withdraw certain conditions they had attached to the abandonment of the privileges. . . . I therefore decided to sacrifice myself especially because everybody knows that the Third Estate daily offers to elect me, I cannot therefore not be suspected of selfish motives [in not resigning again.]"[21] Very confused; La Fayette must have remembered his American problems with the several legislatures—it certainly looked as if he had difficulty in handling deliberative assemblies. The only result of all his argumentation was that he had had to agree to three principles he actually abhorred, and was committed to vote for them at the Estates-General: the first was that all voting was to be by estate; the second that the nobility's privileges were to be defended; and the third that, as a deputy, he would vote according to his constituents' instructions. And even then, he had only received 198 votes out of a possible 393. It was a very unhappy deputy indeed who returned to Paris on April 11.

The Estates-General were to open on May 5, and since the several parties—reactionaries, constitutional monarchists, pure constitutionalists, Orléanists—firmly intended to prevail, the rest of April was a period of intense activity for La Fayette. He held endless meetings with other liberal nobles, with people such as the Abbé Emmanuel Sieyès, who, though a churchman, was resolved to provide a constitution for a new regime, and with the other members of the Club of the Thirties, a gathering of liberals. He was, in fact, always racing around Paris, attending conference after conference. Gouverneur Morris, freshly installed in Paris, recorded in his diary one attempt after the other to see him; he sometimes found Adrienne at home, but the Marquis never.

Frantic though he had become, La Fayette at least knew what he wanted. He had had a good many discussions with his new friends about reform over the preceding four years, and, more important still, the United States had just given itself a new constitution. This was the subject of much correspondence with Washington, and many discourses with Jefferson, in the course of which the Marquis received virtually an education in constitutional law.

From the day the war ended, Washington had been saying that the new nation could not survive without a more perfect union and a more effective federal government. It was a view that La Fayette himself had repeatedly endorsed throughout his American trip in 1784, and the progressive breakdown of the economy, the currency, and, finally, civil peace proved them both right. "The pressure of the public voice was so loud, I could not resist the call to a convention of the States which is to determine whether we are to have a government of respectability under which life, liberty and property will be secured to us,"[22] Washington had written the Marquis on June 6, 1787. When the Constitution was finally ready for approval by the states, the General had let La Fayette know that he was fully satisfied with it.

By then, La Fayette felt he had become a competent judge, although perhaps one with a favorable prejudice. "I have admired [the proposed Constitution]," he wrote back on January 1, 1788, "and find it is a bold, large and solid frame for the Confederation. The electioneering principles in regard to the two houses of Congress are most happily calculated. I am only afraid of two things—1st the want of a Declaration of Rights 2dly the great powers and possible continuance of the President. . . . Should my observation be well founded, I am still easy on two accounts. The first that a Bill of Rights may be made if wished for by the people before they accept the Constitution, my other comfort is that you cannot refuse being elected President."[23] In one respect, of course, La Fayette was quite right, and the Constitution was soon amended to include a Bill of Rights. What mattered, however, was that a few key principles had been established: the necessity of elected assemblies; the separation of powers; a system of checks and balances that prevented any branch of the new government from dominating the others; and a system of elections in which the upper house was kept at one remove from the voters. The Senate, with its minimum age requirement and selection by the state legislatures, could, everyone agreed, be counted on to restrain the violent but ephemeral passions of the people as expressed in the House of Representatives.

As for the powers of the President and his ability to seek an indefinite number of four-year terms, which La Fayette found so alarming, that, clearly, was no example to follow: Louis XVI, after all, was no Washington, and could not be expected to step down. But then again, France was not the

United States and while he wanted to preserve the spirit of the American Constitution, La Fayette realized that a number of major modifications would have to be made. For one thing, virtually no one, in 1789, thought that France should become a republic, and La Fayette least of all, so the King must be given a role. On the other hand, it was expected that he would always try to behave in an absolutist manner, so his powers must be severely curbed. If La Fayette had his way, the King was likely to end up practically impotent, and anarchy was all too likely to replace despotism.

Then there was the vexing question of the veto. The King of England could refuse his assent to an Act of Parliament, but no sovereign had done so since Queen Anne. The President of the United States had a conditional veto that could be overriden by a two-thirds majority in both houses of Congress. What should the King of France have? An absolute veto, a conditional veto, or no veto at all?

The question of the legislature must also be settled. The existence of an elected representative body was at the very core of La Fayette's notion of a free constitution; but how was it to be organized? Should there be a Senate elected by other legislative bodies? Should there be a House of Lords, as in England? While he wasn't quite sure about the veto, La Fayette at least knew he wanted no upper house: the principle of heredity was anti-democratic, the notion of a Senate seemed unnecessary; so there would be the King, to whom a carefully controlled executive power would be assigned; a unicameral legislature to make the laws and vote the budget; and, somehow, an independent judiciary and a jury system. All this, however, depended on two basic ideas: the affirmation of the primacy of the nation over the King, expressed by the electorate,* and the winning of a Bill of Rights.

Early in January 1789 La Fayette sat down and wrote out his Declaration of Rights. He then showed it to Jefferson, who declared it was excellent and asked for a copy to send to Madison. This document embodies precisely what La Fayette meant when he spoke of a free government, and, having set down its principles, he defended them for the rest of his life. These were:

1. Nature has made men free and equal; any distinction necessary to the social order is founded on its utility.
2. Every man is born with inalienable and ineradicable rights: such as

---

*There was no question of universal suffrage, however. The voters were to be chosen among the people paying a minimum yearly sum in taxes. In Paris, for instance, where the population was 750,000, that meant 50,000 voters. And no one at all thought that women ought to have the vote.

the freedom of all opinions; the care for his honor and his life; the right to own property; the full and free disposition of his person, of his industry, and of all his faculties; the communication of all his thoughts by all possible means; the quest for happiness and the resistance to oppression.

3. The only limitations on these natural rights are those which ensure their enjoyment by the other members of the society.
4. No man may be forced to obey laws other than those he or his representatives have consented to, after they have been promulgated and only if they are legally enforced.
5. Sovereignty resides in the people. No body, no individual shall have any authority that is not expressly derived from this.
6. All government has the common welfare as its goal. In consequence, the executive, legislative, and judiciary powers must be separate and fully defined; their organization must ensure the free representation of the citizens, the responsibility of the executive agents, and the impartiality of the judges.
7. The laws must be clear and precise and must apply to all citizens.
8. The expenditure of public money must be the result of the people's free consent and must be equally supported by all.
9. And since the introduction of abuses and the rights of future generations necessitate the revision of all human establishments, it must be possible to have in certain cases an extraordinary meeting of deputies whose sole object will be to look into, and correct if need be, the shortcomings of the constitution.[24]

Life, liberty, and the pursuit of happiness: La Fayette had learned it all in America, and while his style does not rival Jefferson's, his nine principles would transform a feudal, absolute monarchy into a free constitutional state, while always providing a standard against which governments could be measured. The declaration was not original, but it was solid, and it deserved to end up in the empty frame that awaited it in the Marquis's study.

Of course, La Fayette had every intention of offering his declaration to the Estates-General when they met, but, in the meantime, there was much work to be done. It was just at the beginning of the year that he started to correspond with the comte de Latour-Maubourg, one of the liberal young noblemen who formed his circle. Like most of them, César de Latour-Maubourg had gone to America, fought for liberty, and returned to France with a whole new outlook. He and La Fayette found themselves in close political agreement. It was to Maubourg that the Marquis had written that very confused letter from the Auvergne about the instructions he was being made to swallow; and when it looked as if the duc de Polignac, the husband of Marie Antoinette's beloved friend, might ensure Maubourg's defeat in the election, La Fayette wrote him page after page of advice, while calling on all his other friends to turn out and help. It worked. Maubourg was elected and became one of the two people with whom La Fayette, that spring, felt he could be completely open.

The other, of course, was Mme de Simiane. More beautiful, more fashionable than ever, Adélaide believed in Gilbert's future; that they were still lovers seems certain, but they hardly could meet very often. The countess had duties at court while La Fayette was plunged neck-deep into politics. And while his letters to her deal mostly with current developments, they do usually end with an assurance that he loves her as ardently as ever. Adélaide, however, although she undoubtedly loved La Fayette in her cool way, hardly found herself in political agreement with him: she belonged to the reactionary court party and had no inclination toward either reform or liberty.

La Fayette's letters to Maubourg were dashed off hastily; as a result, they are never dated, but their content gives a very strong clue as to when they must have been written. In April, for instance, the Marquis was defending himself against the accusation that he was behind the unrest evident everywhere, and most particularly in Paris. There, from October 1788 on, riots on a varying scale kept occurring. They were due partly to the steadily rising price of bread, partly to the political events. In December 1788, La Fayette had joined the more forward-looking elements in the city when a controversy arose over the mode of election to the Estates-General. Back in 1614, the deputies of Paris had been chosen by its officials; now the liberals wanted them to be elected directly by the people (the 50,000, that is, whose means qualified them). La Fayette, of course, defended the newer method and it was adopted. In return, his enemies at court, all those who had been jealous of him for so long, took their revenge by blaming him for inciting the riots.

Such accusations were outright lies. "People must be mad if they imagine, and really abominable if they say that just a few days before the Estates-General the very man who was the first to ask for them, who has never moved a step but to conciliate nobility and Third Estate, now has the infamous project of creating disorder and violence when we have before us a chance of achieving freedom and happiness in the quietest way possible,"[25] La Fayette complained to Maubourg in mid-April. Friend of the people though he was, La Fayette always kept his taste for order. Not only was the Marquis convinced that the Estates-General would be able to carry out the necessary reforms peacefully and easily, but he also thought that any serious disruption was likely to end the incipient revolution. The King, if sufficiently provoked, would call in the army, crush the rebellion, cancel the Estates-General, and return to his autocratic ways.

Although La Fayette always claimed he acted from the most selfless of motives, he had other good reasons to deplore the riots in Paris. Far from being the spontaneous uprising of an angered people, they were mostly the carefully planned creations of the Orléans faction. Ever since La Fayette had first lost Aglaé d'Hunolstein to the then duc de Chartres, and later taken her away from him, the two men had been on less than friendly terms. Further, the duc d'Orléans was the perfect example of everything La Fayette detested. This prince of the blood royal* was probably also the richest man in France; his yearly income hovered around 3 million livres; but far from using this huge fortune on good works, he squandered it through a course of debauchery spectacular even by eighteenth-century standards. It was not just that he gambled for enormous amounts and spent vast sums on the racehorses he had imported from England; he was also a dandy who gave his clothes endless thought, and aside from having a wife and an official mistress whom he appointed governess to his children, he also presided at mass orgies where the women were cheap prostitutes picked up from the streets of Paris. Finally, he was said to be a coward; he had certainly panicked during the only battle, a naval one, at which he had ever been present. For some time he had been financing both street disorders and the pamphlets of a few violently antiroyalist extremists. It was not, appearances to the contrary, that he was anxious to establish a constitutional government; rather, urged by moderate revolutionaries like Mirabeau and with the example of the English Revolution of 1688 firmly in mind, he thought that if he created enough upheaval and confusion, he would be able to replace Louis XVI on the throne. That, of course, was the very last thing that La Fayette wanted; and already in May he was writing Maubourg a letter in which, as he deplored the differences between the "friends of liberty," he fixed the blame firmly on the duc d'Orléans's plots.[26]

It was thus in a troubled atmosphere that, on May 5, 1789, the Estates-General were finally opened. The ceremony itself was the last of the grand displays of the ancien régime. The King (who was applauded), the Queen (who was hissed), the court, and the members of the Estates-General marched in procession to the Church of Saint Louis with troops on display, flags waving, and music playing. Louis XVI and Marie Antoinette wore sumptuous

---

*His great-great-grandfather, the first duke, had been Louis XIV's brother.

costumes and were covered with gold and diamonds; then came the clergy, the cardinals in red, the bishops in purple, all dripping with precious lace; they were followed by the aristocracy, wearing embroidered silk or velvet and plumed hats; and all the way at the back marched the Third Estate, dressed in black wool and plain hats. The costumes, like the order of the procession, answered to the dictates of the undying etiquette. After hearing Mass, everyone marched back to a hall installed in the palace, with steps, a throne, and draperies at one end. The Third Estate stood while the other orders sat and listened to the King's opening speech, which was much applauded. Then after the King had left, everyone sat to hear an endless, confusing exposition by M. Necker on the financial state of the country. It was more than five hours long and a masterpiece of confusion; as a result, the minister's reputation began to sink rapidly.

From the first day it became obvious that only difficulties lay ahead. Many of the Third Estate deputies had come from their provinces in a suspicious frame of mind. As they saw Versailles for the first time, they were shocked by its splendors—even if they never did find that room with diamond and emerald walls supposedly installed by Marie Antoinette at the Petit Trianon. Now they could see where all the money had gone, why there was such a deficit; and they were urged on by people such as the Abbé Sieyès, already pondering the first of the many constitutions he would author; Mirabeau, passionate lover, and covered with debts, but one of the great orators of his time; and the duc d'Orléans's friends. A solid majority of the nobility, however, though ready and willing to rebel against a king infringing on their privileges, were hardly about to join with the lower orders and topple the whole edifice. The clergy, for its part, was deeply divided between a group of priests who hated the rich and powerful bishops, and the bishops, almost all of whom came from the great noble families and who felt exactly like their relatives of the nobility. The inevitable result was immediate stagnation: the Third Estate asked that all orders verify the powers of the deputies (that is, whether they had been properly elected) together. The other two orders would not hear of it since that implied a vote by headcount, not by estate. And so the first of a series of confrontations was on the way.

High above the fray sat a supposedly benevolent arbiter, but poor Louis XVI, who was indecisiveness personified, lacked the courage of his convictions and quickly allowed the nobility and clergy, whom he favored, to become less and less powerful. As for the Third Estate, it wavered between cheering the King—everyone knew he was well intentioned, after all—and being deeply suspicious of what he, and especially the Queen, might do to thwart the coming changes. The comte d'Artois, whose weakness was a spectacular lack of intellectual capacity, now led a group of reactionary aristocrats, but since he was the King's brother, he might convince him to withhold all concessions. On the other hand, the comte de Provence had taken up a liberal position; but everyone knew that his real ambition was to replace his dim-witted brother on the throne. While everyone argued over the deputies' power, Paris was seething; the price of bread was rising rapidly, a classic cause for riot; men stood up in public and demanded an end to the régime; while in the provinces, the peasants not only stopped paying rents and feudal dues, but, in some cases, burned down the chateaux. All in all, it is a little hard to understand why anybody should have thought that France was on the brink of a Golden Age, but in fact, that was exactly the opinion current in the liberal, aristocratic salons frequented by La Fayette. At Mme de Tessé's in Versailles, or at Mme Necker's in Paris, open-minded and generous noblemen met with intellectuals, economists, lawyers, and pretty women, and all agreed that the Revolution would be over by the autumn, after which the country would enter an era of unprecedented peace, prosperity, and contentment. Perhaps it helped that these gatherings took place in some of the most beautiful rooms ever created, that the pretty women were dressed in the height of a very becoming fashion, that life was quite as sweet as it had ever been: it was impossible for these charmed, privileged creatures to imagine anything going seriously wrong, even if they did forgo that special legal status they now all abhorred. They felt all the safer that, even before the showdown, the villains (no drama would be complete without them) were as good as vanquished: after all, neither Marie Antoinette nor the comte d'Artois was a very formidable adversary. And yet . . .

And yet, everything was going wrong from the very first day of the Estates-General, and for none more than La Fayette. After the Third Estate had asked for the verification in common, the nobility listened to a speech of La Fayette's in favor, then massively voted against the move. Indications could hardly have been clearer: the Marquis was sitting with the wrong order. The very next day, Jefferson wrote him a letter of advice. "As it becomes more and more possible that the Nobles will go wrong," he said, "I become uneasy for you. Your principles are decidedly with the Third Estate and your instructions against them. A complaisance to the latter on some occasions, and an adherence to the former on others, may give an appearance of trimming between the two parties, which may lose you both. You will, in the end, go over wholly to the Third Estate, because it will be impossible for you to live in a constant sacrifice of your own sentiments to the prejudice of the Noblesse. But you would be received by the Third Estate at any future day, coldly and without confidence. This appears to me the moment to take at once that honest and manly stand with them which your own principles dictate. This will win their hearts for ever, be approved by the world, which marks and honors the man of the people, and will be an eternal consolation to yourself."[27]

Jefferson was right, but La Fayette, at this point, was scared. Within a few days, he was writing Maubourg about the possibility of a revolt in Paris, which he thought would be a catastrophe because "one must not play games with a population as numerous as that of Paris where the slightest disturbance can go further than people think. We will content ourselves, I hope, with a protest . . . and will exert our rights by making up a little text embodying our constitutional principles. . . . It is really the summit of folly or wickedness to risk the slightest disturbance. . . . [As for the regulations separating the three estates] I have always thought we should obey them under protest, and not think yet about the reunion of the three orders."[28] These might almost have been the words of Louis XVI, who had, in fact, forbidden the reunion. For the moment it looked as if La Fayette, reluctantly and "under protest," was lining up with the conservatives.

The question of "reunion" was as simple as it was crucial: if the three orders voted separately, then conservatives would always win the day. The three orders, he announced, would meet separately but, on the other hand, he would propose a series of reforms. It took no great acuity to guess that the reforms in question were not likely to limit the King's powers.

These developments left La Fayette in an almost untenable position, as Jefferson had predicted. He disagreed with what the nobility was doing, but was afraid of pressing for violent change. He could see that the Third Estate was beginning to make a revolution all by itself, but he was precluded from helping by the instructions to which he had bound himself in the spring. By early June, La Fayette hoped, implausibly, that Louis XVI might solve his dilemma by proposing some form of constitutional order; and Jefferson again sent the Marquis some advice. "Revolving further in my mind the idea of the King's coming forward . . . and offering a charter containing all the good on which all the parties agree," he wrote, "I have ventured to sketch such a charter,"[29] and he proceeded to enumerate all the principles on which a constitutional monarchy should be based. Like a great many other people, including La Fayette, Jefferson was mistaken: Louis XVI let it be known that he had no intention of coming up with any charter or, indeed, going further than the elimination of a few glaring abuses. La Fayette's position had now become so impossible that he thought of resigning and seeking reelection by the Third Estate. In the meantime, however, he made his opinions known, not in the Estates-General, where he felt legally constrained, but in every salon and every meeting he attended, so much so that Adélaide de Simiane reproached him for the violence of his position.

The letter he sent her in answer, dated simply June 1789 but clearly written near the middle of the month, reveals a crucial evolution in his feelings and position. It was not only a self-justification of the sort the Marquis often indulged in; it was in fact in the nature of a campaign biography—and one that did not hesitate to distort the facts to prettify and buttress the La Fayette myth. It is really the first appearance of what would eventually become his "standard line."

"At the age of nineteen," the Marquis wrote, "I gave myself over to the liberty of man and the destruction of depotism. . . . I left for the New World, impeded by all and helped by none. . . .

"During my last American trip I had the pleasure of seeing that Revolution completed and I said in a speech to Congress printed everywhere except in the Gazette de France: 'May this serve as a lesson to all oppressors and as an example to the oppressed.' The disorder of the Treasury and the first Assembly of Notables made everyone realize that the happy moment was approaching. You know that I was the first to establish the key principles of the nullity of taxation without consent; of individual liberty; of the necessity of the Estates-General. . . .

"I joined all resistances; I used an instrument [that is, the Breton nobility] that will soon have to be broken.* I tried everything except a civil war, which I could have started but whose horrors I feared. A full year ago, I developed a plan whose simplest points looked like follies but which, within six months, will be carried out in full without changing a single word. I also wrote a Declaration of Rights which Mr. Jefferson found so excellent that he demanded it be sent to General Washington; and that declaration will just about become the new catechism of our country.

"You must understand, therefore, that having drawn the sword and thrown the scabbard away, I must be delighted with whatever furthers the revolution, and I try to forecast everything which might prevent us from reaching the goal at which I want us to stop. . . .

"I can swear to you that throughout the twelve years of my public life, while I may have made many mistakes, there is not a single moment of which I am not proud, and among the mistakes I made, there are many I owe to other people's prudence."[30]

Whatever the avowed purpose of this letter, its disturbing aspect is the fact that La Fayette believed what he wrote: the tendency to self-delusion

---

*He meant that since the Breton resistance consisted of nobles anxious to retain their privileged status, they would soon be made to obey the new, more egalitarian order.

already noticeable back in 1780 during the dispute with d'Estaing now emerges as a major component of La Fayette's self-image. He thoroughly—though probably unconsciously—distorts the record. He did not "give himself over to the liberty of man at the age of nineteen," and he did receive help. The oppressors referred to in the speech he cites were the British in Ireland and Canada, not the King of France. Far from being his instruments, the Bretons had used him to gain publicity for their cause. Jefferson had not sent his Declaration of Rights to Washington, but to the much less important Madison. Finally, it is simply not true that he had ever been in a position to start a civil war, and thus his failure to do so is no proof of his moderation.

La Fayette had developed the ability to change facts and to make them suit his new purpose. Anyone who opposed him, or merely disagreed with him, automatically became the enemy of France and liberty. Future events would also be distorted to make them fit into his preexisting framework. Convinced he had achieved far more than he had, and that he was now indeed a second George Washington, La Fayette would consistently underestimate the difficulties and perils of any situation—a dangerous position to adopt at the beginning of the greatest upheaval the country had ever seen. And the discrepancy between his real abilities and his imagined powers would not go untested for long.

All through May and June, as plots thickened and tensions mounted between the King and the Third Estate, La Fayette dithered, while expressing himself with great violence in the salons—so much so, in fact, that Gouverneur Morris,* who was growing increasingly alarmed, begged him to try to cool down people's tempers instead. Polite as always, the Marquis agreed—and did no such thing. Instead, he continued to vacillate while using the most inflamed language as a cover for his hesitation. When, on June 25, the more liberal members of the clergy and nobility joined the Third Estate, La Fayette followed though he felt bound by his previous commitments to abstain from voting. Finally, on July 11, he came to a resolution and offered his Declaration of the Rights of Man to the new gathering that, significantly, now called itself the National Assembly. His draft was immediately taken into consideration and, eventually, better written and somewhat amended, it was adopted. Today it still serves as the preamble to the French Consti-

---

*The new American consul, Morris had only just arrived in Paris. He was a prosperous merchant of markedly conservative views who sided most often with the King.

tution. This time, La Fayette was right to be pleased with himself: it was no mean achievement to have given a Bill of Rights to a country that, until then, had never known any kind of freedom. Had he done no more for the rest of his life, La Fayette would be entitled to fame and gratitude for that one achievement alone.

As of July 11, however, the Bill of Rights was still a proposition. That day in Paris, men gathered and made inflammatory speeches: some sort of explosion was being readied. The angry marquis had written Mme de Simiane: "I am convinced that M. le duc d'Orléans, or at any rate the people who control him, are trying to confuse the issues. I have been told things and solicited. . . . I answered coldly that M. le duc d'Orléans, in my eyes, is only a private citizen richer than I am and whose fate is no more interesting than that of the other members of the minority [that is, the nobility]; and that there is no use in forming a party when one is united with the Nation. . . . In the meantime, I am watching M. le duc d'Orléans and may have to denounce at the same time M. le comte d'Artois as an aristocratic rebel and M. le duc d'Orléans as a rebel using more popular means."[31] This split between the two liberal groups was extremely serious: their mutual hostility, based as it was on personal hatred and political differences, seemed to preclude their ever working together. Since the duc d'Orléans and his friends were literally not on speaking terms with the La Fayette-Noailles-Maubourg group, the reactionaries now had a real chance, especially because La Fayette and his friends had nothing but reprobation for the disorders in Paris.

Suddenly, on July 10, 1789, Louis XVI reunited the liberals by firing Necker and replacing him with the reactionary baron de Breteuil. Despite Necker's incompetence, he had been functioning, in essence, as the guarantee of Louis XVI's good faith. Thus the King's intentions in getting rid of him were perfectly clear: Artois and the Queen had finally imposed their policy; the Assembly would be dissolved, all the reforms would be annulled, and the country would find itself back where it had been before the Assembly of Notables.

The response was immediate and even stronger than expected: on July 11, the Assembly declared a prohibition on its meeting to be treason; on July 13 it elected La Fayette, the symbol of America and republican sentiment, vice-president. Finally, on July 14, the people of Paris rose up in anger and seized that hated symbol of the ancien régime, the Bastille.

A new, irreversible step had been taken. Louis XVI gave in, took Necker back, and promised to be a better king. Artois, several princes of the blood royal, and many great aristocrats emigrated. La Fayette, meanwhile, found himself presiding pro tem over the National Assembly and led a deputation to the King. On July 15, when the King visited the Assembly to eat crow, he found La Fayette at the head of its receiving committee. In just two days, the dithering marquis had become one of the leaders of the Revolution.

It became evident later that day that, when it came to revolutions, La Fayette was the only available expert. The duc d'Orléans was partly responsible for the riots in Paris, but, having helped to start them, he was as helpless as everyone else to stop them. The King, obviously, could do nothing: not only had he provoked the explosion, but the troops that were supposed to keep the city orderly, the Gardes Françaises, had joined the rebels in assaulting the Bastille. So the Assembly filled the power void by sending eighty-eight of its members to Paris and electing La Fayette to head the delegation: if anyone could get the people to listen, it was the Hero of Two Worlds.

By midafternoon, La Fayette, assisted by Jean-Sylvain Bailly, a famous astronomer of liberal tendencies, found himself ensconced at that center of all Paris upheavals, the Hôtel de Ville (city hall). Huge crowds surged back and forth around the building, cursing the Queen and the aristocrats, and madly cheering La Fayette. As the Marquis and Bailly took their place with the city's terrified officials, the applause and shouting became more frenzied still. The new idol came forth and congratulated the Parisians on having achieved their freedom. He read them the speech Louis XVI had made to the National Assembly promising, in essence, to be a good boy. Finally, at a meeting of the Parisian electors to the Estates-General, convened to help resolve the crisis, he heard Bailly proclaimed mayor of Paris and himself commander of the city's militia. Then in a grand theatrical gesture, he swore to sacrifice his life, if need be, to the protection of their liberty.

The next afternoon, a very harried commander managed to find time to write his Adélaide; his letter is a useful corrective to the official picture of the hero leading the people to liberty. "As soon as the idea of my commanding the Parisian militia had been mentioned to me, it suddenly conquered everyone; it became essential for me to accept; it has become essential to stay, and the people, in their delirium of enthusiasm can be moderated by myself only. I wanted to go to Versailles; the leaders of the city declared that the salvation of Paris demanded that I not leave it for an instant. Forty thousand souls are assembled, the fermentation has reached its highest degree, I appear, and one word from me makes them go home. I have already saved the lives of six people who were being hanged in the different quarters;

but this furious, drunken people will not always listen to me. As I write you, eighty thousand persons surround the Hôtel de Ville, claiming that they are being duped, that the troops have not been withdrawn [from the suburbs], that the King was supposed to come. As soon as I go away, they go mad. . . . If I leave for more than four hours, we are lost. In any event, my situation is unlike anybody else's. I reign over Paris, but it is over a maddened people urged on by abominable plots. . . . In this very moment they are uttering dreadful shouts."[32]

On that same day, the sixteenth, having convinced the electors to change the name of "militia" to "National Guard," he was formally appointed commandant-general and promptly decreed, as if it were necessary, that the Bastille would be razed. Then, he completed the arrangements for the King's visit on the seventeenth: the regular Royal Guard, who were known to be faithful to the monarch, would stay outside the limits of the city; within Paris, the monarch's security was to be entrusted solely to the National Guard and its new commander, General La Fayette.

And so the humbled Louis XVI, wearing a plain suit and a plumeless hat, drove through the capital that had exchanged his rule for that of its general, and was received by Bailly, the new mayor of Paris, whom he had not appointed. As La Fayette was soon to tell Gouverneur Morris, on that day he gave orders to 100,000 men, promenaded his sovereign through the streets just as he, La Fayette, pleased, and settled on the exact amount of applause the King was to receive; indeed, he said, he could have kept the monarch as his prisoner if he had so chosen.

But there was another fact he confided to no one but Adélaide. He had neither predicted nor even wanted the uprising on the fourteenth, because he thought a revolution ought to be an orderly change decreed by the Assembly, not the result of popular furor. He had then lived the next three days in terror of what might really happen. Far from being in control, he was petrified at losing his power over the maddened crowd; nor did he think it wise to subject the very man who was to head the new constitutional monarchy to so deep a humiliation: even the peaceful Louis XVI was bound to feel some resentment. As the Revolution progressed, La Fayette developed the habit of pretending that he had favored all along a course of action that, in reality, he dreaded and opposed; then, sure as always that he was right, he began to believe that what he said mattered more than what had actually happened. And people at court and in the Assembly, who should have known better, believed him, at least for the moment.

On July 17, 1789, as the world of the ancien régime slowly and ponderously crumbled into dust, one thing, at least, seemed sure. Neither poor

Louis XVI, driving back to his palace with a blue and red cockade* in his hat, nor Necker, the erstwhile financial wizard, nor even the National Assembly, could any longer claim they were the center of power. In the hot, dirty, frantic city, which was reclaiming the primacy usurped by Versailles, everyone knew that the Revolution had one leader, one idol only—the friend of liberty, the erstwhile marquis-turned-citizen, the commander of the National Guard, General La Fayette.

---

*Blue and red were the colors on the coat of arms of the City of Paris, and they became the symbol of the Revolution.

Lafayette in 1782. Just back from the United States, the newly promoted hero is shown here wearing his French uniform.

The vicomte de Noailles, Lafayette's cousin by marriage, a model of wit, grace, and elegance whom the young Gilbert greatly admired.

The comte d'Artois, Louis XVI's youngest brother. He and Lafayette were taught to ride together and they remained friends until 1789, only to meet again as adversaries when Artois became Charles X and the people of Paris rose against him in 1830.

The good life under the ancien régime, when looks and manners were everything. Three engravings by Moreau-le-Jeune. ABOVE: "Coming out of the Theater." A fashionable young woman receiving the homage of an admirer. BELOW LEFT: "Meeting in a Garden," illustration for Rousseau's sentimental—and highly successful—novel, La Nouvelle Héloise. BELOW RIGHT: "A Gentleman at his Toilette," the sort of scene Lafayette witnessed every time he attended a minister's lever.

LEFT: *Help from Versailles: the comte de Vergennes, the foreign minister who convinced Louis XVI to assist the American insurgents.* RIGHT: *The comte de Maurepas, prime minister in all but name, who ordered Lafayette back from Bordeaux but treated him like a hero when he returned from the United States in 1780.*

General Washington, Father of his Country, Lafayette's hero, protector, and mentor, in an allegorical setting.

American officers:

General Nathanael Greene, one of the most effective commanders during the War of Independence, was a special favorite of General Washington's.

The traitor Benedict Arnold, the only American general officer ever to defect to the British, very nearly captured Lafayette and Washington on their way back to headquarters.

French commanders:

Admiral d'Estaing, whom Lafayette found too prudent, and with whom he quarreled.

Admiral de Grasse, who led the French fleet that blockaded Yorktown.

The comte de Rochambeau, who led the French forces in the United States.

Diagram of the Siege of Yorktown. The French fleet blockades the city from the sea while the combined Franco-American forces surround it by land. Lafayette and his Light Infantry are on the right wing.

The British surrender at Yorktown. Cornwallis is (inaccurately) pictured surrendering his sword to Washington. Lafayette, a hand to his hat, stands at the center.

Marie Antoinette, who laughed at Lafayette when he was just a clumsy young man, admired him when he returned from the United States and finally despised him for his liberal stance.

Louis XVI in coronation robes. An identical engraving hung in Washington's house in Philadelphia; it was removed in 1792 when France became a republic.

The fall of the Bastille, July 14, 1789. Its immediate consequence was the creation of the National Guard, with Lafayette as its commander.

The opening of the Estates-General, May 15, 1789. Louis XVI sits on the throne, Lafayette is lost among the ranks of the nobility on the right.

Lafayette represented by Debucourt in his self-designed uniform of commander-in-chief of the Paris National Guard.

A great occasion: the Fete of the Federation on July 14, 1790. Talleyrand said mass at the altar in the center, Louis XVI swore to observe the nonexistent constitution, and Lafayette was mobbed by the adoring crowd.

Long live Lafayette and France: a laudatory fan celebrating the civic oath sworn by Lafayette during the Fete of the Federation.

Lafayette receives the crown of immortality from Prudence while Truth unveils the plots of the aristocracy: an allegorical print in praise of the General.

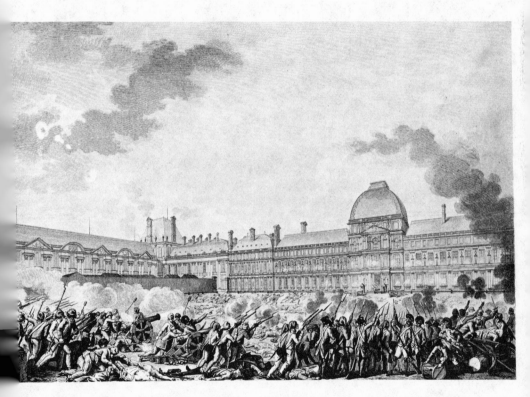

*From Republic to Empire: the Tuileries assaulted by the people on August 10, 1792,
an event that led to Lafayette's emigration.*

The Bonapartist coup d'état on November 9, 1799, which installed the dictatorial government that Lafayette opposed to the last.

View of Lafayette's chateau, Lagrange. There, from 1802 to his death, Lafayette found peace, friendship, and the comforts of a devoted family.

The landing of General Lafayette at Castle Garden, New York, August 16, 1824. It was the start of a fifteen-month ovation for the returning hero.

Louis-Philippe, King of the French. His hand resting on a copy of the Constitution of 1830, the former duc d'Orlèans looks every inch a king—a transformation that Lafayette engineered, then resented.

Lafayette, the hero of 1830. The General, here slightly embellished by an admirer, is seen at bottom as he leads the people who rose against the tyranny of Charles X. This is exactly how the General liked to think of himself in his last years.

Eight

HOSTAGE TO REVOLUTION

When Louis XVI, whom his wife and most of the court had never expected to see again, returned from Paris in the early evening of July 17, 1789, his position was bad but not hopeless. After all, this was not the first time a king of France had had to endure humiliation at the hands of a Paris mob. There were the examples, among others, of Charles V in the fourteenth century, being forced (already) to put on the blue and red insignia of the city; of Louis XIV even, who as a child had pretended to sleep as the suspicious Parisians filed past his bed. As to what should follow such episodes, those precedents made it abundantly clear. The King was to flee to a safe garrison town—Metz, for example—return at the head of his faithful troops, and punish the rebellious city. Admittedly, this time the revolt was unusually widespread. What had worked before would not be so easy, but many observers thought it could be done if only the King were resolute enough. Talleyrand, for one, had tried, just a few days earlier, to get him to act, but it was no use. Louis XVI had an immense capacity for sullenness and resentment, as well as a vague, insistent feeling that it really wasn't nice to shoot his people down, and so, as the Revolution progressed, he managed to resist only in ways that ensured his prompt defeat.

Of course, almost everyone realized that he was outraged by the new status of Paris, and indignant about the creation of the National Guard, but it was crucial for Lafayette (as he now spelled his name) and most of the other liberals to pretend publicly that he accepted the changes. Their plan, after all, called for a constitutional monarchy. Therefore, the King must appear to cooperate. At the same time, even the General—as he was now called—was aware that, in order to create a new régime, he must force the King to accept a form of government he despised. As a result, Lafayette's actions stood in permanent contradiction to his abundant speeches, pretending to respect a man for whom he felt contempt. Meanwhile, pressure from the left could hardly be ignored: revolutions are generally a bad environment for liberal centrists, and Lafayette now had many an occasion to learn this unpleasant lesson.

The proof of his predicament came quickly enough. On July 20, the new commandant-general announced happily that, since Paris was once again peaceful, the theaters would be reopened. But violence was hardly at an end: on the twenty-second, a mob strung up two fermiers généraux, Berthier de Sauvigny and Joseph Foulon, who had been accused of speculating on the rise of the price of wheat. It was the first use, for purposes other than illumination, of the new streetlights and gave rise to the perennial revolutionary cry: "A la lanterne" ("Up on the lamppost!").* For Lafayette, who was nothing if not devoted to the law, this was unacceptable, especially since his attempt at saving the two men by having them taken to jail had been absolutely ineffective. So, on the twenty-third, having been in office less than a week, he resigned. "The people," he wrote Bailly, "have not listened to my advice and, on the day they withdraw the trust they had promised me, I must, as I said I would, resign from a position in which I can no longer be of any use."[1]

A resignation offered insincerely can be a tricky thing, but this time, perhaps because everyone was so new at the game, the General's ploy worked. Lafayette sent word to the districts into which Paris had just divided itself. The electors of whom they were composed were convinced only he could control the mobs and begged him to come back. Sadly but firmly, he announced that his resignation was final; nevertheless he attended a general meeting that evening called specifically to discuss his resignation at which

---

*Replaced, since World War II by the equally minatory "Au poteau!," the "poteau" being the stake to which you tie the person you are about to shoot.

a sobbing elector fell at his feet and, promising Paris would behave, pleaded with him to change his mind. Unable to resist this heartbreaking appeal, which was taken up by the entire Assembly, the selfless hero agreed to withdraw his resignation. Within twenty-four hours, posters were proclaiming: "We, the electors and deputies of the City of Paris . . . promise him . . . subordination and obedience to all his orders so that his zeal . . . may bring to perfection the great enterprise of public liberty."[2] The incident had been very good for Lafayette's image. The trouble was that Foulon and Berthier could hardly be called back to life, their assassins went unpunished, and Lafayette knew perfectly well it had all been pure playacting. On the twenty-fourth, he wrote to Mme de Simiane: "I cannot abandon the citizens [of Paris] who have put all their trust in me and, if I stay, I am in the terrible position of seeing evil done without being able to stop it."[3] Unfortunately, even when Lafayette managed to make such a realistic assessment, he seems to have felt no need to adjust his behavior correspondingly. Instead, he went on firmly pretending to everyone, and himself, too, that his optimistic public statements actually mattered.

For the rest of July, August, and September, the new commander helped organize the new civic government and set up the elected council of the municipality. When Necker came to the council on July 30 and pleaded for the liberation of the innocent baron de Besenval, who was hated as a member of Marie Antoinette's set and was about to be executed, Lafayette added his exhortations to the minister's. This time the two men succeeded, but it is worth noting that the friend of liberty was now dealing, in the most matter-of-fact way, with an insurrectionary and illegal system of justice in which ad hoc tribunals composed of active revolutionaries handed out death sentences without a trial.

In spite of this, La Fayette kept up his work. On July 31, he published the regulations governing the National Guard and gave it a tricolor cockade, thus inaugurating the use of blue, white, and red as the emblem of France. On August 4, he awarded a certificate of achievement to the Gardes Françaises who, having disobeyed orders, had joined in the assault of the Bastille; on the fifth, he fixed the pay of the National Guards; on the sixth, he saved the life of a civil servant guilty of having sent some gunpowder outside of the city; on the ninth, for the first time, he put on the uniform of the National Guard; on the twelfth, he selected the officers who were to serve on his staff, his choice being confirmed on the thirteenth by the electors; on the twenty-fifth, with Bailly, he paid an official visit to Versailles, where the King and Queen, who were learning to dissemble, gave the two men an excellent reception; on September 7, he refused the yearly salary of 120,000 livres that was offered him by the Council of the Commune: he was already

rich enough, he said, and would not take the people's money. And throughout those very few weeks, he managed to mold the National Guard into an
enduring institution.

The principles behind this body were simple and, as so often with
Lafayette, derived from the American model. Since there must be order
and the King could not be trusted to enforce it in a democratic way, the
new institution was to have a double purpose: in time of peace, it would act
as a sort of police; in time of war, it would provide the army with a trained
reserve. Everyone who qualified as an elector (workers, artisans, and domestic servants as well as the poor were thus excluded) was required to
serve in the guard for at least one week a year and was provided with a gun,
a uniform and, while he served, a salary. Such guidelines assured that it
would be the reliable—that is, middle class—part of the people who would
police the city. They could be trusted to protect property, which, after all,
they owned, and to resist, if need be, any attempt by the King at reestab-
lishing his power. Within weeks, La Fayette's system was extended to other
French cities as well.

The new corps, which numbered 31,058 men between twenty and fifty
years of age, was divided into districts, each of which had a battalion, made
up of five companies of a hundred men each. Only one company was on
duty at any given time. The uniform consisted of a dark blue coat with white
cloth lapels and a scarlet collar, lined with white, and adorned with yellow
buttons and badges bearing the arms of the city; the waistcoat and trousers
were made of white cloth, while the gaiters were black for winter and white
for summer; the hat was bordered with blue and sported the tricolor cockade.
As for the commandant-general, he granted himself gold epaulets and a blue,
white, and red plume for his hat. Lafayette had at last emerged from those
frustrating days in America when his division had lacked a proper uniform.

Satisfying as these sartorial details must have been, Lafayette had more
pressing concerns that summer. The trouble was that he neither wanted nor
knew what to do with the power that was now accruing to him. As a result,
he failed to take advantage of his position as the commander of the only
organized force in or near the capital, and the only man, with Bailly, to
whom the Parisians were willing to listen. Further, misapplying one of the
lessons learned from Washington, he manifested the most extreme deference
for the civilian government, in this case the Council of the Commune. The
council, which represented the most revolutionary elements of the most
revolutionary city in France, was no Congress; Paris was not Philadelphia,
and American principles quite failed to help. Unfortunately, power, unlike
other, more solid possessions tends to shrink if it is not used, and that is
just what was happening all through August and September, especially since

there were other people—the duc d'Orléans, for instance—who had every intention of taking advantage of the situation.

Not only had Lafayette become a great national leader but he also found himself surrounded by a great variety of new associates. Of course, all his liberal aristocratic friends still gathered around him and emulated his love of liberty. Thus it was none other than the vicomte de Noailles, claiming the limelight one last time, who on August 4 proposed to the assembled nobility that it renounce its privileges, and saw his motion carried. But now a great many other people had business with the General: deputies who, like him, wanted a constitution; the officers of the National Guard; Bailly, a man of goodwill and a friend of the people, whose effectiveness was uncertain and who constantly needed help; Sieyès, a worldly abbé with a passion for constitutions and equality; the Lameth brothers, the brilliant young officers whom Lafayette had first met at Metz in the 1770s and who were moving closer to the Orléanists; even, for a while, Mirabeau, that debauched, indebted aristocrat-turned-democrat whose extraordinary ugliness was paired with an extraordinary power of seduction, almost unequaled eloquence, and a firm determination to come out of the Revolution as a prime minister. In the midst of all the turmoil, Adrienne, devoted as ever, began to gain a new influence on her husband. Like most of her family, Adrienne deplored the changes then taking place, but neither she nor her mother ever gave up on Gilbert. In 1789, Adrienne wrote of the duchesse d'Ayen: "She could see that M. de La Fayette who was so dear to her, was going to play a great role and she was filled with terror by the symptoms of the Revolution. . . . The storms came soon afterward and my mother, who had already predicted them with great fear, who then saw with every kind of apprehension the role played by M. de La Fayette, judged every detail of his actions with that understanding given by a willing heart. She always saw him on the verge of the precipice, but always worthy of being loved and respected."[4] As Lafayette's role grew, and more and more people began to wish him ill, the love and support he received at home became more and more important to him; and though Adrienne never tried to force a policy on him, she undoubtedly exerted a moderating influence.

The situation in Paris, during the summer, remained a paradox. The life of the city, its theaters, cafés, promenades, salons, and amusements continued as if nothing were happening, only, now and again, violence flared up. Still, many people felt that, while taking the Bastille had been a first step, nothing solid could be achieved while the King remained at Versailles. In 1789 the monarch had not yet stopped seeming to be the incarnation of France. With him present, all would be well; with him away, evil counselors might prevail. Soon the feeling grew that the King really should be in Paris, and since, clearly, he was not going to move there of his own accord, he might have to be fetched. Naturally, the Orléans faction reinforced that mood because they felt confident that the King, once back in the city, would also be in their power.

Lafayette, on the other hand, was firmly opposed to any attempt on Versailles. First, of course, he believed in liberty; second, he loathed and feared mob rule; finally, he, too, was aware that the duc d'Orléans might reap the benefits of the operation. Throughout August and September, however, he was convinced he had the situation in the city well in hand, and worried instead mostly about the royal veto. At the Assembly, where the question was being discussed, the right wanted the King to have an absolute veto. This Lafayette dismissed out of hand, because, he wrote Maubourg, it would be ineffective: it would nullify the will of the people and therefore the King would never dare use it. Instead, he proposed, "The House of Representatives would alone have the power to initiate laws. . . . Once a Bill has passed it will be sent to the Senate (for we must have two houses) and the Senators, elected for ten years or for life, will have a one-year suspensive veto. . . . The King's assent will be necessary for a Bill to become law. The King will be able to withhold his assent for two legislatures but if, during the third legislature, the House of Representatives passes the same Bill again by a two-thirds majority and without any changes, the King would no longer be able to refuse his assent."[5]

In another letter, he added that he was sure a second chamber, not elected directly by the people, was necessary so that a balance could be reached. America, after ten years of unicameral government, had been forced to change its ways. And he ended: "Do not allow the King's prerogative to be more diminished than is absolutely necessary, insofar, especially as the army and foreign policy are concerned."[6] This was quite a change, and it was due to experience. As he watched the National Assembly, swayed by eloquence and sometimes fear, confuse ordinary laws with constitutional decrees, as he noticed how unable it was to govern, he realized that his earlier position in favor of a single chamber had been a mistake.

His first step was to try to convince a sufficient number of deputies. "I beg for liberty's sake you will break every engagement to give us a dinner tomorrow Wednesday," he wrote Jefferson late in August. "We shall be some members of the National Assembly—eight of us I want to coalize as being the only means to prevent a total dissolution and a civil war—the difficulty between us is the King's veto."[7] Not only was Jefferson's house neutral ground, but the American could also be expected to listen and eventually to advise. Among those present at the dinner, all deputies, were

Duport, a liberal lawyer with whom Lafayette had been friends for the past two years; Charles de Maubourg; Antoine Barnave, a lawyer who belonged to the extreme left; Jean-Joseph Mounier, another lawyer who wanted the King to have an absolute veto; Alexandre de Lameth, who could no doubt speak for the Orléanists; and a few others. Jefferson, in his autobiography, describes what happened: "The discussions began at the hour of four and were continued till ten o'clock in the evening; during which time I was a silent witness to a coolness and candor of argument, unusual in the conflicts of political opinion, to a logical reasoning, and chaste eloquence, disfigured by no gaudy tinsel of rhetoric or declamation. . . . The result was that the King shall have a suspensive veto on the laws, that the legislature shall be composed of a single body only, and that to be chosen by the people."[8] It seemed like a fair compromise (except, of course, that the King himself was never consulted). Lafayette got his suspensive vote in exchange for letting go the idea of a second legislative house.

In fact, it was a catastrophic agreement. First, the veto was still likely to be unworkable if the King was left alone facing the Assembly. Without a Senate to cover him, any veto would be seen as a direct King versus the People confrontation, a showdown the King was bound to lose—as the future would abundantly confirm. Worse, the single chamber, which need not reach agreement with a Senate, would be wholly unrestrained and therefore likely to give in to demagogic extremes. Finally, because no time limit was set for the completion of the Constitution, there was bound to be a confusion between pragmatic measures and constitutional principles with, ultimately, an unworkable charter as the result. As Lafayette knew, when the United States had decided to give itself a constitution, it had called a special convention for that purpose only, thus insulating the foundation of its future from the heat of day-to-day politics. By making a disastrous compromise, instead of using the power that was available to him, the General, then the one man who could actually make a difference, failed in his most basic responsibility and helped ensure eventual defeat. At the time, however, he was far too satisfied with his apparent success to worry about the future.

"My situation is indeed extraordinary," he wrote smugly to Mme de Simiane on August 20. "I am engaged in a great adventure, and enjoy the thought that I will come out of it without having had to reproach myself for a single ambitious thought, and that, having put everyone in his place, I will retire with a quarter of the fortune I had when I entered upon my career."[9] Amazingly, it was true: he had no personal ambition other than to be the French Washington, and the Revolution he embraced so ardently was costing him a great deal of money. But it is not sufficient for leading public figures to be disinterested; they must also fulfill their trust, and that is what Lafayette, as he bragged about his integrity, was signally failing to do.

Just how blind he had become to the reality of the Revolution was soon put to the proof. As the commandant-general of the National Guard, Lafayette was supposed to maintain order within the capital; but on the morning of October 5, he found, much to his surprise, that the people had risen again. The church bells were all tolling (which presumes some advance organization), and, in no time, the Hôtel de Ville was seized by the mob. The startled General at least managed to clear the building, but then he realized that the crowd in the big plaza were all shouting "To Versailles! To Versailles!" Had he sent his aides-de-camp among the crowd, he would have discovered that the cry had been started by a number of men, wearing dresses over their clothes, pretending to be hungry housewives. Because of a series of bad crops, the price of bread—the exclusive sustenance of the poor—had been steadily rising. The mass of the poor, women in good part, who now made up the crowd, still relied on the King for help in their distress, so that when agitators started shouting "To Versailles!" they took up the cry thinking that they would go to petition the King to get them the bread they so desperately needed. The Orléanists exploited this genuine discontent as a chance to eliminate, or at least replace, Louis XVI, especially since the King and Queen had just hosted a banquet of the Royal Guard during which, in a provocative gesture, the tricolor cockade had been trodden underfoot.

Lafayette may have been unprepared, but he could see that something very dangerous was about to happen, so he begged the crowd to stay in the city. He was completely ignored. At that point, anxious to retain his popularity, he decided that if he could not stop the Parisians, he might as well join them. Hastily gathering a few regiments of the National Guard, he, too, set off on the road to Versailles.

By the end of the afternoon, as the weather turned drizzly, the mob had encamped in front of the palace, and Lafayette went inside to reassure its occupants. He would protect the court and the Assembly alike, he said; and, having carefully posted a few guards at the various strategic points, off he went to spend the night at the hôtel de Noailles. The gates to the palace courtyard were locked, as they were every night. Not bothering to take any unusual precautions, Lafayette had simply and literally gone to sleep. Louis XVI, who was urged by his courtiers to leave with the royal family by a back road and not come back until he had an army, refused, as usual, to do anything at all; and Marie Antoinette, who had hurried back from the Petit Trianon at the end of the afternoon, went through the ritual of her *coucher* in her state bedroom, while the King did the same in his.

Neither had very much sleep. At 6:00 A.M., the crowd broke the gates and invaded the palace. Marie Antoinette, still in her nightclothes, fled her bedroom through a back passage just in time to avoid a murderous mob who made up for their disappointment by tearing her bed to pieces, and after a long moment during which no one knew whether she was alive or dead, she managed to join the King in his bedroom where the rest of the royal family was already gathered. At last, she was able to dress. As for Lafayette (who, under the circumstances, might well have spent the night in the palace), he, too, was eventually awakened, arriving just in time to stop the massacre of the Royal Guard, already under way. The National Guard, far from protecting the palace, had simply vanished.

As Lafayette joined the King in his study—being told at the door that he was now granted the *entrées du cabinet*—the crowd outside was becoming louder and angrier. At first the King alone went out onto the balcony of the *cour de marbre* and tried speaking to the crowd, but his voice was drowned by shouts of "The Queen! The Queen!" So Marie Antoinette, holding her children by the hand, joined him, but now the shouts were "No King!" and "No Children!" For a minute everyone went back in; but the crowd kept demanding the Queen with increasingly menacing gestures. In an act of great bravery, since she expected to be lynched, Marie Antoinette went out on the balcony. For a while the hostile yells redoubled. The Queen curtsied, and the mob quieted a little; then Lafayette came out on the balcony and, with a bow, bent and kissed her hand. Suddenly a dead silence fell, soon broken by cries of "Long Live the Queen! Long live General Lafayette!" The Hero of Two Worlds had just saved his sovereign.

Still the crowds kept shouting, but now it was "To Paris!" so the King came out again and promised his "loving subjects" that he would go and live with them in Paris. Within two hours, the royal family had been bundled into a carriage, surrounded by the drunken, triumphant crowd, who were yelling "We're bringing back the baker, his wife, and the little apprentice." Lafayette rode the whole way next to the carriage, ready to protect its occupants in case the crowd should turn uglier, but it didn't. After six hours— the Parisians were, after all, on foot—the royal family reached the palace of the Tuileries where they found, naturally enough since the palace had not been in use for over a hundred years, that there were not even enough beds for them all. Still, they were alive—but they were prisoners.

Lafayette put the best possible face on these events by the now-familiar process of adjusting reality to image. Although he had been swept along passively on the fifth and the sixth, he claimed the credit for saving the King and Queen, and for having brought the King closer to his people by moving him to Paris. One thing was certain in any case: at this moment, the General was politically the most powerful man in France. He alone maintained order in Paris, where the Assembly had joined the King. The mobs listened to him alone. And on October 9, after he had presented a deputation of the city to the King, he was appointed commander of all the troops situated within fifteen leagues (approximately thirty-five miles) of Paris. Now, if ever, was the time for him to accede officially to power: he had only to speak if he wanted to become prime minister. Instead, he flew about in a flurry of occupations, congratulating himself all the more easily now that Jefferson had gone home. Had the American still been in Paris, he could have warned Lafayette that he was making a grave mistake and told him that he was wasting precious time.

In one respect, at least, Lafayette had his way. Although the Assembly's attempt at establishing the duc d'Orléans's responsibility never succeeded, it was obvious to all that he had largely provoked the events of the fifth and sixth because his henchman had been seen leading the mob; so now Lafayette offered him the choice of accepting a purely decorative mission to England or staying to face the gravest accusations. The duc was nothing if not pusillanimous, so he went, thus ridding Lafayette of a dangerous rival; but his agents who remained did their best, by a campaign of pamphlets, to turn the Parisians against the General. On October 23, in a letter to Mounier, the royalist deputy who had attended the session about the veto and who had later left Paris in disgust, Lafayette boasted about the way he had disposed of the duc d'Orléans, adding that Louis XVI was perfectly free: the fact that the King had stopped hunting—his chief passion and heretofore a daily indulgence—was not because he could not leave the city; he was just too busy concurring in the great work of national renovation. It is difficult to accept that even the author of such an argument could possibly have believed it; and in an ecstasy of smugness Lafayette went on: "As for me, I am amazed at the immense extent of my responsibilities, but feel in no way discouraged."[10]

Such boasts without consequent action could only strengthen the extremist elements who claimed they spoke for the people. The Assembly, in an orgy of self-liberation, was rapidly making all government impossible, and Louis XVI encouraged the excesses in the mistaken belief that if the situation grew bad enough, public reaction would enable him to restore the ancien régime.

By mid-October, only two men were popular enough to run the government effectively: Mirabeau, because of his eloquence, and Lafayette, because of his popularity. Neither man, however, could form a ministry without the other. Lafayette had come to despise Mirabeau for his debauchery, his drunkenness, and his corruption, failing to appreciate the orator's capacity for swaying opinion, his sharp understanding of the situation, and his genuine love of liberty. Mirabeau, on his side, thought Lafayette was a swollen-headed nitwit, but he was far too practical to let those feelings stand in his way, especially since he had little doubt that, in a Lafayette-Mirabeau administration, he would be the dominant partner. At Mirabeau's suggestion, the two principals opened secret negotiations. From the very first, Mirabeau was decisive and Lafayette hesitant. Mirabeau confided in just one close friend, the comte de la Marck; Lafayette wavered, as usual, and talked to a great many people. He consulted Gouverneur Morris, for instance, who disliked Mirabeau and his reputation for taking bribes from both right and left, and advised the General not to soil himself by an alliance with the less than pristine tribune. On November 3, to further his case against Mirabeau, Morris brought the ambitious and greedy Talleyrand, who was still a bishop, to Lafayette's house. Talleyrand's friendship with Morris was based on their sharing the same mistress: as the lady put it, he had suavity but Morris offered more solid performances. Seeing a Talleyrand-Lafayette ministry in the middle distance and fearing Mirabeau as a rival, the bishop advised Lafayette against the proposed alliance. He watched Lafayette hesitate and contradict himself, and later told Morris with disgust that the General neither knew what he wanted nor what he would do in the end, and that he was obviously a spent political force.

In the meantime, the principals had engaged in a series of intricate steps which got them absolutely nowhere. On October 17, for instance, Mirabeau wrote de La Marck: "The business is hot and Lafayette as decided as he can be without outside help. This morning, he takes me to see Montmorin. . . . We must get Lafayette, scared as he is about the shortage of food and the unrest in the provinces, to make a firm decision."[11] It must have been maddening for the energetic Mirabeau to deal with a man who was apparently incapable of making up his mind but, at least, Lafayette lent him 50,000 livres, a great boon for the always inpecunious politician. Mirabeau promptly returned with a gesture of goodwill. On October 19, he talked the Assembly into offering a motion of thanks to Lafayette and Bailly, despite his assessment of the General as having only the appearance of a great man.

All through October, the conversations continued, although by now they were no longer secret. Mirabeau produced a list for the new government: he would replace Necker, Lafayette would become Minister of War and a marshal of France, and Montmorin would remain Foreign Minister. Mirabeau and Lafayette then agreed to keep Necker after all because he made the King more popular, and on October 29, Lafayette at long last seemed to reach a decision. After receiving a medal from the Assembly, he wrote Mirabeau: "Mutual confidence and friendship: I give them and hope to receive them."[12] But then, almost at once, he began to waver. It seemed safer, after all, not to implement the plans. On November 5, the infuriated Mirabeau wrote de La Marck: "You have seen the man as he really is, equally incapable of reneging on a promise and keeping it ad tempus; besides, powerless except after an explosion."[13] Then Champion de Cicé, the Keeper of the Seals, who would have lost his office in a change of administration, offered and carried a motion at the Assembly forbidding any of its members from taking on an executive function, so as to avoid, he said, undue influence. Always suspicious of the King, the Assembly passed the motion by a large majority, and the proposed ministry was buried. Referring to Lafayette, Mirabeau wrote: "He could not have been more thoroughly fooled."[14]

After this fiasco, the relationship between the two men, fragile at best, cooled off again. On December 1, apparently no longer concerned about diplomacy, Mirabeau told Lafayette just what he thought of him: "The dazzlement of your position and your fatal indecision are [blinding] you," he wrote. "Your preference for mediocre men [will] abort the most promising destiny and will be your undoing along with that of the state."[15] It was an unkind but accurate diagnosis. Actual power frightened Lafayette; he neither understood it nor knew how to use it. As a result, he found it easier virtuously to disclaim all personal ambition. It was the perfect excuse to remain on the sidelines; only, it also meant that he must stand by, passively, while others carried out a revolution.

As 1789 passed into 1790, Lafayette, amid his usual flurry of speeches and oath-taking ceremonies, soon had to confront the contradiction between the appearance of power and its reality. Outwardly, he was as revered as ever. On January 22, for instance, he refused the command of all the National Guards throughout the kingdom: it was too much for any man, he said. Only ten days earlier, 243 guards had mutinied in the Champs Elysées, and Lafayette had managed to have them disarmed and arrested. The uprising remained a worrying symptom, however. Order was breaking down everywhere. To combat this situation, the General changed strategy, and the erstwhile revolutionary now advocated law and order. The Revolution is over, he kept telling the people. On February 20, in a speech asking for the end of a series of upheavals in the provinces, he said, "For the Revolution, we needed disorders; the old order was nothing but slavery and, under those circumstances, insurrection is the holiest of duties, but for the Constitution, the new order must be stabilized, individuals must be secure. . . . The government must take on strength and energy."[16] Unfortunately, although its meaning was perfectly clear, the speech included one fatal sentence—"insurrection is the holiest of duties"—which was immediately taken out of context. The royalists claimed that, far from being a moderate, Lafayette was the bloodthirsty revolutionary they had thought him all along, and the extreme left claimed that the situation had in fact not changed sufficiently for them to dispense with "the holiest of duties."

The problem, as even Lafayette was beginning to see, was that the government had practically disappeared. As he wrote Washington on January 12: "Our revolution is getting on as well as it can with a nation which has swallowed up liberty all at once, and is still liable to mistake licentiousness for freedom. The Assembly have more hatred to the ancient system than experience in the organisation of a new and constitutional government. The ministers are lamenting the loss of power and afraid to use that which they have—and as everything has been destroyed and not much new building is yet above ground, there is much room for critics and calomnies.

"To which may be added that we are still pestered by two parties, the Aristocratic which is panting for a counter-revolution, and the factious [the extreme left] which aims at the division of the [country], and destruction of all authority and perhaps of the lifes of the reigning branch, both of which parties are fomenting troubles."[17]

Since, clearly, all authority was gone, the General now tried to create it anew; so he embarked on a campaign of secret advice to the King. "I place at Your Majesty's feet the gratitude of a pure and sensitive heart which knows how to appreciate your kindness and respond to your trust. We must believe, Sire, that your benevolent intentions will be carried out. When the people and the King are united, who can prevail against you? At any rate, I swear to Your Majesty that if my hopes were to be unrealized, I would shed my last drop of blood to prove my fidelity to you,"[18] Lafayette wrote Louis XVI on February 28. A very moving plea, but since he was unwilling to lose his popularity, there was a constant discrepancy between his alleged desire to reinforce the King's power and his efforts to ingratiate himself with the revolutionaries. As a result, he was trusted by neither side. On April 9, for instance, Montmorin, who had become, in effect, the head of the government, wrote the King: "I think that M. de La Fayette will ask to see Your Majesty. There are rumors about a rapprochement between him and the party from which we have had such difficulty separating him. I still hope it isn't so . . . but felt I must warn Your Majesty who will understand how such a rapprochement, if it is taking place, must limit your trust in him."[19]

That Lafayette's new moderating line was due partly to feminine influence cannot be doubted. Adrienne and Adélaide both kept pressing him to help the King and Queen. In April, he was writing Mme de Simiane: "You have often preached deference to the King and Queen to me; it was not necessary because my own tendencies inclined me in that direction ever since their misfortunes; but, believe me, they would have been better served, and the state too, if I had been a harder man. They are big children who will only swallow salutary medicine when they are threatened with an ogre."[20] He was right as to the problem, but incapable of understanding its gravity; worse, his optimistic public speeches only obscured the truth.

By the end of May, Lafayette was deluging the King with what he considered good advice. "The King must realize that nothing can be done except for and with the people's liberty. . . . Any other system would lose him his servants, myself in particular, but, in order to defeat the extremists . . . the King must neglect no means of becoming popular."[21] So far, so good, but when it came to concrete solutions Lafayette was all symbol and no substance. According to the General, poor Louis XVI was to stop the Revolution, by reviewing the National Guard; by giving horses not just to the division heads of the guard who had been presented at court but to the others as well; by ceasing to require proofs of nobility from those who wanted to attend the court; by having the old tower of Vincennes demolished; and by proclaiming the tricolor as the only legal emblem. A more feeble plan for stabilizing the Revolution is hard to imagine, or a more absolute blindness to the forces on both sides. Lafayette knew, for instance, that by 1790 Louis XVI was trying to make up for what he saw as his failure to rule forcefully by almost unfailingly taking his wife's reactionary advice. He knew also that Marie Antoinette, who considered him a traitor, disliked and distrusted him, and that letters or no, therefore, he had virtually no influence on the King's actions. Meanwhile on the other extreme, the revolutionary left had begun a series of attacks against him. In one short pamphlet entitled *Plan Infernal des Ennemis de la Révolution* ("Diabolical Plan of the Revolution's Enemies") Jean-Paul Marat wrote: "It is not without surprise that we have seen the excessive respect the General has demonstrated for the deputies and all the vile cajoling he has used to fool them. Finally, we have not seen without indignation all the disgusting tricks he has used to make them believe he is the hero of the two worlds."[22] All his honeyed words, Marat warned, would lead to a ministry made up of Mirabeau, Lafayette, and Sieyès, and went on to describe Lafayette as "a traitor to his fatherland who wants to make the King an absolute dictator and whose efforts to bring back despotism never cease."[23]

Marat, a good observer if a vicious polemicist, was right on at least one count: Lafayette did bestow unwonted praise on the Assembly in general and the deputies in particular. This was not so much an attempt to curry favor and power as the result of his conviction that the very sovereignty of the nation was embodied in its representatives. An admirable principle in itself, for Lafayette it served to conceal the reality of an incoherent and often hysterical body. More and more, his utterances took on the character of an incantation: as if by saying something with enough force, it would come true. But by 1790, magic had long since ceased to be effective.

No matter how he felt about Lafayette, Mirabeau at least recognized that something had to be done, so on April 28 he wrote the General, pointing out that the government was paralyzed, the Revolution speeding up, and that only a union of the two men could save the day. The problem was that Mirabeau had been bought by the King and now wanted to be his sole adviser, while Lafayette, who thought himself vastly superior to Mirabeau, had no notion of sharing access to the King—access that he never had. Still, the two men's policies began to coincide. On May 22, for instance, Lafayette supported Mirabeau in proposing to vest in the King and Assembly together, and not in the Assembly alone, the right to make war and peace. By this time the Assembly had managed to retain all three powers to itself—legislative, executive, and judiciary—thus leaving the King and ministers virtually impotent and all exercise of authority impossible. The two men's attempt to be practical merely led to their being immediately denounced by the extreme left. Marat, in particular, pointed out that no man who commanded an army as large as Lafayette's should also be a member of the Assembly since his command, alone, already gave him too much power. In rebuttal, the General made it known that he would serve his country, no matter how unpopular that might make him, and when, on May 25, he saved the life of a perfectly innocent carter who was about to be lynched, he used the occasion to make a widely reported speech on the theme that obeying the law was a sacred duty.

All through these events, Mirabeau continued his efforts, with the full backing of the court, which was trying to enlist the General so as to prevent him from doing further harm to the royalist cause. In a last desperate attempt, Mirabeau, safe in the knowledge that he could outtalk the reluctant hero, offered to make Lafayette prime minister while he himself remained merely a private adviser. Lafayette saw through the maneuver and refused. Once again, Lafayette was afraid of power, especially power controlled by Mirabeau, whom he still did not trust. On June 3, a meeting between the two men failed to produce any results, but on the tenth, as a sop, Lafayette asked Mirabeau to take on the task of delivering a eulogy to the Assembly for Benjamin Franklin, who had died in Philadelphia on April 17. As usual when faced with a hard choice, that of joining the ministry, the General procrastinated or vacillated. On June 19, for instance, he backed the abolition of all titles of nobility in the Assembly, going so far as to prohibit the use of the word "monseigneur" even for use among members of the royal family—

thus infuriating the monarch whose trust he was trying to win. On June 27 he apologized to the King and said he would try to obtain a lax application of the new law, but, of course, it was too late.

At least, in the summer of 1790, Lafayette enjoyed his most spectacular moment yet: the Fete of the Federation. On June 5, Lafayette and Bailly sent the Assembly an address from the citizens of Paris endorsing a new federal union of the National Guard, and it was decided that delegations from all over France would come together in solemn ceremony on July 14, the anniversary of the fall of the Bastille. There was little time, so, as soon as the Champ de Mars, the empty space between the Ecole Militaire and the Seine, was selected,* Paris went mad: a great terraced amphitheater had to be built; soon even ladies of title pushing mahogany wheelbarrows could be seen laboring side by side with the more usual work force.

"The Federation of 1790," Lafayette wrote in his memoirs, "was one of the greatest events of the Revolution. Fourteen thousand deputies, who were lawfully elected by more than three million National Guards along with deputations of all the armed forces, both on land and at sea, came in the name of France to renounce the ancien régime and swear to observe their constitutional liberty and equality."[24] The ceremonies were so grand that they had to be spread over several days. On July 13, Lafayette read the Assembly an address from the National Guards of France, stating: "The Rights of Man have been declared; the people's sovereignty is recognized. . . . The basis of public order has been established. Quickly now you must give the state back its strength and energy. The people owe you the glory of a free constitution; but they ask, they expect at last that peace that cannot exist without a stable and complete organization of the government. . . . As for us, without hesitating, we will swear before the altar of the fatherland the oath that you have prescribed for all soldiers. May the solemnity of this great day mark the reconciliation of the several parties, the oblivion of all offenses and the birth of public peace and happiness."[25] The General was sticking to his new peace-and-order line. He continued to do so when, that same day, he harangued the King, "We like to admire in Your Majesty the most splendid of all titles, that . . . of King of a free people. Enjoy, Sire, the reward of your virtues; let this pure homage, which despotism could never deserve, be the glory and the reward of a citizen King. You have wanted us to have a constitution based on liberty and public order: liberty is now safe, and your zeal is the guaranty that order will be maintained."[26] To this, Louis XVI, with surprising forthrightness replied, "De-

---

*The Eiffel Tower stands there now.

fenders of public order, Friends of liberty and the law, remember that your first duty is to maintain order and ensure that the laws will be obeyed. The rewards of a free constitution must be equal for all. The freer we are, and the graver any attempt against liberty becomes, as do the acts of . . . violence which are not authorized by law."[27] And he added, hypocritically: "Tell [everyone] that their King is also their father, their brother, their friend."

Events the next day were even more spectacular. On one side of the amphitheater stood thousands upon thousands of men; opposite them, up a series of steps, a great altar had been erected; and on the side all could see a platform where the royal family and the deputies sat. First, a High Mass was celebrated by the Bishop of Autun, Talleyrand. Next Lafayette came forward and took a solemn oath: "We swear to be ever faithful to the Nation, the Laws and the King; to maintain with all our power the constitution decreed by the National Assembly and accepted by the King; to protect, according to the laws, the safety of people and property; the free circulation of grains and foods in the kingdom; the collection of public taxes . . . and to remain united to all Frenchmen by indissoluble bonds of brotherhood."[28] The Assembly marched forward and swore to maintain liberty and the Constitution, and finally the King stood up and took the same oath. These ceremonies were followed by thunderous applause. At that point, a witness noted, the King and Queen, greatly to their annoyance, found themselves completely ignored. "The crowd would not let [Lafayette] come down from the altar . . . he had hardly left it when his admirers came rushing toward him; some kissed his face, others his hands, the unlucky ones his clothes. As soon as he had got upon his horse, they kissed whatever they could reach: his thighs, his boots, his saddle and finally the horse itself."[29]

The celebrations had been a great triumph, but in fact, the Federation was all make-believe and hypocrisy. The Constitution, for instance, which the King swore to observe, didn't exist—there was merely a hodgepodge of often contradictory decrees from the Assembly; the "citizen King" who, according to Lafayette had "wanted us to have a constitution" wanted in fact just the reverse, and most of the spectators knew it. The celebrant of the solemn Mass, Tallyrand, was a gambler, a debauchee, the father of an illegitimate child, and probably an agnostic. Except for the physical presence of a great many people, nothing was what it seemed to be. Once again, Lafayette had thought it enough to pretend, but the effect of the great ceremony lasted no longer than the decorations.

The plain fact was that order was unraveling everywhere. In August, for instance, the garrison of Nancy, which was tired of obeying its officers, mutinied. The Assembly, which could see where this might lead, passed a repressive decree. The marquis de Bouillé, the local commander and a friend of Lafayette's, was instructed to put down the rebellion forcibly. He did, and Lafayette, who had supported him publicly, wrote him: "You are the savior of the state, I enjoy it doubly, as a citizen and as your friend";[30] and to Washington, he commented on August 23: "Now we are disturbed with revolts amongst the regiments—And as I am constantly attacked on both sides by the Aristocratic and the Factious party, I don't know to which of the two we owe these insurrections. . . . The people begin to be a little tired with the Revolution and the Assembly."[31]

In fact, disillusioned, the people were beginning to pay more attention to Marat, Brissot, who had now joined the most ardent revolutionaries, Danton, all leaders of the extreme left, and wanted to eliminate the King and Lafayette. On August 3, the General's order of the day to the National Guard sounded an anxious note: "The commandant-general, convinced that the Revolution that has given the people its rights and prepared its happiness, can only take root through public order, considers whoever does not hate license and anarchy an enemy of liberty. . . . Insurrection against the Assembly's decrees and the King's constitutional authority is being preached."[32]

The "massacre of Nancy"—some ten soldiers were probably killed— resulted in a major riot near the Tuileries. After all the centuries of repression, the lower classes, led by the artisans of the Faubourg Saint Antoine, wanted an end to order and social differences. Again, Lafayette was able to disperse the mob, who wanted to assault both the Assembly and the palace, but in the process his popularity dwindled. On September 13, Marat's paper, L'Ami du Peuple ("The Friend of the People") reviled the "shameful tricks used by the man Motier* to lead the Parisian army into covering itself with shame by its approbation for the massacre of the patriots in Nancy."[33] That issue was seized and never distributed, but, a little later, Camille Desmoulins, a fiery and popular speaker, wrote: "The name of Lafayette had died on our lips as that of an ambitious officer whose soul was not great enough to be a Washington and now only awaits the time when he can be another Monk."†[34]

Throughout the summer of 1790, leftist attacks on Lafayette continued. In a leaflet entitled C'en Est Fait de Nous ("We Are Done For"), which was distributed free, Marat claimed that France was about to be invaded by foreign troops under the command of the émigré comte d'Artois, but that

---

*Lafayette's full name was Motier de La Fayette; the revolutionaries now purposely dropped the more aristocratic de La Fayette and used Motier alone; it also had the advantage of creating a break within the people's memory between the current villain and Lafayette, the hero of liberty.

†The general responsible for the English Restoration of 1660.

no one dared to reveal the fact because all were afraid of the ministers, the mayor (Bailly), and "the commander of the Paris militia whose ties with the Court are all too alarming. . . . The head of your militia," he went on, "who knows all that is happening, instead of arresting the ministers, as is his duty, has contrived the escape from prison of the traitor Bonne de Savardin so as to conceal all proof of the ministry's and perhaps his own, perfidy." Marat exhorted the people to march on Saint-Cloud, where the royal family was spending the summer. They should seize the King and bring him back to Paris, jail *l'Autrichienne*, "imprison the General, arrest his staff, and seize the artillery stored in the rue Verte." And then, in an eloquent finale, Marat urged the Parisians to spill a little blood: "Five or six heads taken off their bodies would ensure peace, liberty, happiness. A mistaken humanitarianism has held you back. . . . It will cost their lives to millions of your brothers. Let your enemies triumph but for a moment, and torrents of blood will be shed: you will be murdered pitilessly, they will disembowel your wives and in order to extinguish among you the love of liberty, their bloody hands will tear out your children's hearts and entrails."[35] Stirring stuff, if perhaps not wholly convincing, even to the easily alarmed Parisians. But increasing numbers of people were beginning to listen.

Meanwhile, a new kind of anti-Lafayette pamphlet had also begun to appear. All through the Revolution, sex and politics were to remain strongly linked: the quickest way to discredit a political enemy was to expose his supposed sexual excesses. One of the chief accusations at Marie Antoinette's trial, for instance, was that she had had sex with her nine-year-old son. Now this technique was applied to the General in a pamphlet entitled *Soirées Amoureuses du Général Mottié et de la belle Antoinette par le petit épagneul de l'Autrichienne.** This little tale purports to be the memoirs of Marie Antoinette's spaniel and starts out with the dog's description of his own sexual involvement with his mistress. We then hear the Queen muttering to herself: "I was everything, now I am nothing, and it is to the red-haired general, to that chameleon that I owe my torment. . . . People are really blind when it comes to that man, who is dishonest, hypocritical, ambitious and inept; even though he betrays daily the party which brought him to power, they persist in admiring him stupidly, in considering him as . . . the firmest support of the Revolution . . . from which he profits by fooling the King and the Nation." Marie Antoinette, anxious to take her revenge on the Revolution by using Lafayette's ambition ("He controls the army, he is our

---

*"Erotic Evenings of General Mottié and the beautiful Antoinette, by the little spaniel of the Austrian."

jailer"), decides to seduce him. There follows a detailed description of the
seduction, in the midst of which Lafayette exclaims: "I have only tried to
gain the love of this misled people to bring them back to . . . the respect
they owe . . . the King. . . . And the only way I knew was to pretend approval of the rebellion."[36] Having delivered himself of his true sentiments,
he is about to consummate the love act when Louis XVI appears; after a
number of other interruptions, the door is finally locked, the Queen is about
to give herself freely when, to her fury and frustration, he finds himself
impotent. Although this pamphlet contained not a scintilla of truth, this
story, and others like it, represented an effective weapon against the General.

Still, in the autumn of 1790, there were people who were willing to
praise Lafayette. The Council of the Commune, for instance, officially described him as "a real patriot, a sincere friend of liberty, a fearless defender
of the people's rights,"[37] and once again offered him a salary—this time, it
was 100,000 livres—which he once again turned down. His gesture was
more meaningful than in 1789. Because the Assembly had abolished all feudal
dues, and also because he had been spending carelessly, Lafayette's income
had shrunk by a little over half: once all outstanding debts were paid, he
was left with a little over 55,000 livres a year. His boast to Mme de Simiane
about ending up with a quarter of his original fortune was rapidly becoming
true.

Early in October, the relationship between the only two men who
together might yet halt the government's disintegration, Mirabeau and Lafayette, passed from coolness to actual enmity. It was Lafayette's stubborn-
ness that caused the break. On October 2, the Assembly was to consider
the report of a commission charged with fixing the blame for the events of
October 5 and 6, 1789, when the Parisians had marched on Versailles.
Mirabeau and the duc d'Orléans stood to be either cleared or condemned,
and Mirabeau asked Lafayette to defend him. The General not only failed
to do so but actually stayed away from the Assembly altogether. As it turned
out, the Assembly never actually indicted either man, but Mirabeau never
forgave Lafayette; and when on the twenty-ninth, the King dismissed the
ministry, Mirabeau secretly advised him to avoid appointing a single "Fayettist" so as to publicize the General's decline in influence. At the same
time, of course, he suggested that Marie Antoinette try to "win over" Lafayette, to prevent his continuing attacks. This the Queen failed to do, for
she saw Lafayette as the man most responsible for the Revolution and in
consequence hated him. Thus the General stood in a kind of no-man's-land,
attacked from both right and left, with almost no center remaining to support
him. As for the new ministry, it was too weak to make any difference.

Mirabeau, who had a good eye for political situations, had analyzed

Lafayette's position in a letter to La Marck early in September: "Riots are the ruin of M. de La Fayette because, while they don't give him a single additional supporter, they bring him as enemies everyone who is angry at the current license and who is always ready to blame him for negligence, incompetence, or even complicity. . . . It is possible that the shame of tolerating an insurrection near an army of thirty thousand men may one day bring M. de La Fayette to order his troops to fire on the people. That alone would wound him fatally. Would the people who asked for Bouillé's head because he had shot down some mutineers forgive the commander of the National Guard a battle of citizen against citizen?"[38] Mirabeau was perfectly right: it would take only one more "revolutionary day" and Lafayette would cease to exist as a leader of the Parisians.

The General, however, thought he had found a solution: if only the King placed himself, truly and honestly, at the head of the moderate revolutionaries, everything could still be salvaged. "I will tell [the King and Queen] tonight about the dangers they are incurring; if they are not thoroughly revolutionary, and if they do no want to rely solely on [my advice], I cannot answer for the consequences," he wrote Mme de Simiane on October 20, adding, however, "The political situation is difficult, my own situation excruciating; I am hurt because I do not receive from you that consolation needed by my faded and betrayed heart, which sees the fairest of revolutions endangered by vile passions."[39] Two months later, with the situation deteriorating visibly, he tried again and reported his new effort to Adélaïde: "I have had a long and I think useless conversation with the Queen. I told her about the three parties . . . the Aristocrats led by M. d'Artois; the Orléanist whose despicable leader still manages to provide a center of attraction; and finally the popular and monarchical party, the largest but the least active, through whom alone the King can be saved.

"I explained that if I were accused of not having done everything that might be expected, it was because they wouldn't accept the Revolution. . . . I stated that for me the country came first and the King second. . . . It seemed to me that the Queen was listening to contrary advice and had been angered by false reports; that she wanted to be admirable when in danger rather than safe; that she hated me, respected me and thought that, to keep myself afloat, I needed a coalition with the King"; and then he added a postscript: "If the King wanted, I am sure that with a popular ministry and a wise policy, we could save him and the state . . . but they receive too much bad advice."[40] Whatever the possibilities of a popular government—quite possibly a contradiction in terms—Lafayette, like other liberals, now found himself in an impossible bind: the new government had a slim chance of surviving if the King truly backed it, but since Louis XVI loathed the men and resented the laws of the Revolution, there was no possibility of creating an effective centrist coalition in the Assembly. The system was, in fact, dead from the start, since neither its titular head, the King, nor its enemies wanted to have anything to do with it.

Unfortunately, Lafayette went on behaving as if words alone were enough to stem the mounting tide of disorder. He continued to make fine speeches, on November 2 to the Electoral Assembly of Paris, for instance, and frequently to the Assembly and the National Guard. The young comte de Bouillé, son of the marquis who had commanded at Nancy and a distant cousin of Lafayette's, came to see him in January 1791 and made it very plain that he was a conservative royalist, but, as he did with almost everyone, Lafayette spoke to him freely. He always liked the young, whatever their political position, when they were disinterested and fiery, and had a strong family feeling besides; and their conversation, which was followed by long letters, set out the General's official position in early 1791:

"M. de La Fayette protested with great eloquence . . . that he was attached to the monarchy, and, more particularly to the King's person, that he was a moderate and had no personal ambition. . . .

"The King now serves the Constitution [he said], I need therefore hardly tell you that I am pleased with him. Besides, you know him, he's a nice man, very weak, and I could do anything I wanted with him if it weren't for the Queen who is a great impediment to me. She often seems to trust me but then she doesn't sufficiently follow the advice I give her and which would make her popular. She has everything that's needed to gain the hearts of the Parisians but then her old pride, and a bad temper she doesn't know how to conceal, often alienate them. I wish she would show me more good faith."[41] Bouillé, demonstrating the blindness typical of his party and assuming Lafayette was ruled exclusively by self-interest, suggested a solution: Lafayette would become dictator and save the King. Lafayette, however much complimented, demurred. "He told me that his only ambition was for the people's well-being and the completion of a free and effective constitution; that the only reward he wanted for his services was the respect and esteem of his fellow citizens; that once he had accomplished his task he would take back his rank in the army and retire to the country. . . . Then, he added, 'I will enjoy the fruit of my labors; then I will have acquired an existence that I will owe solely to the purity of my principles; the simplicity of my character and the people's trust will put me above the King himself.' "[42]

Lafayette fooled himself into thinking his well-meaning attempts to help Louis XVI—his suggestions continued to flow thick and fast—had finally convinced the royal couple, but actually the King and Queen no longer argued because they simply were not listening to him. Far from accepting the Revolution, the Queen was already writing her brother to ask that an Austrian army invade France and restore the ancien régime. Louis XVI himself was rapidly reaching the point where he would take any risk rather than continue to be the King of the Revolution; and on the left, moderates were now beginning to be thoroughly intimidated by the extremists. The full measure of Lafayette's tragic isolation can be seen in a royalist pamphlet, for instance, which came close enough to the truth to do real damage. "Everyone asks: is M. de La Fayette a demagogue or a royalist? Does he want to uphold or topple the throne? No one can answer the question and both parties distrust the Parisians' General equally. . . . The circumstances have produced in M. de La Fayette a kind of prudence that looks very much like falseness," and after a long—and unflattering—review of Lafayette's history, the anonymous author concluded: "Weak and irresolute under all circumstances, his behavior is almost always characterized by timidity or hypocrisy. . . . Meant by nature to play a secondary role, M. de La Fayette needs to be led. . . . He has, in his folly, thought he could emulate Washington; but what a difference in men and circumstances."[43]

A more impartial observer, Gouverneur Morris, at this time came to similar conclusions in a letter to Washington. After saying that Lafayette had "hitherto acted a splendid part," Morris went on: "Unfortunately both for himself and his Country, he has not the Talents which his situation requires. This important Truth known to so few from the very beginning is now but too well understood by the People in general. His authority depends on Incidents and sinks to nothing in a Moment of Calm so that if his Enemies would let him alone his twinkling light would expire. He would then perhaps raise Commotions in order to quell them. This his enemies have long charged him with, unjustly I believe. . . . The King obeys but detests him. Whoever possesses the royal Person may do what he pleases with the royal Character and authority. Hence it happens that the [new] Ministers are of Lafayette's appointment . . . Lafayette thinks that these his Creatures will worship their Creator, but he is mightily mistaken."[44] In fact, the King had appointed ex-Fayettists—men who had followed the General earlier on, but now simply tried to survive on their own.

The one group Lafayette always felt he could count on was the National Guard. Order had to be maintained and with Bailly constantly asking for help, the General was kept busy; but there, too, as Lafayette apparently moved to the center, the loyalty of the troops became increasingly uncertain. The Assembly began to adopt ever more extreme measures, the mobs grew angrier and the King more unpopular. On February 26, Bailly had to ask the General to post sentries along the terrace of the Tuileries to stop the people who, standing right under Louis XVI's windows, were shouting insults. Around the same time, a band of extremists had to be prevented from razing the old fortress of Vincennes; on this occasion, sixty-four men were taken prisoner, and Lafayette was blamed by the mob for his "reactionary" attitude. Then, there was an incident right in the palace—a few misguided noblemen armed with knives, who had formed a secret body sworn to protect the King, were discovered; and since it was the role of the National General to look after the King, Lafayette disarmed them. Even then, the General was blamed for the incident by the right, who resented his action, and by the left, who said the incident was proof of laxness on Lafayette's part. The left thought the noblemen should have been jailed, while Louis XVI manifested his displeasure at the disbanding of the nobles by asking the General to deny publicly a rumor that he had been appointed captain of the King's Guard. This he did in print.

Now events speeded up. The Assembly had passed laws creating a French church separate from the universal Roman Catholic communion— the *constitution civile du clergé*—and requiring all churchmen to swear obedience to this new body. The Pope condemned both the new church and the laws governing it as schismatic, forbidding all priests and bishops to obey; and the King, who was a devout Catholic, found that he had had enough. He did not dare veto the new law; but he determined he would not observe it himself, and Lafayette's effort to persuade him was in vain. The first confrontation came when, rather than take Easter Communion from the hands of a constitutional priest—there were a few—Louis XVI decided to spend the holiday in Saint-Cloud where he could more easily bring in a nonjuring priest. Lafayette, himself, had no objections to the King's wishes. After all, not only did he believe in religious toleration—and now orthodox Catholic priests were in the same position as Protestant ministers a few years earlier—but also Adrienne, like the King, had refused to countenance the constitutional clergy, and she, too, was looking for a nonjuring priest since most were already in hiding. Unfortunately, the National Guard who were being rapidly radicalized by events, did not feel as tolerant as their General. Thus when the King got into his carriage the morning of April 18 on his way to Saint-Cloud, the guards on duty in the Tuileries Palace courtyard, who had guessed his reason for leaving Paris, refused to let him go. They harassed the royal family, who could only sit helplessly in its carriage.

Lafayette had no doubt as to where the real blame belonged; "I knew the stupidities of the Court would lead to this," he wrote Mme de Simiane that evening. "The extremists have taken advantage of it and I'm afraid public affairs are in a very bad state. . . . The day has been disastrous and a little dangerous [for me]. I will at least end it pleasantly by telling you of my tenderness for you."[45] Lafayette reasoned that the incident was all the King's fault because, instead of sneaking off to Saint-Cloud, he should have overtly demanded a nonjuring priest. That, in fact, would have provoked a worse riot.

And now there could be no blinking of the fact Louis XVI was a prisoner in his own palace, denied the very religious freedom supposedly guaranteed by the Constitution; worst of all, the National Guard, ordered by Lafayette to let the King go, had refused to obey—an obvious insult to their commandant-general.

It took the General three days to come to a decision, but finally, on April 21, he resigned his command. It was, of course, the same stratagem he had used in 1789, after the lynching of Foulon and Berthier. Then, after his resignation speech to the Council of the Commune, he fainted dead away: whether or not the faint was genuine, all present enjoyed the drama. The very next day, after the council begged him to resume his office, he came down to the Hôtel de Ville and delivered another long address. "I cannot believe," he said, "that the National Guard has seen with indifference the causes of my discouragement: the lawful authorities ignored, their orders held in contempt, the forces of order refusing to carry out the laws whose protection they must ensure. We are citizens, we are free, but if the laws be not obeyed, nothing remains but anarchy, confusion, and despotism. . . .

"I admit that in order to command [the National Guard] I must be sure that it believes unanimously that the fate of the Constitution rests on the rule of law, that sole sovereign of a free people; that personal and religious freedom, the safety of the home and the respect for all legitimate authorities would be as sacred for the Guards as for myself."[46]

Then Lafayette again refused to reconsider his resignation. Hundreds of guards followed him home, calling after him, and, kneeling before a statue of Liberty that had been set up before his door, begged him to be their general once more. This time, in a great display of emotion, he accepted. Touching, perhaps, but the main issue remained unresolved: the General might be back in apparent command, but the guards, much as they wanted him back, still had no intention of allowing Louis XVI to leave his palace. In 1789, Lafayette's resignation had helped him to reestablish some measure of order. In 1791, it merely confirmed the erosion of his power.

By now both the ladies in Lafayette's life had become seriously upset by the turn of events. Although she still worshiped her husband, Adrienne was troubled by the new religious laws as well as by the increasingly dreadful situation of the royal family. She did not blame Gilbert, but begged him to help; as for Mme de Simiane, she was simply horrified. Although it seems very probable that, at this point, their relationship had become more epistolary than physical—Lafayette, who was always in public, literally had neither the time nor the opportunity to see his mistress—Mme de Simiane had stayed on in Paris, partly out of devotion to the Queen, partly because she knew the General could still protect her, and partly, no doubt, because she still hoped to convert him to her own brand of conservative royalism. At any rate, she never hesitated to criticize him; and, sometime in May, Lafayette was writing her: "I cannot tell you how much sorrow your letter has caused me. This Revolution that I had long wished for, that my efforts have, in part, provoked, that I defend with all my might, is making all those I love unhappy. I will be devoted to it until my dying day but all the charms it had for me have been poisoned by the effect it has on the people dearest to my heart."[47] The clear dawn of a new age was rapidly turning into the dreariest of sunsets.

Then, on June 20, 1791, disaster struck. If Lafayette had looked out of his carriage window as he left the Tuileries that evening, he might well have noticed a very familiar figure hurrying away across the terrace, her face concealed by a hat and a veil. Within a few minutes, she climbed into a waiting carriage, there to be joined by several other people; the coachman jerked his reins and they were off. The lady was Marie Antoinette; bright and early the next morning, June 21, Lafayette was given the appalling news that the royal family had run away. And even the moderate royalists, who were devoted to the person of the King, suddenly found themselves in an impossible position: were they to follow the monarch, in whose person the government was incarnate, or disown their most cherished beliefs?

It should have been no surprise, really. Louis XVI had made it very clear that he resented being held prisoner and that his inability to see a nonjuring priest was torturing him. Of course, the King had repeatedly promised not to leave, and Lafayette had believed him. Now he found himself confronted with a dangerous dilemma: there could be no constitutional monarchy without a king. Adrienne, as Morris described her later that day, was "half wild." Obviously something had to be done, and fast, before the government collapsed. As Lafayette describes it in his memoirs, he immediately summoned Bailly and Alexandre de Beauharnais, the current President of the National Assembly.* " 'Do you think,' he asked them, 'that the arrest of the King and his family is necessary for the country's good and can alone prevent a civil war?' There could be no doubt about the answer. Then, he said, 'I will take that responsibility.' And, right here, he wrote out, on a sheet of National Guard official stationery: 'Order to arrest the King. The

---

*And husband of the future Empress Josephine.

enemies of the Revolution having kidnapped the King, this messenger will warn all good citizens. It is ordered in the name of the Fatherland in danger to free [the King] from their hands and to bring him back to the National Assembly. It will meet soon but, in the meantime, I take upon myself the full responsibility of this order,' "[48] and, signing his name, he sent couriers galloping after the fugitives.

That the King had been abducted by enemies of the Revolution was a convenient but wholly transparent fiction. Obviously, if it were officially admitted that the King had fled, the whole constitutional setup would collapse. "The intention of the Assembly, I find, is to cover up the King's Flight and cause it to be forgotten," Morris noted a few days later, adding: "This proves to me a great Feebleness in every respect and will perhaps destroy the monarchy."[49] And indeed, on the twenty-first, the Assembly passed a motion stating that it "had learned of the attempt made the previous night on the King and a part of his family in the foolish hope of subverting liberty in France."[50]

Nothing could have been more stupid. For one thing, the comte de Provence, the King's constitutionalist brother, had also fled; for another, Louis XVI had left a manifesto behind denouncing the Revolution and all its works. Sure enough, when the King and his family, waiting for fresh horses at the little post-inn of Varennes, were recognized by the post-master, who compared the profile on a coin to that of the gentleman sitting in a corner of the carriage, they were arrested and held in one of the upstairs rooms of the inn. There were no abductors in sight anywhere. The anti-royalists, of course, saw their chance. Not only did they now begin to demand a republic—there was, after all, no longer a king—but they also attacked the commandant-general of the National Guard: at the Jacobins, Danton thundered: "M. le commandant-général promised on his head that the King would not leave; we must have the person of the King or the head of M. le commandant-général."[51] However, because Alexandre de Lameth, one of the "Americans," opposed the motion, it failed, but only barely, to pass.

By June 25, the royal family, accompanied by the three official commissioners sent at the Assembly's orders—Maubourg and the declared republicans Barnave and Jérôme Pétion—arrived back in Paris where they were treated like runaway convicts. The troops lining the streets were ordered not to salute; the crowds shouted insults. When the carriage finally drew up in front of the Tuileries, and its passengers, amid the jeers, reentered the palace, Marie Antoinette, whose hair had until then been blond, was seen to have turned gray overnight. Lafayette, on the other hand, appeared as jaunty as ever. "Sire," he told the King, "Your Majesty knows how attached I am to you; but I have always said that if you were to separate your cause from that of the people, I would remain on the people's side."

"Yes," Louis XVI answered, "that's true, you have followed your principles, it is all a question of party. I will tell you frankly that I had thought you were surrounding me with a whirlwind of people of your opinion, but that the French did not agree with you. I have seen clearly, during this trip, that I was wrong, and that yours was the prevalent opinion."[52] With that, guards were posted at every door, and when Lafayette asked the King whether he had any orders to give, Louis XVI, in an unusual moment of irony, answered: "It seems to me that your orders matter more than mine." At least the General, contrary to the Assembly's decree, decided it was not necessary to isolate the various members of the royal family or to have a man spending the night inside the Queen's bedroom. The King was declared suspended from his royal functions, and everyone waited for the cover-up.

It came immediately. Officially, a pall of forgetfulness descended on the whole episode; it was, however, contradicted by the fact that the King was still suspended. Either he had fled, and he ought not to reign, or he had been abducted, was innocent, and should not be penalized. A halfway measure such as the one adopted was self-defeating; and all the moderates wondered what to do next. By July 1791 they had found a solution. Since the Assembly was not ready for a republic, the constitutional monarchy had to be set up anew: it was time, at long last, to produce a proper constitution. This the Assembly proceeded to draft in the midst of great confusion. Lafayette, of course, participated in the effort and was responsible for the exclusion of the *constitution civile du clergé* from the final document.

All the way across the ocean, President Washington, who, now that he represented his country, usually abstained from comment on the events in France, sent Lafayette a warning. "The tumultuous populace of the cities," he wrote, "are ever to be dreaded. Their indiscriminate violence prostrates for the time all public authority, and its consequences are sometimes extensive and terrible. In Paris we may suppose these tumults are particularly disastrous at this time, when the public mind is in a ferment and when (as is always the case on such occasions) there are not wanting wicked and designing men, whose element is confusion and who will not hesitate in destroying the public tranquillity to gain a point. But until your constitution is fixed, your government organised and your representative Body renovated, much tranquillity cannot be expected."[53] As usual, Washington was right, but unfortunately, the French deputies had only the most theoretical notions of how a constitution would actually work; and at that very time— July 28—they were busy producing a completely unworkable document.

Even as Lafayette, partly under the double influence of Adrienne and

Adélaide, was pressing the Assembly to crown its constitution with a monarch, and to let that monarch be Louis XVI—he was, after all, the only Bourbon still residing in Paris—his outward life in Paris still remained unchanged. "I dined frequently with General Lafayette," wrote the young Lord Holland, a Whig aristocrat then visiting Paris. "He kept a sort of open table for officers of the National Guard and other persons zealous and forward in the cause of the Revolution. I was pleased with the unaffected dignity and simplicity of his manners, and flattered by the openness with which he spoke to me of his own views and the situation of the country. He was loud in condemning the brutality of Pétion, whose cold and offensive replies to the questions of the royal prisoners on their journey back from Varennes were very currently repeated; and he was in his professions, and I believe in his heart, much more confident of the sincerity of the King than common prudence should have allowed him to be. . . . Lafayette was, however, then as always a pure, disinterested man full of private affection and public virtue, and not devoid of such talents as firmness of purpose, sense of honour, and earnestness of zeal will, on great occasions, supply. He was indeed accessible to flattery and apt to mistake the forms or, if I may so phrase it, the pedantry of liberty for the substance."[54]

Lord Holland's presence in the middle of the Revolution is one of the curious footnotes to the history of this period; until the late summer of 1792, tourists from across the Channel kept streaming into Paris as if it were still the capital of pleasure. Looking back, the French Revolution often seems a long orgy of revolt and blood, but for the contemporaries, at least until the beginning of the Terror, life went on much as before. Even if somewhere in Paris men were marching with pikes and menacing shouts, on the Champs Elysées elegant women still strolled undisturbed. Unlike the English, who were known to be violent, the French had such a reputation for urbane civilization that very few people foresaw the later horrors of the guillotine.

Still, by mid-July, a new turn was being taken. The fourteenth, with its celebration of the two great anniversaries, the fall of the Bastille and the Federation, passed quietly; but then on the sixteenth, a mob started gathering in the Champs de Mars to demand that Louis XVI be deposed. Whatever loyalty the mob still retained the King had lost by his flight; besides, absolute equality—a republic—had become an accepted goal. A monster petition, organized by the Orléanists, was to be signed by all present. Soon, signatures seemed too tame; by the seventeenth a major riot was under way.

That morning, Morris wrote, "Two Men were lanterned and mangled in the parisian Taste. This occasioned some little Stir. There had been a pretty general Summons to the friends of Liberty, requesting them to meet in the Champ de Mars. The object of this Meeting was to perswade the Assembly by the gentle Influence of the Cord to undo what they had done respecting the imprisoned Monarch."[55] In fact, the Orléanists quickly lost control of the crowd to the republicans; and the Assembly, with its anti-Orléans and antirepublican majority, saw this as the perfect occasion to restore order. Bailly, told to act, requested Lafayette to bring in the guard and the riot was suppressed by force. The General was shot at and narrowly missed; some twelve rioters, after due warning, were killed by the guards, and the fracas was over. To all appearances Lafayette, Bailly, and the forces of order had won.

In fact, the government lost all its support; and Lafayette from the day he raised weapons against "the people"—rioters or not—was seen as a murderer and lost all influence over the Parisian populace. Now the Revolution was able to proceed unhampered: only the left—Girondins and Jacobins—had any power in Paris; the Assembly itself was becoming irrelevant. At the same time, and for a while longer, the political process continued to function. In August, the Constitution was finished. In September, Louis XVI was reinstated so that he could accept it (no one contemplated the possibility that he might refuse it); on the thirteenth, at the King's suggestion, a general amnesty was decreed; on the eighteenth, the Constitution was officially proclaimed; on the thirtieth, the National Assembly, after having forbidden its members to serve either in the forthcoming Assemblée Législative or in the executive branch of the government, dissolved itself. And on October 8, Lafayette, in turn, resigned his command. He had, he said, completed his task. France had a free constitution, the Revolution was at an end, and he could at last retire to Chavaniac. The National Guard voted him a gold-handled sword, the commune had a medal struck in his honor, and he was off to the Auvergne.

When cowboys at the end of a Western ride into the sunset, the audience can relax, safe in the knowledge that the bad guys have been taken care of, but when Lafayette drove off to the Auvergne, he was leaving behind him a highly explosive situation. Bailly resigned as mayor of Paris, and Pétion, the republican who had arrested the King and a known enemy of the General, decided to run. A group of Fayettists, thereupon, put up Lafayette's name for election—with his consent. The vast majority of the electors prudently abstained: since there was no secret ballot, it was too dangerous to appear in public as a moderate. When the votes were in, Pétion had won by 6,728 to 3,123.

With the city administration now in extremist hands, Louis XVI, hardly even able to take a walk in the Tuileries gardens, could only hope for a war in which France would be defeated by his brother-in-law, the Emperor

Leopold, whose army would crush the Revolution. Since the left also wanted a war, thinking that it would provoke a burst of patriotic, antiroyalist feeling, the King decided to play along. He appointed new ministers and the country headed for a conflict with Austria. What no one quite realized yet, however, was that both King and Constitution had become largely irrelevant. Policy, more and more, was determined in one political club, the Jacobins. Set up like an assembly, with motions, speeches, and votes, the club represented the most extreme section of the left. It thus pushed the Girondins toward the center, a fatal position for a revolutionary party, and endeared itself to the Parisian mob with whom, increasingly, all power rested. A government of laws had been replaced by the rule of violence.

In the meantime a new Assembly had been elected and the Constitution of 1791 had come into effect. The charter had been composed solely by the National Assembly; neither the King nor the ministers had been allowed even to make suggestions. And since the memories of the ancien régime were still so fresh, the Assembly had bent over backward to make sure the executive branch could never again become despotic—but this overcompensation so hobbled the executive branch as to make all government impossible.

All real power was vested in a 745-member Assemblée Législative whose deputies were forbidden to serve two consecutive terms. The Assembly could be neither dissolved nor prorogued except by itself. The King was allowed to read his messages in person, but, as soon as he had done so, the meeting was suspended. The ministers could ask to be heard; they could also be questioned, accused, or impeached. The Assembly reserved to itself the right, along with the regular judiciary, to arrest, try, and convict. Only the Assembly could initiate or pass a law; if it voted that there was an emergency, the law could be passed within the day, a great convenience on those occasions when an angry mob filled the public's tribune. The Assembly alone decided on the budget and taxation: the King had nothing to say about that at all; he wasn't even allowed to use his veto on them. He could, however, veto any other law, unless three successive legislatures had passed it.

Opposite this all-powerful Assembly, the King was left naked. Although, theoretically, the King's person was inviolable—the ministers were responsible for all political decisions—the corollary was that he was paralyzed. He was allowed neither a private fortune nor the ownership of any land: he must live wholly off his civil list.* He could be dethroned if he left the kingdom or even a fifty-mile circle around Paris, if he led the army, or if he refused

---

*The yearly income given him by the Assembly.

to swear obedience to the Constitution. He was given guards but was refused the right to command them himself or select their commander. He appointed the ministers but they could be impeached. Two-thirds of all army officers, all civil servants outside Paris, all judges, all priests were to be elected, and the King could not fire them. If there was a rebellion, the King was forbidden to do anything unless it involved an entire department, and even then, after notifying the Assembly, he still needed to receive a formal authorization to reestablish order. He was forbidden to give pensions or grants of money, to declare war or to make peace. A look across the Channel for comparison showed the extent of Louis XVI's predicament. George III was a constitutional monarch, but he appointed all army officers, civil servants, and judges; he was allowed to have a private fortune, he could move around as he pleased, controlled his guard, gave pensions, and, all in all, enjoyed powers not far removed from those of the President of the United States today.

With the Constitution immobilizing the executive branch of government, the country began to come apart. The courts were open to the worst kind of electioneering. There was no reason why any civil servant should obey orders since he could not be promoted or fired. Even Lafayette admitted that "the executive and the efficacity of the government had been enfeebled,"[56] but that was only in private. In public, he claimed that the Constitution was flawless and that the country was now ready for a new era of peace and prosperity. On October 20, he wrote Adélaide de Simiane, describing his trip to Chavaniac in glowing terms. "Forced to stop everywhere, to cross cities and towns on foot, to receive enough civic crowns to fill the carriage, I can no longer travel as fast as I once did. I left Clermont at night; the city was illuminated throughout. We were surrounded by the National Guard and by men carrying torches: it was really a charming spectacle. . . .

"It is as a lover of liberty and equality that I enjoy the change which has put all citizens on the same level and given preeminence only to the lawful authorities. I cannot tell you with what delight I bow to a village mayor. . . . Only the duty of defending us could now take me out of my private life."[57]

In fact, that charming side of Lafayette, the good family man, loving father, and devoted husband, had once again come to the fore. For Adrienne, away at last from Paris, its storms and its beauties, it was a golden moment. "M. de Lafayette having remained unchanged after three years spent amid such storms, retaining that simplicity of habits, that freshness of feeling for his aunt and the place of his birth, was happy to be surrounded by his children, happy to find himself cherished by the two mothers [his aunt and his mother-in-law] whom he was so fond of,"[58] Adrienne wrote. Their lives

were idyllic: the old castle, the devoted peasants—unlike most of the countryside, Chavaniac was largely untouched by the Revolution—added to the
satisfaction of accomplishment; and the strong link to Adrienne, perhaps
grown a little weaker as Gilbert fell in love with other women, was now
regaining its strength, but all that happiness lasted a mere five weeks. On
December 15, 1791, the Lafayettes returned to Paris—France was on the
brink of war.

Three separate armies had been raised to defend the north of France
where the Austrians were expected to attack. Rochambeau was given one
of the commands, the veteran maréchal Nicolas de Luckner another, and,
at the Minister of War's insistence, Lafayette was given the third by a very
reluctant Louis XVI. Seldom has a conflict been awaited with more opposed
feelings by different classes of a nation. The left thought of it as the way to
win the Republic; the moderates dreaded the uncertainty of what the war
might bring, knowing full well it was unlikely to work to their advantage;
and the court hoped for a prompt defeat that would allow the invading forces
to reestablish the ancien régime. Louis XVI therefore did as much as he
could to hamper the war effort; the Assembly, meanwhile, convinced that
France was invincible, saw no reason to vote special credits. That left the
frantic Louis de Narbonne, a liberal nobleman and the Minister of War,
who, almost alone, was trying to raise, supply, and organize armies. By
January 1792, most of the officer corps had deserted: they were, after all,
aristocrats who loathed the new regime, and in any case their soldiers, who
felt that liberty should be universal, at best refused to obey them and at
worst tried to murder them. Not only was it virtually impossible to find
trained replacements for the deserting officers but two-thirds of all new
candidates had to be elected by their troops, a system calculated to abolish
discipline very quickly. Finally the central administration, never a model of
efficiency, had been thoroughly disorganized by the Revolution. It is easy
to see why Louis XVI and Marie Antoinette were so looking forward to the
declaration of war: as they and all Europe knew, the French army had
become a laughingstock.

With his usual blind optimism, Lafayette disregarded all difficulties.
On December 24, he was admitted to address the Assembly, assured it of
his respect and "his unchanging and ineradicable devotion to the Constitution."[59] He then went to thank the King, who received him very coolly,
for his appointment. By the end of the month, he had joined his army in
Metz.

There, he found a rabble of undisciplined men, a critical shortage of
officers, and hardly any supplies. This might have proved daunting to an
ordinary general, but for Lafayette, it was a thoroughly familiar situation

and he promptly set about improving it. "I am going, and I am the only one whose popularity can stand it, to establish in spite of the [political] Clubs and the Jacobine clamours a most severe discipline and I think afterwards the army will do pretty well,"[60] he wrote Washington on January 22; and, for a while, he was indeed successful. He used all the methods he had learned in America: he badgered the government for supplies, and, while maintaining the most exact discipline, made himself popular with the men by unflagging attention to their well-being; he inspected hospitals and food supplies, tasted the soldiers' soup, got them better clothing.

Of course, there was a great difference between the Continental army and the forces gathered at Metz. For one, the central government had been undermined on two sides—by the King who wanted a quick defeat and by the left who wanted to take over. For another, the Revolution itself was constantly creating new difficulties. In January, for instance, Provence and Artois, the King's two émigré brothers, were declared traitors for having left France; on February 9, the Assembly decreed the confiscation of all émigré property. Nonjuring priests began to be in serious danger. In Paris the temper of the crowds grew hotter every day. At the end of February, it looked as if the government would fall apart. Narbonne called in the commanders for a conference, disagreed with them about the opening operations of the as yet undeclared conflict, and resigned. With great difficulty he was convinced to stay; and it was agreed that, as soon as war was declared, Lafayette would march into the Austrian Netherlands (today's Belgium) with forty thousand men, that Rochambeau would follow and assist him, and that Luckner would defend the Rhine.

On March 6, Narbonne asked the Assembly for more money. The government had floated a paper currency, the assignat, and now found that the scrip did not inspire confidence and consequently tended to depreciate, so more funds were needed for the army. The Assembly granted the new credits, but it kept moving to the left; and on March 14 Louis XVI was forced to appoint a new government chosen among the Girondins, who were outflanked by the Jacobins only. Jean-Marie Roland, a republican who despised Lafayette, became Minister of the Interior, and de Graves, an incompetent, Minister of War. As usual, the General tried to take a positive view, but this time his worry began to show: "The King has chosen his Council amidst the most violent party. . . . [This is] more fit to make deserters from than converts to our cause. The new ministers, however, being unsuspected, have a chance to restore public order and say they will improve it. The Assembly are wildly uninformed and too fond of popular applause, and the King slow and rather backward in his daily conduct,"[61] Lafayette wrote.

In fact, far from being "slow and backward," Louis XVI was doing his best to encourage the rashness of his Girondin ministers. He was confident that the French army would collapse on its first contact with the Austrians, and that, within days, absolutism would be restored in a cowed and occupied Paris at the order of Marie Antoinette's brother, the Emperor. Naturally, what he said in public was quite different: he spoke of defending France's honor and crushing the enemy—a task so easy, he said, that it was not even necessary to waste effort or money on further preparations.

As a result, Lafayette found himself in a no-win situation: the King wanted to see him defeated, the government reached an extreme degree of incompetence, the speakers at the Jacobin Club concentrated their attacks on Lafayette while he was simultaneously assaulted by a recrudescence of pamphlets comparing him alternately to Monk and to Cromwell.

Back in Metz, Lafayette continued to look after his troops, but he was now seriously worried that France might soon slip into a new kind of despotism, that of the extreme left. On April 20, when France declared war on Austria because it had concentrated troops in the Netherlands, he asked the Assembly to decree that the most severe discipline was to be maintained— the few officers that remained were deserting in droves. Indeed, the first consequence of the declaration of war was chaos. Lafayette's advance was stopped by news of general uprisings in the advance guard who had panicked and murdered their commanding officer. Occupying the fortified camp of Maubeuge, unable to go forward, he wrote, "I cannot conceive how the war could have been declared, since nothing was ready."[62]

Meanwhile, in Paris, the war was having the opposite effect from what Louis XVI had expected: that of uniting the left and increasing its popularity. For now the people began to perceive, rightly, that the King and court were obstructing the war efforts while communicating military secrets to the Austrians on the borders. They began to think the generals must also be in cahoots with the enemy because no victories had yet been won. On May 9, Servan, also a Girondin, but a reasonable man, took on the War Ministry just in time to commend a retreat skillfully led by Laurent de Gouvion, one of Lafayette's lieutenants; but Roland was proving constantly more hostile, and Lafayette's position, consequently, grew ever more precarious.

The temper of Paris grew increasingly dangerous. Soon, even the Girondins began to look too moderate. On June 13, Louis XVI, no longer free to appoint men of his choice, changed his ministry again under pressure from the Assembly. This time, Lafayette decided to act, and on June 16, he sent the Assembly a letter. This, in itself, was a mark of boldness, despite appearances to the contrary. Having once proclaimed himself a constitutional monarchist, Lafayette, in spite of changing circumstances, was keeping to his old beliefs—an act of no small courage. In fact, for the first time since July 1789, Lafayette refused to abandon principle for popularity.

"The state is in peril," the General wrote, "and the fate of France depends mainly upon its representatives. The Nation expects its salvation from them; but when it gave itself a constitution, it also prescribed for them the only way in which they could save it. . . .

"Can you refuse to see that . . . the Jacobine faction has caused all the disorders? I accuse it now of this. Organized like an empire throughout the country, blindly led by a few ambitious men, this sect forms a separate body amid the French people whose powers it usurps by subjugating its representatives. . . . Because we must fight the foreigners who want to intervene in our domestic quarrels, must we not therefore free our fatherland from a domestic tyranny? . . .

"Let the royal power remain intact, for it is guaranteed by the Constitution; let it be independent for that independence is one of the mainstays of our liberty; let the King be revered, for he is imbued with the Nation's majesty; let him chose a ministry free from the bonds of faction; and if there be conspirators, let them perish under the sword of the law."[63]

It was so daring a letter that many people thought it apocryphal, and it created the final break between Lafayette and the revolutionary left: the promoter of the Revolution had changed sides, or so it seemed to the King and Jacobins. The "republican" was defending the King.

That his new and enthusiastic backing of Louis XVI owed something to the objurgations of both Adrienne and Adélaide de Simiane cannot be doubted; that, also, he felt a sort of compassion for the now powerless monarch is extremely probable; but above all, he believed in the Constitution. Only its strict observance, he thought, could ensure permanent freedom for the French and, increasingly, the charter was being disregarded by the all-powerful Assembly. Finally, Lafayette had always disliked street violence, the very weapon the Jacobins were using to intimidate the government and destroy his own popularity, something he had made great efforts to preserve.

The General's letter immediately caused great indignation: an army commander, some deputies said, had no right to make political suggestions. Naturally, the Jacobins went even further: Danton, on June 18, exclaimed, "There can be no doubt that Lafayette is the head of the nobles who are allied with the tyrants of Europe," while Robespierre, who always had a preference for radical methods, added, "Strike Lafayette and the nation is safe."[64]

Then, on June 20, 1792, the people of Paris (or, at any rate, the politically active fraction thereof) rose yet again. This time, the mob invaded the Palace of the Tuileries, cornered Louis XVI, forced him to put on a red hat and drink a toast (in red wine) to the Revolution, and kept him there, amid pikes and drawn knives, for several hours. It was now clear that the monarchy was in the gravest trouble and that the Constitution was fast becoming irrelevant. Away in Metz, Lafayette tried to convince Luckner to join him in a march on Paris where, together, they would reestablish order, dispose of the Jacobins, and reinstate the King to his rightful constitutional place, but the aging Luckner was not about to take unnecessary chances, and he refused.

Once again, therefore, Lafayette decided to rely on the ghost of his popularity. In an order of the day, he told the army he was off to Paris, and, without warning the War Minister, as was his duty, he appeared in the capital on the twenty-eighth, went straight to the Assembly, and demanded to be heard.

There, he explained that, having provided for the army's safety, he had come to protest the invasion of the Tuileries, and affirmed that his June 16 letter was indeed authentic. He then made a plea for a return to a strict application of the Constitution. A violent debate followed, with the left demanding the General's head, but many of the deputies still warmly remembered the Fete of the Federation, and in the end, a majority approved Lafayette's actions. But even at the time, since he was under violent attack by the Jacobins, it was easy to see that majority was not likely to survive for long. The King and Queen, whom Lafayette visited next, received him with the most distant politeness: although he might now disapprove of the course of the Revolution, they blamed him for starting it in the first place.

The next day, after having been applauded by some crowds near the Assembly, Lafayette returned to Maubeuge. His trip, however much it may have salved his conscience, had absolutely no effect. The days when the Hero of Two Worlds could influence an Assembly were long past.

Even Lafayette could see this, so he decided, some time in June, that he must save the King and the Constitution by stronger means. He wrote secretly to Louis XVI to suggest a plan: the King would go to the Assembly and announce that he would spend the summer at his palace in Compiègne, just inside the constitutional limit within which he was permitted to move, under the protection of the National Guard. Lafayette would then march his army to Compiègne, meet with the King, arrest the Jacobins, and restore the proper constitutional order. Later, Lafayette claimed that the royal couple rejected his plan because they resented his role as the protector of liberty; Marie Antoinette, in particular, was not about to undertake so risky an operation with a man she so thoroughly distrusted. More likely, however, the King and Queen must have realized that the plan was simply foolish. Well aware of the King's attitudes, the Assembly would never have allowed him to leave Paris; the National Guard would not have protected the departing royal family; and very likely, Lafayette's army would not have followed him to Compiègne. Still, the plan did have an important use to Gilbert: it allowed him to feel that he was not responsible for the King's ultimate fate.

By now it was obvious, even across the Atlantic, that a bloodbath was on the way. "I assure you, my dear sir," Washington wrote Lafayette on June 10, "I have not been a little anxious for your personal safety; and I have yet no grounds for removing that anxiety; but I have the consolation of believing that, if you should fail, it will be in defense of that cause which your heart tells you is just."[65]

These sentiments were not very reassuring, and the war, too, was going badly. On July 6, Luckner wrote the War Minister that he lacked the means to resist an attack and that he was retreating from La Capelle to Montmédy. At that point, the government, which was beginning to worry about its generals' loyalty, switched Lafayette and Luckner without a word of explanation. Their motive, however, was obvious: by removing Lafayette to the Northern Army, where he had not yet made himself liked, the ministry ensured that the General would not be able to march on Paris. "Freedom will be in danger as long as Lafayette is at the head of an army,"[66] Robespierre had just proclaimed: changing soldiers on him would help, at least.

In Paris itself, the situation was deteriorating quickly. On July 15, one of the deputies, Basire, demanded that Lafayette be indicted for treason. The Assembly refused to do so, but the trend was obvious, and a letter from the General flatly denying the accusations made against him had very little effect. Then, on July 24, Lajard, who had been Minister of War for a little over a month, was replaced by Abancourt. Lafayette, who had been friendly with Lajard, saw this as a blow aimed directly at him; and when, on August 4, Abancourt wrote the General a friendly letter, its recipient didn't even bother to answer. When Charles Dumouriez, who had been one of the Girondin ministers, was given a command, both Lafayette and Luckner refused to have him in their armies, and although Dumouriez was finally placed in a separate corps under Arthur Dillon, Lafayette sent the minister a strong protest.

By now, it was obvious a crisis was coming. On July 20, Robespierre once again asked for Lafayette's arrest: "If Lafayette is not punished," he told the Assembly, "it means we have no constitution, for there can be no constitution where a man is above the law."[67] On August 4, a recently established committee backed Robespierre's demand. Again the Assembly refused, 406 to 224, to indict the General, but this time the refusal incited a major new riot. Six days later, on August 10, the mob again invaded the

Tuileries. The royal family took refuge in the Assembly whence, after much debate, they were sent to prison. The King was declared suspended, a condition, as Lafayette pointed out, that was unknown to the Constitution: either the King was deposed or he reigned. Although the Republic was not formally declared for another six weeks, it was obvious that the monarchy had ended and that the King's life was in grave danger.

For Lafayette, this was the breaking point. On August 12, from Sedan, where he had established his headquarters, he demanded an explanation from the War Minister. On the thirteenth, his order of the day told the army about the King's suspension and asked it to rally around him in defense of the Constitution. On the fourteenth, rather than receive the three commissioners sent by the new government, he had them arrested. Then he tried to galvanize his troops into a march on Paris; just now hopeless this was he realized when, instead of swearing an oath of loyalty to "The Nation, the Law, the King," as prescribed by the Constitution, the men, who scarcely knew him, swore spontaneously to "Liberty, Equality and the National Assembly." In Paris, the National Assembly was appointing Dumouriez to Lafayette's command and giving out an order for his arrest. The General, surrounded by some thirty of his officers, decided to flee. Before he left, he wrote the Sedan Municipal Council, on August 19, 1792: "The best way I can serve [you] is to remove a man proscribed by all the enemies of liberty and who will never bend to any despotism. . . . My only consolation will be that the sacred cause of liberty and equality, profaned . . . by the crimes of a faction, will not for long be enslaved."[68] With that, the little troupe set out for the Belgian coast where they hoped to take ship for the United States.

Nine

PRISONER OF
EUROPE

W hen Lafayette crossed the French border, on August 19, 1792, a little more than three years had passed since the beginning of the Revolution. In that short time, the Hero of Two Worlds, the Washington of France, had become a man almost universally loathed—in France, where he had joined the ranks of the aristocratic party, or so the Jacobins said; in most of Europe, where the several monarchs, alarmed by the spread of revolutionary ideas, considered him a dangerous firebrand; and among the other émigrés, all now ultraroyalists. Only a man as profoundly and foolishly optimistic as the General could have thought he would be allowed to proceed safely through the Austrian army. The French Revolution had yet to be crushed, but here, an easy prey, was one of its chief instigators. As soon as the Austrian authorities realized just which French officer it was who asked for passage to the coast, they had him arrested.

The eighteenth century, that amiable and civilized era, ended in 1789, but few people yet realized it, so the fleeing Lafayette expected to be treated as he would have been, for instance, if he had decided to ride through the

English lines at Minden. The letter he wrote Count d'Harnoncourt, who commanded the Austrian troops in the area, was obviously based on that assumption. It was also a first manifesto against the excesses of the Jacobins.

"The undersigned, French citizens, torn by a number of extraordinary and irresistible circumstances from the happiness of serving, as they have never ceased doing, the liberty of their country, and being unable to resist any longer the violations of the Constitution established by the will of the nation, declare that they cannot be considered as enemy soldiers because they have given up their commands in the French army and even less [do they belong] to that section of their compatriots whose interests, feelings or opinions are absolutely opposed to theirs and who have become linked with the foreign powers now at war with France. They are foreigners who claim the free passage guaranteed them by international custom, which they need in order to travel with all possible speed to a territory whose government is not at the moment at war with their country."[1]

The most remarkable part of this self-righteous missive is, without question, the contemptuous reference to the émigrés. At that very moment, they had joined the Prussians and Austrians who had coalesced to attack France, and they all feared and despised the very constitutional principles that Lafayette was now invoking to demand free passage. In all probability, nothing could have prevented his arrest; but the letter was bound to provoke his captors. His temporary captivity began on the evening of August 19 and was rapidly transformed into more permanent custody, despite the fact that the General had been seized on the territory of the Bishopric of Liége, then an independent and neutral state.

At first, Lafayette protested that he couldn't be arrested in a country that was not at war with France; then he demanded an interview with the local commander in chief; unfortunately that turned out to be the prince de Lambesc, a cousin of Marie Antoinette's who on July 12, 1789, had led a charge of dragoons against Parisians marching across the place Louis XV, a preliminary to the attack on the Bastille. The prince refused the interview, and the prisoners were moved to Nivelle. There, most of them were freed; only four men who had played an important role in the National Assembly were detained: Alexandre de Lameth, Maubourg, Bureaux de Puzy, Lafayette's aide-de-camp, and the General himself.

Naturally, Lafayette kept on protesting, this time to the Governor General of the Austrian Netherlands, Duke Albrecht von Sachsen-Teschen who, as it happened, had married one of Marie Antoinette's sisters. Keeping his prisoners firmly under lock and key, the duke sent to the Emperor for further instructions; in the meantime, he wrote General d'Harnoncourt: "M. de La Fayette cannot deny having been until now our declared enemy, he made war, he comes to our country not as an émigré but still imbued with his old principles, he would have continued to be our enemy if he didn't now risk being massacred by the same populace he has led against his King; further, they came upon our advanced posts without any warning and without having received any permission to do so, therefore, according to all the rules of war, he is our prisoner."[2] This somewhat breathless epistle clearly shows the terror that Lafayette could inspire in an otherwise civilized, if obtuse, personage. Then, a few days later, the duke put it all very plainly in a letter to "the monster."

"You are under arrest not as a prisoner of war," he wrote on September 12, "or as a member of the National Assembly, or as an émigré, but since you are responsible for the Revolution which has upset everything in France, since you have put your King in chains, deprived him of his legitimate rights and power and held him back in bondage [an allusion to Varennes], since you have been the main instruments of the calamities from which this unfortunate monarch suffers, it is only right that those who are working to reestablish his throne hold you until the moment when your master, having recovered his freedom and his sovereign power, will, according to his justice or his clemency, pronounce on your fate."[3] Given that France was an independent power, it was not for Austria to decide which of its citizens ought to be imprisoned, but Europe had entered the age of ideology from which the world has been suffering ever since. Lafayette was now caught, essentially, by the very image he had created: he deserved neither the glory nor the blame implied by the duke's letter, but the very reputation that he had been at such pains to build had crossed France's borders and now made him seem one of Europe's most dangerous men. Not only was he supposedly responsible for Louis XVI's misfortunes, but, if allowed to remain free, there was no telling where else he might start a revolution.

At the end of August 1792, a conference of Prussian and Austrian representatives was held to decide on the fate of the man who had become the prisoner of Europe. Its outcome boded ill for the General: Lafayette, it announced, was guilty of the crime of lèse-majesté. As the enemy of kings and a danger for all European states, he must be held under close watch in a fortress until the day when Louis XVI, reestablished on his throne, would be willing to decide his future. Short of a successful invasion that would leave Louis XVI in allied hands, there was no chance of a restoration, so the General's future looked grim indeed; nor did his prospects improve when, to everyone's surprise, the Austro-Prussian army was beaten by the French at Valmy.

Still, Lafayette was an uncomfortable possession, so the Austrians turned him over to the Prussians; they interned him in the fortress of Wesel north of Berlin, a combination of arsenal and state prison at the edge of a marsh where he was kept in a dank, cold cell and treated with great harshness. His jailers were obeying the personal order of Frederick William II, that same amiable and civilized prince whom Lafayette had met and liked at Potsdam in 1786.

Unpleasant, and even dangerous as the conditions of Lafayette's imprisonment may have been, however, they did provide him with one boon. Resisting the Jacobins in France had placed him in an extremely awkward position. Now, at last, he could go back to being himself: the man who symbolized liberty. The fact that he was jailed by the monarchs of Europe was rapidly restoring the shine to his rather tarnished halo, and it enabled him to strike his favorite pose: "It is rather strange to see La Rochefoucauld [a very liberal duke] and Barnave under the iron of the Jacobins, myself and my friends chained by the Austrians. The friends of liberty are assaulted on both sides. I can therefore feel that the only right place for me is a prison,"[4] he wrote secretly, on August 26, to his friend the princesse d'Hénin.* The man who preferred being right to being powerful, to whom fame and reputation were everything, was storing up credits as a martyr, for the future—provided his imprisonment did not last too long, of course.

From the moment of his arrest, Adrienne once again became the most important person in his life. On August 21 he was already writing her: "I could, with more ambition than morals, have had an existence very different from this; but there can never be anything in common between crime and myself. I have been the last to maintain the Constitution I had sworn to uphold. You know that my heart would have been republican if my reason had not given me a nuance of royalism, and if my fidelity to my oaths and to the nation's will had not made me the defender of the King's constitutional rights; but the less others dared to resist, the louder I spoke, and I became the object of all the attacks. The mathematical demonstration that I could no longer usefully resist crime and that I was about to be the victim of yet another crime has forced me to remove myself from a struggle in which it was obvious that I would perish fruitlessly. . . . I will not apologize to my children or to you for having ruined our family; there is none among you who could wish to owe his fortune to a behavior that would go against the dictates of my conscience. . . . Farewell, my dear heart."[5] Now that he no longer bore the impossible responsibility for the King's constitutional po-

---

*The princesse d'Hénin had been one of the most fashionable ladies at court and a friend of Marie Antoinette. She managed to combine extreme sensitivity with an amiable, if slightly excessive, promiscuity. It seems likely that Lafayette was one of the many elect.

sition and the royal family's lives, the General could now move further to the left and become a real republican, thus identifying more closely with the form of government adopted by the United States. An advantage perhaps, since it seemed fairly certain that Washington and the prisoner's other transatlantic friends would soon intervene.

Uncomfortable as the fortress of Wesel may have been for Gilbert, France was hardly a better place for Adrienne. She had been staying at Chavaniac and was enormously relieved when, on August 24, she heard that Gilbert had escaped, especially since she did not yet know of his imprisonment. However, as a woman with three young children, the wife of an émigré, and bearing a name that, in Paris, was arousing violent hatred, she had to look to her own interests. On August 10, Brissot, Lafayette's former friend, had accused him of wanting to become a dictator and demanded his arrest; within a few days his wish was satisfied. On August 19, the decree of accusation against the General was adopted by the Assembly. "The National Assembly, considering that General Lafayette used the most odious stratagems to trick the army whose command had been entrusted to him," it read, "considering that he tried to cause it to rebel against the authority of the representatives of the nation, and that he has turned against the fatherland the very weapons of the Fatherland's soldiers, considering that he accused of the crime of rebellion against the law, of plotting against freedom and of treason to the nation, decrees . . . Article 1. Motié La Fayette is hereby indicted."[6] The decree went on to order the General's arrest and to forbid the army to obey him. Lafayette had officially become an outlaw.

It was no doubt a great disappointment when, on the twenty-first, Servan, the Minister of War, informed the Assembly that the villain had emigrated. As compensation, the deputies were at last able to hear what a criminal Lafayette had been all along. The district of Crépy near Paris, for instance, sent an address to the Assembly on August 23, which turned out to be a perfect example of the new revolutionary style: "Motié Lafayette has surpassed by his audacity and his treasons Catilina, Cromwell and the other criminals who have been the bane of humanity. In an access of rage, he dared to call you slaves, but his atrocious invective is actually your praise. The Nation's sword is suspended over his criminal head and if he soils the free and equal soil of France with his impure blood, he will take to his tomb the malediction and execration of the entire universe while you will receive its blessings."[7] War naturally tends to bring on hysteria, but in this case, the violence was purely political. And on September 1, Bouquet, an ambitious soldier from the General's last army, came up to Paris from the border in an access of righteous indignation, to tell the Assembly: "We have left our camp to come and unveil before you the perfidious maneuvers of the criminal Motié de Lafayette. . . . [Our defeats] are due to his perfidy and treachery combined. . . . This monster, tainted with the blood of his brothers murdered in the Champ de Mars . . . turned against us the knives he had been secretly sharpening."[8] By December, Agier, the chief judge of the second arrondissement, claimed he was able to prove that even Lafayette's popularity was a fraud: the General, he said, would pay people two livres a day to go and applaud him when he spoke at the National Assembly.

It must have been highly frustrating for the new authorities to be unable to punish the traitor, but, at least, they might confiscate all he owned; his wife, however, was still free in Chavaniac. So Adrienne claimed the entire estate as her property and, while fighting eviction, installed herself in the neighboring town of Brioude so that no one could say that she, too, had fled the country. As an émigré, Lafayette would have all his property seized; by claiming it as part of her marriage settlement, and therefore her property, Adrienne hoped to save it because she herself had remained in France.

It was a good plan—or would have been without the excesses of the Terror. By moving to Chavaniac, she had placed herself under the protection of the Lafayette tenants, among whom she was popular, while keeping herself out of the limelight; and since the wives of émigrés had not yet lost their civil rights, she would be able to save her husband's property. Then, after a few days in Brioude, she returned to Chavaniac, only to be arrested, on September 10, by order of the Committee of Public Safety and Roland, the Minister of the Interior: Lafayette's name, after all, was too heavy to bear. Boldly, she protested she was perfectly innocent and appealed to public opinion, but Alphonse Aulagnier, the Commissioner of Police in Brioude, answered: "Today, Madame, the courts are public opinion."[9] From the castle she was taken to Le Puy, the capital of the Auvergne. There, she placed herself under the protection of the local government with which she knew she was popular, claiming that its administrators were the representatives of the people, and announced that, henceforth, she considered herself their prisoner.

Luckily, Aulagnier was a compassionate man. He knew that in Paris most of the people kept in prison, a majority of them liberals, had been massacred, while still in their cells, by the bloodthirsty mob, and that there was every chance that Adrienne would be torn from limb to limb the moment she arrived in the capital, so he took it upon himself to keep her at Le Puy and allowed her to write Brissot on September 12.

"I really believe you are fanatically devoted to the cause of liberty," the letter said. "This is an honor, right now, that I grant to very few people. . . . I think that while you want to achieve your party's goals with passion, still the means now being used are repugnant to you. I am sure that you esteem M. de La Fayette as a faithful and courageous friend of liberty even as you attack him because he holds opinions contrary to yours,"[10] and she asked to be allowed to join her husband in England, where she thought he meant to go, or else to be allowed to remain at Chavaniac on parole. It was a courageous letter; it was also clever inasmuch as it reminded Brissot that Lafayette and he had once been friends—and it worked. Brissot went to see Roland who, although he hated Lafayette, liked to think of himself as the last of the Romans and agreed to let Adrienne move back to Chavaniac.

Remarkably, dauntlessly, the "Citizeness Noailles-Lafayette" kept trying to get permission to join Gilbert, in late 1792—a time when the guillotine had started to work overtime in Paris. She wrote Brissot again, telling him she only wanted to share her husband's captivity; she even begged Roland, who answered her, in surprisingly polite tones, that the trip was impossible. Her name would make it too dangerous for her to travel, but later conditions might improve.

In the meantime, she worked to free her husband, although by no means sure that she was not already a widow. She wrote diligently to the King of Prussia, to his sister, to Washington—all to no avail. Then all her property was seized and she found herself utterly destitute, unable even to feed her family. She was rescued by a loan from Gouverneur Morris, still in Paris as America's envoy. Soon, however, she had become too conspicuous. The Girondins, now too moderate, were supplanted by the Jacobins; Roland left office and then died, and Adrienne lost her protector. On November 13, 1793, Adrienne was arrested again at Chavaniac where she had been allowed to live on parole. This time, there were no old friends to save her. Louis XVI had gone to the guillotine. Even Washington, who had sent money in January, was powerless to intervene.

Away in Germany, Lafayette, too, was being moved, from Wesel to the fortress at Magdeburg. On his way, his carriage passed that of the comtes de Provence and d'Artois, on their way to army headquarters, who made no secret of their pleasure at seeing the General thus captive. The conditions, at the new jail, a moated East Prussian fortress, were even worse than at Wesel. Although Lafayette paid for his own food—the United States had provided 10,000 florins—it was bad and insufficient; worst of all, he was allowed neither to receive nor to send letters. Finally, in May, American pressure on the King of Prussia made it possible for the flow of mail to resume, but the letters were opened and read by the authorities.

Still, now and again, Gilbert managed to have a secret letter smuggled out, mostly addressed to the princesse d'Hénin, since she was free and in England. Much as he would have liked to, he was unable to write Adrienne since he did not know where she was—or even if she was alive; so he could only worry about her. "Imagine an opening dug out from under the rampart of the fortress," he wrote Mme d'Hénin on March 13, 1793. "It is surrounded by a tall, thick palisade. It is through this that, by opening, one after the other, four doors each of which is reinforced with chains, padlocks and steel bars, one reaches, not without trouble or noise, my cell which is three steps wide and five and a half steps long. It is lugubrious, damp, and offers me, as its sole ornament, two French verses which end with *suffering* and *dying.* . . . The wall near the moat is moldy, the one in front lets in the day, but not the sun, through a tiny barred window; add to that two sentries who stare down into my basement but stand outside the palisade so they cannot talk to us, observers independent from the guard, a great number of walls, moats, ramparts, and guards in and out of the fortress . . . and you will agree that the Powers are neglecting nothing in order to keep me within their states.

"The noisy opening of my four doors takes place in the morning, to let in my servant; at lunchtime, to eat in front of the commanders of the guard and the fortress; and in the evening to take my servant back to prison. After all the doors are locked again, the commander takes the keys with him to the room where, ever since my arrival, the King has ordered him to sleep. . . .

"All my letters from my wife, my children, and my other friends have been so thoroughly intercepted that I am still in the most painful incertitude about the fate of all those I love.

"I have books from which the blank pages are torn, but no newspapers, no communications, neither ink, nor a pen, nor paper nor a pencil. It is only through a miracle I have this sheet and I am writing to you with a toothpick. . . .

"My health worsens every day, my body needs freedom almost as much as my spirit. The little amount of air which reaches this cave is destroying my chest; a fever makes it all worse; no exercise; no sleep."[11]

While it is interesting to note that, even at its most repressive, the eighteenth century still allowed a wellborn prisoner his servant, there is no doubt that the description of the harshness of prison life given by Lafayette is accurate. It was all the more impressive, therefore, that, when he was given a chance to lead a normal life again by cooperating with the Prussian army, he refused without a moment's hesitation.

"Enclosed for more than three months in the most dreadful place, deprived of all communications and all news, forced night and day to endure the indescribable torture of the surveillance by a noncommissioned officer whom they change every two hours so that I will always be watched, abandoned to diseases of the chest and the nerves, to insomnia, to fevers and especially to all the moral tortures they enjoy practicing on me, I dare say that never has the watchfulness of revenge and tyranny been brought to so eminent a degree," Gilbert wrote Mme d'Hénin on June 23, 1793. "A letter from the King [of Prussia] offered to better my condition if I would give him a [war] plan against France. . . . I answered that the King was being thoroughly impertinent in linking my name to such an idea and that, although his prisoner, I would not stand any insult from him. . . .

"I will not give you the details of the precautions with which I am surrounded; these people must think they have imprisoned the devil himself. . . . Whether a miracle gets me out of here, or whether I soon adorn a scaffold, liberty and equality will be my first and last words."[12] In fact, dreadful as the conditions of his imprisonment may have been, Lafayette was lucky to be alive. There were a great many powerful people, in Prusssia and Austria, who thought he would remain a danger to the coalition as long as he breathed.

The harshness with which Gilbert was being treated scandalized a substantial portion of the civilized world, but while the United States was ready to provide funds for the prisoner, there was little else they could do: not only were they the most minor of powers, but Washington opposed committing the nation to a political intervention based solely on interest in the fate of one individual. Still, he did what he could. "It would be agreable to me," he wrote the Secretary of State on March 13, in an attempt to mitigate the anti-Lafayette sentiment in France, "that Mr. Morris [still Minister to France] should be instructed to neglect no favorable opportunity of expressing *informally* the sentiments and the wishes of this country regarding M. de La Fayette."[13] And to Adrienne herself, the President sent a letter of sympathy, which, however, went on to say: "The measures you were pleased to intimate in your letter are perhaps not exactly those which I could pursue. . . . But be assured that I am not inattentive to his condition, nor contenting myself with inactive wishes for his liberation."[14]

The form taken by the President's wishes was that of a request that Lafayette at least be treated more humanely. In Parliament, Charles Fox, the great Whig leader, spoke eloquently in favor of the prisoners of Europe, and he was seconded by a wide majority of the members; then, in its turn, the powers took up Lafayette's cause. The outcry eventually had some effect: by August Gilbert was allowed to take daily walks in the fortress garden. This made it easier for him to sneak letters out and also to plan for an escape: no matter how agonizing the circumstances, he refused to let himself be crushed; and while he never gave up his demand to be released, he was fully determined to make a break for freedom as soon as he could. For a nobleman like Lafayette to be kept in such close and harsh confinement was altogether unique in 1793, and many another man, no matter how brave on the battlefield, would have given up. Just as Gilbert had been at his best in the United States when the situation was most difficult, he now could draw again on strengths that had seemed altogether absent during his days of triumph.

Of course, Gilbert's well-established tendency to think he had always been right now stood him in good stead: his very martyrdom confirmed his self-appointed role as the incarnation of liberty, and he was therefore all the more disposed to resist, as best he could, this new manifestation of tyranny. "You are surprised, my dear princess, to hear that [captured] members of the Convention [the current French Revolutionary Assembly] are better treated than we are," he wrote Mme d'Hénin on July 16. "Are you not aware of the regard tyrants have for one another? What have these poor Jacobins done? They have abolished freedom of the press, punished opinions, usurped all power, violated the national trust and all principles of justice. Well, say the crowned heads, we are tyrants, too. They hate the constant and sincere friend of liberty, equality, and the legal order, the enemy of all aristocracy and despotism. We too, the coalition powers say, we really hate him. . . .

"I think that some action by the United States would be the most proper way of freeing me from my bonds, but I fear the complications, slowness, and perfidy of European politics."[15]

By bribing his jailers and writing with lemon juice on pages torn out of books, Lafayette had already managed to send secret letters to Thomas Pinckney, the United States Minister to Northern Europe. On July 4, 1793, he had written: "Encircled as I am by ditches, ramparts, guards, double sentries and palisades, shut up in a quadruple-gated, barred, chained, locked, grated, narrow, moisty subterraneous dungeon, and doomed to the moral and bodily hardship which revengeful tyranny is heaping on me, let it be today my frolic, so far to cheat the crowned gang and their vile agents as to be enabled first to scribble, then to convey this homage of a sympathetic heart."[16]

By the end of 1793, Gilbert was beginning to realize that there was very little chance of his being released in the near future. "It has become obvious to me that the Powers hate my principles, my character and my person too much for me to limit my hopes of freedom to either one of these possibilities: that of a well-planned escape, or that of a demand from the United States who must cease all negotiations with lying governments and embarrass them by an open éclat which would be more suitable to the dignity of America and, in any case, more satisfying for me. As for the idea of seeing my wife lower herself by begging before all these thrones, you will allow me not even to consider it,"[17] he wrote Mme d'Hénin on November 16; and when, on December 11, he thanked Pinckney for "the cessation of that absolute gloomy silence respecting the fate of every person I hold dear, a torture the most diabolical which revenge could invent"—he thought that his family was safe in Chavaniac—he quickly went on to ask: "Am I not an American officer now unconnected with European service? Wa'n't I an American citizen long before there could be such things as citizens in France?"[18] But no one in America thought of Lafayette as more than an adopted friend, and there could be no question of mobilizing the resources of the nation for the release of a private person who was not even native-born.

Furthermore, his efforts to outside support may have turned out to be self-defeating. As 1794 began, in fact, the conditions of his life deteriorated further.

On January 14, in Philadelphia, "at a meeting of the heads of Departments at the President's . . . it was propounded by the President whether in consideration of the eminent services of M. de La Fayette to the United States and his present sufferings, it was not advisable for the President, in a *private* and *unofficial* character, to address the King of Prussia a letter, requesting his release on parole founded on motives of personal friendship only. The opinion is, that such a letter is proposed to be written." Frederick William, known for his greed and cowardice, might well have realized now that he was keeping a man sufficiently popular to make trouble for him, especially since he was, at this time, allied with Great Britain. Since the Prussian King could hardly free the man, he instead had him transferred, on May 17, 1794, to the custody of Emperor Francis II, who was altogether beyond the reach of scruple, apprehension, or pity.

Lafayette was now separated completely from Maubourg and Bureaux de Pusy, whom, until now, he had seen, occasionally, from a distance, and held, alone, at the fortress of Olmutz, in Moravia, where his servant was taken from him, along with his watch and shoe buckles. He was denied all contact with the outside world and even stripped of his name: he had become simply prisoner number two.

To make everything worse, Adrienne, a prisoner herself, could no longer receive letters. Late in May 1794 she was transferred to Paris. At least her children were safe—she had carefully hidden them near Chavaniac in the house of two of her former tenants. Still, she saw her daughters before she left and did her best to reassure them. After all, she was not scheduled to appear before the revolutionary tribunal—from which the only exit led straight to the guillotine—nor had she, in fact, been charged with any crime. And since she was now quite penniless, the new occupants of Chavaniac allowed her daughters—no longer in hiding since, after all, there was no attempt at arresting them—and aunt to reside there in a small suite of rooms.

Her prison in Paris was overcrowded and dreadfully uncomfortable; there were no beds, only filthy straw mattresses and no facilities of any kind. Food was insufficient, light and air were scarce, but the inmates all belonged to the best families in France: among them were her sister, the vicomtesse de Noailles; her grandmother, the old maréchale; and her mother, the duchesse d'Ayen. The men of her family—the duc d'Ayen, the prince de Poix—had emigrated early in the Revolution; the vicomte de Noailles, still a liberal, had remained a little longer, but then he, too, had fled; only one of the Noailles women, the liberal comtesse de Tessé, had also left in time. Until the last moment, the Noailles ladies had resisted emigration, in order to save the family fortune. Although in semihiding at the hôtel de Noailles—they almost never left the premises and lived very modestly—they were arrested in the fall of 1792. They had been in prison for several months when Adrienne joined them. Immediately she took over the care of her grandmother, and like the other Noailles women—indeed like all the other titled women who had been suddenly thrust from their gilded salons into jail—she behaved with perfect dignity, calm, and courage; but, even more, she stood out from her fellow prisoners by her undaunted cheerfulness and her readiness to help. Many of the great ladies who faced death with absolute equanimity had retained their old habits of intrigue and backbiting even in their cells. Adrienne, almost alone, remained aloof from these affairs. All through that late spring and early summer of 1794, the executions continued, and of course, she fully expected to die. On July 4, the octogenarian maréchale de Noailles, her daughter, and her granddaughter were guillotined.

Now only Adrienne remained. That she was spared was probably due to Gouverneur Morris's personal and unauthorized intervention with Robespierre, a virtual dictator after the elimination of Brisson and Roland. It was not in the interests of France to alienate the United States and so, while the "Incorruptible" took no official notice of Morris's memo, Adrienne's case failed to come up before the revolutionary tribunal. Then, on July 10, suddenly, the Terror ended. Robespierre followed his victims to the scaffold and all remaining prisoners were safe.

Still, there was no question of freeing the Citizeness Noailles-Lafayette, even as the other prisoners were released: the name she bore was far too potent. However, she was transferred to a supposedly less uncomfortable prison, where she remained for the rest of the year. All through her long ordeal, Adrienne had demonstrated new qualities of tenacity, courage, and intelligence. She had always been an admirable wife and mother, but also always under someone else's aegis, first her mother's, then her husband's. When circumstances forced her to fend for herself, she found she managed

admirably, far better, in fact, than almost everybody she knew, and it taught
her a lesson she never forgot.

Although both Lafayettes now languished in prison, they were not without friends. James Monroe, in particular, who had replaced Morris as Minister to France—Morris, implacably hostile to the Republic, was unpopular
in Paris and clearly unable to analyze the complicated French situation with
objectivity—worked hard and persistently to convince the new French government that it was high time to release Adrienne. It took six months but,
finally, on January 21, 1795, she was granted her freedom. She moved in
with the Monroes, who were settled in a large and luxurious house, and
they nursed her back to health. Then she began to plan her next move; she
had been away from Gilbert far too long.

There was, at that point, very little hope of obtaining Lafayette's release.
France was at war with the rest of Europe and therefore in no position to
claim him even if it wished to do so. The several sovereigns of the coalition
still thought of the General as a very dangerous man indeed, and Francis
II was convinced that his prisoner was responsible for the entire Revolution
and its most appalling consequence—the execution of his aunt, Marie Antoinette. On the other hand, since the Austrian emperor was receiving
English subsidies and there was a large body of support for Lafayette in
Westminster, it seemed pointless to make waves by having "the monster"
executed; anyway, with luck, the cold and damp of Olmutz would take care
of the problem. The only power really interested in Lafayette's fate was in
no position to do anything. In June 1795 Washington wrote Adrienne to
congratulate her on her recovered freedom, but he added: "To touch on the
case of M. de La Fayette in this letter would be still more delicate and,
under the present circumstances, as unavailing as it would be inexpedient."[19]

Realizing himself that his situation was hopeless, Lafayette continued
to plan his escape. As before using lemon juice in place of ink, he had
managed to correspond with two confederates, Justus Erich Bollman and
Francis Huger, the son of Major Benjamin Huger in whose house Lafayette
had spent his first night on American soil. Both American citizens, Huger
and his friend were devoted to the Hero of Two Worlds; quite on their own,
therefore, with much effort, delay, and money, they managed to arrange
his escape from Olmutz. Some guards were to be bribed, others would be
overcome, horses would be ready, so that, as he took his daily walk outside
the fortress, Lafayette could be rescued. The plan worked. Losing a piece
of a finger to the bite of a guard and wrenching his back, Lafayette managed
to escape; he found a horse waiting for him at the appointed place and
galloped off. Then the road forked: one side led out of Austrian territory,
the other meandered, then petered out. Unfortunately, just outside town,

the General took the wrong turn; soon, he was recognized and stopped. By the next day he was back in his cell.

There was nothing, therefore, for Adrienne to do if she wanted to see her husband but to go to Austria. It was no easy undertaking. For one thing, France and Austria were at war; for another, she needed money. Luckily, since neither her mother, the duchesse d'Ayen, who had been beheaded, nor she herself had ever emigrated, and since all arbitrarily confiscated properties were now being restored to their rightful owners, she was able to recover a good deal of land. There was not much hard cash to be had, but she managed to get enough for her trip. Then she went to Chavaniac, saw to it that Lafayette's old aunt, who had lived in one barely furnished room, was reinstalled in comfort in the castle, met again with her daughters and with one of her sisters, Rosalie de Grammont,* and sent her sixteen-year-old son off to America. Then she returned to Paris where, with Monroe's help, she and her two daughters were granted passports giving them the right to travel to the United States. Before leaving Paris, selflessly, she visited Adélaide de Simiane, now completely out of touch with Lafayette and who, like her, was alive but ruined, and promised to give Gilbert her love.

The three took the stagecoach to Dunkirk and, on September 5, 1795, boarded an American packet ostensibly bound for New York; but when the ship sailed for Hamburg instead, Adrienne was, to say the least, not very surprised. Once there, she convinced the American consul to issue her an American passport under the name of Mrs. Motier of New York, as well as some money with which she bought a carriage. Then, still with Anastasie and Virginie, she set off for Vienna. It was a slow trip, on bad roads, with long waits at each post-inn.

Even in the imperial capital, a small city with ramparts but full of grand baroque palaces and dominated by the bulk of the Hofburg, she was no closer to seeing her husband. But she was not a Noailles for nothing. Having taken lodgings under her assumed name, she called on a distant relative, Prince Rosemberg, revealed her true identity, and asked him to obtain an audience with the Emperor. That Rosemberg eventually succeeded was nothing short of miraculous, for Francis II was a conscientious but not very bright young man with a high notion of his obligations to the monarchy and an almost slavish regard for his advisers' opinions; Baron Franz von Thugut, his Foreign Minister, was a fanatical, and very stupid, reactionary to whom Lafayette was anathema. To Rosemberg's surprise, Adrienne actually con-

---

*She had been in hiding and so had kept out of prison.

vinced the Emperor to let her move in with Lafayette at Olmutz. What followed, Adrienne herself told Mme de Tessé in a letter sent from prison on May 10, 1796.

"Had I traveled under my own name," she wrote, "I could never have entered the Emperor's states; and if I had not carefully hidden myself in Vienna until M. de Rosemberg had arranged my business, I could never have succeeded. I have told you about my visit to the Emperor who, as he allowed me in the most polite way to be locked up with M. de La Fayette, told me that *his business was complicated and did not depend on him alone*; but he assured me that *he was very well treated* and that *my presence would be yet another pleasure for him*. I was so far from suspecting the truth that I mentioned that, in Prussia, at the beginning, M. de La Fayette had been kept in ignorance of our fate: but I added that since I knew nothing about his present condition, I was not accusing H.I.M. of such barbarity. The Emperor also allowed me to write him directly. I then saw M. de Thugut, the most influential of the ministers, and the one most opposed to us; and when I pointed out that the governments of the Coalition attributed too much importance to a single man he repeated several times *too much importance!* in a tone and with a grimace which proved to me that he thought [Lafayette] very important indeed."[20] Adrienne chose to concentrate on her permit of incarceration and the fact that she would soon see Gilbert, but she knew now that there was very little chance that her husband would be released; by saying that this was a matter which involved his allies, the Emperor had neatly removed all responsibility from himself; and while in England the Whigs were pro-Lafayette, they were also out of power, and William Pitt, the Prime Minister, was bound to go against the Opposition's wishes; and, therefore, he did nothing.

At least, Adrienne and her two daughters were allowed to travel on to Olmutz, encouraged by the right the Emperor had given them to write him directly, and by their expectation of living not too uncomfortably. "Just imagine how M. de La Fayette must have felt," Adrienne wrote, "when after eight months spent seeing only his jailers, who refused to tell him whether we were still alive, suddenly, without any preparation, he saw us walk into his cell!"[21]

What Adrienne saw, in turn, was the ghost of her husband. Gilbert's escape, in November 1794, had been followed by an illness that had brought him close to death several times, and he was now pitifully weak. He was, Adrienne wrote, "left without any care at all, at first without light, then with light only until nine o'clock, with no possibility of receiving help during the fourteen-hour nights since the keys were, as they still are, at the other end of town; reduced to two shirts and unable to get a change for the one he soaked with sweat during the bouts with fever, the surgeon who came in to treat his finger scarcely daring to speak to him, pressed by the officer to leave right away and allowed neither reflexion nor advice. Add to these physical details the extreme rudeness of his jailers . . ."[22] In an age when this kind of barbarous treatment was still unheard of, Adrienne had every right to be outraged; and, in fact, given his history of tuberculosis in 1788 and 1789, it is nothing short of miraculous that Gilbert survived his detention in a dank, unheated cell that he was never allowed to leave. Until Adrienne arrived, his only—and very imperfect—communication with the outside had been through a servant of Maubourg's who, standing outside the fortress, whistled in something a little like the Morse code. The fact that Maubourg and Bureaux de Pusy had by now also been transferred to Olmutz did not help, since the three men were kept absolutely separate. Adrienne, at least, was allowed to send and receive letters, so her presence, among other benefits, meant that Gilbert was once again in touch with the outside world.

The reunited Lafayettes were treated like animals. Brought together with her daughters, who had a separate cell, at eight o'clock for breakfast, Adrienne was kept apart from Gilbert until lunch; then the family stayed together until, at eight, Anastasie and Virginie were again locked away. Since it was Adrienne who paid for the food, it was abundant, but indescribably poor and served in filthy wooden bowls. It was a wonder, in fact, that the two girls remained relatively healthy.

"As for me," Adrienne went on, "I must admit that my health could be better. I have headaches and there are signs that my blood . . . is altered; but that is not dangerous and, besides, you understand that we cannot contemplate the idea of leaving M. de La Fayette. The positive effect of our presence is not limited to the pleasure of seeing us; his health is really not as bad since our arrival. You know the influence of feeling on him . . . ."[23]

Lafayette, in fact, although still thin and weak, was, at least, no longer in danger of dying. It was real progress. But, in worrying only about Gilbert as usual, Adrienne was being stoical. She was actually quite ill, and when she wrote to the Emperor to ask if she might go to Vienna for a week so she could consult a physician, the answer came back after several months that she could indeed leave but must not expect permission to return to Olmutz. She can hardly have been surprised: even the efforts she made to recover the three silver forks, seized when she entered Olmutz, were to no avail: the family had to continue eating with their fingers. And while it seems unfair to criticize this loving and heroic woman, one wonders why she allowed her teenage daughters to live in this hell. That they were a comfort to Lafayette is certain, as is the fact that both girls remained astonishingly cheerful, and never manifested the slightest resentment at having to share their parents' captivity.

As time passed, the treatment meted out to the Lafayettes became better known—Adrienne was writing continually—and it seemed intolerable to growing numbers of people. Those who cared about religion thought it dreadful that the family wasn't even allowed to attend Mass on Sundays; all agreed that it was monstrous to have placed them in a cell contiguous to the fortress latrines, with their unavoidable stench.

From Philadelphia, Washington wrote Pinckney on February 20, 1796: "I need hardly mention how much my sensibility has been hurt by the treatment [Lafayette] has met with; or how anxious I am to see him liberated therefrom; but what course to pursue . . . is not quite so easy to decide on. . . . Yet such is my wish to contribute my *mite* . . . that I have no objection to its being made known to the Imperial Ambassador in London (who, if he thinks it proper may communicate it to his Court) that this event is an ardent wish of the people of the United States."[24] This was, to say the least, a prudent communication. Washington was, as usual, held back by his old fear of putting private feeling before the public interest. On May 15, finally, he could stand it no longer and wrote directly to the Emperor: "I take the liberty of writing this *private* letter to your Majesty. . . . Permit me only to submit to your Majesty's consideration, whether [Lafayette's] long imprisonment, and the confiscation of his Estate, and the Indigence and dispersion of his family—and the painful anxieties incident to all these circumstances, do not form an assemblage of sufferings, which recommend him to the mediation of Humanity? Allow me, Sir! on this occasion to be its organ; and to entreat that he may be permitted to come to this country . . ."[25] Francis II was the very last man to respond to this sort of appeal, but the letter was not altogether useless: the Austrian government now knew that if ever it chose to release Lafayette, it could, at the same time, send him so far away that he would no longer be dangerous.

Of course, Gilbert had many friends who were urging the President to adopt a firmer tone, but that was out of the question. On August 8, Washington answered a letter from the duc de Liancourt who had fought at Yorktown and was then traveling in the United States: "Altho' Fayette is an *adopted* citizen of this country, the Government of it, nor the people themselves, notwithstanding their attachment to his person and the recollection of his services, have any right to demand him as *their* citizen by the law of nations."[26] It was not encouraging.

Around this time, a new kind of hope arose. On July 25, Adrienne, always friendly to anyone her husband loved, was writing the princesse d'Hénin: "Our situation is altogether the same; but still there is a visible change in the politeness of our guards. After every French victory, after every strong publication in our favor, we perceive yet an additional nuance . . . ."[27]

In France, not only was the Terror over but a new, moderate government, the Directoire, now ruled. It was not unfriendly to Lafayette especially since, through Adrienne's letters, he had carefully made it known that he fully approved of, and felt he owed allegiance to, the Republic, while at the same time he considered it would be highly premature for him to return home. This was exactly the right attitude, since the Directors weren't about to help a royalist, and, even if they pressed for the prisoner's release, the very last thing they wanted was to have him in Paris, adding to the already excruciating fragility of the government. Luckily, they were also aware that it did not look well for a world-famous French citizen to be arbitrarily imprisoned in Austria; so, in early 1797, they decided to demand his release.

This move was only possible because the French armies in Italy, under the command of General Bonaparte, had been inflicting a series of stinging defeats on the Austrians. By the spring, peace talks were under way. The liberation of all prisoners was normally specified by a standard clause; but on April 24, 1797, the Directoire wrote a letter to Bonaparte, who was also the chief negotiator. "We desire to have these prisoners, viz. Lafayette, Latour-Maubourg, and Bureaux de Pusy freed without delay," the letter said. "All facilities must be given them to travel, if they wish, to North America without, however, passing through France.

"We also desire, Citizen General, that this demand be stipulated among the secret articles of the treaty under discussion."[28] Lafayette and his companions, uniquely, were to have a clause all to themselves. Ironically, it was the Foreign Minister, Charles Delacroix, who forwarded this letter—the very man who had been presiding over the National Assembly when Lafayette was declared an outlaw.

Unfortunately Thugut, an obstinate ultrareactionary, was dead set against giving up the prisoners; so, a few days later, Bonaparte had to insist. He wrote the Austrian plenipotentiary another letter demanding the prisoners' release, adding that he felt "no doubt that the Emperor would give this additional proof of his humanity, would feel some desire to oblige the Directoire, and help, in the circumstances, to consolidate the interior tran-

quillity of the Republic."[29] Bonaparte's victory at Rivoli spoke louder than
this rather embarrassed plea, and it began to look as if the doors of Olmutz
would soon open. But the very fact that Bonaparte had insisted made the
Austrians think that perhaps the French government would be willing to
make some concessions in order to gain Lafayette's freedom, and the talks
ground to a halt. On May 5, Lazare Carnot, one of the Directors, was writing:
"Our national honor demands that they be freed from the cell where they
are detained only because they started the Revolution."[30] With this encouragement, Bonaparte insisted again, while at the same time making it
clear that he was not willing to change an iota of the draft treaty.

It worked. The preliminaries were signed, along with the article providing for Lafayette's release but excluding him from France, and late in
July, the Emperor sent an emissary to Olmutz, who explained to the Lafayettes that they would be free just as soon as they signed a promise never
again to set foot on the territory of the Empire (which, under the Emperor's
nominal sovereignty, included many independent German states), and to
sail to America at the earliest possible opportunity. What happened next is
detailed in a December 1797 letter from Reinhard, the French Minister in
Hamburg, then a free city, in a letter to Talleyrand, the new Foreign Minister.

"Lafayette is awaited here in a few days. The Imperial Minister has at
any rate announced that he was free again. . . . I am told that the Court of
Vienna would prefer to have it appear that it followed the wishes of the
United States government rather than those of France. It first offered Lafayette his freedom provided he would embark immediately for America.
He answered that he could agree to no conditions and that there was a
country that had sacred rights over him. It would seem, however, that this
condition has been agreed to without and in spite of him. . . ."[31] Still, when
the Lafayettes finally reached Hamburg, their first move was to visit the
French consul, to seek permission to go home to France in the spring.
Indeed, Louis Romeuf, who preceded them, made it very plain that the
prisoners were well aware that they owed their freedom to General Bonaparte and the Republic.

"The next day," Reinhard continued, "around six in the evening, Lafayette and his companions came to my house. As I was out, they left their
cards."[32]

At this point, the consul found himself in a dreadfully awkward situation.
After all, while Lafayette owed his freedom to the French government, he
was still an outlaw, and therefore ought to be treated as such by any French
diplomat, but then again, Lafayette was proclaiming his gratitude to the

government of the Republic. He had been feted all through Germany precisely because he was now considered a republican, and France might as well take credit for his freedom since it proved its power. Last but not least, Reinhard thought he had better find out exactly how Lafayette felt about the Directoire: after all, once free, his voice was likely to be heard both in Europe and the United States. So, having solved the embarrassing dilemma of whether he ought to take official notice of a man who, despite all his fame, was still legally a criminal, Reinhard managed to be home the next time he came, especially since Lafayette had notified him that "his first endeavor . . . had been to visit the Minister of the Republic to congratulate him on the triumphs of France and to thank the government for its intercession. . . ."[33]

He now learned that the prisoners had been out of jail for fifteen days; that they had been escorted by an Austrian major who prevented them from communicating with strangers until they reached the border with Saxony; but that there they found relatives and friends awaiting them. "It was then that they heard for the first time about the events of the last two years; that Bonaparte's name was first mentioned to them. . . . For two years no political news had reached them; for the last few months, it was forbidden on pain of death to write them even the most ordinary letters. Everything that has been published on their atrocious treatment is true. . . .

"Lafayette then spoke of the Republic and the [new] Constitution. He said that he found this Constitution infinitely superior to that which he had felt a duty to uphold, that he would always bow to the will of the people and that no one could impugn his republican principles."[34] So far, so good. Only, unfortunately, the Directoire had recently maintained itself in power by dint of arresting a number of right-wing deputies, canceling their election, and sending them off to Devil's Island. Always a stickler for constitutionality, Lafayette disapproved, but was prudent enough to try to change the subject when Reinhard first mentioned the event, which had taken place on the 18 Fructidor.* When pressed, however, Gilbert asked Reinhard whether the government's coup had broken the law. The consul acknowledged that it had, explaining, however, that it had been the only way to save the Republic. At that, Lafayette protested that he knew the men who had been transported, and that they were republicans, leaving the consul to answer feebly that in five years people had changed, and that Gilbert was no longer able to ap-

---

*Fructidor: Twelfth month of the calendar of the first French Republic, from August 18 to September 11.

preciate either men or events. Still, the consul concluded, Lafayette could be relied on as a good citizen; and any opponent using his name was doing so without his consent.

Despite this last encomium, Lafayette had just, as usual, made his life more difficult. Since he disapproved of the seizure of 18 Fructidor, there was obviously no possibility that he would be allowed back in France. Exiled from his homeland, almost destitute, Lafayette could only look to a singularly bleak future. He was free, at last, but to what purpose?

Ten

A QUIET LIFE

When they reached Hamburg on October 4, 1797, Gilbert and Adrienne de Lafayette looked quite unlike that glamorous young couple whose Paris house had been open to all. They had both aged in jail. Although he was only forty, Gilbert had begun to look like an old man; he was still tall and spare, but he had become bald and looked worn; Adrienne was very ill, suffering from the heart disease that had taxed her strength in jail. What she needed above all was quiet, rest, and care. She had also changed in another respect: she still loved Gilbert as much as ever, but she had become the active, responsible, and competent half of the couple. While still in France, she had saved part of their estate; now, with Gilbert forbidden to reenter the country, the family's financial future had become her problem, all the more so because Gilbert, who until 1792 had always had a steward to do it, was incapable of managing his own affairs. Adrienne's having become the financial manager altered the balance of the marriage in her favor. And there was a further change in the family's status: the title that Gilbert had renounced on August 4, 1789, was now officially dropped from his name, and for the rest of his life he gave up the aristocratic "de" and became plain M. Lafayette.

Otherwise, however, Gilbert remained very much himself. His long imprisonment had, if anything, added to his fame; it had clarified his somewhat murky political position and made him, once again, the hero of liberty. No sooner had he reached Hamburg than he was presented with an address from the American community residing there: "Beholding in you, Sir, the genuine friend of national liberty and good government," it said, "our astonishment has been less excited than our indignation to have found you the object of the vengeance of every species of tyrants who, that nothing should be wanting to your suffering, added those of a virtuous and innocent family. But while we have deplored this injustice, we have rejoiced that you ever have exhibited to the world your upright intentions and the undeviating principles of an enlightened and true patriot."[1] Gratifying as this must have been, a letter sent from Paris on June 22 by Mme de Staël must have given the exiles even more comfort.

"Come straight to France!" she wrote. "There can be no other country for you. There you will find the Republic that your opinion already favored when your conscience still bound you to the monarchy; you will find it ennobled by victory and freed from the crimes that sullied its beginnings; you will support it because liberty, in France, can no longer exist without it, and because you are, as a hero and a martyr, so closely united with liberty that I use that word or your name indifferently when I express my wishes for the honor and prosperity of France."[2] Mme de Staël had now reopened the salon in which, before 1792, she had gathered the brightest of the liberals, and as a writer, she had gained even greater fame. Since she was known to have great influence on Barras, the most powerful of the five Directors, and on Talleyrand, now Foreign Minister, her endorsement was valuable indeed, but, as Lafayette must have discovered from his visit to Reinhard, Mme de Staël was promising more than she could deliver. His disapproval of the 18 Fructidor had aligned Gilbert with the opposition to the régime.

Politics, however, although never very far from Lafayette's mind, were not quite yet again his first preoccupation. Within forty-eight hours of his arrival in Hamburg, he wrote two important letters. The first went, naturally, to the newly retired Washington, and was almost incoherent with joy. "In vain would I attempt, my beloved General, to express to you the feelings of my filial heart, when, at the moment of this unexpected restoration to liberty and life, I find myself blessed with the opportunity to let you hear from me—this heart has for twenty years been known to you—words that, whatever they be, fall so short of my sentiments, could not do justice to what I feel—But you will be sensible of the affectionate and delightful emotions with which I am now writing you. . . . With what eagerness and pleasure I would hasten to fly to Mount Vernon there to pour out all the sentiments of affection, respect and gratitude which ever bound me and more than ever bind me to you—your paternal goodness to my, to our son* was not unexpected but was most heartily felt—your constant sollicitude on my behalf I have enjoyed as a consolation in captivity. . . . My own health, altho' it is impaired could, I think, tolerably support a voyage. My daughters are not ill. But Mrs. Lafayette's sufferings in this cruel unhealthy captivity have had such a deplorable effect upon her that . . . it would be an act of madness to let her embark in this advanced season of the year."[3]

The second letter, more important still, went to Lafayette's liberator, the young man whom all expected to play an important role in the future, General Bonaparte, on October 6:

"Citizen General," it read, "The prisoners of Olmutz, happy that they owe their deliverance to the benevolence of their fatherland and your ir-resistible armies, have enjoyed, in their captivity, the thought that their liberty and their lives were linked to the triumphs of the Republic and to your own glory. . . . How sweet it would have been for us, Citizen General, to offer you in person the expression of our feelings, to see the theater of so many victories. . . . In [this] solitary retreat . . . we will join with the wishes of our patriotism for the Republic the most lively interest in the illustrious general to whom we are even the more grateful for the services he has rendered the cause of liberty and our fatherland than for the private obligations we glory in owing him. . . ."[4] Although the letter was signed by Maubourg and Bureaux de Pusy, Lafayette's contorted, courtly style is un-mistakable; and while the vocabulary is wholly republican, the young general must have recognized the courtliness of the ancien régime in its extravagantly grateful phrases. Lafayette did not yet know that, more strongly even than the timorous Directoire, it had been Bonaparte who had stipulated that Lafayette must remain in exile. The reason was plain enough: the new hero wanted no competition from his predecessor; and while he cared about the greatness of France, liberty seemed to him an idea whose time had passed.

Within a few days, the Lafayettes and Maubourg left Hamburg for Wittmold, some four hours away from Hamburg in Holstein, a large agri-cultural estate owned by Adrienne's aunt, Mme de Tessé. This liberal grande dame, whose salon at Versailles had seen the beginnings of the Revolution, was not only intelligent and kind but sensible as well. As soon as events had

---

*In fact, Washington had carefully maintained his distance from George Lafayette for fear of compromising the U.S. government.

begun to turn for the worse, she had sent a large sum of money outside the country with which, eventually, she bought the estate of Wittmold. There the Lafayettes were reunited with Pauline de Montagu, one of Adrienne's two surviving sisters; and it was in an atmosphere of family affection that the prisoners began to come back to life.

"Gilbert is as kind, as simple in his manners, as affectionate in his caresses, as moderate in discussion as you have ever known him to be," Mme de Montagu wrote her other sister, Mme de Grammont. "He loves his children tenderly and is, despite his cool exterior, extremely amiable to his wife. He behaves in an affable way, with a detachment I can easily see through and a secret yearning to be where he can act. I avoid as best as possible any discussion with him about the Revolution, both about the things he defends and those he condemns. . . . That poor Gilbert! May God preserve him from being ever again on the world's stage."[5]

For a while it almost seemed as if Lafayette, too, shared that attitude. On October 11, he wrote a friend: "My political life is over. I will be full of life for my friends, but for the public I will be like a painting in a museum or a book in a library; I admit that, politically, I have never felt younger; that liberty and everything connected with it excites me today as it did when I was nineteen; but since most hearts are too constricted, too timid, too apathetic to allow for the complete development of truth, liberty and justice, my reason tells me that there will never be anything for me to do."[6] It was not a convincing disclaimer, but even if, secretly, Lafayette hoped that he would once again ride his white horse through Paris at the head of a cheering crowd, there was, at the moment, no possibility at all of transforming the dream into reality. In France, the Directoire seemed firmly entrenched, and while it was disorganized, inefficient, and corrupt, it also served the interests of several powerful groups who had emerged intact from the turmoil of the Revolution: the bankers; the army suppliers, who were making millions; the generals, former members of the Convention, especially the so-called regicides*; and the remnants of the old liberal intellectual circles meeting once again in Mme de Staël's salon. Curiously, the Directors and their ministers were all the more powerful because the new Constitution was more complex; and since the government kept going by alternately outlawing the right and left, the very last thing it wanted was someone capable of symbolizing what France was supposed to be—a liberal republic—when in fact it suffered from a peculiar, erratic but repressive de facto dictatorship. In law, Lafayette could not return so long as his name remained

---

*Those who had voted for the death of Louis XVI.

on the list of émigrés; and the Directors had no intention whatever of crossing it off.

After a while, the Lafayettes and Maubourg, whose family had also emigrated, decided they wanted a house of their own, so, pooling their resources, they rented a large, not very comfortable manor house at Lemkuhlen, just across the lake from Wittmold. There they were joined by Mme de Simiane. Now that the political situation in France had settled down, Adélaide was able to come out of hiding and obtain a passport; she was still penniless, however, so it was an act of kindness on the part of the Lafayettes to take her in. And while it may seem a little bizarre that Gilbert's wife and his mistress were thus brought together, Adrienne had extraordinary tolerance for anything that would make her husband happy. Since, furthermore, she was still a very sick woman, it seems quite probable that, by inviting Adélaide, she was also providing for Gilbert's sexual needs.

It was at Lemkuhlen that it soon became obvious that Anastasie and Charles de Latour-Maubourg, the younger brother of Lafayette's friend, were falling in love. The parents were delighted, of course, and on May 9, 1798, the young people were married.

Otherwise, life was quiet. In February, George had arrived from the United States, to his parents' great pleasure. He found his mother still seriously ill, but the warmth of the spring and summer helped, and at the end of August, Adrienne set out on a journey to France, this time to settle her mother's inheritance and to look after the few little properties she had recovered earlier. It was just as well that she went without Gilbert, since he was still utterly incapable of behaving in such a way as to propitiate the powers-that-be. Adrienne was far too practical to mind paying a few visits to the ministers if it meant recovering an estate; indeed, as a nonpolitical figure, she could do so more easily. Besides, she was providing for her husband and children and did not feel that soliciting the powerful to restore her own property need in any way bruise her pride. Soon afterward, and for the same reasons, Mme de Simiane followed her.

Although Gilbert was not left alone—he had returned to Wittmold when the lease expired at Lemkuhlen and was staying with Mme de Tessé and his sister-in-law—he missed Adrienne greatly. His letters to her now began to reflect a new kind of dependence. "Your letter came at last after nine days, my dear heart," he wrote on September 14, "and although the distance which separates us does not appear to me any less, I feel considerably cheered by the fact that when you wrote me so tenderly, you were a little closer. . . ."[7]

How little he considered himself retired from politics was now becoming all too clear. "Here is a task which I am very anxious to have you carry out," he wrote Adrienne on September 26. "The aristocrats and the royalists are deafening the universe with the delights of the ancien régime. You would think, to hear them, that the French had been the happiest people in the world. . . . So many misfortunes and so many crimes have sullied the Revolution that they always serve as a ready reply to those who speak of the ancien régime so that it seems one cannot hate it without being a partisan of Robespierre. . . . It would be necessary to have some literate man who was a patriot and a good writer produce a little account of what they modestly term the old abuses."[8] It hardly needs saying that such a pamphlet, in attacking the ancien régime, would necessarily have praised the champion of liberty.

At this time Lafayette was also longing to return to America. Although Adrienne was at first too ill, then too busy in France to go with him, he thought very seriously of sailing over by himself and would undoubtedly have done so had Washington not told him firmly to remain in Europe. It seemed, for most of 1798 and 1799, as if France and the United States might soon go to war over their commercial differences; eventually, these difficulties were ironed out, but Washington wisely saved Lafayette from further compromising his position. So with a feeling of keen disappointment, Gilbert put off the trip.

It became obvious that Adrienne would henceforth have to spend a great deal of time in France, so Lafayette decided to move to Vianen, near Utrecht, in Holland, a short distance from Paris. Holland was a republic defended (and occupied) by a French army, so that he could be in one of the few countries not at war with France. And the Dutch, who remembered his aborted command in 1787 and liked his brand of liberalism, made Gilbert feel very welcome. "As for my situation here," he wrote on March 9, 1799, some three months after his arrival, "it is happy, quiet, and altogether appropriate. . . . I have been received by old friends with the most touching emotion and must add that, among the proofs of Dutch affection, I have also noticed in our compatriots the same [good] dispositions as those I enjoyed before leaving France."[9] In the meantime, Adrienne continued to make arrangements for a new life in France, when and if it again became possible. She had inherited from her mother an estate at Lagrange-Bléneau, some fourteen leagues (about forty miles) east of Paris. Aside from a farm and a considerable amount of land, it also boasted a handsome old chateau in need of restoration and decoration. This time, with what little money she could gather, Adrienne was going to start making it livable; soon, she and Gilbert hoped, they would once again have their own house.

Or at least so he said. In fact Lafayette had simply developed a new pose to conceal his ambitions. It was obvious to everyone, in 1799, that the current régime could not last much longer. It was simply a question of what was to replace it. To the erstwhile commandant-general of the National Guard it seemed that, having started the Revolution, he should also end it by creating the free government of his dreams. Already, on April 4, he was writing longingly: "If I were elected to the Council of the Five Hundred,* if, in a motion recalling me to France, I were asked to come to the Council and explain my behavior . . . it would be easy for me to sweep away all prejudice due to malevolence or stupidity. . . . Then could I speak a language worthy of my friends and myself. . . . In any case I may be able to . . . render liberty and my fatherland services peculiar to my situation."[10] He could hardly have spoken more clearly; only, it was hardly relevant. The situation in Paris had changed so radically since 1792 that an exile could no longer even hope to find a place in it. Lafayette, it is true, was not completely forgotten, but the people in power, the Directors, thought him dangerous to the régime, and Talleyrand, the one man in Paris who was effectively preparing for the next stage, had measured Lafayette's political incapacity in 1789 and 1790. The sad truth was, no one really disliked Lafayette, but no one wanted him back.

Although pleased with his garden, with Adrienne in Paris he felt lonely. "I returned to the house feeling sad and lonely, my dear Adrienne, and although I cannot consider this separation the way I did last year's, it is still more than enough to afflict me. Already I feel that impatience of seeing you that usually results from the approach of our reunion: I am really starting early. . . . Adieu, my dear Adrienne, my heart follows you, yearns for you . . . and loves you tenderly."[11] Never forgetting that he was in exile, he tried to plan for the future. "My letter will probably find you at Lagrange, my dear heart," he wrote on May 29, "in that retreat where we are fated, I hope, to rest together after the vicissitudes of our life. That idea will help to alleviate your present troubles. . . .

"You must write me many details about Lagrange; first what the house is like and an answer to all my ideas about lodging; then the farm. I would like to know the number of living animals, large and small, which are kept there, how much it all costs, how many servants take care of them; then a little word on the park and the woods. Liancourt has lent me some of Arthur Young's books; I am deeper than ever in the study of agriculture."[12] There were, apparently, several ways of being the French Washington: if Lafayette could not be the Father of his Country, at least he could, at Lagrange, replicate the squire of Mount Vernon. There was, after all, something to be

---

*One of the two legislative bodies of the Directoire.

said for retiring to the country and watching over the cultivation of your property while you waited for the world to need you again. It was dignified, it was safe, it might even be effective.

He continued to watch the political situation in France. General Bonaparte had just returned from Egypt; something was obviously about to happen. On October 17, Lafayette wrote Maubourg with unusual understanding about Bonaparte's ambitions: "Bonaparte thinks only of his own ambition and, until now, has not found glory in serving liberty. . . . He may do so today. . . . Ever since the coalition has been defeated, the malcontents hope their salvation will come from inside the country. The moment is therefore very favorable to Bonaparte. He will risk no personal advantage for the sake of liberty. He has proved that his soul could quite happily watch and even cooperate in its violation. If, however, his fame and his ambition demand that he put himself forward in defense of the cause, he will do so. His wish must be to establish the Republic on a solid foundation of liberty and justice. He might even want to be President for life. I should quite like that arrangement; it would be an interesting experiment."[13]

Bonaparte was indeed about to take over, but the young general, far from being indifferent to the idea of liberty, was in fact hostile to it. He wanted a strong government armed with solidly repressive laws, a censored press, and the faculty to arrest dissidents at will—everything that Lafayette most hated. And how far the exile was from perceiving this is shown by a letter he sent Louis Romeuf, his former aide-de-camp, on October 29. "It is obvious that [Bonaparte's] interest is to be united specifically with me," he wrote, "since my position forbids me from coveting the possible objects of his ambition, and I would give my vote very cordially to make him President of a free, just and well-organized republic."[14] In fact, Bonaparte had no need at all for Lafayette's vote, approval, or support.

Helped as he was both by his lofty principles and Adrienne's hard work, Lafayette could afford to strike noble poses, but Adrienne herself, busily retrieving what little of the family's fortune she could, took a more practical position. It was, in particular, clearly a good idea to court Bonaparte, and by now Gilbert was becoming accustomed to doing what he was told. "Here is the letter for Bonaparte you have asked me to send," he wrote his wife on October 30, 1799. "It is short and perhaps a little curt. . . . The people who are jealous of Bonaparte think I will oppose him in the future. They are right if he decides to suppress liberty; but if he is good enough to serve it, I will be the man he wants, for I do not believe him stupid enough to want to be a mere despot. . . .

"As for me, dear Adrienne, whom you see with terror ready to reenter public life, I protest that I am no longer sensitive to many attractions that once I prized too highly. The needs of my soul are the same, but they have taken on a more serious character, they are more independent of any followers, and the public whose approval I now value closer to its true worth. To end the Revolution so as to benefit humanity, to influence some measures useful for my contemporaries and for posterity, to reestablish the doctrine of liberty . . . would be pleasures that could still thrill my heart, but I am more disgusted than ever, irrevocably so, by the idea of taking root in the government, I would only enter it for a brief, energetic effort; then nothing, I swear it on my honor, on my tenderness for you and the memory of those we mourn, will convince me to give up the retirement I have decided on and in which we shall spend the rest of our lives quietly. . . .

"There is an existence that would suit me very well, in which, without an official position . . . I would exert my personal influence in favor of my principles."[15] Nothing, really, had changed: here was the same intention to retire—just as soon as things could be set right—that Lafayette had professed in 1790, 1791, and 1792; the same yearning for influence without responsibility. Luckily, Adrienne can't have worried for long: just a day after the letter was sent, Bonaparte organized a coup d'état that toppled the Directoire and made him First Consul; and it rapidly became obvious that there was no place for the hero of liberty in the new régime.

Lafayette's letter to Bonaparte had not been so very curt. "Citizen General," it read, "I only needed to love liberty and the fatherland for your arrival to fill me with joy and hope. . . . I rejoice in all my obligations to you, Citizen General, and feel the happy conviction that cherishing your glory and wishing for your success is a civic act as well as a proof of attachment and gratitude to you."[16]

Unfortunately, it did not convince Bonaparte to cross him off the list of émigrés. Gilbert's yearning to be home at last was almost unbearably strong so Adrienne, relying now on boldness, sent Gilbert a passport bearing an assumed name. Sieyès, his friend, was Second Consul; Bonaparte could not be ill-disposed toward the man he had freed. The guillotine had long been shut down—the risk was worth taking. Lagrange was not yet fit to be lived in, so Lafayette, exhilarated, left immediately for Paris. Once there, he discreetly kept hidden for a few days, but then wrote Bonaparte to announce his presence. "I thought that the continuation of my proscription suited neither the government nor myself. Today I have arrived in Paris. Before leaving for the distant country house [forty miles!] where I will gather my family, even before seeing my friends, I do not waste a moment in addressing myself to you, not because I think I can be out of place in any country where the Republic is founded on worthy bases, but because my duty and my feelings alike urge me to send you the expression of my gratitude."[17] A straightforward appeal for clemency would probably have worked. With its bland assumption that by rights he belonged in France, the letter was calculated to irritate the new chief of state. And indeed, Bonaparte's reaction was an explosion of rage, made all the more violent, no doubt, because he realized that his brand-new government could hardly take on the onus of arresting the hero of liberty. He was so furious, in fact, that, the next day, both Sieyès and Talleyrand, whom the Lafayettes consulted, advised them to return to Holland, but this time, Gilbert refused to flee. Instead, he discreetly retreated to Lagrange, there to await events.

The chateau of Lagrange-Bléneau was an old feudal building, with a moat, a stone bridge, and a gate flanked on each side by a big round tower. One of its four wings had been torn down in the eighteenth century, and the rest of it modernized, so it was open to air and light. On the whole, it was a noble house, but it had stood empty for a long time, so the Lafayettes found themselves busy trying to make it even minimally comfortable. With ready money in short supply, furniture was a problem, and they were only able to buy a few pieces of it at a time; but Adrienne threw herself into the task of making the chateau warm and inviting and she soon succeeded. The house itself was surrounded by lawns and woods, then came the farmland that produced the bulk of the Lafayettes' income; and aside from developing a penchant for trying to seduce the maids, Gilbert now became the perfect patriarch, kind to all, amiable, hospitable, busy looking after his land and his produce.

He might have felt quite happy, in fact, but for a crushing blow: Washington had died on December 14, 1799, and Gilbert was devastated by his loss. The last link with his glorious past was gone now with the person he loved best in the world. Washington had been right when he had written that sad letter on parting, back in 1784: the two had never met again. Although he was now living the quietest of lives—after all, by law he could have been arrested and executed—he took umbrage when, early in 1800, he found himself excluded from the Paris memorial for Washington and unmentioned in Bonaparte's dedication speech.

Still, Lafayette soon had reason to rejoice. In March 1800, the First Consul decreed that the members of the original National Assembly would henceforth be crossed off the list of émigrés. So, almost eight years after he had crossed the border, he was once again legally entitled to reside in France. As the formalities had to be carried out in Paris, Lafayette returned there and went in person to thank Bonaparte, who received him with a good deal of amiability and acceded to Lafayette's request that his son be given a commission. By May, young George Lafayette had been appointed a sub-lieutenant of Hussars, and it looked as if the whole family was reconciled to the new régime.

It had become Bonaparte's new policy to bury the excesses of the Revolution by uniting men of all opinions in the new government—regicides were to work side by side with former royalists in founding the new France— and to a very large extent, he succeeded. Lafayette, as the standard-bearer of the liberals, was obviously a desirable recruit, so he was promptly offered a seat in the Senate—a body of well-known men appointed by the consul— given a large salary, and expected to support the government. Gilbert declined politely, explaining that, if he were to become a Senator, he would often find himself compelled to disagree: much better, he said, for him to remain obscure. But his obscurity was rapidly taking on a shade of disapproval; to counter this, Talleyrand now offered him the French Embassy to the United States. Once again, Lafayette declined, this time on the grounds that he could hardly represent France adequately when he felt like an American himself. It was a deadlock, but Bonaparte, who was nothing if not persistent, still tried to seduce him. In October 1800, when a new treaty of friendship and commerce was concluded with the United States, Lafayette was one of the guests at the three-day fete given by Joseph Bonaparte at his chateau of Mortefontaine; and there, the consul, one afternoon, took him aside for a long chat.

"One of the first things he said to me," Lafayette later recalled, "was that I must have found that the French had lost their enthusiasm for liberty.

" 'Yes,' I answered, 'but they are able to receive it.'

" 'They are thoroughly sick of it,' he answered. 'Your Parisians, for instance, oh, the shopkeepers don't want it anymore." There was obviously not much the two men could agree on, especially since Bonaparte had no desire at all to listen to a man he considered an impractical ideologue. Still, Lafayette was impressed. "I found in general that his conversation had the simplicity of genius, that his mind was deep and his glance wise."[18]

That December there was an attempt on the consul's life, and afterward Lafayette came in person to congratulate him on his escape. He found Bonaparte in a reflective mood. The consul had received offers, he said, from the pretender, Louis XVIII, the former comte de Provence, who had even offered him a statue in exchange for a restoration; but, he went on, he had a feeling they might keep him chained to the statue. Yes, Lafayette answered, and even inside the pedestal. He then listened with approval as the consul extolled the Revolution and its achievements, asked and was granted the Tessés' removal from the list of émigrés, and left convinced that liberty might yet prevail.

In fact, the two men were absolute opposites. Bonaparte thrived on power while Lafayette dreaded it; the younger believed in order, the elder in liberty. Already in 1801, Bonaparte told his secretary Louis Bourrienne, "M. de Lafayette may be right in theory; but then, what is a theory?" The truth was that Gilbert belonged to the category of men the consul feared and despised most—those who, with the best of intentions, brought about the worst of catastrophes. But for a while, Lafayette was treated, if not exactly with favor, at least with consideration. His plantation in the Indies, La Belle Gabrielle, had naturally been seized by the government during the Revolution; now he was finally paid for it. And in April 1802 he was officially retired from the army at his own request with a yearly pension of 6,000 francs (about $27,000).

However, soon the situation began to deteriorate. When the Legion of Honor was created, Joseph Bonaparte told Lafayette that he was on the list of recipients. Bonaparte's purpose was to stabilize France by re-creating social categories that, unlike the ancien régime's, would be open to all who deserved them. Gilbert promptly asked that his name be crossed off: he was opposed, he said, to all such orders of knighthood, and, since he held no official position, he could conceive of no reason why he should accept this invidious distinction. Lafayette's refusal rankled, and with it the hero of liberty joined the opposition.

In May 1802 the French had been asked to vote on a Senate proposal that Bonaparte be given the office of First Consul for life. Despite his earlier approval of the presidency for life, in his letter to Maubourg of October 1799, Gilbert unhesitatingly stood against the change. It was undemocratic, he proclaimed, and sent the consul a long letter of explanation. "It is impossible," he wrote, "that you, General, the first among that order of men whose [fame] straddles the centuries, should want that such a revolution, so many victories and prodigies, so much blood and pain have no other result for the world and for you than an arbitrary government. The French people have known their rights too well ever to forget them, and today more than in the moment of their effervescence, they may be able to recover them and make good use of them; and you, by the strength of your character and of the public's confidence in you, by the superiority of your talents, of your existence, of your fate, you can, as you restore liberty, avoid all danger and reassure every apprehension. I therefore have nothing but patriotic and personal reasons to wish you . . . a permanent office; but it suits the principles, the commitments and the actions of my whole life to wait and see [that the office] become worthy of the nation and of you before I give it my vote."[19] No words could have been more exasperating for Bonaparte: the harping on principle and liberty, the chiding about his arbitrariness, the demand that he liberalize the Republic. Such demands were all the more maddening since Bonaparte intended, in short order, to seat himself upon a throne. And so, little by little, as the régime became more authoritarian, Lafayette's opposition became more total. He watched Napoleon's imperial charade with disgust, the re-creation of an aristocracy with anger. By 1807, a time when the opponents of the new emperor could be counted on the fingers of both hands, Lafayette stood prominently among them. His stance so angered Napoleon that George Lafayette was forced to resign his commission. From then on, all connections between the conqueror of Europe and the hero of liberty were severed.

Estranged from political life, Lafayette continued to cultivate his family. There was his old aunt in Chavaniac—in 1802, she was eighty-two—whom he visited periodically. There were his children. On June 7, 1802, George married Emilie Destutt de Tracy, the daughter of an old liberal friend, and on April 20, 1803, Virginie wed the comte Louis de Lasteyrie. Both Gilbert and Adrienne loved their children-in-law, and the family circle at Lagrange was a rich and constant source of pleasure for both of them even if Adrienne's health still worried everyone: clearly, her heart disease was weakening her. More than ever, Lafayette studied and practiced agriculture, so that the estate flourished. He was among the first in France to own a flock of merino sheep, for instance, which by 1811 reached the imposing size of 720. Adélaide de Simiane, no longer Gilbert's love, was still a very dear friend, and often came to stay.

Late in February 1803, as he crossed the Place de la Concorde, Gilbert slipped on the ice and broke his thigh. Unfortunately, he was friends with a doctor who had just invented a new machine for setting bones, so, disregarding the agonizing physical pain he was warned he would have to endure for forty days, he volunteered to be the machine's first guinea pig. As it turned out, the device was a failure and the patient, besides enduring agonies, was left with a very stiff leg and a permanent limp. He would have suffered infinitely less, and recovered completely, if he had refused to be the subject of an experiment. As it was, in July 1804 he was sent off to take the waters at the Mont d'Or, which were supposed to be good for the bones. From there he began to correspond with his daughter-in-law, Emilie, whom he discovered he could love both as a father and a friend. His letters have all the easy charm, all the relaxed intimacy, that endeared him to all who knew him well.

"I take advantage, my dear Emilie, of your husband's absence to write you," he noted on July 13. "George, who is faster than I, never gave me a chance to take my turn, but I enjoyed watching him give you our news which soon he will communicate in person. He will have been better able to tell you about the beauties of the Mont d'Or. We traveled, the ladies and I, in coffin-shaped conveyances . . . and I saw nothing until I was unpacked in the ditch [deep and narrow valley] where we are now." Going on to say that Adrienne was exhausted and in poor health, he continued: "I will tell you, dear Emilie, that [my health] will be greatly improved by my stay here because I can already feel that the pleasure it will give you will greatly increase that of my recovery, especially once I am able to take walks with you. . . . I would think myself too optimistic, had I not been able to kneel, yesterday night and this morning, next to my bed. I called in witnesses to my pious posture, and even if you insist it does not mean I have been converted, you will at least admit it shows a marked limbering of my legs."[20]

After all the years of turmoil, Gilbert had at last come to rest: surrounded by an adoring wife and loving family, freed from any serious money problems by Adrienne's inheritance—600,000 francs ($2,700,000) besides La-grange—he still complained bitterly when he was forced to concern himself with money matters: in that, and in his manners, the republican always remained an aristocrat. In a letter written from Paris to Emilie in 1806, for instance, he moaned, "I leave after having drunk to the bitter dregs the annoyance of pecuniary affairs." In truth, although not nearly as rich as before the Revolution, he was still very well off; and the annoyance in question did not prevent his adding in the same letter: "Give me a good filial benediction; I will be satisfied with the consolation of telling you that I love you madly, that you give my life an indescribable charm and happiness, and that all my feelings come together to adore my dear Emilie."[21] Then, in August 1806 Emilie, who had given birth to a daughter, felt great distress because she found herself unable to feed her baby and had to have it weaned, so Lafayette consoled her. "My dear beloved Emilie, I want to tell you how much I share in your sorrow about the weaning. . . . Just think that your baby is, will be, in perfect health and that many people cleverer than we think that an early weaning is the best thing for the child, but when your heart feels sorrow dear Emilie, it afflicts mine as well."[22]

Although Lafayette had always been greatly loved in his own family, he had had little occasion, until Lagrange, to spend much time at home. Now he reaped domestic pleasure to the fullest; he often went to the theater and was an admirer of Talma, the leading tragic actor of the time; he saw a great deal of his friends. But by the fall of 1807, Adrienne's illness took a turn for the worse; she could barely breathe, her legs were swollen, but she tried bravely to fight on despite the terrible pain caused by the ghastly medical practices of the time (mostly cauterizing and blistering). And she never ceased telling Gilbert that she loved him. He wrote: "That night, she told me: 'If I go to another place, you know how much I will be thinking of you there. The sacrifice of my life would be little indeed, if it ensures your eternal happiness. . . . There was a period,' she told me a few months ago, 'when as you were returning from America, I felt such violent feelings that I almost fainted as you came into the room, but I was afraid of being a bother, of imposing a constraint on your delicacy. I tried therefore to moderate myself. You can not be dissatisfied with what was left over.' "[23] She was too deeply exhausted to fight on, however; and on December 24, with all her family around her, she passed on to what she firmly believed would be another life.

For Gilbert, it was a devastating blow. He had always been solicitous of Adrienne's health, but without really facing the fact that he might lose his most devoted admirer. Of course, he loved her, but she worshiped him, gave him the sort of security he needed so badly, and looked after him and his interests. Adrienne had been not just a wife but a parent and an adviser as well.

A few days after her death, Gilbert sent Maubourg an immense letter expressing his feelings of loss—it covers some fourteen pages, in small print— a curious mixture of real sorrow and disappointed egotism.

"I had not yet written you, my dear friend, from the bottom of the abyss of sorrow in which I am plunged; but I was close to it when I sent you the last proofs of her friendship for you, of her confidence in your feelings for her. You will already have heard about the angelic end of this incomparable woman. I need to tell you more about it. My pain likes to talk to the most constant and dearest confidant of all my thoughts in the midst of those vicissitudes when I often thought myself unhappy. Until now you have found me stronger than the circumstances; today the circumstance is too strong for me. I shall never get over it.

"During the thirty-four years of a union in which her tenderness, her kindness, the elevation, the delicateness, the generosity of her soul charmed, embellished, honored my life, I felt so accustomed to everything she was for me that I did not separate it from my own existence. She was fourteen and I was sixteen when her heart embraced all that could matter to me. I thought I loved her, needed her, but it is only as I lose her that I can untangle what is left of myself for the rest of a life which has appeared to have so many pleasures and for which, nonetheless, neither happiness nor comfort are any longer possible. . . .

" 'What thanks I owe to God,' she would tell me during her illness, 'for the fact that so violent a passion was also a duty for me! How happy I have been!' She told me the day she died: 'What a role to be your wife!' And when I spoke to her of my tenderness for her, 'Is it true?' she answered in the most touching tones. 'What? Is it true? How good you are. Repeat it again. I have so much pleasure in hearing it. If you think you are not loved enough,' she told me, 'you must blame God: I used all the powers he gave me. I love you,' she told me in the middle of her delirium, 'in a manner Christian, worldly, passionate, voluptuous, even, if I still had sensual feelings! . . .'

" 'You are not a Christian,' she was asking one day. And as I did not answer: 'I know what you are: you are a Fayettist.'

" 'You must think me very vain,' I answered, 'but aren't you a Fayettist yourself?'

" 'Oh, yes!' she answered, 'with all my soul. I'm sure I could give my life for that particular sect!'

"The last day, she told me: 'When you see Mme de Simiane, you will give her my tender feelings. . . .' "[24]

As he lost her, Lafayette learned to appreciate his wife. It is impossible, however, not to wonder whether a less saintly woman might not have been better for him: admiration does not encourage change. Had Adrienne been more critical of her husband's positions and actions, she might have dispelled some of his illusions and forced him to behave in more effective ways. With all her superb qualities, loving criticism is just what Adrienne had never given him.

Now Gilbert had to stand alone, make his own decisions, and look after his own estate. At least he had his children and grandchildren, and he drew ever closer to them. He now took on a slightly more patriarchal quality. At fifty, he was older than anyone in his entourage at Lagrange, largely restricted to his family and a few old friends because of his estrangement from the government.

As the American Revolution receded into the past, he seemed, more and more, to belong to a generation whose day was done. The Empire, in France, was a time for young men, and the years that preceded 1789 seemed remote indeed. In America, then in France before 1792, he had always had something to gain by professing republican beliefs; but, after 1800, the reverse was true. Yet, unhesitatingly, he continued to stand for liberty and equality. Little by little, his enforced distance from politics had begun to pay off. Because he had refused all connection with Napoleon's despotism, thus renouncing great financial advantages, he came, more and more, to be seen as an enduring incarnation of liberty, so that, on the ruins of his career, a new, towering structure of trust and respect began to appear.

Still, there wasn't much he could do. Even his dislike for that "curious mixture of grandeur borrowed from the Revolution and counterrevolutionary groveling,"[25] as he wrote Jefferson in 1810, remained largely silent. And when, by chance, some dignitary of the régime met this survivor, he generally reacted with an irritation born, perhaps, of the fact that, deep down, those men of the Revolution resented the pomp, pageantry, and absolutism of the new monarchy.

General Thiébault, a former republican, meeting Lafayette in a bookstore sometime in June 1810, asked him why he did not belong to the Senate. "I refused a seat there," Lafayette answered. "The government's arbitrary practices preclude my having anything to do with it." As soon as he got home, Thiébault, who felt the implied criticism, gave vent to his rage. "The dignity of this citizen of the two worlds, the calmness of his face, the manners of this aristocratic demagogue, his courtly airs and politenesses . . . all that contrast between his refined manners and his political behavior, have never let me consider him as anything but factious, just as his overdelicate feelings contrasted with his revolutionary role have always made me think he was a dupe of himself and others."[26]

What a lot of acrimony against a man so thoroughly devoid of any public role! As the violence of this letter reveals, what the Bonapartists resented about Lafayette, aside from the fact that his manners were so much better than theirs, was that he was a revolutionary by conviction and not, unlike them, by necessity. They had entered the great upheaval because all doors were closed to them and had come out of it with new fortunes and freshly minted titles. He had lost almost everything but not given up liberty.

Thiébault was a faithful mirror of his imperial master. As he grew more absolute, Napoleon's resentment against the very few people who failed to fall in line preoccupied him more and more. "Everyone has learned his lesson," he said in 1812; "only one man still hasn't, and it's Lafayette. He has never given up an inch. You see him quiet, now; well, I will tell you that he is ready to start all over again."[27]

It was astonishing how eloquent one man's silence could be. All over Europe, now, people knew that the spirit of liberty survived at Lagrange; this was so patent that when General Claude Malet, a disgruntled, retired officer, launched an ill-planned, but briefly successful coup, he was found to have put Lafayette on the list of his provisional government. Since, however, this had been done completely without Lafayette's consent or knowledge, he was not indicted; but when the returning Napoleon (he had been in Russia at the time of the attempt) proceeded to apportion the blame, he exclaimed: "Who proclaimed that insurrection was a duty? Who flattered the people by proclaiming a sovereignty it is incapable of holding? Who destroyed the respect due to the law, its sanctity, by making them depend, not on the sacred principles of justice, the nature of things and civil justice, but only from the will of an assembly of men devoid of all knowledge of the civil, criminal, administrative, political, and military laws?"[28] The Emperor hardly needed to name Lafayette; everyone knew who he meant.

Later that year, 1812, away in Chavaniac, his ninety-two-year-old aunt died, and with her, Gilbert lost the last link to his childhood. Meanwhile, Lafayette worried about friends and relations who were fighting in the Russian campaign. "I have lost General Romeuf at the Battle of the Moskowa," he wrote on December 22. "He was an intimate friend who had been my aide-de-camp and to whom I was bound by the most tender ties of affection and gratitude. My daughter-in-law's brother, Victor Tracy . . . was made a prisoner. We fear he may be wounded. Communications are almost impossible and who knows when we may hope to see him again? Finally, my poor nephew, Alfred Noailles [son of the vicomte] . . . has just been killed crossing the Beresina."

While Napoleon's war continued, however, Lafayette went right on farming. "I do not rise above my agricultural occupations," he wrote in the same letter. "By dint of countless exchanges, I have put together more than five hundred acres of farmland which, together with the woods and plantations, give me seven hundred acres altogether. I only have a master carter under me and, without making any great scientific claims, I can say that with a little theory and ten years' experience on the same terrain, I have become . . . quite a good farmer. That occupation gives the body and mind a little exercise without fatigue."[29] It was a peaceful, not unpleasant life, and there was no reason to think that it would ever change.

The day the enemy entered the city," Lafayette wrote about March 31, 1814, "I locked my door and burst into tears."[1] Napoleon had been defeated and the Allied armies—Russian, Prussian, Austrian—were encamped on the Champs Elysées.

How startling an event this was can be judged by the fact that, for a long time, the Allies had hung back for fear of falling into a trap: it seemed almost beyond belief that the greatest military genius of modern times should have left his capital open to the enemy. And with his military defeat, Napoleon lost his throne.

In that spring of 1814, Lafayette was too remote from power to help with the despot's fall. He did speak to an anonymous marshal at the turn of the year, suggesting that the army depose Napoleon and declare France a republic, but of course to no avail. As downcast as his patriotic heart might be, however, the hero of liberty could see distinct advantages to the Emperor's downfall. After all the years suffered under the most crushing of despotisms, in France and throughout Europe, a new era was about to dawn that might well see constitutions, legislative assemblies, and the return of Lafayette to public life.

Nevertheless, the shock of military defeat was hard to take. Like many others, Gilbert had grown accustomed to victory; there had been, after all, almost twenty years of battles won and countries conquered, so the invasion of France seemed doubly humiliating. At least there was someone—Napoleon and his insensate ambition—to blame for the catastrophe. After the tyranny and incessant wars of the Emperor, any change seemed for the better; but since the allied sovereigns were in Paris, the possibilities were few. A republic was obviously out of the question; the best the liberals could hope for was a constitutional monarchy. When, in fact, it became clear that some such régime was in the making, Lafayette, like most of his compatriots, set about accepting it—even though it was the Bourbons who were now restored to the throne. "I would have felt a few scruples about recalling the Bourbons," he wrote a few years later, "and yet such is the strength of early impressions [that is, his childhood at Versailles] that I saw them again with pleasure, that seeing the comte d'Artois in the street moved me deeply and that, forgiving their sins, even those against the fatherland, I wished with all my heart that liberty might attach itself to the reign of the brothers and daughter of Louis XVI."[2] Luckily for Louis XVIII, the former comte de Provence (of the prodigious memory), Talleyrand felt no scruples at all about recalling him. By dint of clever maneuvers and the fact that Tsar Alexander I trusted him implicitly, Talleyrand engineered the restoration.

Just because Louis XVIII now sat on the throne of his ancestors, however, France was not about to return to the ancien régime. Before he entered Paris on his way from London, that selfish but intelligent monarch "granted" (as if it had been purely of his free will) the Charter, a constitution that established a parliamentary system representative of the upper and upper-middle classes, a responsible ministry, and just about all the liberties then considered possible—equality before the law, freedom of religion, freedom of speech, partly limited freedom of the press. Further, no man could be prosecuted for his acts during the Revolution or under Napoleon (even the regicides, for instance, were safe), and the properties that had been confiscated and resold by the state were specifically stated to belong irretrievably to their new owners. All in all, except for the fact that the Charter was dated from the nineteenth year of the new King's reign, this was the most democratic arrangement* that France had yet experienced: it was therefore perfectly possible even for the "republican" Lafayette to accept it.

---

*With the exception of the unworkable and promptly violated Constitution of 1791.

Of course, institutions are, to some extent, what men make them. And with the return of the King came a flood of émigrés yearning for the good old days. Soon, in the freshly reopened salon of his old friend, Mme de Staël, Lafayette met Alexander I, who complained that the Bourbons were "incorrigible."[3] One of the small, irritating issues, for instance, was the replacement of the tricolor flag, ennobled by a hundred victories, with the white flag of the Bourbons. It seemed like a deliberate insult, but most Frenchmen were too exhausted really to mind; besides, as Lafayette wrote, "In the midst of all these disappointments, France now had recovered more liberty than it had had since Napoleon had come to power."[4] Perhaps if he rallied the new régime, Lafayette thought, he could help make it more liberal. So he put on his old uniform of the National Guard, pinned a white cockade to his hat, and went to the Tuileries, where he was received by Louis XVIII and the comte d'Artois with great politeness.

The atmosphere, however, was not friendly to the former revolutionary. The French wanted neither argument nor trouble; Gilbert himself deplored the laws restricting the freedom of the press; the behavior of the émigrés, who were being odious to everyone; the reappearance of the old etiquette; and, worse, the re-creation of the old Royal Guard. There was one man, however, who stood out from all this: Louis-Philippe, duc d'Orléans, the son of Lafayette's old enemy. Intelligent and open to his time—although careful not to make trouble, he was not without his father's ambition—he promptly set himself up as the one member of the royal family who was also a liberal. And since Lafayette was a symbol of the center-left, Orléans proceeded to court him by reminding him that he, too, had fought for France in 1792; by explaining that he deplored the disappearance of the tri-color flag; and generally by flattering the always susceptible Gilbert as he referred to his past with devout admiration. It worked. Lafayette was often seen at the Palais Royal, the duc d'Orléans's residence, and even as he regretted the behavior of the other Bourbons, he extolled that of their liberal cousin.

Still, there wasn't much to be done in Paris, so in August Gilbert returned to Lagrange and the quiet life. He did spend part of the following winter in Paris, assiduously frequenting Mme de Staël's salon, where he met and disliked the duke of Wellington, but he was in the country in March 1815 when the electrifying news came that Napoleon had escaped from Elba and had landed in Provence. Clearly, Paris was the place to be when such great events were under way. Once there, however, Lafayette, as in 1814, found himself in a quandary. On the one hand, he felt that the expulsion of the Bourbons would be all to the good; on the other, he dreaded a return to the old despotism. So having flirted once more with power and plots, he retreated to Lagrange and waited out events that came one upon the other very quickly.

The unstoppable Napoleon reached Paris in mid-March and Louis XVIII fled the country. Once back at the Tuileries, however, the Emperor realized that few would follow him unless he gave France at least as substantial a dose of liberty as the Bourbons had. Having very little choice, he pronounced himself transformed into a new, liberal Napoleon, promised a new constitution, and pledged that, as the best proof of his conversion, he would henceforth pick all advisers from among the liberals. Lafayette described these maneuvers in a letter to his old friend, the princesse d'Hénin* on May 15. "Napoleon, republican in Provence, semirepublican in Lyon, absolute emperor in Paris, has realized his only salvation lay in becoming a constitutionalist. His mind and his character are like two opposed currents; we see a bizarre mixture of imperial, terrorist, and liberal measures; but public opinion is stronger than he is, and since he is prodigiously talented, he gives in to what he cannot avoid with a cleverness that the others [that is, the Bourbons] can never hope to equal."[5]

The Emperor was clearly going to need every famous liberal he could get. To this end he published the *Acte additionel aux Constitutions de l'Empire*, which embodied his liberal reforms, and while Lafayette objected to the title—what "constitutions of the Empire?" he asked—he accepted the content just as he had the Charter. As a further assurance, Joseph Bonaparte, who had been successively King of Naples and King of Spain, and was now again helping his brother at home, invited Lafayette to come to see him. At the interview he explained that Napoleon meant what he said. Although Lafayette did not believe him, he went on to say that Gilbert's name was the very first on the list for the new House of Peers. With great amiability, Lafayette, who thought, rightly, that as soon as Napoleon had won a victory he would free himself of all constitutional trappings, firmly refused. Since he would accept public functions from none but the people, he said, he would run for the Chamber of Representatives, which, unlike the Peers', was to be elected. Meanwhile he used the occasion to stress the fact that he expected elections to be called immediately.

When, at last, on May 1, an election was announced, Lafayette received a letter from Benjamin Constant, a fellow liberal, the former lover of Mme de Staël, and the author of the *Acte additionel*, who urged him to run for the Chamber. That was just the kind of encouragement Lafayette wanted. He became a candidate from Meaux, near Lagrange, and, on May 10, was

---

*Mme de Tessé, another recipient of frequent letters, had died in February.

elected a deputy by fifty-six out of seventy-nine votes.* Famous as he was, it is nevertheless unlikely that Gilbert owed his success to his reputation; instead, in all probability, the votes went to him as a landholder known for his wealth and easy charity. Indeed, when he offered himself as a candidate for President of the Chamber of Representatives on June 4, he was soundly defeated by Jean Lanjuinais, a man of doubtful honor but unquestioned practicality; and only with the greatest difficulty did he finally become Third Vice-President. Still, he had a double consolation: his son, George, who had also been elected, sat next to him; and, after twenty-three years of enforced political abstention, at long, long last, he was back in public office.

Two days after the election, it began to look as if the days of the first National Assembly were returning, as the Chamber discussed the oath that would be sworn to the Emperor. Lafayette first opposed the very idea of an oath: the sovereign, he reminded his colleagues, was the French people. When this approach didn't work, he encouraged the deputies to take the oath as a body instead of individually. This, he reasoned, would nullify it, as oaths were individual, not mass commitments. When told about Lafayette's obstructions, Napoleon was furious, of course, and the very next day, he came face to face with his opponent. "During the great session," Lafayette wrote Emilie, "I had remained in my seat next to George's, forgetting that the officials belonged in the deputation, when they came to fetch me in order to greet the Emperor upon his arrival. It was in the salon where he stopped that we renewed our acquaintance. 'It has been twelve years since I have had the pleasure of seeing you,' he said. I answered rather drily, 'Yes, Sire, it has been that length of time.' . . . You will be pleased with his speech; I was not satisfied with his face, which looked to me like that of an old despot angered by the role that his position was forcing him to play."[6] Lafayette was perfectly right: Napoleon had nothing but contempt for the Chamber, which had been forced on him.

On June 10, as the deputies discussed the address to the Emperor, Lafayette stuck to his guns, demanding that the Emperor be referred to not as "a hero," but merely as "a great man." It did not really matter. The armies of Europe were arrayed once again and the fate of France would be decided on the battlefield. Within a week, on June 18, Wellington defeated Napoleon at Waterloo. The Allies had refused to deal with Napoleon; so, now, it seemed, there were two possibilities: either a new government would seek an armistice from the Allies on the grounds that, with Napoleon gone, there was no reason to continue the war, or Napoleon could try raising new troops

*Only people who could prove a substantial income were allowed to vote.

to fight on. Naturally, the Emperor favored the second solution; he rushed back to Paris and considered dissolving the Chamber so that he could go back to his old way of governing. Others, however, had already foreseen such a possibility and taken measures against it. On the afternoon of June 21, Lafayette stood up in the Chamber. "For the first time in a great many years," he said, "I speak with a voice that the old friends of liberty will still recognize."[7] He went on to propose a resolution stating the nation's independence to be in jeopardy; declaring the Chamber in permanent session and that any attempt to dissolve it would be treason; further proclaiming that the army and generals were entitled to the gratitude of the fatherland; and finally, requesting that the police, the Ministers of War, Interior, and Foreign Affairs immediately come to the Assembly. After that, it was too late for Napoleon to recapture his power. The end of the drama took another twenty-four hours. The ministers came, offered little information, and moved on to the Tuileries with the President and Vice-Presidents of the Chamber, where they deliberated fruitlessly until three in the morning; at some point in the evening, Lafayette asked that the Emperor be deposed but none of the others would agree. By the next day, June 22, however, the ministers realized that their position had become impossible, so they asked Napoleon to abdicate after all; he refused. Lafayette then sent the Emperor a message: either he abdicated or he, Lafayette, would ask the Chamber formally to depose him. There was nothing the Emperor could do. He signed an act of abdication transmitting the crown to his son* and retired to Malmaison.

Now France needed a new government. Lafayette assumed he would be part of it but, with his customary inability to judge men and events, failed to see that Joseph Fouché, Minister of the Police and a regicide, had already started a maneuver of dazzling brilliance that was to make himself the Police Minister of the restored king. A first-rate intriguer, Fouché got rid of Lafayette by a simple device: he convinced the Vice-Presidents to amend a resolution stating that the members of the provisional government would be selected *from* the members of both Chambers (Representatives and Peers) to one stating that they must be chosen *by* the members of both Chambers. Fouche himself, who was neither a Peer nor a Representative, could now be elected, and he brought his entire team in with him. As a result, Lafayette, who would surely have been among the deputies elected to the government, now trailed behind men like Fouché himself, who were far more practical. However, even if excluded from the government, Lafayette could still be-

---

*His son, unfortunately, had been taken to Austria by his mother, the Empress Marie-Louise.

come a nuisance; so Fouché turned down his request for appointment as commander of the National Guard and instead sent him off to negotiate an armistice with the foreign armies nearing Paris. It was a fool's errand. The foreign leaders, who had been warned by Fouché, simply ignored Lafayette and his delegation, while impeding their travels. Eventually, he gave up, returned to Paris, and reported his failure to the government on July 6. The very next day, Blücher, the Prussian commander in chief, entered Paris, and, on the eighth, Elie Decazes, the Prefect of Police just appointed by Louis XVIII, locked up the doors of the Palais Bourbon where the Chamber had been sitting. Lafayette protested, of course, but to no avail: the King was back and the Chamber dissolved. All he could do was return to Lagrange. "The white flag waves over the Tuileries," he wrote Mme d'Hénin on July 11. "It is defended by Prussian and English troops who keep a lighted fuse on their cannon. . . . We have at least, my friends and I, the consolation of thinking that we have neglected nothing in order to avoid the catastrophes that afflict us. I must add that while our Chamber may have made a few political mistakes, its intentions have always been above reproach and its behavior noble and independent. You may be sure that this Assembly, and the immense mass of the people gathered, after Napoleon's fall, under the tricolor flag, are the true national party."[8]

Whatever its intentions and errors, the Chamber's actions could in no way have modified the outcome of the Hundred Days. The Allied armies were in charge, not the deputies, and France, with or without Napoleon, could not resist them. Not only did Lafayette remain wholly oblivious of that unpleasant fact but he also failed to realize that France, even with a monarch who had returned in the Allies' baggage, was better off than ever before. The Charter was revised in a liberal direction, and, aside from some excesses committed in the south of the country by bands of ultraroyalists, the government was at least as democratic as that old model, its English counterpart. Besides, Louis XVIII, who was far from stupid, did learn a lesson from the speed with which France had rallied to Napoleon's banner in the spring; and this time he conscientiously set about creating something very close to a real parliamentary régime.

The restored monarchy had a number of flaws. The first, and most serious, was that so few people—about 90,000 for a population of over 20 million—were entitled to vote; it must, however, be said that the same situation prevailed in England, then considered the most democratic of all European nations. Another was that the freedom of the press, while incomparably greater than under the Empire, was still limited. Then, too, by its deliberate emphasis on continuity with the ancien régime (a good case of appearance obscuring reality), the court, led by the reactionary comte d'Artois,* managed almost to conceal the power of the two Chambers, focusing all the attention on the ruling family. What actually mattered was not that a Bourbon occupied the throne, but that government depended on the consent of the people, and that everyone was safe from arbitrary arrest or dispossession.

Blind to the political reality, Lafayette concentrated instead on small irritants. "Although it is now proved that the royal persons will never cease hating me or wanting to harm me," he wrote Lord Holland on December 15, "I would prefer them still if I could be convinced that they will at last understand their own best interests and their safety, and that they will [cease trying to destroy] the rights and interests of my country."[9] In fact, Louis XVIII was, at that very moment, busy restraining the ultraroyalists, and he soon dissolved the Chamber elected immediately after Napoleon's fall. The new Chamber was far more moderate, and the liberties of France—as well as its finances—began to prosper.

Although theoretically retired, Lafayette quickly became one of the leaders of the left-wing opposition to the government. It was at this time, in fact, that his political position became more radical. Letters, long, long letters, went out to a variety of correspondents to prove that the great man had always been a republican (a patent untruth) and always right (a gross inaccuracy). Now, in his implacable resistance to the régime, Lafayette began to attack not its very real shortcomings, which were not spectacular enough, but imaginary, and far more entrancing, defects. He began to seem more and more a caricature of himself. To practical people, Lafayette appeared not as the rallying point of the liberals, but as the Quixote of liberty. The duc de Broglie characterized Gilbert's behavior: "You had to love M. de la Fayette for himself, which was in fact very easy," he wrote, "because there was nothing to be gained by being one of his close friends; he hardly made any difference between an honest man and a blackguard, between intelligence and stupidity. The only difference he made was between the people who said, and those who didn't say, what he had been saying himself. He was a prince surrounded by people who flattered and robbed him. That handsome fortune, nobly earned, nobly offered, nobly received was dissipated in the hands of adventurers and spies.

"There was nothing to be gained either in taking him as one's chief: for he was always ready to start a new enterprise on the first appeal by some

---

*Artois had emigrated on July 15, 1789, and ever since then belonged to the most extreme wing of the exiled aristocracy. Even now, he favored a return to the ancien régime pure and simple.

stranger just like a knight of old who would fight for the pleasure of fighting, the excitement of danger and the desire of obliging a friend.

"What I say here . . . I told him a hundred times during the course of an intimate friendship that ended only with his life."[10]

Lafayette's retirement did not last long. In 1817, he failed to be elected to the Chamber in Paris, but, on October 26, 1818, he became once more a deputy from Le Mans. "The King," a courtier wrote, "has taken M. de la Fayette's election very seriously and is pained by it."[11] Perhaps Louis XVIII remembered 1789 too vividly. In the new France, Lafayette could not be more than a gadfly, irritating at times, but never politically dangerous.

As soon as he reentered the Chamber of Deputies, Lafayette identified himself with the extreme, antidynastic left, and took his stand as the champion of the persecuted. In August 1819, for instance, he was writing the Keeper of the Seals, the comte de Serre, about "an exile, originally from the department of the Pyrenées Orientales, whose unfortunate family, composed of a wife and seven children, begs that he be allowed to return home."[12] The man, a regicide who had served the government during the Hundred Days, was finally amnestied. And in the Chamber itself, Lafayette spoke out repeatedly for liberty. On March 8, 1820, he was deploring the antilibertarian excesses of the Revolution and the ancien régime alike. "All the sufferings of France," he said, "are due far less to the perverseness of the wicked and the exaggeration of madmen than to the hesitations of the weak, the compromises with conscience, and the eclipses of patriotism."[13] A little later, when the electoral law was discussed, Broglie tells us, "M. de Lafayette took the speaker's stand three times. He had written his speech because he was afraid it might be thought too violent. The effect he made was all the worse; there was something noble and imposing about his manner, an accent of the ancien régime that contrasted strangely with the revolutionary ideas and expressions that filled his speech."[14] Since the horrors of the Revolution were still present in everyone's mind, Lafayette offered an easy target, and on that occasion, Broglie reports, M. de Serre answered, "When a civil war rages, the blood being spilled is on the head of those who started it. The last speaker knows this better than most: more than once, he has discovered with dread and shame that he who encourages that mob is forced to follow it and almost to lead it."[15] Most people, the duc de Broglie concluded, found this a telling answer, but Lafayette was deaf to the voices of his opponents.

Strangely, it was Lafayette's egotism that worried the government most: he seemed to have some secret knowledge, and they wanted to find out. While the Restoration was willing to concede a measure of liberty, it relied, as Napoleon had, on a host of police informers and feared daily the beginnings of a new revolution. For instance, when Lafayette visited his constituents at Le Mans in September 1820, the Minister of the Interior received a stream of reports from a variety of officials describing the smallest event of the trip. A hundred young men had ridden out to greet Lafayette, one report anxiously stated, while confirming that a large body of troops had been brought into town, just in case. The Minister of War was informed that the mayor of La Ferté-Bernard, an unimportant little town, had received Lafayette and attended the ensuing banquet; the mayor must be fired, the minister wrote angrily to his colleague of the Interior. Luckily, the prefect was able to write that the banquet at Le Mans had been gloomy and ill-attended; Lafayette must be disappointed; but all street gatherings were carefully dispersed, all the same. One would think it was Robespierre *redivivus*, and not a lame old gentleman, who was disturbing the peace of Le Mans.

Still, the years 1820 to 1823 saw a number of plots form and almost succeed. Although most Frenchmen were patently satisfied with the régime and were not about to stage another revolution, various groups of republicans and Bonapartists had attempted coups d'état. First came the Waterside Plot (its members met by the side of the Seine) to murder the royal family and, in the ensuing disorder, to proclaim a revolutionary government; then the plot of the Four Sergeants of La Rochelle, the regiment that would start a military rebellion; and many others followed. The men who took part in these attempts generally lacked both substance and reputation, except for one—Lafayette. Until now he, more than anyone, had stood for honesty and openness, but in order to reestablish a republican government, of which he would be part, he was willing to encourage assassination attempts and other dark and discreditable goings-on. Once again, he was demonstrating his lack of common sense and risking a great deal in the wrong way for the wrong goal. That he seemed so little to understand the difference between revolution and assassination is consistent with his steady move to the left. Lafayette emerged from this unpleasant phase untouched, and, with a few other deputies, was cited, though not indicted, in the trial of the Four Sergeants; for the next few years, the prefect of Seine and Marne was instructed to keep a careful eye on Lagrange.

That Lafayette should have felt the need for these clandestine and dishonorable activities seems all the odder for the fact that he could, when he spoke up, be extremely effective. On March 3, 1823, for instance, Manuel, a young left-wing deputy, made a speech in the Chamber of Deputies that sounded like an apologia for the execution of Louis XVI. His expulsion was ordered amid great tumult, and the National Guard was called in. "The Guard came in. From all sides came shouts of 'No National Guard.' M. de Lafayette stood up and, with a paternal air, signaled to the guards that they were to leave. He found himself, suddenly, just as he had been thirty years earlier. The officer hesitated, went for orders, returned, stammered, and finally turned to the sergeant who refused to obey the expulsion order. Then, on every side, cries of 'Long live the National Guard' were heard,"[16] Broglie recounted. There, obviously, was Lafayette's strength: whenever he was really defending liberty, the people listened, and his old influence was found to be intact; but that still did not translate into political influence.

Lafayette also made himself useful in another area. Even though almost half a century had passed, he remembered the care with which the Continental Congress of the United States had husbanded its funds. It is, of course, a mainstay of all democracies that their parliaments control, scrutinize, and often try to reduce public expenditure. In 1821, however, the French Chamber felt that once it had voted the budget its role was over, and it expected the budget largely to reflect the requests of the executive branch. Now Lafayette started the practice of analyzing the proposed budget, pointing out, for instance, that the civil list was far too costly, or that too many pensions were being paid. He objected to the current custom of giving each ministry a block grant, which the minister could then apportion as he pleased. In his fight for a sound economy, Lafayette was placing himself alongside a number of British statesmen, the most famous of whom, today, is probably Gladstone. Unfortunately, his arguments were marred by a number of absurdities, such as his assertion that it would have been cheaper to fight the Allies in 1815 than to give in; or that even at his most despotic Napoleon had at least accepted all the principles of the Revolution, or when, sounding a theme which became his leitmotif, Gilbert demanded a return to the unworkable Constitution of 1791, forgetting that, earlier, he had admitted that even the Constitution of the Directoire had been an improvement on its predecessor.

His attitude toward the Revolution was typical of his faulty thinking. "The Revolution," he would say, "means the victory of right over privilege. It means emancipation and development of human faculties, the restoration of the people."[17] But every time he made that point, he would promptly spoil it by going on to make ridiculous and impossible claims for the Revolution—whatever else it may have done, it had not brought the French peace and prosperity. His attacks on the régime confirmed Lafayette's position as one of the key figures of the liberal party, even as his illogical lapses precluded him from ever leading it. He remained on the fringe. The men who surrounded him were those whose motives were most likely to be tainted by greed and ambition, and they used him ruthlessly.

Further, Lafayette's constant equation of the government with the ancien régime was self-defeating because it was so patently untrue. In a country with a parliament, constitutional equality before the law, and an independent judiciary, who would believe him when he said, as on July 23, 1822: "The counterrevolution has mastered all the power of the state, all its institutions, all its influence; it is upheld by the European coalition of all the despotisms, all the prejudices, all the abuses. . . . Let the French people realize that . . . it will soon be informed . . . that all the liberties, all the advantages wrested from the ancien régime by the national revolution of 1789 are passing, illegitimate and revocable usurpations"?[18] Such were the themes he repeated again and again, to the people who reelected him in 1822, and again, to his constituents in 1824. Only in 1824 they did not find him convincing, and he was soundly beaten.

The defeat, however, was a blessing in disguise. Ever since Adrienne's death, Lafayette had been mismanaging his financial affairs. Ever the grand seigneur, he spent freely, helped the needy, financed a variety of liberal causes and men, all without worrying where the money was to come from. Eventually, the inevitable happened, and Lafayette cheerfully told his family that, in order to pay his debts, he would have to sell his Brittany estate. The response was consternation. The young Lafayettes had nineteenth-century principles about the sacredness of capital and the need to live within one's means. Luckily, at that very moment, President Monroe, who knew of these difficulties, invited Lafayette to visit the United States, hinting that Congress was disposed to do something generous for the man who, when it mattered, had helped America. On February 7, 1824, Congress passed a resolution offering Lafayette a warship for his passage. With that fine sense of appositeness that he seemed to develop whenever he dealt with his adopted country, Lafayette refused the warship as an unnecessary expense and accepted the invitation. He would sail on a packet instead, he said, and leave Paris in July. Not only was he likely to return richer than he had left but a warm reception abroad could only boost further his already growing popularity in France.

From the first, Lafayette's journey proved irritating to the French government, always worried about anything that might further the cause of "international revolution." Even at Le Havre, from which he sailed on July 13, 1824, he was greeted by cheering crowds, to the alarm of the police and the fury of the Minister of the Interior. While, at this point, the voters were basically satisfied with the Charter, the mass of the population was still disfranchised. Politically, dissatisfaction with this condition mattered little since, by definition, it could not be expressed legally. Still, they could cheer the old hero of liberty, the avowed republican.

On August 16, as he arrived in New York, his reception exceeded even the most radiant acclaim of his past. Thus the baron de Mareuil, who was French Minister to the United States, found himself compelled to send home

a long series of gloomy dispatches. "There is at the moment only one occupation in America," Mareuil reported on August 19, "and that is the arrival
of M. le Marquis de La Fayette. The presence of the *Marquis*, as the old
Americans say, although the gazettes make a point of referring to him as
General Lafayette, will certainly produce, in every part of the country he
will visit, explosions of joy and enthusiasm that will not be simply the expression of the country's gratitude. The party spirit, the democratic spirit and
the opposition to our European doctrines that are rife in this country will
play a large part in the warmth of his reception. I am prepared for this hurly-
burly. I will show no concern but will miss no occasion of saying what I
think while respecting whatever is only gratitude . . . and treating with
contempt whatever may be inspired by a desire to honor in M. de La Fayette
the patriarch and the friend of the European revolutionaries."[19]

The French Minister may have been annoyed, but in America he was
a solitary quibbler. For the thirteen months of his visit, Lafayette moved
constantly amid cheering, enthusiastic crowds, from reception to reception,
from speech to speech, and from banquet to banquet. In the most spectacular
and unprecedented outpouring of love, the entire country turned out to
view and applaud the old hero; everywhere people pressed forward in passionate gratitude. Gilbert was so overwhelmed that he hardly found time to
write home; when he did, however, his letters were characteristically addressed to the ladies of the family. "All through this trip of two hundred
leagues," he exulted on September 5, "we have felt everything which can
touch or flatter the human heart. . . . I found more old soldiers of the Revolution than I had hoped for and I have felt a great satisfaction in seeing the
memories I have left in their hearts. . . . I respond as best I can to the
unexpected duty of answering speeches among a multitude of listeners,
luckily well disposed and who think my accent barely perceptible and my
English excellent. It would not be so in the streets of London, but here
everything is all right because they are so well disposed."[20]

He became the chief newsmaker throughout the country. Not only did
he provide the papers with a daily headline, he also was the subject of
endless articles, and his every movement, his every smile, his every article
of clothing, even, was reported in the fullest detail. In Europe, the papers
picked up the American press reports, and all Lafayette's friends passed
around the letters written by George, who was accompanying his father. As
for the hero, he was drunk with happiness. This, after all, was what he had
always yearned for: immense popularity in a republican country, with no
responsibility to go with it. "A grand ball will bring together some six thousand persons," he wrote from New York on September 13; and, on the way
to Philadelphia, "A very amiable group of ladies will accompany us on a

steamship which is as comfortable as a floating hotel. In the midst of the gatherings, of the revues, of the fetes, we go to church on Sundays. The other day we asked God to grant the freedom of both hemispheres: this sort of religion suits me better than the counterrevolutionary anathemas of Europe. . . . I see deputations that arrive from every corner of the United States, towns and villages, and they have come all this way to ask me if I will spend an hour with them. When I see men and women come from two hundred miles just to touch my hand for a few moments, must I not feel shame that I am unable to respond in writing to their addresses?"[21] And on October 10, in Baltimore, where Washington's tent had been uncovered from the archives and set up for Lafayette's reception, he continued: "We have been kept here by the most touching of circumstances; we all cried when we embraced my old comrades under General Washington's tent; and every day they find a new way of proving the tenderest public affection."[22] Two weeks later, from Norfolk, Virginia, he went on: "You will have heard . . . the details of this unprecedented continuation of kindnesses addressed to the nation's guest. I am on excellent terms with the ministers of South America; the Greek envoys* in London have also written me with great friendship and trust; but the European diplomats do not see all this with the same pleasure."[23]

Indeed, at home, the French government watched the scene with disgust and anger, which M. de Mareuil regularly fueled. "In New York," he wrote on August 27, "in the midst of the homages offered to him, they did him the disservice of making him sit on an armchair that had belonged to Louis XVI, to the king martyred by the Revolution; on another occasion, they made him drink a toast to Napoleon's memory."[24] All this was bad enough for poor M. de Mareuil, but, worse, Lafayette was about to arrive in the nation's new capital, Washington, D.C. "The head of state, the Secretaries . . . will want to welcome the man of the hour. . . . [The Russian Minister and I] have agreed to refuse any invitation, even from the President, to any festivity for M. de Lafayette. . . . Even if one didn't know [his] feelings and his political intentions, he has been careful, ever since his arrival in America to manifest them highly and every one of his words . . . is less a homage to America than an appeal to the revolutionary passions in Europe, a wish for their success and for the complete triumph of democracy."[25] Mareuil was right; although he scarcely refrained from speaking out at home, Lafayette was now seizing his golden opportunity with enthusiasm: not only could he say exactly what he pleased, but, carried away by the ovations of

---

*Greece was then fighting for its independence from Turkey.

the delirious crowds, he went a good deal further than he might have otherwise.

Of course, in a country justifiably proud of its democratic institutions, Lafayette's strong words only added to the national guests's overwhelming popularity, and he continued to go from triumph to triumph. Then, too, there were meetings with the few surviving leaders of the American Revolution. On November 8, for instance, Lafayette was writing from Monticello: "I have been received with much emotion by Mr. Jefferson, whom of course I found greatly aged after a separation of thirty-five years, but carrying his eighty-one years admirably and enjoying the full vigor of his mind and soul, which he uses mostly in the foundation of a superb university."[26] The two old friends had much to talk about, and while, everywhere else, Lafayette insisted on speaking English, here he deferred to Jefferson's request and conversed in French. During his time in Virginia, he also went to pay his respects to the tomb of his adopted father. There, uniquely, he asked to be left absolutely alone, sending even George away. And when, after an hour, he reappeared, he was uncharacteristically silent.

Plaudits and ovations were immensely satisfying, but Lafayette had also been led to expect a more substantial proof of the United States' high regard, and soon it was forthcoming. In a move of unprecedented generosity, Congress decided to award the illustrious visitor a cash grant of $250,000 (close to $3 million 1983 dollars) and twenty-five thousand acres of Federal lands, which Lafayette eventually sold. At one blow his financial difficulties were solved. In the 1770s Lafayette had spent freely to help America; now the United States paid back its debt and made him wealthy for the rest of his life. Of course, there were formal ceremonies as well. Lafayette was the first foreigner ever to address Congress. He described the scene in one of his letters home. "I have come from an imposing ceremony," he wrote on December 10. "I have answered, in English, a speech that Mr. Clay, the famous orator and Speaker of the House of Representatives gave from his presiding seat. That admirable hall was filled with two thousand spectators of both sexes; the Senators were sitting in their reserved places; the foreigners, the diplomats, among whom I recognized the English legation but not the French Minister, were also there. A great deputation of twenty-four men came to fetch me and took me to the Capitol. Hardly had I entered into that vast hall where the usher announced me in a loud voice, as he did yesterday in the Senate . . . but everyone stood up. After hearing the Speaker's speech and sitting down, I had to stand again, along with everyone present, and answer in English, which was far more daunting than anything I had done so far. They thought I would fish my glasses and my speech out of my pocket but I took my chances and answered as you will see. They tell me I managed quite well."[27] Lafayette was being unduly modest: he was a splendid success and received many cheers as he talked about the United States and liberty.

The dazzling procession then continued, monotonous almost in its succession of triumphs. From Fayetteville, for instance, on March 5, he reported: "We are here, in that North Carolina town of which you have seen a rendition at Lagrange; we are given honors, tenderness, fetes and escorts around our carriages and houses which, for the last seven months have accompanied us at every step, at every hour of the day . . . throughout our two-thousand-league journey surrounded by feelings of gratitude and affection."[28] There was, in fact, no town where Lafayette was not anxiously awaited, no state which could bear to miss his visit. The United States, in 1825, was a real nation, with a booming economy, a sound currency, and good roads. The cities were larger, the population more numerous. The early promise had come to fruition. The Revolution, as a consequence, had become a golden memory, the myth all Americans lived; and these feelings found their incarnation in the person of "General Lafayette."

The smooth sailing was briefly interrupted, on May 8, in the most literal way: as it steamed up the Ohio, Lafayette's ship collided with a tree trunk and sank to the bottom. Luckily, no one was killed or even hurt, and only luggage was lost, but it was a dramatic and widely reported episode. Poor M. de Mareuil, writing his endless reports, must have wished not just the boat but its passengers at the bottom of the Ohio, especially since, by now, press reports of the journey's success were reawakening memories at home: after all those years, everywhere in France except at court, Lafayette was again the Hero of Two Worlds.

In America, also, people were remembering the past. On June 17, 1825, the fiftieth anniversary of the Battle of Bunker Hill, a massive celebration took place to celebrate the laying of the cornerstone of a monument. There, Lafayette basked in the enthusiastic applause of some 200,000 people. "I was received yesterday by the legislature and executive branch of the State of Massachusetts," he wrote home, "and today, in the finest weather in the world, we have celebrated the great anniversary. . . . Nothing can give you an idea of the effect made by that republican prayer spoken before an immense multitude by an old chaplain who had fought at Bunker Hill, of the survivors of the day uncovering their white hair when the president of the association, the orator of the day, spoke to them. And I too, I rose at the head of all the other revolutionary soldiers as we were given our compliment! We will send you Mr. Webster's admirable speech; we sat down at a table where four thousand places were set, and where I announced that having now celebrated . . . the liberation of the American hemisphere, the toast for the next fifty years would be *To the liberation of Europe!*"[29]

The provocative toast, which was widely reported, thrilled the oppressed in Europe as much as it angered their governments. In fact, well before Karl Marx propounded the theory that history had a direction, Lafayette had discovered how much can be done by invoking the future: if you represent what must surely come, then your adversaries, at best, are fighting a rearguard action.

To commemorate the historic visit of Lafayette, many cities published small books. A typical one, produced in Savannah, Georgia, gives a minute description of every festivity and every participant, running to some seventy-three pages of small print.* Naturally, it starts with Lafayette's arrival by steamer and the address delivered by Governor Troup.

" 'General,' " the Governor said, " ' 'Tis little more than ninety years since the Founder of this State first set foot upon the bank on which you stand. Now, four hundred thousand people open their arms to receive you. Thanks to a kind Providence, it called you to the standard of liberty in the hopelessness of our early revolution; it has preserved you that in your latter day the glory of a great empire might be reflected back upon you, amid the acclamations of millions.

" 'The scenes which are to come will be for you comparatively tranquil and placid, there will be no more of dungeons, no more of frowns of tyrants. Oh, Sir! What a consolation for a man who has passed through such a sea of trouble, that the million of bayonets, which guard the blessings we enjoy, stand between you and them. But enough! Welcome, General, welcome, thrice welcome to the State of Georgia!' "[30]

The report went on to say that Lafayette listened with an attention all the more meritorious in that he had heard many speeches like this before, and he replied simply by offering his thanks to the governor and people, with a few words for the United States and liberty. Then a procession was formed; it moved to the town proper where the mayor greeted the crowd, made a speech, and listened to Lafayette's response. Then there was a dinner for three hundred people at which thirteen toasts were offered, ranging from "To the Constitution of the United States" to, simply "Woman!"; then there were volunteer toasts; then the company listened to a song written in honor of that glorious day; then there were illuminations; and finally everyone went off to bed, only to start again on the following day. It must have taken all

---

*It fails to mention, however, that, there as elsewhere, all of Lafayette's expenses were picked up by the local governments.

Lafayette's taste for popular acclaim to withstand this kind of schedule, but he did more than survive it: he positively thrived on it, to the continuing despair of M. de Mareuil.

On his way to America, Lafayette had refused the offer of an American warship; now the offer was made again for his return and he accepted it, partly because it was so pressing, partly because he had accumulated so many gifts—several tons' worth—that he could not have taken them home on an ordinary packet. On September 6, he attended a farewell and birthday dinner given him by the new President, John Quincy Adams; by October 3, he was back at Le Havre where once again the people treated him to an enthusiastic welcome.

Both by his physical presence in the land of liberty and by the speeches he had made there, Lafayette had, once more, identified himself with freedom and democracy. The authorities in France were angry and worried; but the disfranchised now saw him as the symbol of all their aspirations. As he spoke for them when he demanded democratic reforms, they loved and cheered him.

On the fifth a reception at Rouen was canceled by order of the police. On October 9, when Lafayette returned to Lagrange, four thousand people had gathered to celebrate his return with illuminations, songs, music, and a triumphal arch inscribed "To the Friend of the People." The next day, a group of young women brought him flowers and sang songs praising him; they were followed by a deputation of the local National Guard; and on the following Sunday, there was a ball and fireworks. What a contrast to the sentiments of M. de Mareuil who, in his most recent dispatch, had expressed the hope the old revolutionary would be arrested as soon as he set foot on French soil.

Paradoxically Lafayette, as he returned, was in rather better odor at the court than before. Louis XVIII had died in 1824 and been succeeded by his brother the comte d'Artois, who now reigned as Charles X. Although the new King was dense, reactionary, and a religious bigot, he lacked meanness of spirit. Disagree with Lafayette he might, but he also remembered they had been adolescents together; besides, since he was a model of unchanging obstinacy himself, he rather esteemed that characteristic in others. "I only know two men who have always professed the same principles," the King told M. de Ségur, "myself and M. de Lafayette: he as the defender of liberty, and I as the King of the aristocracy. I have a high regard for M. de Lafayette; and if the circumstances ever allow it, I should enjoy seeing him."[31] And to Pierre Royer-Collard, a conservative politician, he had said a year earlier: "I must do him justice: he has no more changed than I have. In 1787, at the Assemblée des Notables, he was in my commission and we had a very heated discussion about gamekeepers. He wanted them abolished, and I said I could not see why poachers, who are always blackguards, should be allowed to operate freely."[32] During a visit to Meaux in 1828, when Charles X inquired about Lafayette, the bishop and the prefect looked shocked, but the King answered, "Ah, but you see, I know him so well. He has rendered our family the kind of services one cannot forget. We were born the same year; we learned how to ride together in the Versailles academy. . . ."[33]

It seemed that France was entering a new era of amiability. The new King, people thought, understood that he reigned but did not rule, and the irritation caused by his reactionary convictions was mitigated by his affable manners. And the King's very political incompetence also seemed to be a good sign: he would meddle far less than his brother had tried to do.

Ultimately, the monarch's fondness for the aristocracy proved a boon for Lafayette. Partly to please the King, the Prime Minister, M. Jean de Villèle, decided to compensate the nobles whose estates had been seized during the Revolution with 4 percent government bonds to the total amount of a billion francs. The expenditure to the state actually amounted only to 40 million francs a year, since the bonds were perpetual, but there was a great outcry from the liberal party. Despite the protest, Lafayette, as an heir of the duc d'Ayen, accepted quite happily the 325,000 francs he was offered.

Neither this money, however, nor Charles X's friendliness deflected the hero of liberty from his accustomed course. It was in the late 1820s, in fact, that he extended his field of operations to encompass the whole of Europe and, indeed, the world. He corresponded with, helped, and, whenever possible, invited to Lagrange Spanish and Portuguese liberals, Italian nationalists, Greek envoys, and Polish protesters. He followed with anxiety and approval the liberation of the Spanish colonies from the mother country. Thus, on December 16, 1826, he was writing Bolivar: "Nothing can surpass the high value I put on your esteem and friendship; my admiration and my wishes for you, my dear general, date back to your first efforts for the patriotic cause."[34]

Until his death, Lafayette remained a sort of one-man propaganda center for liberal causes all over; such activities naturally added to his already immense burden of letter writing, an occupation to which he now gave several hours every single day. And in France, too, he continued his efforts. Jacques Manuel, the deputy whose expulsion he had prevented and one of the leaders of the antidynastic left, died in 1827. Although he was too young to have been active during the Revolution, Manuel was a sworn enemy of the Bourbons and never stopped attacking their régime in eloquent, sometimes demagogic, speeches. In France, all through the nineteenth century, funerals were the occasions of political manifestos, and so Gilbert chose the occasion to make an ardent speech by the side of the tomb. He called Manuel an "eloquent defender of national liberty," reminding his listeners that "as a young man, during the prodigious campaign of our army in Italy, Manuel was at one with the immense glory of the tricolor flag," that his expulsion had been "the most shocking injustice ever perpetrated against a deliberating assembly," and ending, "Manuel . . . wanted his country to be free. As for us, citizens, it is by the tomb of this faithful servant of the people [that we show] our respect . . . and commitment to its ineradicable rights."[35] The address was almost seditious; worse, it was soon printed and the publisher was indicted for rebellion. Immediately, Lafayette demanded that he be indicted himself since the pamphlet had only reproduced his words. It would have been a splendid opportunity, but unfortunately, the prosecution was dropped, and no new martyrs were created.

Far more serious was Lafayette's crusade for a free, state-run educational system. While there was a government-funded university, the local schools had remained the responsibility of the church, and they tended to be insufficient in numbers, badly run, and poorly staffed. On June 23, 1828, for instance, Gilbert told the Chamber, to which he had been reelected a year earlier, "National education, gentlemen, and especially primary education, that great supporter of public reason, practical morality, and the people's tranquillity, has become today the population's main need, and the government's main obligation."[36] He was perfectly right—and fifty years ahead of his time. There was also his never-ending fight to trim the budget, which spawned a lengthy, and soon published, correspondence with the American author James Fenimore Cooper, already a famous novelist and a fighting liberal; his constant pressure on the ministry to help the Greeks free themselves from the Turkish yoke; and finally his growing worry about the government's direction. "The machinery of government is pulled forward by people who don't walk at the same pace," he wrote his granddaughter in December 1828, "from side to side by the priests and the Court, and backward by the King. . . . My information about the prefect of the Haute Loire is worse and worse. Maubourg came by yesterday and told me that he is a man, with the help of his friend the bishop, to set the department aflame."[37] In fact, at the impulse of the King, the government was clearly moving to the right. The church was claiming, and slowly regaining, a dangerous degree of influence; and it began to look as if a crisis was in the making.

None of this really changed the even tenor of Lafayette's life. All through the 1820s, he kept up a steady stream of little notes to Emilie, mostly undated, often about daily amusements. "Yesterday's ball I thought very pleasant,"[38] he would write one day; or "I have reserved a box at the Italian theater, my dear Emilie; the idea of taking our two youngsters is full of charms";[39] or "I must admit that I had forgotten the American lady and her son. Please ask her to come tomorrow at noon";[40] or "I have decided not to go out for dinner because one always ends up eating more than one would like. I have some very urgent letters to write and will rest until seven";[41] or "You won't forget that I have four tickets for the Opera and that they're giving La Sylphide preceded by Le Rossignol. . . . My dear Clémentine [a granddaughter] must not pine because she missed yesterday's ball, the crowd was so packed that there was hardly any room for dancing, at least during the half-hour I spent there."[42] Sometimes the letters were about politics— the change of ministry, the elections, the new ministers—and sometimes about more practical matters—the illness of a grandchild, the purchase of a special liqueur made in Grenoble, or that of a book on how to raise silkworms. At this time, Lafayette alternated between Paris, where he resided in an apartment on the rue d'Anjou, near the Place de la Concorde, and Lagrange, which continued to prosper.

He now developed a new, more aggressive attitude in foreign affairs, partly because France had now been at peace for a while, and partly because he believed it capable, still, of conquering Europe. The French, he felt, should once again take up their old role as the exporters of revolution. "It is France, since it is in closer sympathy with the ideas of the new civilization, which ought to be at the head of this civilization; there is its glory, its interest; there could be its ambition; there it would also find the dignity and safety of its government," he told the Chamber on July 9, 1829. "But in order to fulfill that noble task, the government would have to decide it no longer feared the nation as electorate or the source of an army, and then it would be able to tell the foreign powers. After God, it is to the French people we owe our place above your influence and outside your speculations."[43] But, in fact, France was in no condition to repeat the Napoleonic era, and luckily, Lafayette completely failed to convince his compatriots.

When it came to civil liberties, however, his was a powerful voice. As he asked for greater freedom of the press, agitated for a wider electorate (without, however, going as far as universal suffrage), and demanded a better system of education, Lafayette commanded attention. But with the appointment of the conservative prince de Polignac as Prime Minister, it seemed that the King was on his way to doing something foolish. Ever since his accession to the throne, Charles X had been chafing under the restraints imposed on him by the Charter. Now, at last, he was ready to embark on the realization of his dream, the return to the ancien régime, and Polignac was eager to help him. Unfortunately, Charles X believed, with some reason, that he was popular. He had made a journey through France the preceding autumn and been given a warm reception—largely a response to his own openness, which made it appear that he had at last understood what his predecessors had ignored. However, he chose to interpret things differently. As Lafayette wrote Emilie, "The King's trip, instead of opening his heart to liberalism, has made him sure he doesn't need it because his people love him."[44]

To show liberal strength, in July and August, Lafayette canvassed the Auvergne, Grenoble, and Lyon. Everywhere he was greeted with great enthusiasm, especially by the middle class, as the prefect reported from Clermont-Ferrand. Although there were no disorders, the régime was being cautioned: the electorate was largely middle class, and its disaffection, showed by the outpouring of liberal feeling, would have great weight in the next elections. Still, the régime seemed to have grown such strong roots that no one could believe that Charles X would put it in jeopardy. "Would they dare, by using royal decrees, to invalidate the election and rule illegally? Without doubt, the people who advocate such measures will remember in time that the government's strength comes from the arms and the pocketbooks of its citizens who, together, make up the nation. The French nation knows its rights, and it will defend them,"[45] Lafayette said in Lyon. It was a warning; no one really thought that any more would be needed.

By January 1830 the situation was beginning to look more serious. The duc d'Orléans, now more the darling of the liberals than ever, began to dissociate himself from the government in the most visible way. On January 7 Lafayette wrote: "The government and the Court are spreading the rumor that they are watching for the Chamber's first imprudence in order to dissolve it, to start a coup d'état, etc. The goal of this tactic is, I believe, to worry the so-called moderates . . . so as to push them away from a vigorous Address*. . . . I see with pleasure that, in all this, I am at one with my constituents."[46] In fact, quite legally and without starting a coup d'état, the King did dissolve, and in the election which was held on the twenty-third, Lafayette was easily reelected and the new Chamber's majority was clearly liberal: it now seemed obvious that Polignac would have to go.

As it turned out, however, the King chose to ignore the elections. As

---

*The session of the Chambers of Deputies, each year, began with a speech from the Throne and the answering Address from the deputies.

long as he wanted to keep Polignac, he felt, the Chamber must put up with him—a position contrary to the very nature of the Charter—and so he proceeded to scold the deputies. In his Speech from the Throne, he spoke of "an opposition to my government I neither can nor want to expect," making it clear that Polignac was to stay in place. Obviously, a clash with the new liberal Chamber was in the making. Still, the deputies thought, the King might be obstinate, but he was not mad, and they proceeded to make their feelings known tactfully: "Our fidelity, Sire, forces us to tell you that the government has no support."[47] Lafayette, always the alarmist, was already talking of refusing to vote the budget, but everyone else assumed that, when the pressure became sufficient, the King would dismiss the Prime Minister. Instead, on May 16, he dissolved the Chamber and set new elections for July 12. He was within his rights, as everyone admitted, but he caused great irritation in fighting the 221 deputies who had voted the anti-Polignac Address by every possible means.

By now, people were beginning to worry, since an upheaval was the last thing anyone wanted. "The situation, the royal family are so unreasonable that . . . we are still in the midst of a very unpleasant uncertainty," Lafayette wrote on May 4. "However bad the ministry may be that is not where the real evil lies. The King means to govern by himself. . . . M. de Polignac, frivolous, presumptuous, and reactionary as he is, thinks himself capable of re-creating the monarchy and the church of old." Charles X did not much care for the exercise of power, but he did want to go back to the ancien régime; and the incapable Polignac really thought he was the man to do it.

Still, the elections took place on schedule. Enough of the 221 opposition deputies were reelected to keep the Chamber liberal. At first the liberals feared that Charles X might simply not call a session of the Chamber for months; but the letters-patent convoking the deputies for the August session were, with great publicity, being sent off. It looked as if everything might yet be all right. "There have been, in the last councils, great discussions about the coup d'état they speak of in the King's entourage [that is, a royal dictatorship with Polignac at the helm] as if it were a simple undertaking. It seems, however, that they have given up the idea for now," Lafayette wrote from Lagrange on July 26. That very day, several royal decrees were published. They dissolved the Chamber, drastically modified the composition of the electorate, and abolished the freedom of the press. Lafayette heard about this on the twenty-seventh. On the twenty-eighth, from Paris, he was writing: "I thought that, in the circumstances, I should meet with my colleagues and so I arrived [here] yesterday night. . . . If things become serious, it will not be our fault but that of the people who have destroyed the pact with which the nation was satisfied."[48] For a day or two, the incredulous people watched a King foolish enough to affront them unnecessarily. Everyone knew a major explosion was on the way; indeed, it seemed very likely that, at age seventy-two, Lafayette would find himself in the midst of a new revolution, and no one who knew him could suppose that he would remain merely a disinterested spectator.

Twelve

THOROUGHLY
REPUBLICAN
INSTITUTIONS

If someone had asked Lafayette, on January 1, 1830, to make a wish for the coming year, he might have asked for the fulfillment of any one of his usual goals, but even he would have been unlikely to answer, a revolution. It was simply too unlikely. To extreme stupidity, however, nothing is impossible, and it would have been hard to find two more simpleminded men than Charles X and his prime minister, the prince de Polignac. Together, they managed to produce what even Lafayette had given up ever seeing again in his lifetime: a bona fide libertarian uprising. This was what the hero of liberty had been waiting for. He had started the great revolution of 1789 (or so he thought); now he would bring it to its logical conclusion and, in so doing, recover his old place as idol of the Parisians. It was almost too good to be true, yet, by July 27, it had become a distinct possibility.

Almost as soon as he reached his apartment, on the evening of Tuesday, July 27, Lafayette wrote Emilie, who was still at Lagrange, to tell her that the people of Paris had risen against the anticonstitutional decrees promulgated by the King and Polignac; already the government's authority prevailed only in a small part of the central city. "We have arrived safely," he wrote, "but this is not a peaceful place. Our first encounter after the Jardin des Plantes was that of a regiment loadings its guns. Much animation in the streets. At the Place Louis XVI [today the Place de la Concorde] part of the Royal Guard and some artillery. Elsewhere there were gatherings of people and troops. They have fired at the people near the Palais Royal and in front of the hôtel de Polignac where some working men had met. There were several killed or wounded, including a young law student whose friend I have seen. . . . You can see in the enclosed how well the newspapers [that is, liberally] are behaving. Two have already had their presses seized. The Globe, whose protest you will notice, is working tonight on one last issue. . . . We are trying to send them [the papers] to the provinces. . . . Thirty-two deputies met this morning at Casimir Périer's. A protest is being prepared. We will meet again at M. de Puyraveaux's house. I hope that two principles will be established, the first is that we are still deputies, the second that the Charter having been torn up by the government, there must be an immediate refusal to pay taxes. . . . The King went out hunting yesterday, I don't know what he is doing today in Saint-Cloud. The Vincennes artillery blocks the road. . . . A few factories have sent their workers home, many shops are closed, government bonds dropped 7 francs yesterday and 3 today." And the next morning, from his bed, he added: "Three gendarmes were killed trying to force a barricade. . . . Most printers have left their workshops. . . . Paris is showing more energy than the Court expected."[1]

The Revolution was under way, and it was a sign of M. de Polignac's exceptional incompetence that so little was done to stop it. Of course, there were some troops in Paris, but not many, and although the coup d'état had long been planned, no military preparations had been made. The Prime Minister simply kept repeating in reassuring tones that the disorders were nothing to worry about; the Virgin Mary had promised him that everything would be all right. Apparently that week the Virgin was on strike because, in fact, the Revolution grew almost unimpeded. On July 28, some fifty newly elected deputies had reached Paris. "[We] regard ourselves as nondissolved," Lafayette wrote Emilie, "and the social pact as no longer in existence. . . . The crisis is acute . . . and France wants to be free. Paris is giving the signal. The King is in Saint-Cloud; one cannot understand the madness of their behavior when the people only asked to live in peace under the Charter."[2] Blindly confident that he would prevail, the King stayed at the summer palace just outside the city, and as Paris began to explode, even

urgent messages were delayed by the complexities of the old-fashioned etiquette: Charles X could not be disturbed in the middle of a game of cards;
and the situation was allowed to drift while M. de Polignac smiled beatifically.

Already on the twenty-eighth, the deputies had decided they needed
a new government, if not a new king. At their next meeting, on the twenty-
ninth, it was decided to appoint a municipal commission that would run the
city from the Hôtel de Ville. When it came to choosing its members, the
deputies turned to Lafayette and asked him to do the job—an impressive
tribute. Those quiet years under Napoleon, the advocacy of libertarian causes,
the trip to America, and the old memories of 1789 all paid off: when it was
a question of reclaiming their liberty, the Parisians knew where to turn. No
matter what his position, Lafayette would automatically have been a part of
the uprising; now he found himself placed at its head by the spontaneous
and direct wish of the people. And the situation was obviously grave. "The
stage coaches are no longer leaving," Lafayette wrote Emilie, "there are
barricades all over the streets that make communications difficult and I am
sending you a special messenger because you must be worried. The admirable resistance of Paris continues. . . . The people are fighting energeti-
cally."[3]

Popularity was fine; responsibility was much less alluring, so Lafayette
refused to choose the membership of the municipal commission. It would
be undemocratic, he said; the deputies should do it themselves. There was
another call, however, that he felt no temptation at all to refuse. The National
Guard, dissolved by the government in 1827, had now spontaneously come
back into being, and as it did so, it turned to its old commander. "I have
received this morning the news of my nomination as commandant of the
National Guard," he wrote. "It is plain to me that a great number of citizens
want me to accept, not as a deputy but as an individual. . . . An old name
of '89 may be useful in the present crisis."[4]

From that moment on reality became good enough to be fantasy. In
this new revolution everything seemed to be going right. Once more Lafayette found himself at the head of an erupting city; once more he was
issuing proclamations which were placarded on every wall. "The confidence
of the people of Paris calls me once more to the command of its public force,"
he announced on the twenty-ninth. "I have accepted the duties entrusted
to me with devotion and joy and, as I did in 1789, I feel strengthened by
the approval of my honorable colleagues gathered today in Paris. I will not
explain my position: my feelings are well known. The behavior of the people
of Paris in these last difficult days makes me more proud than ever to be at
its head. Liberty will triumph or we will die together."[5] And the same day
another poster was dedicated to the National Guard. "The Paris National

Guard is back in existence,"[6] it said, and after a reminder that it was responsible for preserving public order, the proclamation went on to call on the officers to assemble at the Hôtel de Ville. By then, the troops had nearly stopped fighting. The Tuileries had been taken. Charles X had canceled his decrees, fired M. de Polignac, and made the duc de Mortemart, a liberal aristocrat, Prime Minister instead. It no longer mattered, however. By now, the Chamber refused to deal with the monarch at all. At that very moment, in fact, they were busy looking for a replacement.

All through the restoration, the duc d'Orléans had made himself conspicuous by his liberal positions. Politically, he stood with the center-left; privately, he stressed his democratic convictions by sending his sons to public school and by giving splendid parties, inviting the middle class instead of the court. Now Charles X had disqualified himself; the heir to the throne, who was married to Louis XVI and Marie Antoinette's daughter, was even more reactionary than his father, the King; and the next heir, Charles X's grandson, was only seven years old. The duc d'Orléans, however, was descended directly from Louis XIV; he was the head of the younger branch of the Bourbon family; and his father, Lafayette's old enemy, had played an important role in 1789. Then, too, people remembered that when, 150 years earlier, James II of England had proved too reactionary, he had been replaced by a more enlightened relative: many liberals now thought it was time to stage a similar replacement in France, with the duc d'Orléans playing the role of William and Mary. Prudently, the duc stayed out of the way while his friends worked for him: he would have succeeded easily, except for Lafayette.

The problem for the Orléanists was not merely to convince Lafayette, but to dislodge him. As everyone knew, the people of Paris wanted nothing more than to turn the government over to their general. He could be whatever he wanted, dictator (in the old Roman sense), president of a new republic, lieutenant general—that is, regent—of the kingdom. He had only to speak. He had always said that he wanted free institutions, and here, at last, was his chance to bring them into being. At age seventy-two, he could finally become, if he so wanted, the French Washington. And if he did, the duc d'Orléans would have lost his chance.

Luckily for the duc, the very last thing Lafayette wanted was real power. He reveled in the cheers of the crowd, thrilled at his command of the National Guard, but there his ambition stopped. As in 1789, he wanted to be sage, not dictator; oracle, not regent. He wanted a government that would follow his instructions and take his advice but without imposing painful responsibilities. Yet, although he rejected it for himself, he could not allow others to wield power either. Expecting others to behave as he did, Lafayette was deeply suspicious of anyone willing to take up the burden he had refused. So he dithered, unable to decide either for himself or Orléans, apparently not realizing that evasiveness could harm his cause. After two days, he saw that the Chamber had grown tired of waiting and was about to take action, so he sent over Odilon Barrot, one of his aides who, shortly, was to become prefect of police. "General Lafayette fears that if we announce, at noon, a head of state who will make more or less radical concessions, we will end up returning to the theory of divine right," Barrot told the deputies. "The General thinks that, in order to end all disputes and give the revolution that unanimity that alone can ensure its strength and permanence, he thinks that before making a firm decision it would be better to start by stipulating . . . the conditions desired by the people, so that the crown would be given at the same time as the stipulated guarantees would be proclaimed."[7] And across the river, at the Hôtel de Ville, Lafayette, pressed for answers, at least eliminated one possible solution. "I am asked for an explicit answer on the situation of the royal family. . . . All reconciliation is impossible and the royal family reigns no more."[8] That disposed of the possibility of a regency: Lafayette would not run France in the name of the seven-year-old duc de Bordeaux, Charles X's grandson, in favor of whom the old King had abdicated.

Lafayette's statement narrowed the field to two men. The Chamber still debated, but now that Lafayette had said it, everyone knew that the Bourbons were finished. The only possible choice, therefore, was between the duc d'Orléans and Lafayette himself. The deputies knew, perhaps better than Gilbert himself, that he did not want power. Within hours, they voted to make Orléans lieutenant general of the kingdom; it was obviously only a matter of time before he became King.

By the end of that day, July 30, Lafayette felt he had the city under control; he canceled his order of the previous day closing its gates. "Circulation is now entirely free," he proclaimed. And with that, he was off to bed. The next morning, however, he awoke to the same problem. What government was France to be given? All morning long at the Hôtel de Ville he postponed any decision; then, both the Chamber and the lieutenant general asked him to take on the command of all the National Guards in France. It was apposite, flattering, and designed to force Lafayette's hand, bringing Orléans one step closer to the throne. But still he vacillated: "In the glorious crisis during which the energy of Paris has conquered our rights, all still remains provisional. The only certainty is that of the sovereignty of our national rights."[9]

In the meantime, the Hôtel de Ville was surrounded by an increasingly nervous crowd. Inside, everyone who had a cause to defend tried to gain

Lafayette's ear. Among the Orléanists who tried to convince the General that the duc was the man of the hour, one, François Guizot, a liberal deputy and publicist, was a friend and a good observer. "The choice was between a new monarchy and the Republic, between the duc d'Orléans and M. de Lafayette," he wrote. " 'General,' M. de Rémusat, his grandson-in-law said to him, 'if there is to be a monarchy, the duc d'Orléans will be King. If there is a republic, you will be President. Will you take the responsibility for a republic?' M. de Lafayette appeared to hesitate more than he actually did. Nobly disinterested, but very self-conscious, and fearing responsibility almost as greatly as he loved popularity, he liked speaking for the people but did not want to govern it."[10]

Finally the crowds forced his hand. Lafayette had to choose, and since he still feared a republic, he announced he was ready to back the duc d'Orléans. The lieutenant general was sent for, but, when he arrived at the Hôtel de Ville, he was received by the mob with marked coolness. After all, the throng represented the politically active element of the population; and while neither France, as a whole, nor even the middle class alone (the peasants were notoriously conservative) was ready for a republic, the Parisians felt that they had earned the most democratic government possible; the replacement of one king with another was not good enough for them. Only Lafayette could bring them around to accepting a constitutional, democratic monarchy; and this he now proceeded to do. He described what happened next in his Address to the electors of Meaux in 1831.

"You know," Lafayette said to the duc d'Orléans, "that I am a republican and that I consider the Constitution of the United States as the most perfect there is."

"I agree with you," the duc d'Orléans answered, "it is impossible for anyone who, like me, has spent two years in America not to see this; but do you think in the situation of France and according to public opinion, that we are in a state to adopt it?"

"No," Lafayette answered, "what the French people need today is a popular throne surrounded by republican, thoroughly republican institutions."

"That is just how I see it," said the prince.[11]

The General was satisfied. After all, Orléans had always been a liberal; he must, therefore, be speaking the truth. The thought that the duc, who was a clever man and realized he needed Lafayette, might say anything the other man wanted to hear, never occurred to the always naïve hero of liberty. So, seizing a huge tricolor flag, he wrapped himself and Orléans in its folds and went out to the window. There was a brief silence; then Lafayette, in a spectacular gesture, embraced Orléans. "A shout came out of the guts of

the multitude," Barrot wrote, "and the shout, unanimous now, was: Long
live the duc d'Orléans! Long live Lafayette!"[12] The die was cast: Lafayette
had just created the July Monarchy. Never has a throne been acquired under
less dignified conditions, but the duc d'Orléans didn't mind. He knew very
well that he was acquiring the reality of power, and for that he was willing
to smile, flatter, and abase himself.

The first order of the day, now that the form of the régime was settled,
was to reform the Constitution. Lafayette knew just what he wanted: the
program of the Hôtel de Ville, so called because it was put together in that
building on August 1.

This program consisted of seven points: the sovereignty of the people
was to be formally recognized in the Constitution; there would be no more
hereditary peers; the judiciary would be completely renewed; cities, towns,
and townships were to have officials elected by universal manhood suffrage
instead of government appointees; all lower court judges were to be elected;
all government monopolies (on tobacco, for instance) were to be abolished;
and finally, the reforms would be presented to the electorate for its approval.
That last clause marks a radical departure in Lafayette's thinking. Until then
he had believed that the will of the people was best expressed through its
elected representatives; now, bypassing the Chamber of Deputies, he advocated consulting the people directly. As for the renewal of the judiciary,
this was rapidly becoming a French tradition: when the régime changed, so
did the judges.

Some of Lafayette's program did, in fact, become law within the following year. The sovereignty of the people was expressly recognized; the
hereditary peers were replaced by life appointees; the judiciary was partly
renewed; but because the other points were not implemented, the General
soon began to complain—and this in spite of the fact that other reforms he
had not thought of demanding were now carried out: the freedom of the
press was guaranteed; Catholicism now became equal in law with all other
religions; royal decrees were abolished; the initiative of the laws, formerly
reserved to the government, was now extended to the deputies; and finally,
the amount of tax needed to become a voter dropped from 300 francs a year
to 200 francs a year, thus raising the number of voters from 90,000 to 300,000.
It was not enough, but it was better.

Within a week of the accession, on August 7, however, enough changes
had taken place for the King to come to the Chamber of Deputies and swear
to observe the new Constitution. This moment was a triumph for the General, and on more than one level: the immediate reforms were gratifying,
to be sure, and besides, the King had made it exceedingly plain that he
relied on Lafayette's advice. Seeming proof of the General's new status came

when the King announced his regnal name. Most of his advisers had favored Philip VII, which would have stressed continuity; instead, the duc d'Orléans decided to listen to Lafayette and became Louis-Philippe I, King of the French (not King of France), emphasizing the fact that, in the new era, the King reigned by the consent of the people and not by divine right. Of course, it is fair to say that the new monarch liked to think of himself as the founder of a new dynasty, and that he might very well have behaved in exactly the same way even without Lafayette's advice; but the General did not know that.

And there were more satisfactions for General Lafayette as well. As commander of the National Guard for the entire country, he now found himself thrown into just the sort of whirlwind he liked best. There were endless small decisions to be made, appointments to be considered, parades to be organized: it was like 1789, only better, because this time there were no rude interruptions by other, more successful revolutionaries. Indeed, the last five months of 1830 took on the appearance of a Lafayette festival. Every time the General appeared in the street, he was cheered. Songs were composed about him: there was an updating of the "Marseillaise," for instance, called "La Parisienne," with words by Casimir Delavigne, a popular author; soon it had become the popular revolutionary song and could be heard all over Europe. One of its verses ran:

> Pour briser leurs masses profondes
> Qui conduit nos drapeaux sanglants?
> C'est la liberté des Deux Mondes,
> C'est Lafayette en cheveux blancs.[13]

> To break up their serried ranks
> Who leads our blood-stained flags?
> It is the liberty of the Two Worlds
> It is the white-haired Lafayette.

This was flattering, if untrue: Lafayette had not been involved in any of the fighting. Then, in November, another song came all the way from New York. Composed by a printer, its rather clumsy lines, which were to be sung to the tune of the "Marseillaise," read:

> Immortal Lafayette, we hail thee
> The friend of equal rights on earth
> . . . Thou first of heroes, best of sages.[14]

And there was a host of laudatory poems, letters, and prints.

Never, probably, was Lafayette happier than in that month of August 1830. "It is with a childlike joy that I see the tricolor flag flying everywhere,"[15] he wrote on August 12; on the fifteenth, there was a banquet for 350 in his honor at the Hôtel de Ville at which toasts were given to the French nation, General Lafayette, and the glorious people of Paris. And even as cynical a man as Stendhal wrote: "The admirable Lafayette is the anchor of our liberty." And it was all the more enjoyable that Lafayette felt he could patronize the King. "It has seemed proper to us," he told the Chamber on August 7, "to raise a new* national throne and I must say that my wishes for the Prince whose choice is today's business has become stronger as I have grown to know him better."[16] No one would be allowed to forget that, without Lafayette, there would have been no Louis-Philippe.

But the new King was no Louis XVI. Far from being helpless, he soon demonstrated a remarkable talent for getting people to see things his way. He was shrewd, eloquent, ambitious, and willing to dissemble; for the moment the General was very useful indeed and could be expected to be treated as the King's savior. One way to keep the ever touchy Lafayette happy was to flatter him, so a stream of holograph letters, in Louis-Philippe's tall, legible handwriting, now started coming from the Palais Royal. On August 10, the King was acknowledging a letter of advice: "I want to thank you myself," he wrote, "for your excellent note which has touched me deeply. I feel proud of the feelings you have for me";[17] and after reminding the General that the door was always open to him, he signed himself Louis-Philippe, adding underneath in English: "You see you have carried the point."[18] On August 29, after a grand parade of the National Guard, the King sent off a long letter, asking Lafayette "to be my interpreter to that glorious National Guard whose patriarch you are and to transmit all the admiration it has made me feel today. Tell them that they have surpassed all my expectations. . . . A witness, myself, of the Federation of 1790, in that same Champ de Mars, as well as of the great élan in 1792 when I saw our army . . . grow by forty-eight battalions provided within three days by the city of Paris and who contributed so greatly in stopping the invasion at Valmy, I am able to compare: and it is with ecstasy that I tell you that what I have just seen seems well above what I then found so beautiful and our enemies so threatening."[19] When you flatter royalty, Disraeli said, it is best to lay it on with a trowel; when he fawned over Lafayette, Louis-Philippe went straight for the shovel, and the General loved every word of it. As soon as he received the letter he sent back a request

---

*The old national throne being that of Louis XVI under the Constitution of 1791.

for permission to have the letter made public. Needless to say, the King agreed.

The correspondence also went the other way. There were people to be introduced, favors to be asked, advice to be given. Considering that Lafayette was by no means the only difficult personage the King had to deal with, those last months of 1830 must have been hard work indeed. On September 27, for instance, he answered a letter about the slave trade: "How grateful I am to you, my dear General, for your letter and the details you give me. You realize, of course, that this is too weighty a matter for me to answer you before I have had time for reflection, but we will talk about it at the earliest opportunity."[20] Another day, when Lafayette asked if he could present Maubourg and some Americans to the King, a letter came right back: "I will be enchanted as always to see you tonight . . . with your friends. It is always with pleasure that I am able to refresh my American memories, especially through you."[21] A few days later, off went a little note thanking him: "I appreciate at their true worth the great services you are rendering the country."[22]

The letters continued. Fresh from the National Guard parade of August 29, Lafayette felt he had to have still another. On October 3, the King declared himself delighted to participate in the new parade; on the eighteenth, when there had been some alarming riots, a few quick words came from the Palais Royal: "I am warning you in a great hurry, my dear General, that I would like to consult with you at nine tomorrow morning on maintaining public order."[23] Perhaps the urgency resulted from a certain lack of trust—Louis Philippe evidently felt Lafayette incapable of solving the problem himself—and later that day, the always cautious monarch went on: "Your order of the day is admirable; in one word, it is worthy of you."[24] The government was having Lafayette's order posted all over the city, and wanted the General to do something about the mob gathering in the Faubourg Saint-Antoine. On October 29, the King was thanking Lafayette for his recommendation that the Legion d'Honneur be given to the Prime Minister's brother and telling him he would be glad to meet with the artillery of the National Guard.

By November the King was wondering how he could get rid of the demanding general, especially since their first disagreements had started to appear. Louis-Philippe's great aim, in those last days of 1830, was to establish his régime's respectability in the eyes of Europe, and the General was proving a great embarrassment. It was not just that the King wanted to assert his own policies; more than ever after the "Three Glorious Days," Lafayette had become the symbol of liberty for all Europe, and that streak of aggression he had displayed in the 1820s now formed the basis of his policies. France had freed itself, Lafayette reasoned frequently and publicly; now it must do the same for Europe. There was Belgium, for instance, fighting to break its bond with Holland; Poland rebelling against the tsar; Spain, where Ferdinand VII was oppressing his people; Italy subjugated by Austrian armies; now, as once before, the invincible French armies must come to the help of downtrodden peoples everywhere. On his own, Lafayette did what he could. On October 12, for example, he was writing General Mina, a Spanish liberal: "I tried to raise money on your signature, but since no one was willing to lend anything, my intervention is limited to 10,000 francs which I give you from my own pocket,"[25] and he went on to provide Mina with reams of advice. As long as Lafayette's actions went no further, fine; but soon Louis-Philippe found himself subject to increasingly frequent demands that France intervene, at a time when the chief aim of French policy was to prevent an invasion by the so-called Northern Powers (Russia, Prussia, Austria) who were thought anxious to reestablish Charles X on the throne, thus discouraging revolution everywhere. The Chamber, except for a small minority, shared the King's anxieties. It thus became increasingly obvious that Lafayette was an unnecessary burden, especially since street rioting had become almost continuous, and the General seemed unwilling to stop it.

Although Lafayette always proclaimed in virtuous tones that he would maintain order in Paris even if it meant losing his popularity, the riots actually solidified his position as the indispensable man. While the constant upheavals that disturbed Paris during the second half of 1830 were actually nothing more than surface effervescence, they looked like the beginnings of another, more drastic, revolution and alarmed the government and the bourgeoisie. Sometimes, however, the disorders became a huge joke. Poor Louis-Philippe, for instance, found himself forced to pop on and off the balcony of the Palais Royal dozens of times every day because there always seemed to be a crowd gathering and calling for him. In fact, it eventually became clear, some street children were offering to make the King appear if the passersby would pay them a few cents. Curious as always, the strollers would pay up. They would be told to shout, and out Louis-Philippe would come. The disorders in the working-class quarters seemed a good deal more worrisome, however. Since the National Guard was charged with keeping the peace, the responsibility fell on Lafayette, but most of the time he did too little, or nothing at all. Amid the turmoil, the trial of Charles X's ministers was to take place in late November. While the former monarch and his family had been allowed to leave the country unscathed, the ministers, much to the new government's distress, had let themselves be caught. Louis-Philippe fretted about security at the trial: should the crowd seize Polignac and his colleagues and tear them from limb to limb, the massacre would set off a new revolution patterned after the Terror of 1793.

To the King's and the government's consternation, however, Lafayette had done little to tighten the lax security around the Luxembourg Palace, where the trial was to be held; they noted that when mobs formed and started surging forward, Lafayette tended to smile and do nothing. In the end, the commanders of several of the units proved to be more conscientious than their general and, by dint of removing the prisoners from the palace ahead of schedule, they averted tragedy. But the lesson was clear all the same: Lafayette, in 1830, was no more able to control unruly crowds than in 1790, only this time, ironically, the duc d'Orléans—now King—wanted order and Lafayette the reverse. This time both the King and the Chamber of Deputies were united in feeling that consolidation, not further revolution, was the order of the day. Still, Lafayette could hardly be fired: that, in itself, might start a new uprising. If, however, the Chamber decided to abolish the post of national commander as inimical to the planned decentralization of the guard, Lafayette would, so to speak, be "resigned" whether he liked it or not.

The next afternoon, Louis-Philippe sent for Lafayette, saying, "Of course, I want to keep you [in office]," but before the two could meet the General had sent in his resignation. "Sire," Lafayette wrote, "the resolution taken yesterday by the Chamber of Deputies with the agreement of the King's ministers . . . expresses the feeling of the two branches of the legislative power, and especially of that to which I have the honor of belonging. I should be lacking in respect for it if I awaited any other formality before sending to the King, as I do herewith, my resignation. . . . The Prime Minister has offered to give me the title of honorary commander. He will realize, and Your Majesty will think, that these nominal decorations suit neither the institutions of a free people nor myself."[26]

The King, whose relief must have been overwhelming, answered in his canniest style. "It is," he wrote, "with acute sorrow that I receive the letter you have just sent me. I cannot answer its contents since I have read neither yesterday's debate nor the resolutions of the Chamber. I will do so with all possible speed and you may be sure it will be with all the consideration I feel, deservedly, for your exalted character, your devotion to the fatherland and the great services which you have always rendered the cause of liberty as well as with the deep and sincere friendship I feel for you from the bottom of my heart and which will never change."[27] And he added a postscript: "I hope you will not mention any of this until we have met and spoken. . . . I have to attend the Council at one . . . but will be free at five and hope to change your mind." That last note was a simple delaying tactic while precautions were taken, but the gist of the letter was clear enough even for Lafayette, and, in essence, came down to two words: *at last!*

The General was attempting, of course, to repeat his old standby, the resignation in a huff. In 1789 and 1791, it had worked; he had been called back by a repentant crowd. This time, everyone breathed a sign of relief and wished him well in his retirement. Naturally, Lafayette found this extremely annoying, so he switched tactics. "Today my conscience for public order is fully satisfied," he threatened in the Chamber on December 27. "I must admit that this is not true of my conscience of liberty. We all know the program of the Hôtel de Ville: a popular throne surrounded by republican institutions. It was accepted but we don't all give it the same meaning; it has not been understood by the King's advisers as it has by myself: I am more impatient to see it enacted than some others."[28] In 1789, after a speech like that, no doubt, the mob would have marched on the Assembly and forced it to recant. In 1830, nothing at all happened. Lafayette had misjudged the situation.

That the General bitterly resented his enforced resignation cannot be doubted. His pain and anger show clearly in his lengthy last address to the National Guard. "A short time ago," he complained, "I was entrusted with an immense command. Today, I am only your old friend." After congratulating himself on his role during the recent revolution and on the efficiency of his administration of the guard, he continued, "Fears that no remembrance could justify, I am entitled to say, had arisen . . . ; they could be quieted only by a *complete and unreserved* resignation of power." In other words, the Chamber had feared he might use the guard to take power—unjustifiably, since he had not done so in 1789 and 1790. Then, after claiming, in passing, that the Revolution had revived the principles of 1791, but not thoroughly enough, and that six thousand men had died for liberty in July,* he bemoaned the conservatism of the Chamber, called for immediate elections and a Senate instead of the House of Peers, protested once again that he had no thought of a coup d'état, and menacingly reminded the King that his was a fragile position. "If the constitutional order conquered during the great days . . . if the popular throne erected by our hands were ever menaced by whoever it might be, the whole nation would rise to defend them."[29]

In its immediate effect, Lafayette's proclamation was an utter failure. The National Guard was willing enough to praise him and to regret him: it had no intention of rising for the sake of its former commander. It was, in fact, the General's constant miscalculation that, from late July 1830 on,

---

*Sixty would have been more accurate.

he thought he was reliving the Revolution of 1789. Within a few days of August 1, however, it became obvious that any attempt at rousing the people was bound to fail, since the Chamber with its memories of 1793–94, was determined to resist popular disorder. Still, Lafayette's idea that 1791 equaled 1830 was now the basis of his political views. It was a disastrous idea, for it encouraged his old habit of ignoring reality and tempted him to make demands completely unsuited to the times. From January 1, 1831, on, the General, although still a famous and popular figure, in effect lost all power and influence, and he had no one but himself to blame.

Nevertheless for a week or so after his resignation on December 31, Gilbert blamed the King's entourage. "I know I weigh like a nightmare on the Palais Royal; not on the King and his family, who like me, are the best people in the world and whom I love tenderly, but on all those who surround them,"[30] he wrote his cousin Philippe de Ségur on December 30. Soon, he was blaming Louis-Philippe as well. A report, in particular, maddened him: one that claimed he had said the July monarchy was the best of republics. That, he protested, was all wrong: America was the best of republics, and the current régime a travesty. He would have preferred that France become a proper republic, but since that seemed impossible, he had settled for "thoroughly republican institutions." Since Louis-Philippe himself was helping spread the canard, Lafayette wrote him a stiff letter in which he reminded him that he, Lafayette, was responsible for the régime "to the people, your sovereign and mine."[31] It seems that the letter was never sent, but Lafayette made his feelings abundantly clear and proceeded to rejoin the left-wing opposition. Of course, his political alignment did not stop his stream of letters to the King asking for a variety of favors—help for the persecuted Italian patriots, support of the liberal refugees, or even the assurance that M. Barrier would be kept in his post as head gardener of Trianon.

Still, despite these political disappointments, life remained pleasant for the old hero. All through 1830 his salon had been as thronged as he might ever have wished. "From eight o'clock on, every Tuesday, a motley crowd which had come on foot, in cabs or in carriages went up, without any ceremony a staircase as plain as the apartment to which it led," the vicomte de Beaumont-Vassy recorded.

"In the first room, which was a dining room of austere appearance where the furniture was indicative of republican mores, one would already meet and jostle the celebrities of the day. . . . From the dining room one went into a second room, the salon, which was furnished just as simply as the dining room, and where the eye was drawn at first by a circle of women and young girls, belonging mostly to M. de Lafayette's family, and whose fair hair and attractive dresses caught one's attention. . . .

"Finally, in an angle of this very simple salon, surrounded . . . by a triple circle of friends and followers attentive to his every word and his every gesture, stood M. de Lafayette: pale face, brown wig, tall and hefty; his expression concealed under a look of kindness and optimism the still very lively political passions of the old man.

"The visitor was prevented from seeing him at first by the compact group which surrounded him with a more or less respectful curiosity. . . . Refugees from every country and republicans wearing their hair cut *à la malcontent* and pointed beards that were meant as an indication of their political beliefs made up . . . the chorus, so to speak, of this curious salon. . . . The prince de Talleyrand, recently appointed Ambassador to London, came, as if to cleanse himself of his old sins against liberalism, on visits to the salon . . . and Lafayette, surprised but, in fact, pleased, repeated to everyone, 'Talleyrand hadn't set foot in my house in thirty years.'

"M. le duc d'Orléans [the heir to the throne] . . . came several times without ceremony, and struck his audiences with the elegance and variety of his conversation. He obviously wanted to shine and seduce."[32] The crowds lessened somewhat in 1831, but Lafayette's Tuesdays remained a polar attraction for French and foreign liberals on the outs with their governments.

At Lagrange, too, life went on pleasantly. Despite all the excitements of the Revolution, Lafayette had sincerely deplored being stuck in Paris. With his release from the National Guard, he was again free to spend almost as much time there as he liked. Jules Cloquet, his doctor and admirer, described him at this time. "Lafayette was tall and well proportioned; his pronounced bulk stopped short of obesity. . . . His face was oval, with regular features; his forehead tall and uncovered [he was bald]; his eyes were gray blue and protruding . . . his nose aquiline . . . his complexion light and free of wrinkles. . . . He was vigorous, in good health . . . he had perfect vision but was a little deaf. . . . He carried himself with nobility and dignity."[33] He still limped, of course, and now and again suffered an attack of gout.

As ever, his tastes were simple. He dressed in a plain gray frock coat, ate only fish or chicken, never meat, and drank no liquor at all, not even wine; his only eccentricity was that, by the standards of the time, he was exceedingly clean and bathed every day.

As for Lagrange, it had prospered. The estate now spread over eight hundred acres; the park around the castle was pleasantly shaded by apple and chestnut trees, while the castle walls disappeared behind a thick coat of ivy. Fish swam about in the moat, and a great lawn extended beyond the open courtyard. In the house itself, pleasantly but simply furnished in the Empire style, there was a large dining room that sat fifty on the ground floor, then two salons, one of them a round room with striped silk on the walls, a room that served as a Lafayette museum, and several apartments for members of Lafayette's family. His own, on the first floor, consisted of a small antechamber, a modestly furnished bedroom, upholstered in yellow silk, and a library where the shelves were held by elegant white columns surmounted by cameos of Washington, Franklin, Bailly, La Rochefoucauld, and others. And all through the house, mementos of the two revolutions, the American and the French, abounded.

Every day, Lafayette spent a great deal of time in his library. There he wrote his innumerable letters and prepared his speeches; from there also, using a loudspeaker, he shouted his instructions to the farmer whose house adjoined that wing of the castle. There was much to supervise: over twenty-two hundred sheep, including one thousand merinos; forty cows; pigs, chickens, horses. Then there were the fields to be checked, the vegetable garden; even, for a time, a little zoo graced by the presence of a gray bear originally caught in Missouri. And Lafayette made a point of handling the accounts himself, a radical departure from his earlier lofty disregard for such things.

In the morning, the patriarch rose between five and six; he breakfasted at ten and dined at six. The early hours were spent on correspondence; then Gilbert paid a visit to the rooms where Adrienne had lived and which remained exactly as they had been at the time of her death. After breakfast, he spent some two hours looking around the farm; then it was back to letter writing; by then the newspapers had come and had to be read. His evening meal was unusual in one respect: all the children were allowed to attend it, so there were seldom less than twenty-five at table. The food was simple but fresh—it came mostly from the farm—and well prepared. Everybody, even the children, took part in the conversation, which continued out on the lawn in summer and in the salon in winter. It was a simple, dignified sort of life, the sort that suited Lafayette best. Most of the time, there were two or three refugees. The park was open to all, and, in the winter, two hundred pounds of bread were given to the needy every week.

In Paris, of course, Lafayette was busier still. "It is two o'clock," he wrote Emilie one day, "and since I woke up I haven't had time to shave. Some twenty friends have been here discussing with me the advantages of solitude and of silence. I still found time to send off thirty-two letters and to read about an equal number."[34] And there were endless good causes. "There will be a reunion of the Lithuanian Society to celebrate the anniversary of their insurrection,"[35] he wrote her another day; or again, about a charity dance: "The business of the ball is being done *the least ill* possible although there are five or six other balls where people will dance in aid of the orphans of [the Revolution of] July, the orphans of the cholera, political prisoners, fined journalists, etc."[36] There was a steady correspondence with the General's new protégée, the great singer Maria Malibran; there were various salons to be attended, that of the duchesse de Broglie in particular, where one day he met Alphonse de Lamartine and was much impressed; so, the next morning, he was reading his poetry. And there were the children, the grandchildren (eleven), and great-grandchildren (twelve). It was a busy, well-filled life in which Gilbert received much love and felt highly useful.

It was just as well that Lafayette felt so happy in his private life. From 1831 on, politics provided him with nothing but failure and frustration. It wasn't just that the Revolution had stopped, in his view, much too soon. Now his own positions had become so extreme that he could no longer hope to lead the main body of the liberals, especially since he was more convinced than ever that he had been, was, and always would be uniquely right. There were very few people who agreed with him, unfortunately. The policies he advocated, if put into effect, would have had the most catastrophic results. France was to send its troops into Belgium instead of negotiating its independence as Talleyrand was successfully doing in London; it was to intervene in Poland where the people had risen against their Russian masters (quite how the French army was to get across Germany was never made clear); it was to back the liberal claimant to the Portuguese throne, Dona Maria, against her wicked absolutist uncle, Dom Miguel; it was to secure the independence of Romagna, in Italy, then rebelling against the Pope's government—and all this was to be done at once. It would have been an impossible program even for a genius like Napoleon. Given the relative strength of France and the rest of Europe in 1831, it was simply laughable.

On January 15, 1831, Lafayette was telling the Chamber: "Every time a European country, no matter where it may be, wants to recover its rights but is prevented from doing so by foreign intervention, that is a direct attack against us because it is as if they told us: 'Wait, we'll smash your natural allies, the friends of liberty in all other countries; and when they cease existing, we will attack you with all our strength.'" And on the twenty-eighth, he took this still further: "Every time a people . . . wants to recover its rights, any intervention from a foreign government to stop them will be considered a direct and formal declaration of war against France. . . . If these principles have war as their consequence, then fight we must."[37] Had the government and the Chamber followed him, France would have been at war with Russia, Prussia, Austria, and, in consequence, England within a month.

Louis-Philippe, who was nothing if not sensible, thought Lafayette's plans the most pernicious nonsense; luckily, so did most everyone else. And even though most people in France sympathized with the Poles, whose insurrection was being repressed with extreme brutality by Tsar Nicholas I, then, as on a number of later occasions, it was all too clear that the Western governments were in no position to help, except through pleas for mercy. As a result, Lafayette's calls to action got him nowhere, but at least he had the satisfaction of a large increase in his letter-writing duties. On April 21, for instance, after he had been made an honorary member of the Polish National Guard, he wrote Count Ostrowski: "All my wishes go to the noble dangers and the sublime resolutions of the admirable nation whom the universe considers with respectful and grateful enthusiasm," and on April 16, 1832, he actually tried to enlist that supreme realist, Talleyrand: "Ancient memories reawaken old habits. Thus I need to say three words to a comrade and friend of the Revolution of 1789 become the diplomat of that of 1830. (1) The King and Chamber are in honor bound to prevent Poland from going under. (2) The same is true for the political institutions of Romagna. (3) Any decisive demonstration in favor of the constitutional Queen of Portugal would ensure the success of her expedition."[38] Talleyrand didn't bother answering; but at least, a few years later, Lord Palmerston, the British Foreign Secretary, did arrange Queen Maria's triumph over Dom Miguel.

By mid-1832, Lafayette was actually at daggers drawn with Louis-Philippe. The King and government, he claimed, were reneging on their earlier promises, going back to the bad ways of the restoration. Nothing could have been more offensive to the court, since it sounded like a call for yet another revolution. Whatever residue of influence Lafayette might have retained was now lost. The old general decided to fight harder. "You tell me to be patient," he wrote Odilon Barrot on August 26, indignantly pointing out that he had had occasion to exercise that virtue under the ancien régime, in prison, during the Empire, and then all through the Restoration. "I would still be patient today, in spite of the indignation I feel when I see promises broken or denied, if I did not see the liberty of France and Europe sacrificed to a system we helped to establish and whose cowardice and selfishness dishonor us as Frenchmen."[39] There was, he went on, no hope that the court would return to the principles of July. Louis-Philippe had become a hopeless reactionary, and that way lay anarchy.

Once again, Lafayette ignored reality. While it was true that Louis-Philippe loved power and tried to rule through his ministers, he did so in a thoroughly reformist spirit; in fact, to the Chamber and most of the electorate, it seemed as if the problem was to restore stability to an overly liberal system. All through 1831 and 1832, riots had continued to shake Paris, and that wily old politician, the duc de Dalberg, wrote Talleyrand: "When the masses are erupting, are pushed forward by agitators, by Lafayettes, who will stop them?" In fact, the régime, at this point, was far more stable than it appeared, but it remains that Lafayette's attitude was a compound of personal resentment and hardened prejudice rather than a fair response to conditions prevailing in France. Nor was it a very good sign that Lafayette found himself in effective alliance with the Legitimists in an effort to discredit, and if possible end, the July Monarchy. Of course, Lafayette wanted a republic, and the Legitimists the return of Charles X, so the understanding between them could hardly go very far; but when it came to blind and constant attacks on the régime, they were in perfect accord.

In mid-June 1832, Lafayette received a letter written by a moderate deputy and friend, Camille Tesseire, a serious document in which the writer tried to expose the fallacies of Gilbert's position. Only through peace and calm could liberty triumph, Tesseire pointed out: war would bring defeat and tyranny. Most of the republican leaders were simply ambitious for themselves and Lafayette was too good for that. Finally, Tesseire argued, it wasn't right to embrace Louis-Philippe, then, a year later, denounce him when he had been following the same policy all along. Tesseire's letter, coming as it did from a fellow liberal, should have held some weight, but Lafayette was well past listening to reason. "You will see how poor Tesseire has sunk into the juste milieu,*" he wrote Emilie. "It is high time he got himself out of it. I can almost hear the government telling its good friends in Vienna and Berlin that it is far from complaining about the measures that will be taken to maintain public order and the discipline of the German press. . . . M. de Metternich must be thrilled by the attitude in Paris."[40] In fact, Louis-Philippe's government was viewed, in Prussia and Austria, with the greatest alarm; it was allied with England, the only other liberal power, and seemed dangerously revolutionary to the rest of Europe. What Lafayette's paranoid fantasy was based on, of course, was his memory of Louis XVI; but 1832 was no more 1792 than 1830 had been 1789.

Lafayette did not stop at a page or two of explanations in his answer to Tesseire; instead, he sent off an enormously long letter in which he explained exactly how he saw himself. Of course, his arguments were often inaccurate and distorted, but it is important to remember that none of these were deliberate lies: Lafayette's capacity for self-delusion, never small, had expanded considerably during the last years of his life.

"Throughout the course of a long life," Lafayette wrote on July 12, 1832, "since I entered the world during the reign of Louis XV, my compatriots

---

*The *juste milieu*, or "exact center," was a term used to describe the liberals who formed a middle party between the Legitimists on the right and the republicans on the left. They supported the régime.

have passed through so many conditions, preventions, and opinions that in order to deserve the praise or blame of having always stayed the same I have had to endure successive and contradictory criticism, and even sometimes a kind of isolation in which, later, people would come to join me in great waves.

"Thus, after my devotion to the American cause had provoked the strongest irritation from the government and a part of my family, two years had barely passed when that cause became that of France, and the young madman became the object of exaggerated enthusiasm and boundless trust.

"When my republican ideas and my plans, realized in 1789, were considered in society, at the French and other courts, notably that of Frederick the Great, as pleasant but impractical utopias that could never be realized in Europe, there turned out to be, in 1792, a great many people who, before the Revolution, had never thought of liberty, and who, nonetheless, proscribed me for having wanted to stop, in my wisdom, with the popular monarchy of 1791.

"In my prison, instead of going into ecstasies with all the other republicans of Europe about that fine coup d'état of the 18 Fructidor, I preferred to remain in exile rather than approve the violation of civil and political rights that, under the pretext of saving the Constitution, dealt it a death blow.

"When the First Consul, whose genius I recognized and for whom I felt gratitude, moved toward despotism and the gradual destruction of all the liberties of '89 by making use of the dreadful memories of '93; and when my constitutional friends, my Jacobin adversaries, my aristocratic enemies in the salons, as well as the kings of Europe, all blamed my republican obstinacy, I remained firm and stood up alone to the colossus without, however, wanting to throw myself with the rest of France, into the hopes arising from the 'freely granted' Charter and the new devotion to the monarchy; and, similarly, during the period of the Hundred Days, I joined Bonaparte to defend our independence and fought him so as to prevent him from dissolving the Chamber of Representatives. . . .

"Well, when during our fine revolution of July 1830, the majority of the combatants who surrounded me preferred the proclamation of the republic, when the Bonapartists would have accepted it with an imperial presidency, when very liberal propositions regarding the reign of the duc de Bordeaux [Charles X's grandson] were reaching me, when the Hôtel de Ville was stronger than the Chamber, I preferred to remain one with the deputies in an Orléanist solution while wishing that, the Lieutenant General once chosen, the constitution be written by a truly national convention. I sacrificed even that wish to the will of my colleagues, to the need for internal

union and foreign peace, but only after I had protected the principle of the
people's sovereignty and the arming of the whole nation [in the National
Guard] from the grasp of the monarchy and the Chambers alike. . . .

"A republican monarchy, *a popular throne surrounded by republican,
thoroughly republican institutions* coming as close as possible to what he
himself called a *model government*, that is what I brought about at the Hôtel
de Ville.

"Louis-Philippe has no obligation to me. I had neither commitment to,
nor friendship with, him. Far from helping his father to become king, I
caused him to leave France. . . . My behavior in July and August 1830 was
motivated only by the thought that [the new monarchy] was the solution
best suited to the interests of freedom and the fatherland, but with the
necessity that the program of the Hôtel de Ville be carried out."

Lafayette then went on, at length, to defend his system of intervening
to help the Spaniards, the Italians, the Poles, the Germans, and continued:
"Our *republican institutions* are reduced to 200,000 electors for a population
of 32 million while the aristocratic British monarchy will have 1,200,000
voters for a population of 20 million.* For two years now we have expected
to hear about the attributions of the townships, their elected councils, free
education, primary instruction, and the responsibility of government em-
ployees. Twenty-two Frenchmen cannot meet legally.† The accused can be
detained for four or five months when their supposed offense deserves at
most a week in prison. The initiative of the Chamber is constantly impeded.
The intention of returning to a quasi-legitimate monarchy, to a quasi-
restoration, to the Charter of 1814 is plainer every day. . . . Shall I tell you
what I really think, I am sure that the government has agreed with its foreign
friends that it would kill the spirit of liberty in France and refrain from
opposing the absolutist governments in the rest of Europe. The error of the
system is in believing that the antilibertarian coalition will go no further. I
think that when our foreign auxiliaries [that is, the other liberals] have been
disarmed, discouraged, and even made to feel angry at us, they [the Powers]
will feel that French turbulence, the Paris and provincial press and the
usurpation of a younger branch demand a repression that will then look
easy."[41]

This letter is typical of everything that made Lafayette such an irritating,
yet respectable, figure to his contemporaries. His self-satisfaction, his claim
that he had always been right, his gross distortion of the government's record,

---

*Lord Grey's great Reform Bill had just taken effect.
†The law prohibited public meetings of more than twenty-one persons without a permit.

his illusions about his own achievements, all tend to make him both annoying and ridiculous. Even in 1832, and without the benefit of hindsight, it was clear enough that the government was not pining for a return to the Charter of 1814; that there was no agreement with the Northern Powers; and that an invasion of France for repressive purposes simply wasn't in the cards. On the other hand, when Lafayette pointed out that the electorate was far too small, he was quite right; it was Louis-Philippe's continued refusal to enlarge it that provoked the Revolution of 1848. Some of the other criticisms listed in the letter—education, the organization of the townships, the length of prior detention—were, in part at least, legitimate; only, there, Lafayette was so much ahead of his time that most of the reforms he demanded were only carried out many years later. What is certain, however, is that his extraordinary mix of self-conscious rectitude, radical views, and inability to judge others—Louis-Philippe, for instance—reduced him to the position of ineffective left-wing critic.

Of course, he was still a deputy and could speak in the Chamber, but he found himself spending more and more time in that curious twilight world of often penniless refugees where fiery speeches were all, and where he could still play his favorite role, that of the benevolent adviser who must be heeded. Although, by now, age was catching up with him—he was seventy-six in 1833—Gilbert was as active as ever, as politically involved, and although he bitterly attacked the régime, one cannot help wondering whether, after all, he did not find opposition the most comfortable of positions.

In his last major speech to the Chamber, on January 3, 1834, Lafayette remained unchanged: "Under the charm of our tricolor flag, thanks to a change of dynasty and the replacement of the aristocracy, we are now walking down a retrograde road toward the system of the restoration that the people blew away during its great week,"[42] he said and then went on to his other usual themes. On the twenty-sixth, he said a few words in favor of the Polish refugees; and on February 1, he took to his bed with a nasty cold.

At first, everyone expected he would recover without difficulty, but the vigor he had always manifested seemed to fade. He continued to write letters, read newspapers, and see his family, but for the first time, he was visibly declining and his cold, settling on his chest, was turning into bronchitis. He had, after all, always had a weak chest, as his attack of tuberculosis back in 1789 had shown. On March 24, feeling too ill to attend the debate on a treaty with the United States, he sent his speech over to be read for him. Still, he expected to recover. By early May, he was feeling better. On the first, he wrote one of his endless letters to Mr. Murray, the chairman of the Glasgow Society for the Emancipation of Negroes. On the ninth, he felt well enough to go for a drive. It was a bad mistake. The bronchitis turned into pneumonia. On May 20, at four in the morning, pressing a medallion bearing a portrait of Adrienne to his lips, surrounded by his family, he expired peacefully.

The reaction to his death was prompt and immense. In the United States, Congress passed resolutions praising the dead man and regretting his loss, and John Quincy Adams, now a member of the House of Representatives, read a long speech in praise of the friend of liberty. There was also an order of the day to the army from President Andrew Jackson setting a time of national mourning. In Paris, everyone acknowledged the event with fulsome praise and equally fulsome (if perhaps insincere) regret: the King, the royal family, the Chamber of Deputies, the National Guard, the press. And the General's funeral, on May 27, became a national manifestation attended by all who mattered. Chateaubriand, France's greatest living writer, watched the funeral procession. "I was in the crowd when M. de Lafayette's convoy went past," he wrote. "At the end of the boulevard, the hearse stopped; I saw it, shining gold in a passing ray of sunshine over the helmets and weapons; then the shade returned and it disappeared."[43]

Remembering perhaps other political funerals, Lafayette had specified that only members of his family were to enter the Picpus cemetery, where he was buried next to Adrienne. There, his remains lie today, honored once a year by a ceremony in which the ambassador of the United States pays homage to America's friend.

Within a short time, his children published seven volumes of his writings, letters, and memoirs, all carefully edited so as to reflect nothing but glory on their father's memory, but it was only some sixty years later that the first serious biography was published. By then, the name of Lafayette had died out. Lagrange had passed on to Virginie de Lasteyrie's heirs, and the library, with its multitudinous boxes of papers, remained closed at the express wish of reactionary descendants who were ashamed of their liberty-loving granduncle.

AFTERWORD

$\mathbf{M}$. de Lafayette became important because he lived. . . . By an extraordinary effect, the result of his action was often in contradiction to his thought: as a royalist, he ended, in 1789, a monarchy that had lasted for eight centuries; as a republican, he created in 1830 the kingdom of the barricades; he went away giving to Philippe the crown he had taken from Louis XVI. . . .

"M. de Lafayette had one idea only; luckily for him, it was that of the century. The fixity of this idea gave him a kingdom; it served him as a pair of blinders; it stopped him from looking to the right and left; he walked a straight line with a firm step; he went forward without falling into the precipice, not because he could see it, but because he didn't; blindness served him as genius might have."[1] So wrote Chateaubriand. It was a judgment with which many of his contemporaries would have agreed.

That Lafayette was a man of genius is a thought that cannot for a moment be entertained. He had great qualities and a greater amount of obstinacy; immense opportunities that he seized, then wasted; and more than his just deserts of popular applause. He was greatly loved by all who knew him well, greatly admired by many who didn't. Fatherless, he seemed ready-made for adoption by the childless Washington; and as long as the relationship remained close, he made very few mistakes. From his idol, he learned that nothing mattered more than liberty: it was indeed the idea of the century; and yet, once he came home, his efforts—ceaseless, often selfless—went wrong. Admirable as it was in many respects, the French Revolution soon traded liberty for terror; and the ensuing five years Gilbert spent in dungeons can hardly be considered a mark of success. Then, in 1830, the General set up a régime only to denounce it within the year. What, then, was the flaw?

Any number of people would have answered, simply, stupidity. From the moment Lafayette became famous, the French word *niais* was applied to him by a wide variety of credible observers; it means not just stupid but also naïve, gullible, and there it touches on one of Lafayette's main failings: his endless appetite for flattery. All his life, he trusted any man, or woman, who appeared to think him a great man. It was as true of Louis-Philippe in 1830 as it had been of General Conway in 1777; and the numerous people who detected this were quick to take advantage of it, either for their own enrichment and aggrandizement, or to enlist Lafayette's help in a variety of dubious causes. This is indeed a serious failing: a public man so easily bamboozled will be prone to serious error and do neither himself nor his cause any good.

The problem, bad as it was, became a thousand times worse when Lafayette discovered the pleasures of popularity. In order to remain popular, he was prepared to use any rationalization; nor was he conscious of what he was doing. In 1791, for instance, when he took back his resignation as commander of the National Guard—since he had failed to win the kind of discipline from the guard and freedom for the King that he claimed were essential—clearly, he had given up his principles in order to retain his popularity. While this would be a severe indictment of any statesman's actions, it matters even more in this case, since Lafayette's great claim was that he had always remained true to his principles.

In fact, the young Lafayette did not go overseas in 1777 because he wanted to fight for liberty any more than he wanted the Bastille to be taken in 1789. He was no republican in 1792. During the French Revolution, he often found himself following the people he was supposed to lead and had to adjust his principles after the fact. One feature of Gilbert's character that remained unchanging, however, was his need to prove that he had always been right. Nothing, of course, could have been more likely to exaggerate an already present tendency to self-delusion. The result was that Lafayette spent much of his life in an unreal world, responding less to outside stimuli than to his own inner compulsions. It is little wonder, really, that people described him as naïve and impractical.

Of course, there were reasons in Gilbert's childhood to explain this. His early years at Chavaniac, during which he was the obvious center of his universe, made him feel that he was a very important person, capable of achieving almost anything, one whose word was not likely to be disputed. With his move to Paris he became an insignificant little boy, of obscure family and small fortune, an awkward provincial, an object of ridicule, and even when he became rich, he went on being a figure of fun. It is easy to see how the little boy who had been the king of his castle became a terrifyingly insecure young man, longing to be loved, famous, and admired. Then, mostly through the machinations of the comte de Broglie, he was given the first of his great opportunities and, in short order, his fantasy became reality.

Nothing corrupts faster than success: it brings with it, all too often, the belief that it is due solely to one's own qualities. As long as Washington was there to reassure, advise, and restrain, Lafayette was able to deal with his rapidly increasing fame, partly because he admired his adopted father and listened to him as he did to no one else; partly because he was able to find all the security, the reassurance he needed. Thus it was that, in the United States, on the whole, Major General the Marquis de Lafayette deserved his success, but as soon as he returned to France, the combination of basic insecurity and inflated ego went to work. No one could take up Washington's role—not Adrienne, who worshiped her husband, not Mmes d'Hunolstein and de Simiane, and certainly not any of the men of the court or the Revolution.

Still, while this may be an explanation, it is no excuse, and even less a justification. If we fail to overcome the disabilities of childhood or adolescence, then, finally, the fault is ours, not the world's; and, in fact, Lafayette never grew up. The seventy-six-year-old revolutionary remained, in all essentials, the boy of 1777. And although adolescents full of fire and enthusiasm can make convincing popular leaders, they never become statesmen. In that sense, what appeared to be Lafayette's luck, his early success in America, was really his doom since, instead of growing up, he used his popularity as a crutch and thereafter sedulously avoided the painful efforts required of all of us as we pass from childhood to maturity.

Even so, Lafayette was able to do much good. Countries occasionally need a figure of unbending principle; there was much to be said, between 1783 and 1834, for having someone tirelessly repeating to the French that liberty mattered more than anything. Appearances to the contrary, France easily lets itself be ruled by men who, to an Anglo-Saxon, would appear intolerably domineering: General de Gaulle is a recent example. All through his life, Lafayette fought this national failing. He deserves a great deal of credit on that account alone.

In Lafayette's own lifetime, another figure, that of Talleyrand, symbolized the practical statesman, always ready to renounce his sworn allegiance to king, emperor, or republic but, at the same time, always able to further the country's interest. Talleyrand, himself, had nothing but contempt for Lafayette, but there perhaps he was blinded by his own need for self-justification. For, when all is said and done, and whatever his limitations, it is to Lafayette's glory that the one idea he seized on was that of liberty. Nothing can replace the right to speak, think, organize, and govern freely: from this all benefits derive. With all his vanity, his obstinacy, his self-satisfaction, his thirst for popularity, Lafayette never lost sight of that all-desirable principle. For that, he deserved the gratitude of his contemporaries and the esteem of later generations. In a world where liberty is in very short supply, there are worse heroes than a man who never stopped worshiping freedom.

NOTES

Most of the material used in researching this book is unpublished, and listed in either French or American catalogues of Lafayette's papers in my bibliography. It has not seemed necessary to indicate page numbers for the published material, which, in any event, is used chronologically. Anyone willing to spend a few months in dank French archives can easily find my references.

The following abbreviations have been used:

Lafayette, Mémoires correspondance et manuscripts: Mems
Lafayette, Correspondance inédite: Corr.
The letters of Lafayette and Jefferson: L. Jeff.
The letters of Lafayette to George Washington: L. Wash.
The Writings of George Washington: GW
Archives du ministère des Affairs étrangères: A.E.
Archives Nationales: Arch. Nat.

CHAPTER ONE

1. Talleyrand, *Mémoires*.
2. Adrienne de La Fayette, *Notice . . . Ayen*.
3. Bacourt, *Mirabeau-La Marck*.

4. Ibid.
5. Ibid.
6. Mems.
7. Segur, *Mémoires*.
8. Mems.
9. Ibid.

CHAPTER TWO

1. Mems.
2. Cited in Gottschalk, *Lafayette Comes to America*.
3. Mems.
4. A.E.
5. Mems.
6. Adrienne de Lafayette, *Notice . . . Ayen*.
7. Cited in Gottschalk.
8. Ibid.
9. Mems.
10. Ibid.
11. A.E.
12. Ibid.
13. Ibid.
14. Du Deffand, *Lettres à Walpole*.
15. Adrienne de Lafayette.
16. Cited in Gottschalk.
17. Ibid.
18. Mems.
19. Ibid.

CHAPTER THREE

1. Cited in Gottschalk, *Lafayette Joins the American Army*.
2. Ibid.
3. Mems.
4. Cited in Gottschalk.
5. Mems.
6. GW, May 17, 1777.
7. Gottschalk.
8. Mems.
9. Ibid.
10. Ibid.
11. GW, August 19, 1777.
12. Gottschalk.
13. Mems.
14. Ibid.
15. Ibid.
16. Ibid.
17. Kapp, *Leben . . . Kalb*.

18. Mems.
19. Ibid.
20. GW, November 1, 1777.
21. L. Wash., November 26, 1777.
22. GW, November 26, 1777.
23. Cited in Gottschalk.
24. L. Wash., December 3, 1777.
25. Mems.
26. Ibid.
27. Ibid.
28. Ibid.
29. L. Wash., Decmeber 30, 1777.
30. GW, December 31, 1777.
31. L. Wash., January 1, 1778.
32. Gottschalk.
33. Ibid.
34. Mems.
35. GW, February 8, 1778.
36. L. Wash., February 19, 1778.
37. Ibid.
38. Gottschalk.
39. L. Wash., February 23, 1778.
40. Mems.
41. Ibid.
42. Gottschalk.
43. GW, March 10, 1778.
44. Mems.
45. Ibid.
46. Ibid.
47. Gottschalk.
48. Ibid.
49. GW, July 18, 1778.
50. GW, July 24, 1778.
51. Gottschalk.
52. Ibid.
53. GW, September 1, 1778.
54. GW, September 8, 1778.
55. GW, September 25, 1778.
56. A.E.
57. GW, December 18, 1778.
58. L. Wash., January 11, 1779.

CHAPTER FOUR

1. Mems.
2. Cited in Charavay, *Le Général La Fayette*.

3. Mems.
4. Mems.
5. A.E.
6. L. Wash., June 12, 1779.
7. Cited in Gottschalk, *Lafayette and the Close of the American Revolution*.
8. A.E.
9. Arch. Nat.
10. L. Wash., June 12, 1779.
11. Mems.
12. Ibid.
13. L. Wash., October 7, 1779.
14. Ibid.
15. GW, October 20, 1779.
16. Mems.
17. Ibid.
18. Ibid.
19. Ibid.
20. L. Wash., March 27, 1780.
21. A.E.
22. GW, May 11, 1780.
23. Cited in Gottschalk.
24. GW, May 16, 1780.
25. L. Wash., July 4, 1780.
26. GW, July 15, 1780.
27. Ibid.
28. GW, July 16, 1780.
29. A.E.
30. L. Wash., July 29, 1780.
31. GW, July 27, 1780.
32. GW, July 29, 1780.
33. L. Wash. August 1, 1780.
34. GW, August 3, 1780.
35. Cited in Charavay.
36. Rochambeau, *Mémoires*.
37. Mems.
38. Rochambeau.
39. Mems.
40. Lafayette, *Letters . . . Noailles*.
41. L. Wash., August 14, 1780.
42. Mems.
43. Ibid.
44. Cited in Maurois, *Adrienne*.
45. Cited in Gottschalk.
46. GW, October 9, 1780.
47. GW, October 30, 1780.
48. GW, November 26, 1780.
49. Cited in Maurois.

CHAPTER FIVE

1. L. Wash., December 4, 1780.
2. L. Wash., December 5, 1780.
3. L. Wash., December 9, 1780.
4. Ibid.
5. GW, December 14, 1780.
6. Mems.
7. L. Wash., February 23, 1781.
8. Ibid., March 2, 1781.
9. Ibid., March 7, 1781.
10. Ibid., March 8, 1781.
11. Ibid., April 8, 1781.
12. GW, April 11, 1781.
13. L. Wash., April 14, 1781.
14. GW, April 21, 1781.
15. Ibid., April 22, 1781.
16. Mems.
17. GW, May 5, 1781.
18. Cited in Gottschalk, *Lafayette and the Close of the American Revolution.*
19. Ibid.
20. L. Wash., May 24, 1781.
21. Ibid.
22. GW, June 4, 1781.
23. Ibid., May 31, 1781.
24. L. Wash., July 20, 1781.
25. GW, July 30, 1781.
26. Ibid.
27. L. Wash., July 30, 1781.
28. Ibid., August 11, 1781.
29. Cited in Gottschalk.
30. GW, August 21, 1781.
31. Mems.
32. GW, September 2, 1781.
33. Mems.
34. GW, September 15, 1781.
35. L. Wash., September 8, 1781.
36. Archives du ministère de la marine.
37. GW, October 15, 1781.
38. Mems.
39. Ibid.
40. A.E.
41. Archives du ministère de la guerre.
42. Cited in Gottschalk.
43. A.E.
44. Cited in Gottschalk.
45. L. Wash., December 23, 1781.

CHAPTER SIX

1. Cited in Charavay, *Le Général La Fayette*.
2. L. Wash., January 18, 1782.
3. Ibid., January 30, 1782.
4. Cited in Gottschalk, *Lafayette and the Close of the American Revolution*.
5. L. Wash., April 12, 1782.
6. Ibid., June 25, 1782.
7. GW, October 20, 1782.
8. Ibid., October 28, 1782.
9. Cited in Gottschalk.
10. John Adams, *Diary*.
11. L. Wash., October 24, 1782.
12. Ibid., December 4, 1782.
13. Talleyrand, *Mémoires*.
14. A.E.
15. L. Wash., February 10, 1783.
16. GW.
17. Ibid., April 16, 1783.
18. Cited in Maurois, *Adrienne*.
19. Cited in Gottschalk, *Lady in Waiting*.
20. Ibid.
21. GW, March 23, 1783.
22. L. Wash., November 11, 1783.
23. Cited in Gottschalk, *Lafayette between the American and the French Revolution*.
24. Franklin, *Writings*.
25. A.E.
26. GW, February 1, 1784.
27. Mems.
28. Mems.
29. GW, April 16, 1783.
30. Ibid., December 8, 1784.
31. L. Wash., December 21, 1784.
32. Mems.
33. A.E.
34. Jefferson, *Writings*.
35. L. Wash., February 6, 1786.
36. Cited in Mitford, *Frederick the Great*.
37. L. Wash., February 6, 1786.
38. A.E.
39. Ibid.
40. Cited in Gottschalk.
41. Brissot, *De la France*.

CHAPTER SEVEN

1. L. Wash., January 13, 1787.
2. Cited in Gottschalk, *Lafayette between the American and French Revolution*.

3. L. Wash., May 5, 1787.
4. Mems.
5. L. Wash., May 5, 1787.
6. Ibid.
7. Mems.
8. L. Wash., August 3, 1787.
9. Cited in Maurois, *Adrienne*.
10. Cited in Charavay, *Le Général La Fayette*.
11. Cited in Gottschalk.
12. L. Wash., October 9, 1787.
13. Cited in Charavay.
14. Mems.
15. GW, April 28, 1788.
16. L. Wash., January 1, 1788.
17. Ibid., May 15, 1788.
18. Cited in Maurois.
19. GW.
20. Mems.
21. Arch. Nat.
22. GW, June 6, 1787.
23. L. Wash., January 1, 1788.
24. Arch. Nat.
25. Ibid.
26. Ibid.
27. Jefferson, *Writings*.
28. Arch. Nat.
29. Jefferson, *Writings*.
30. Cited in Maurois.
31. Ibid.
32. Ibid.

CHAPTER EIGHT

1. Cited in Charavay, *Le Général La Fayette*.
2. Arch. Nat.
3. Cited in Maurois, *Adrienne*.
4. Adrienne de Lafayette, *Notice . . . Ayen*.
5. Arch. Nat.
6. Ibid.
7. Cited in Gottschalk, *Lafayette in the French Revolution*.
8. Jefferson, *Writings*.
9. Cited in Maurois.
10. Arch. Nat.
11. Bacourt, *Mirabeau-La Marck*.
12. Ibid.
13. Ibid.
14. Ibid.
15. Ibid.

16. Lafayette, *Discours au corps municipal.*
17. L. Wash., January 12, 1790.
18. Arch. Nat.
19. Ibid.
20. Cited in Maurois.
21. Arch. Nat.
22. Marat, *Plan Infernal.*
23. Ibid.
24. Mems.
25. Mems.
26. Lafayette, *Adresse au Roi.*
27. Arch. Nat.
28. Ibid.
29. Mems.
30. Bouillé, *Mémoires.*
31. L. Wash., August 23, 1790.
32. Arch. Nat.
33. *L'Ami du Peuple.*
34. Desmoulins, *Revolutions.*
35. Marat, "C'en Est Fait."
36. Anon., *Soirées Amoureuses.*
37. Arch. Nat.
38. Bacourt.
39. Cited in Maurois.
40. Ibid.
41. Bouillé.
42. Ibid.
43. Rivarol, *Vie politique.*
44. Morris, *Diary and Letters.*
45. Cited in Maurois.
46. Lafayette, *Discours . . . du 22 avril.*
47. Cited in Maurois.
48. Mems.
49. Morris, *Diary.*
50. Arch. Nat.
51. Cited in Charavay.
52. Mems.
53. GW, July 28, 1791.
54. Holland, *Foreign Reminiscences.*
55. Morris.
56. Ibid.
57. Cited in Maurois.
58. Adrienne de Lafayette.
59. Arch. Nat.
60. L. Wash., January 22, 1792.
61. Ibid., March 22, 1792.
62. Arch. Nat.
63. Lafayette, *Lettre à l'Assemblée.*

64. Cited in Charavay.
65. GW, June 10, 1792.
66. Arch. Nat.
67. Ibid.
68. Mems.

CHAPTER NINE

1. Mems.
2. Corr.
3. Corr.
4. Mems.
5. Corr.
6. Arch. Nat.
7. Ibid.
8. Ibid.
9. Lasteyrie du Saillant, *Mme de Lafayette.*
10. Ibid.
11. Mems.
12. Ibid.
13. GW, March 13, 1793.
14. Ibid.
15. Mems.
16. Ibid.
17. Ibid.
18. Ibid.
19. GW, June 11, 1795.
20. Cited in Maurois, *Adrienne.*
21. Lasteyrie de Saillant.
22. Cited in Maurois.
23. Ibid.
24. GW, February 20, 1796.
25. Ibid., May 15, 1796.
26. Ibid., August 8, 1796.
27. Lasteyrie du Saillant.
28. A.E.
29. A.E.
30. A.E.
31. A.E.
32. A.E.
33. A.E.
34. A.E.

CHAPTER TEN

1. Mems.
2. Ibid.
3. L. Wash., October 6, 1797.

4. Cited in Chanson, *Lafayette et Napoléon.*
5. Cited in Maurois, *Adrienne.*
6. Arch. Nat.
7. Cited in Maurois.
8. Ibid.
9. Arch. Nat.
10. Corr. Ined.
11. Cited in Maurois.
12. Ibid.
13. Arch. Nat.
14. Mems.
15. Cited in Maurois.
16. Arch. Nat.
17. Ibid.
18. Mems.
19. Cited in Chanson.
20. Arch. Nat.
21. Ibid.
22. Ibid.
23. Mems.
24. Ibid.
25. L. Jeff.
26. Thiébault, *Mémoires.*
27. Cited in Chanson.
28. Ibid.
29. Mems.

CHAPTER ELEVEN

1. Mems.
2. Ibid.
3. Ibid.
4. Ibid.
5. Ibid.
6. Arch. Nat.
7. Mems.
8. Ibid.
9. Holland, *Foreign Reminiscences.*
10. Broglie, *Mémoires.*
11. Arch. Nat.
12. Ibid.
13. Ibid.
14. Broglie.
15. Ibid.
16. Ibid.
17. Arch. Nat.
18. Ibid.
19. A.E.

20. Mems.
21. Ibid.
22. Ibid.
23. Ibid.
24. A.E.
25. A.E.
26. Mems.
27. Ibid.
28. Ibid.
29. Ibid.
30. Anon., *Reception . . . Savannah.*
31. Hugo, "Choses vues."
32. Ibid.
33. Mems.
34. Ibid.
35. Ibid.
36. Arch. Nat.
37. Ibid.
38. Ibid.
39. Ibid.
40. Ibid.
41. Ibid.
42. Ibid.
43. Ibid.
44. Ibid.
45. Mems.
46. Arch. Nat.
47. Ibid.
48. Ibid.

CHAPER TWELVE

1. Arch. Nat.
2. Ibid.
3. Ibid.
4. Ibid.
5. Lafayette, Proclamation . . . 29 juillet.
6. Lafayette, Ordre du jour . . . 29 juillet.
7. Barrot, *Mémoires.*
8. Ibid.
9. Guizot, *Mémoires.*
10. Ibid.
11. Arch. Nat.
12. Barrot, *Mémoires.*
13. Delavigne, *Parisienne.*
14. Arch. Nat.
15. Ibid.
16. Ibid.

17. Ibid.
18. Ibid.
19. Ibid.
20. Ibid.
21. Ibid.
22. Ibid.
23. Ibid.
24. Ibid.
25. Mems.
26. Arch. Nat.
27. Ibid.
28. Ibid.
29. Le Général . . . Parisienne, 1831.
30. Arch. Nat.
31. Ibid.
32. Beaumont-Vassy, *Les Salons.*
33. Cloquet, *Souvenirs.*
34. Arch. Nat.
35. Ibid.
36. Ibid.
37. Ibid.
38. Ibid.
39. Ibid.
40. Ibid.
41. Mems.
42. Ibid.
43. Chateaubriand, *Mémoires.*

AFTERWORD

1. Chateaubriand, *Mémoires.*

BIBLIOGRAPHY

UNPUBLISHED SOURCES

The following repositories in Paris shelter numerous documents either by or regarding Lafayette: the Archives Nationales, the Archives du ministère des affaires étrangères, the Archives du ministère de la guerre, the Archives du ministère de la marine. A repertory of these can be found in: Lafayette, Documents conservés en France, Archives Nationales, Paris, 1976.

All the speeches to French deliberative assemblies quoted in this book can be found, either as manuscript journals or printed pamphlets, in the Archives nationales, Paris.

For Lafayette documents in the United States, Louis Gottschalk, *A Guide to the Letters . . . in the United States* (Cornell University Press, 1975) can be profitably consulted.

PUBLISHED WORKS

A complete bibliography of works by, about, or mentioning Lafayette would almost deserve a volume by itself; only works relevant to this biography are listed here.

Essential periodicals: *L'Ami du Peuple; Le Journal de Paris* (1788–92).

Adams, John Quincy, *Oration on the life . . . of Gilbert Motier de Lafayette* (Washington, 1835).

———, Life of General Lafayette (New York, 1851).

Anon., *Reception of General Lafayette in Savannah* (Savannah, 1825).

Anon., *Vie privée . . . de M. le marquis de Lafayette* (Paris, n.d.).

Anon., *Soirées amoureuses du Général Mottié* (Paris, n.d.).

Anon., *Adresse à l'Assemblée nationale* (Paris, 1792).

Bacourt, A. de, ed., *Correspondance entre le comte de Mirabeau et le comte de la Marck* (Paris, 1851).

Barbaroux, C. O., *Voyage du Général Lafayette aux Etats Unis d'Amérique* (Paris, 1825).

Barras, Vicomte Paul de, *Mémoires* (Paris, 1895).

Barrot, Odilon, *Mémoires posthumes* (Paris, 1876).

Beaumont-Vassy, vicomte de, *Les Salons de Paris sous Louis-Philippe Ier* (Paris, 1866).

Bouillé, marquis de, *Mémoires sur la Revolution Française* (Paris, 1821).

Brissot, J., *De la France et des Etats-Unis* (Paris, 1786).

Broglie, Achille, 3ème duc de, *Souvenirs du feu duc de Broglie* (Paris, 1886).

Chambrun, René de, *Les Prisons de Lafayette* (Paris, 1977).

Chanson, Paul, *Lafayette et Napoléon* (Lyon, 1958).

Charavay, Etienne, Le Général La Fayette (Paris, 1954).

Chateaubriand, *Mémoires d'Outre-tombe* (Paris, 1954).

Cloquet, J. G., *Souvenirs sur la vie privée du Général Lafayette* (Paris, 1836).

Deffand, Mme du, *Lettres à Horace Walpole* (Paris, 1864).

Delavigne, Casimir, *La Parisienne* (Paris, 1830).

Desmoulins, Camille, *Révolutions de France et de Brabant* (Paris, 1790).

Deslandres, Maurice, *Histoire constitutionelle de la France* (Paris, 1933).

Franklin, Benjamin, *The Writings of Benjamin Franklin* (New York, 1905–07).

Gottschalk, Louis R., *Lady in Waiting* (Baltimore, 1939).

———, *Lafayette and the Close of the American Revolution* (Chicago, 1950).

———, *Lafayette between the American and the French Revolution* (Chicago, 1950).

———, *Lafayette Joins the American Army* (Chicago, 1965).

———, *Lafayette Comes to America* (Chicago, 1965).

———, and Maddox, Margaret, *Lafayette in the French Revolution through the October Days* (Chicago, 1969).

Guizot, François, *Mémoires* (Paris, 1858–67)

Holland, Lord, *Foreign Reminiscences* (London, 1850).

Hugo, Victor, "Choses Vues," in *Oeuvres* (Paris, 1938).

Hume, E. E., *Lafayette and the Society of the Cincinnati* (Baltimore, 1934).

Idzerda, Stanley, ed., *Lafayette in the Age of the American Revolution* (Cornell University Press, 1978).

Jefferson, Thomas, *The Writings of Thomas Jefferson* (Washington, 1904–05).

Kapp, Friedrich, *Leben des Amerikanischen Generals Johann Kalb* (Stuttgart, 1862).

Klamkin, Marian, *The Return of Lafayette* (New York, 1975).

Lameth, Théodore de, *Mémoires* (Paris, 1913).

Lasteyrie du Saillant, M.A.V. marquise de, *Vie de Madame de Lafayette* (Paris, 1868).

Lewak, Adam, *Le Général Lafayette et la cause Polonaise* (Warsaw, 1934).

Marat, Jean-Paul, *C'en Est Fait de Nous* (Paris, n.d.).
——— , *Infernal Projet des Ennemis de la Révolution* (Paris, n.d.).
Maurois, *Adrienne ou la vie de Mme de Lafayette* (Paris, 1961).
Mitford, Nancy, *Frederick the Great* (London, 1970).
Morris, Gouverneur, *The Diaries and Letters* (New York, 1888).
Necker, Jacques, *De l'Administration des Finances de la France* (Paris, 1785).
Rivarol, *Vie politique de M. de La Fayette* (Londres, 1792).
Rochambeau, comte de, *Mémoires* (Paris, 1809).
Segur, comte de, *Mémoires* (Paris, 1824–26).
Staël-Holstein, Germaine de, *Considérations sur la Révolution Francaise* (Paris, 1843).
Talleyrand, Charles-Maurice, prince de, *Mémoires* (Paris, 1891).
Thiébault, General baron, *Mémoires* (Paris, 1897).
Thomas, Jules, *Correspondance inédite de Lafayette (1793–1801)* (Paris, 1903).
Washington, George, *The Writings of George Washington* (Washington, 1931–44).
Woodward, Samuel, "Ode" (New York, 1830), printed on silk scarves.

The author has also drawn on the following printed works by Lafayette and Adrienne de Lafayette:

The Letters of Lafayette to Jefferson (Paris, 1929).
The Letters of Lafayette to George Washington, 1777–1799 (New York, 1944).
Lettres inédites du Général Lafayette au vicomte de Noailles (1780–1781) (Paris, 1924).
Correspondance inédite (1793–1801), Thomas, ed. (Paris, 1903).
The Letters of Lafayette and Jefferson (Baltimore, 1929).
Mémoires, Correspondance et manuscripts (Paris, 1837–38).
Lafayette and Louis XVI: Discours du Roi . . . à l'Assemblée des Notables le 23 avril 1787 suivi du Mémoire de M. le marquis de La Fayette, Paris, 1787.
Réglement de l'Infanterie Nationale Parisienne, Paris, 1789.
Adresse au Roi, Paris, 1790.
Discours au Corps Municipal de Paris, Paris, 1790.
Discours . . . du 22 avril 1791, Paris, 1791.
Discours de M. de Lafayette sur la Constitution, Paris, 1791.
Déclaration . . . concernant la dénonciation, Paris, 1792.
Lettre de M. de Lafayette à l'Assemblée Nationale, Paris, 1792.
Opinion de M. de Lafayette . . . sur le budget, Paris, 1821.
Le Général Lafayette à MM. les Electeurs de la Sarthe, Paris, 1822.
Proclamation au Peuple de Paris, 29 juillet 1830.
Le Général Lafayette aux Gardes Nationales du Royaume, Paris, 29 juillet 1830.
Ordre du Jour aux Officiers de la Garde Nationale, 30 juillet 1830.
Le Général Lafayette à la Garde Nationale Parisienne, Paris, 1831.
Adrienne de Noailles, marquise de La Fayette, *Notice sur la vie . . . de la duchesse d'Ayen*, Dampierre, an XI *(1800)*.

INDEX